WORLD

WORLD

WORLD

WORLD

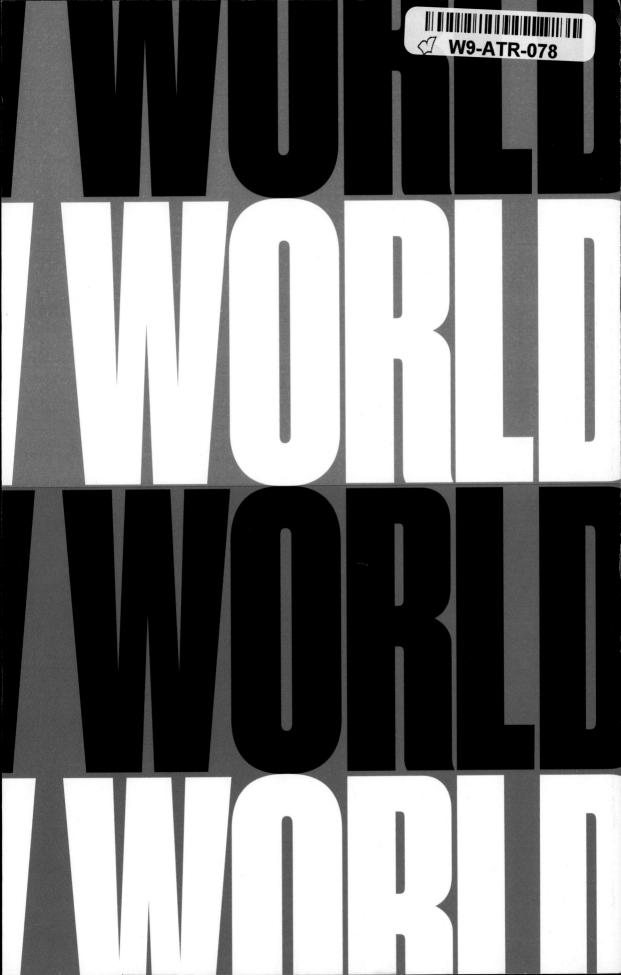

THE
NEW
WORLD

Writer	Aleš Kot
Artist	Tradd Moore
Color Artist	Heather Moore
Flatters	Yesflat (Chapter 1)
	Ludwig Olimba (Chapters 2–5)
	Heather Moore (Chapter 5)
Letterer	Clayton Cowles
Designer	Tom Muller
Production Artist	Ryan Brewer
Cover Art	Tradd Moore
Cover Colors	Heather Moore
Cover Design	Tom Muller

Originally published as THE NEW WORLD #1–5

CHAPTER 1

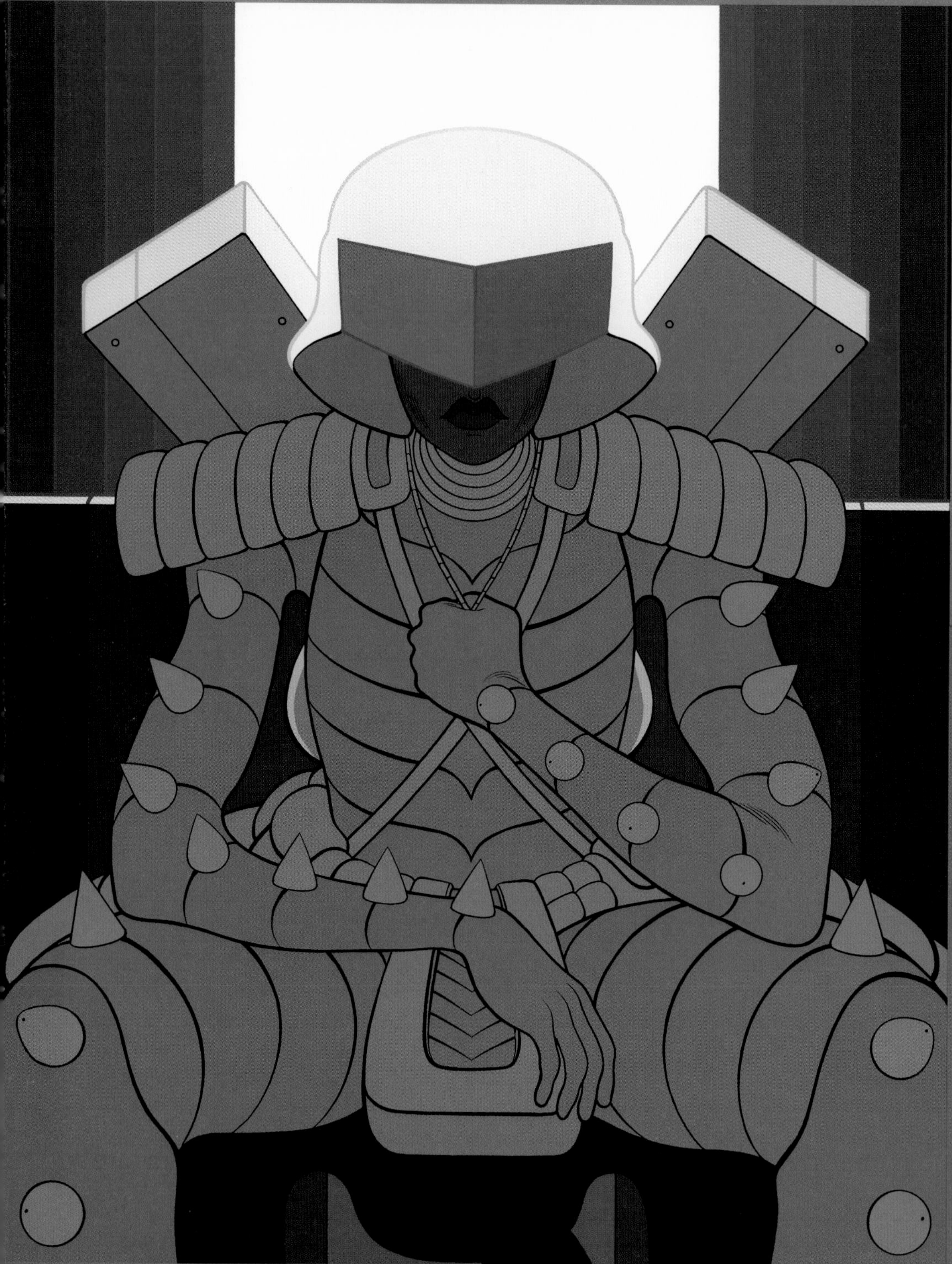

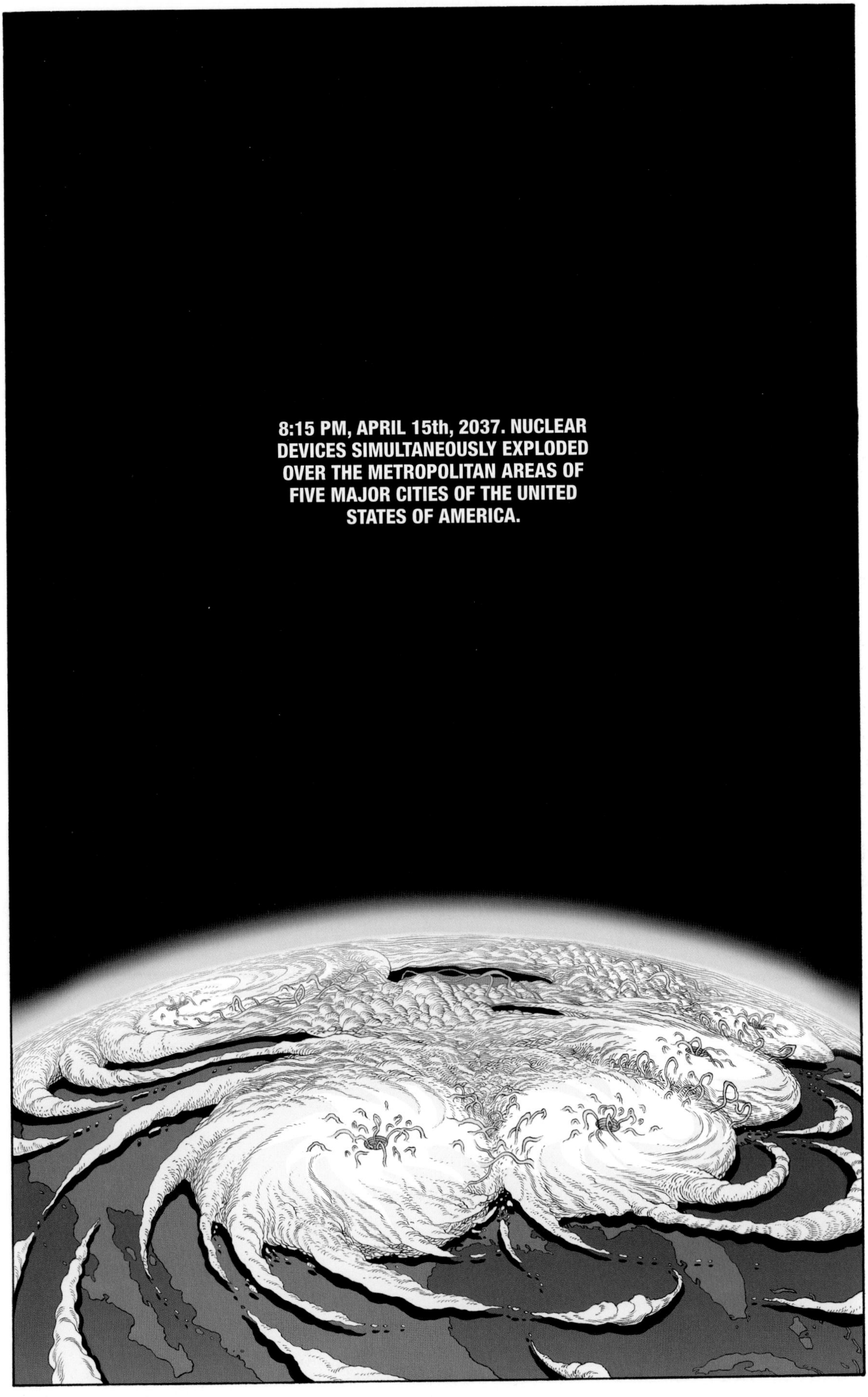
8:15 PM, APRIL 15th, 2037. NUCLEAR DEVICES SIMULTANEOUSLY EXPLODED OVER THE METROPOLITAN AREAS OF FIVE MAJOR CITIES OF THE UNITED STATES OF AMERICA.

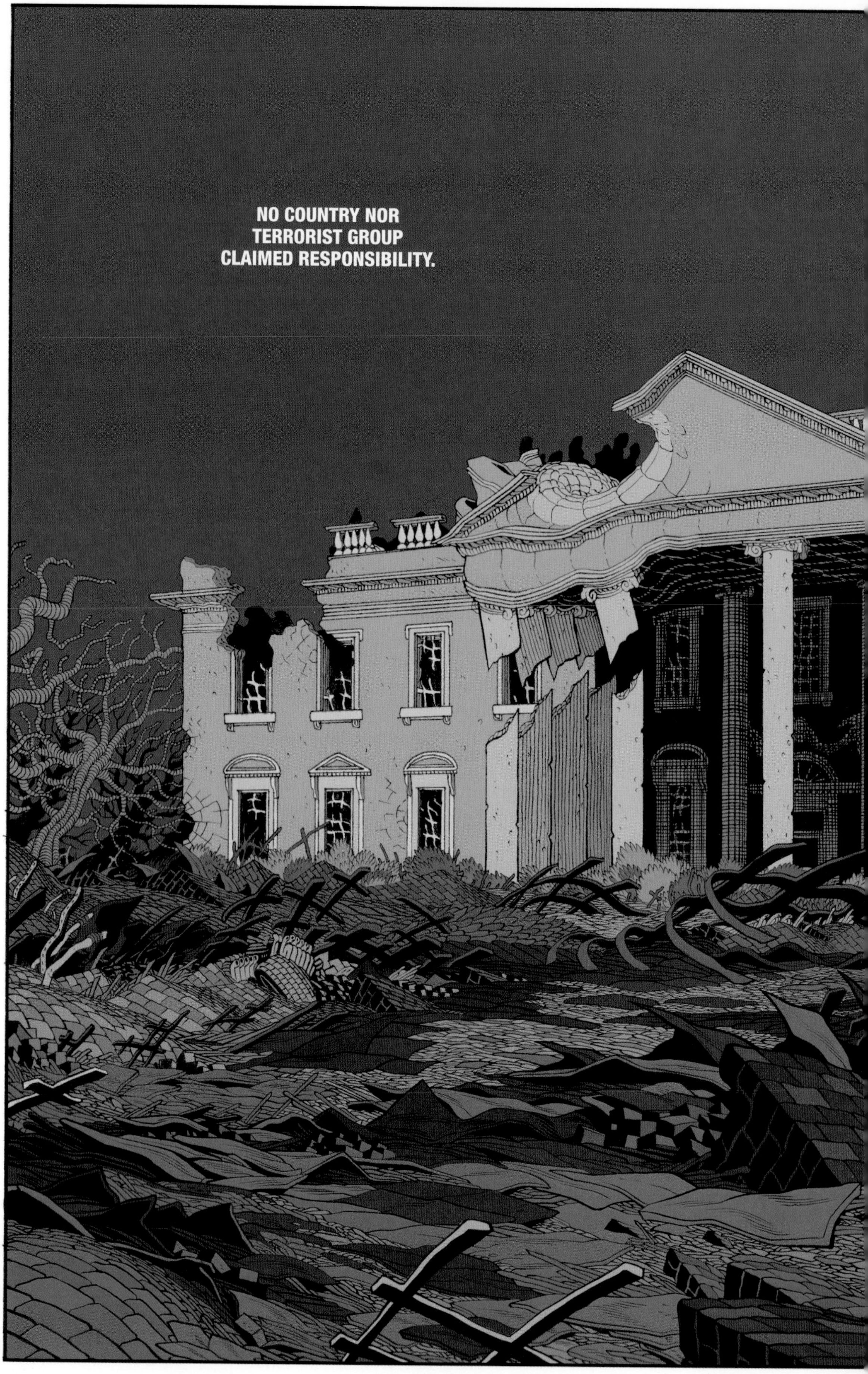
NO COUNTRY NOR
TERRORIST GROUP
CLAIMED RESPONSIBILITY.

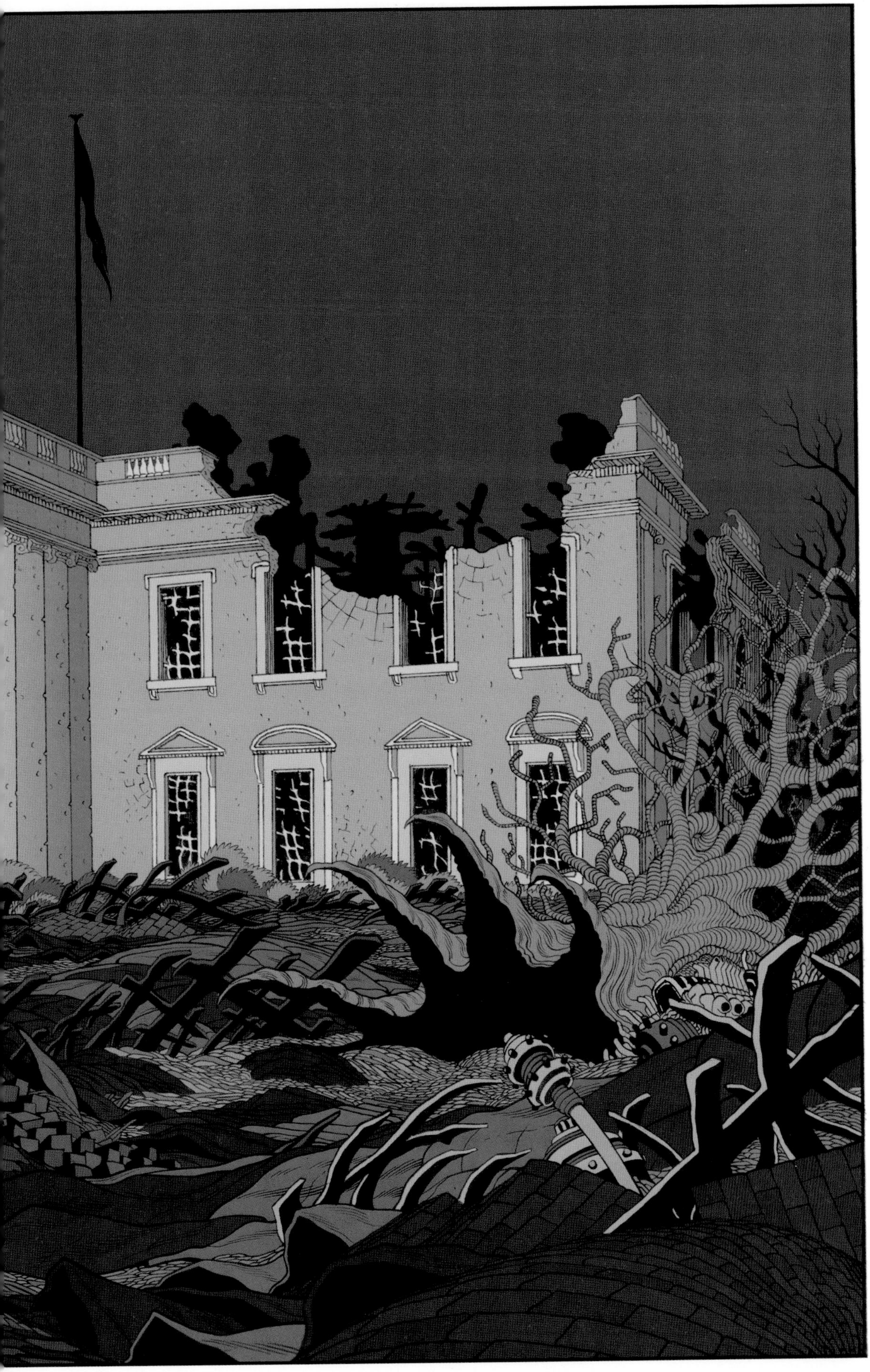

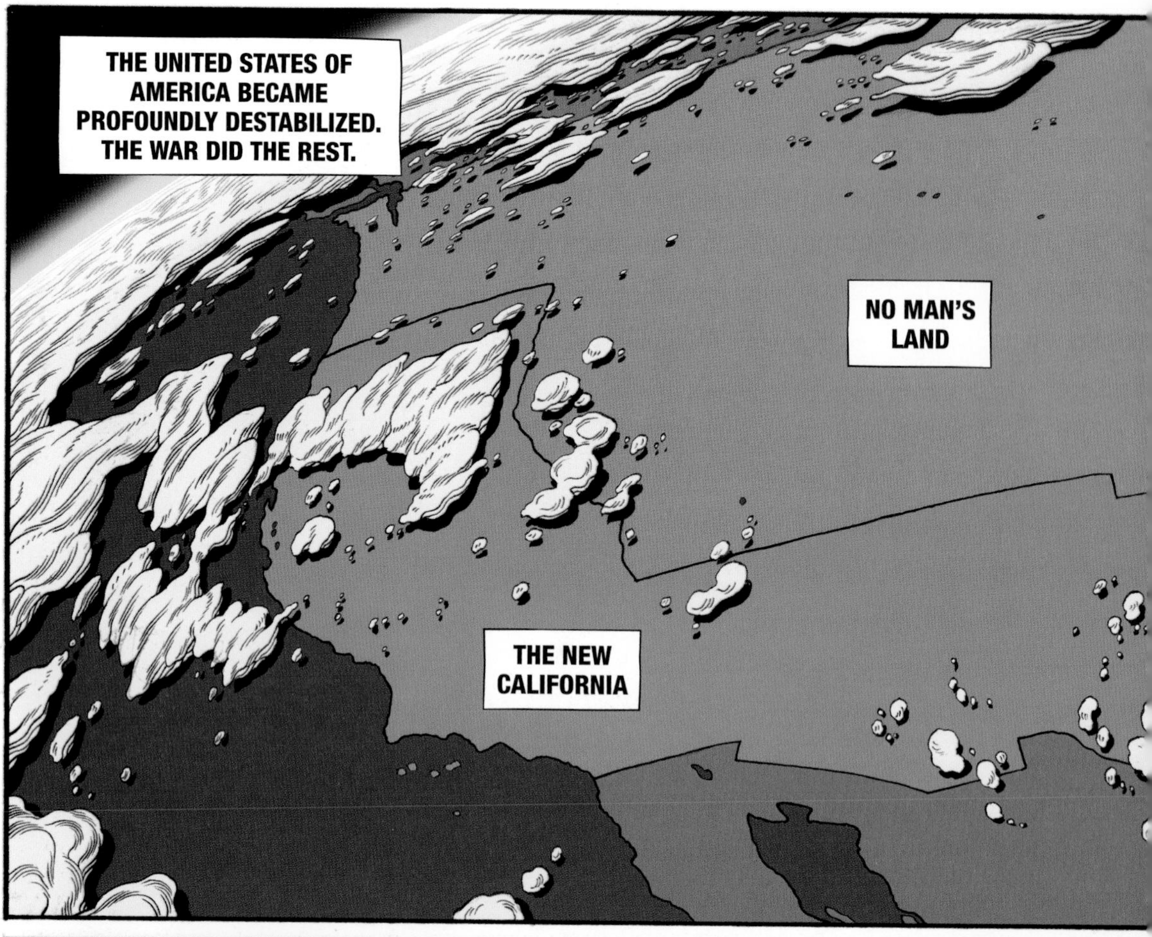
THE UNITED STATES OF AMERICA BECAME PROFOUNDLY DESTABILIZED. THE WAR DID THE REST.
NO MAN'S LAND
THE NEW CALIFORNIA

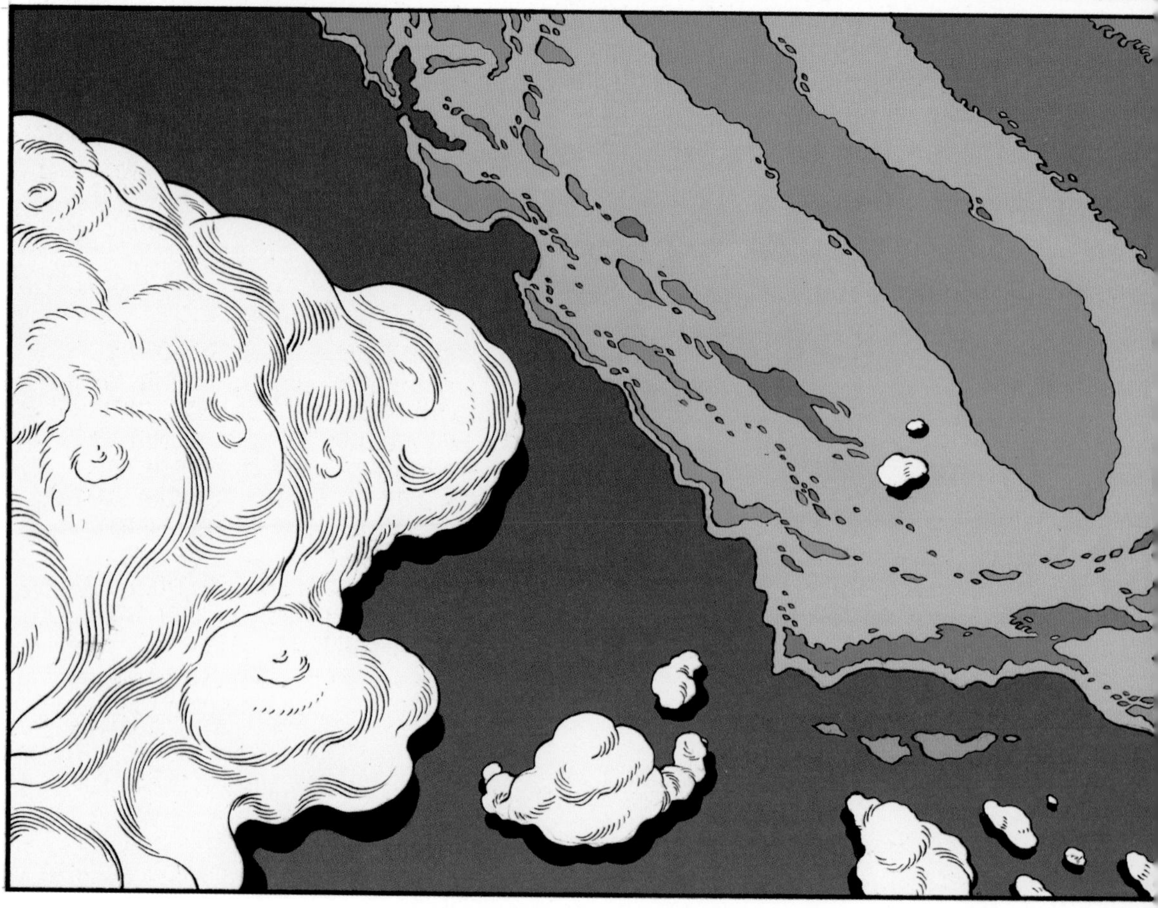

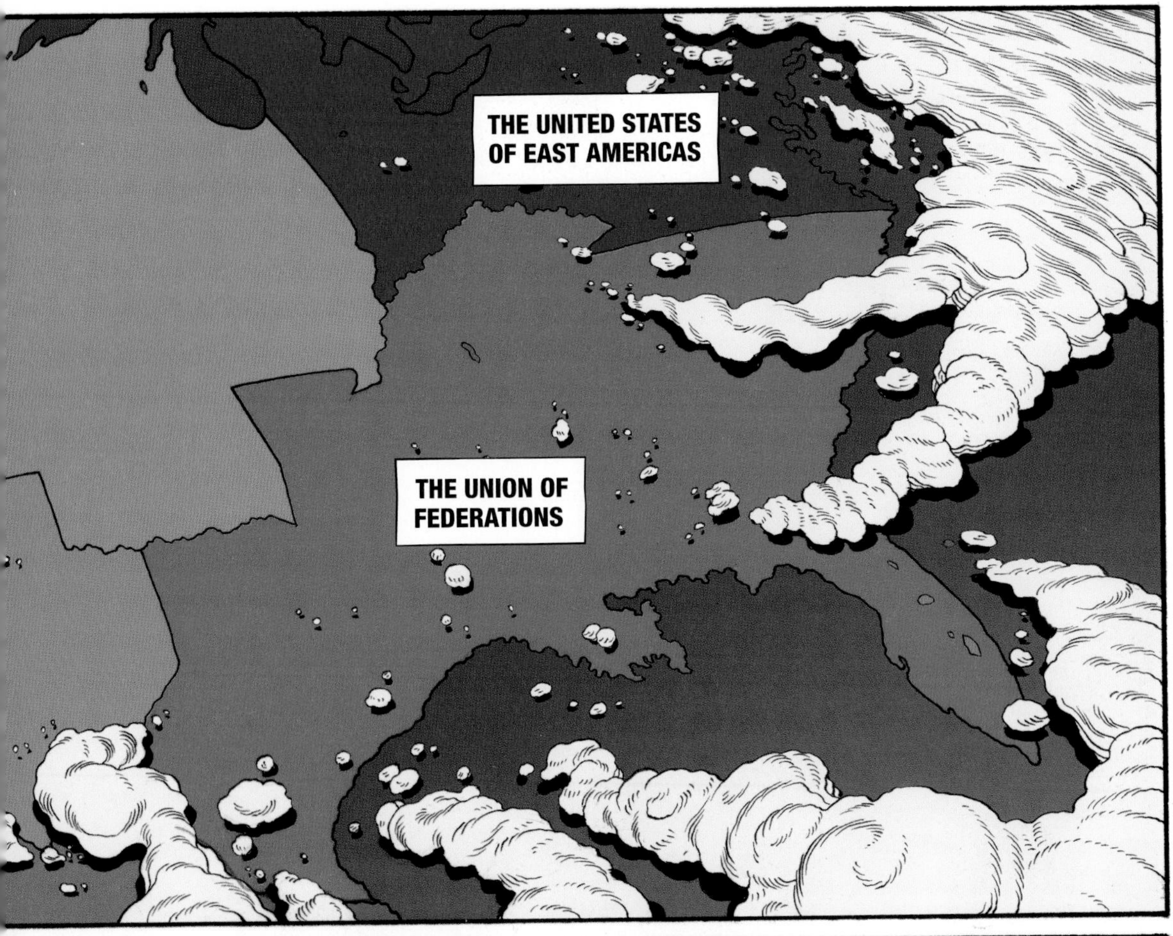
THE UNITED STATES OF EAST AMERICAS
THE UNION OF FEDERATIONS

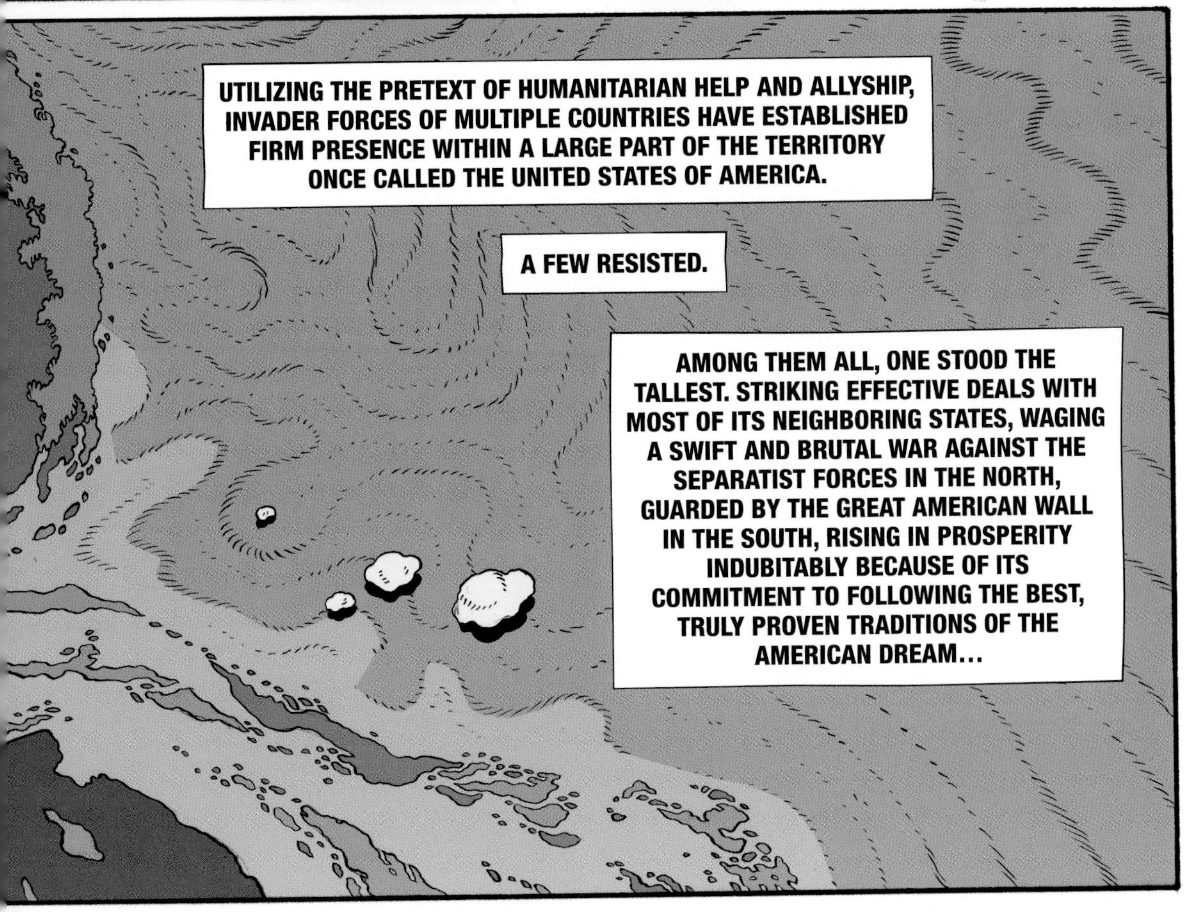
UTILIZING THE PRETEXT OF HUMANITARIAN HELP AND ALLYSHIP, INVADER FORCES OF MULTIPLE COUNTRIES HAVE ESTABLISHED FIRM PRESENCE WITHIN A LARGE PART OF THE TERRITORY ONCE CALLED THE UNITED STATES OF AMERICA.
A FEW RESISTED.
AMONG THEM ALL, ONE STOOD THE TALLEST. STRIKING EFFECTIVE DEALS WITH MOST OF ITS NEIGHBORING STATES, WAGING A SWIFT AND BRUTAL WAR AGAINST THE SEPARATIST FORCES IN THE NORTH, GUARDED BY THE GREAT AMERICAN WALL IN THE SOUTH, RISING IN PROSPERITY INDUBITABLY BECAUSE OF ITS COMMITMENT TO FOLLOWING THE BEST, TRULY PROVEN TRADITIONS OF THE AMERICAN DREAM…

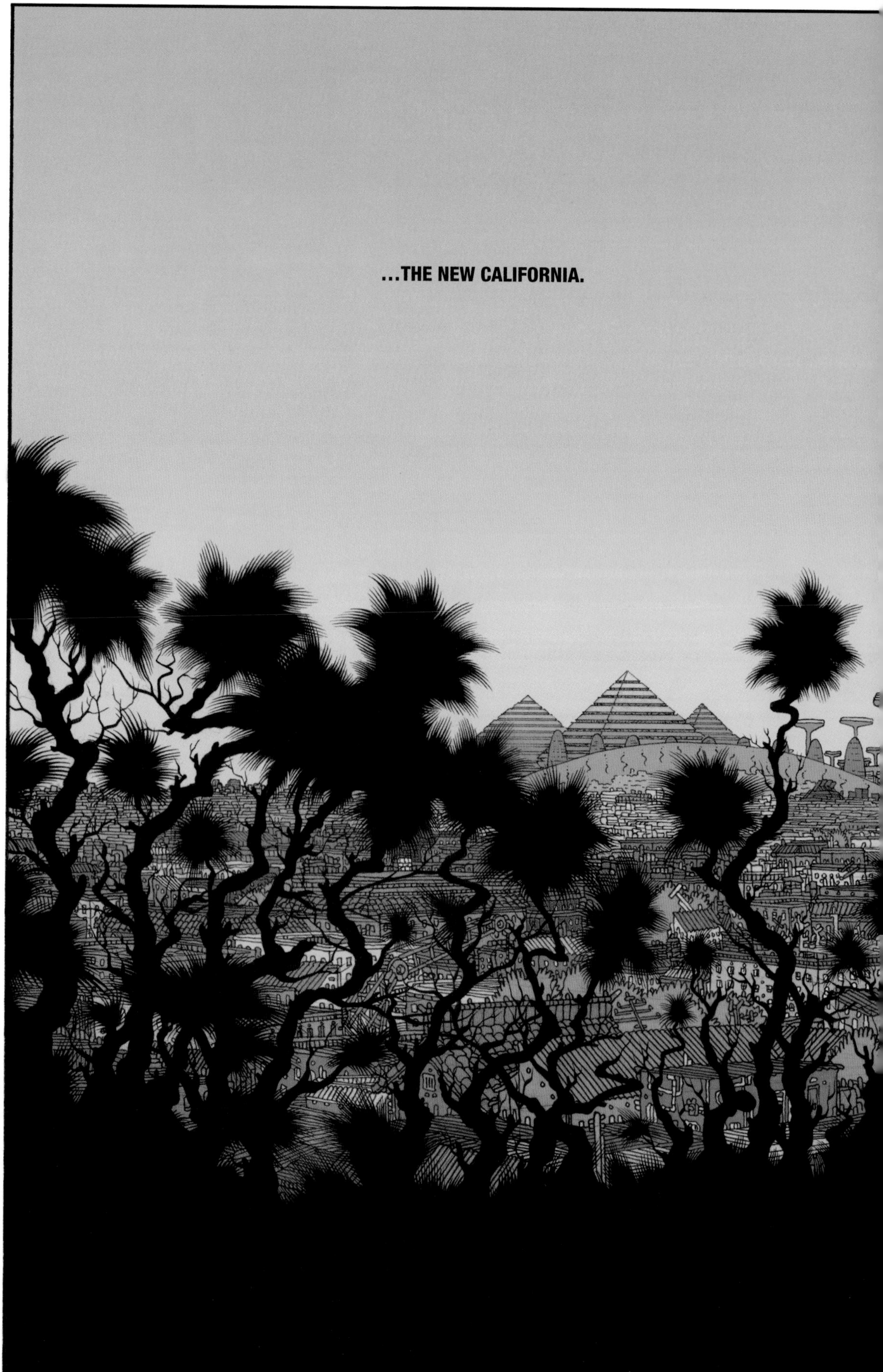
...THE NEW CALIFORNIA.

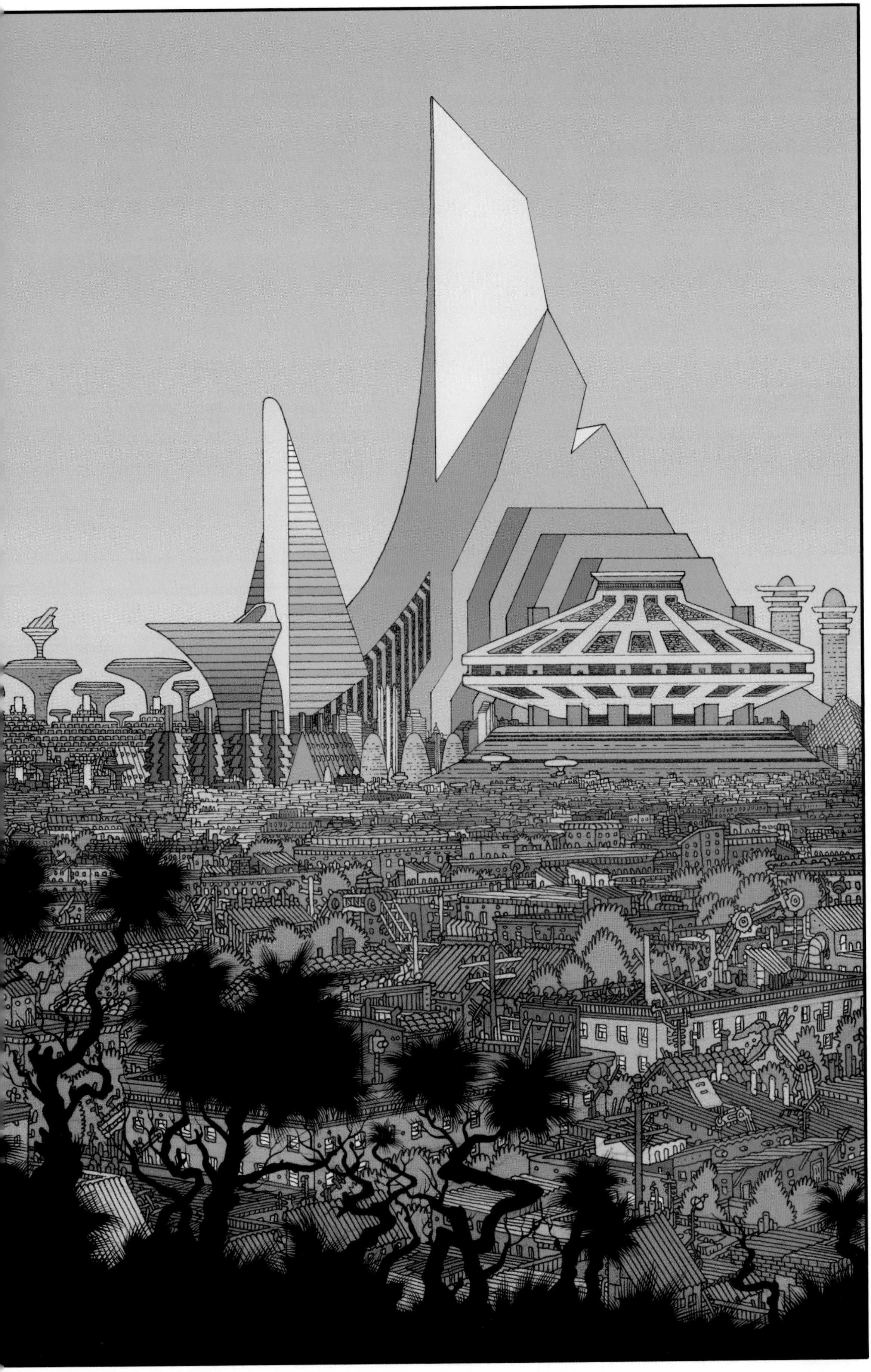

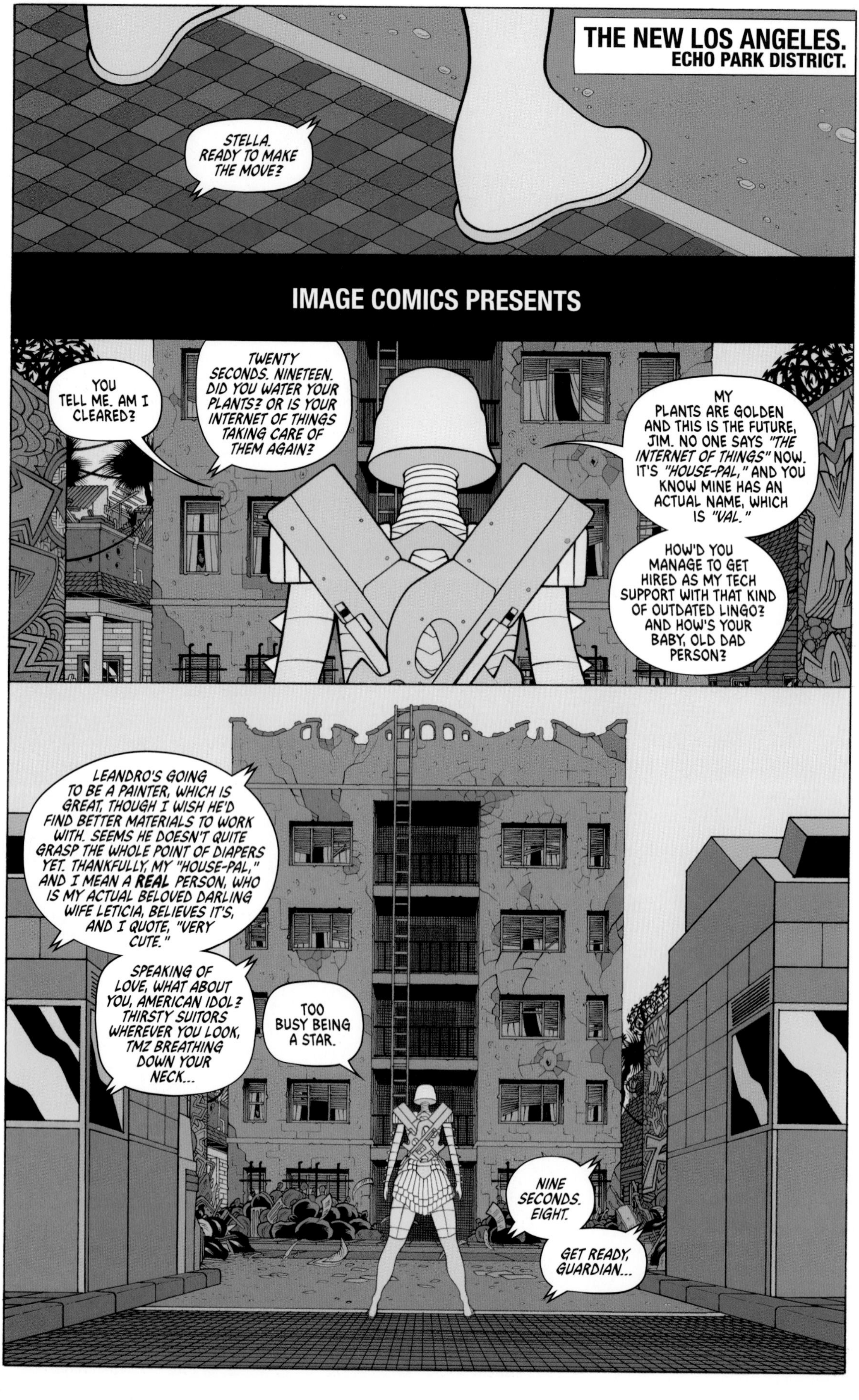
THE NEW LOS ANGELES. ECHO PARK DISTRICT.
STELLA. READY TO MAKE THE MOVE?
IMAGE COMICS PRESENTS
YOU TELL ME. AM I CLEARED?
TWENTY SECONDS. NINETEEN. DID YOU WATER YOUR PLANTS? OR IS YOUR INTERNET OF THINGS TAKING CARE OF THEM AGAIN?
MY PLANTS ARE GOLDEN AND THIS IS THE FUTURE, JIM. NO ONE SAYS "THE INTERNET OF THINGS" NOW. IT'S "HOUSE-PAL," AND YOU KNOW MINE HAS AN ACTUAL NAME, WHICH IS "VAL."
HOW'D YOU MANAGE TO GET HIRED AS MY TECH SUPPORT WITH THAT KIND OF OUTDATED LINGO? AND HOW'S YOUR BABY, OLD DAD PERSON?
LEANDRO'S GOING TO BE A PAINTER, WHICH IS GREAT, THOUGH I WISH HE'D FIND BETTER MATERIALS TO WORK WITH. SEEMS HE DOESN'T QUITE GRASP THE WHOLE POINT OF DIAPERS YET. THANKFULLY, MY "HOUSE-PAL," AND I MEAN A REAL PERSON, WHO IS MY ACTUAL BELOVED DARLING WIFE LETICIA, BELIEVES IT'S, AND I QUOTE, "VERY CUTE."
SPEAKING OF LOVE, WHAT ABOUT YOU, AMERICAN IDOL? THIRSTY SUITORS WHEREVER YOU LOOK, TMZ BREATHING DOWN YOUR NECK...
TOO BUSY BEING A STAR.
NINE SECONDS. EIGHT.
GET READY, GUARDIAN...

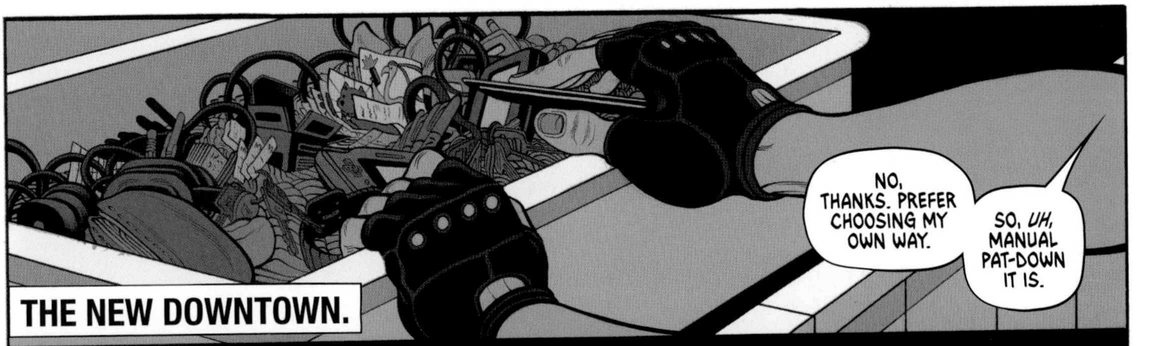
NO, THANKS. PREFER CHOOSING MY OWN WAY.
SO, *UH*, MANUAL PAT-DOWN IT IS.
THE NEW DOWNTOWN.

ALEŠ KOT

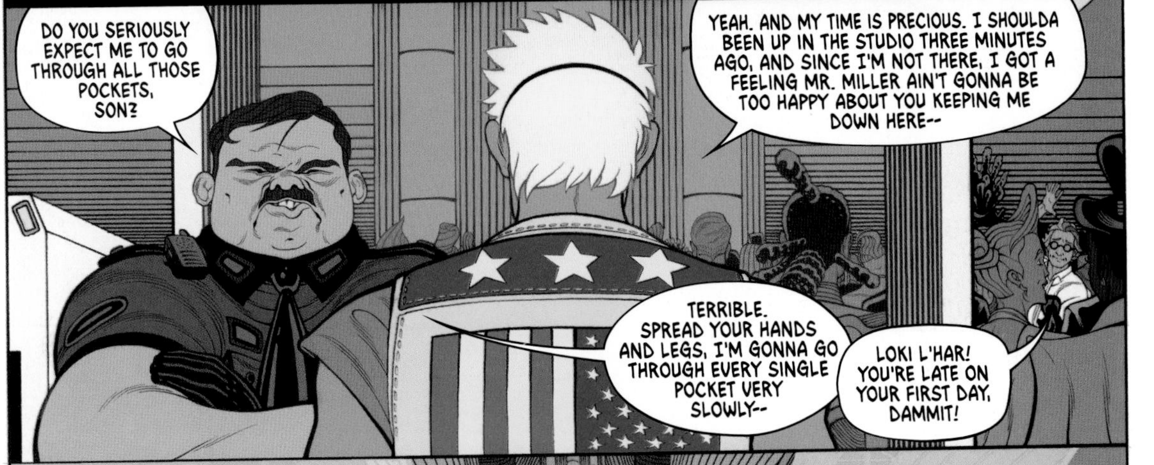
DO YOU SERIOUSLY EXPECT ME TO GO THROUGH ALL THOSE POCKETS, SON?
YEAH. AND MY TIME IS PRECIOUS. I SHOULDA BEEN UP IN THE STUDIO THREE MINUTES AGO, AND SINCE I'M NOT THERE, I GOT A FEELING MR. MILLER AIN'T GONNA BE TOO HAPPY ABOUT YOU KEEPING ME DOWN HERE--
TERRIBLE. SPREAD YOUR HANDS AND LEGS, I'M GONNA GO THROUGH EVERY SINGLE POCKET VERY SLOWLY--
LOKI L'HAR! YOU'RE LATE ON YOUR FIRST DAY, DAMMIT!

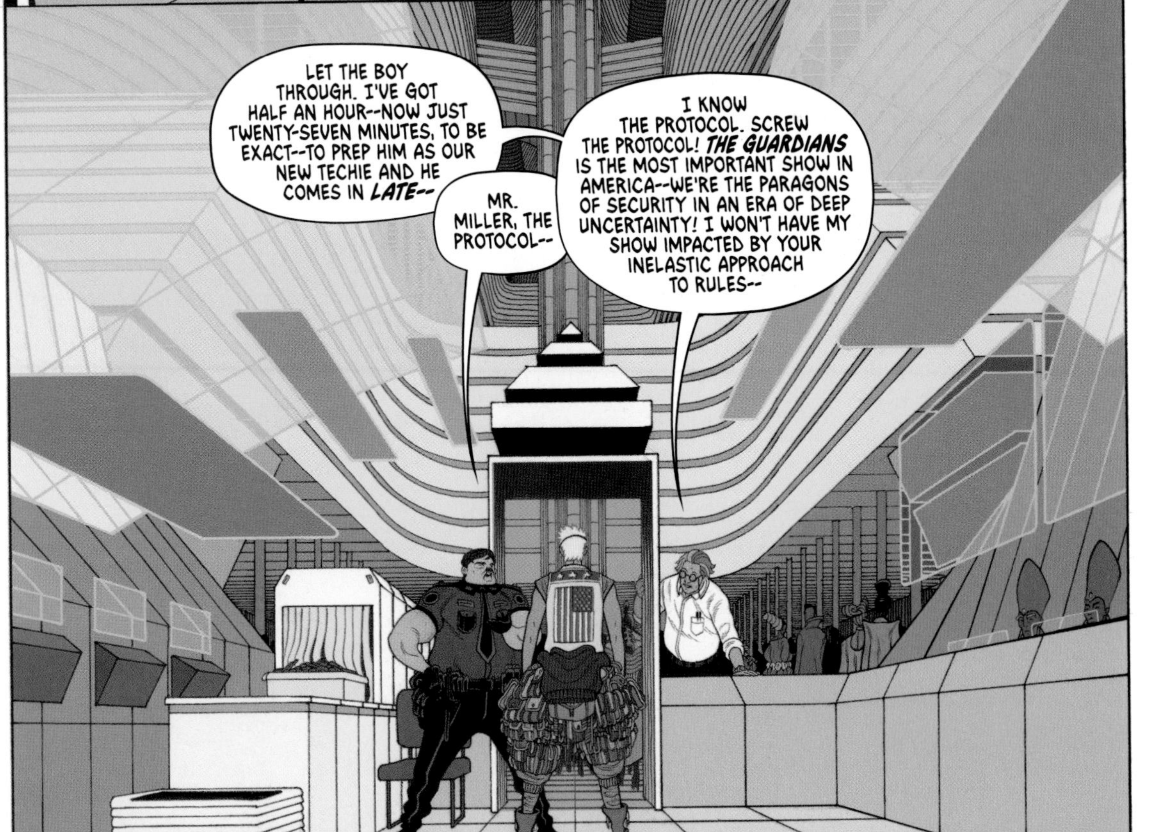
LET THE BOY THROUGH. I'VE GOT HALF AN HOUR--NOW JUST TWENTY-SEVEN MINUTES, TO BE EXACT--TO PREP HIM AS OUR NEW TECHIE AND HE COMES IN *LATE*--
MR. MILLER, THE PROTOCOL--
I KNOW THE PROTOCOL. SCREW THE PROTOCOL! ***THE GUARDIANS*** IS THE MOST IMPORTANT SHOW IN AMERICA--WE'RE THE PARAGONS OF SECURITY IN AN ERA OF DEEP UNCERTAINTY! I WON'T HAVE MY SHOW IMPACTED BY YOUR INELASTIC APPROACH TO RULES--

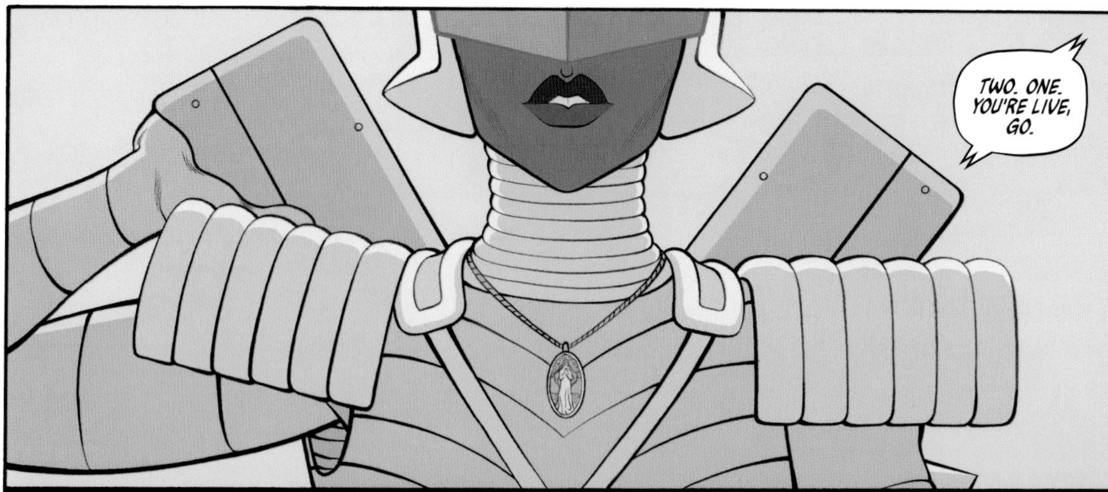
TWO. ONE. YOU'RE LIVE, GO.

TRADD MOORE

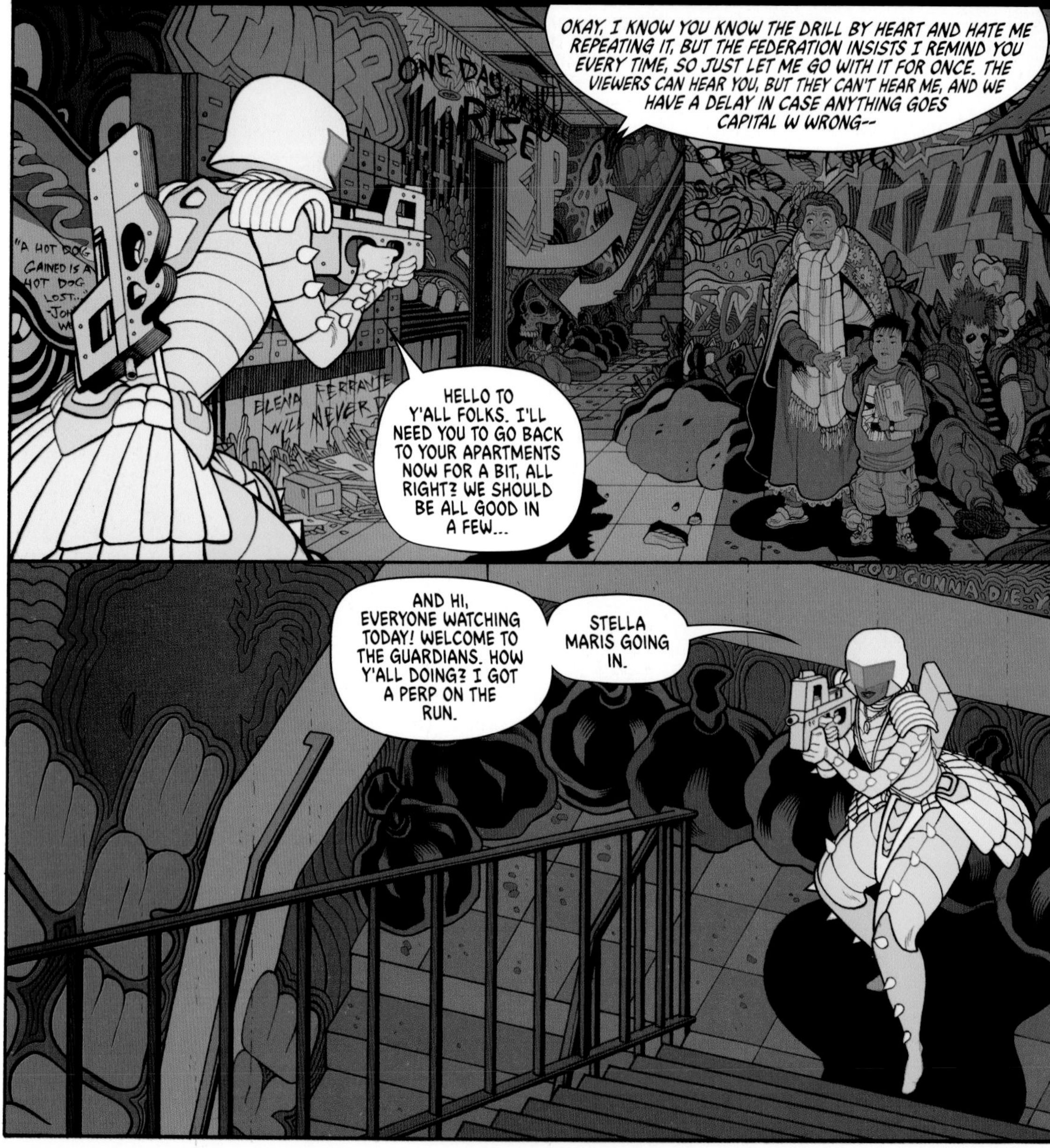
OKAY, I KNOW YOU KNOW THE DRILL BY HEART AND HATE ME REPEATING IT, BUT THE FEDERATION INSISTS I REMIND YOU EVERY TIME, SO JUST LET ME GO WITH IT FOR ONCE. THE VIEWERS CAN HEAR YOU, BUT THEY CAN'T HEAR ME, AND WE HAVE A DELAY IN CASE ANYTHING GOES CAPITAL W WRONG--
HELLO TO Y'ALL FOLKS. I'LL NEED YOU TO GO BACK TO YOUR APARTMENTS NOW FOR A BIT, ALL RIGHT? WE SHOULD BE ALL GOOD IN A FEW...
AND HI, EVERYONE WATCHING TODAY! WELCOME TO THE GUARDIANS. HOW Y'ALL DOING? I GOT A PERP ON THE RUN.
STELLA MARIS GOING IN.

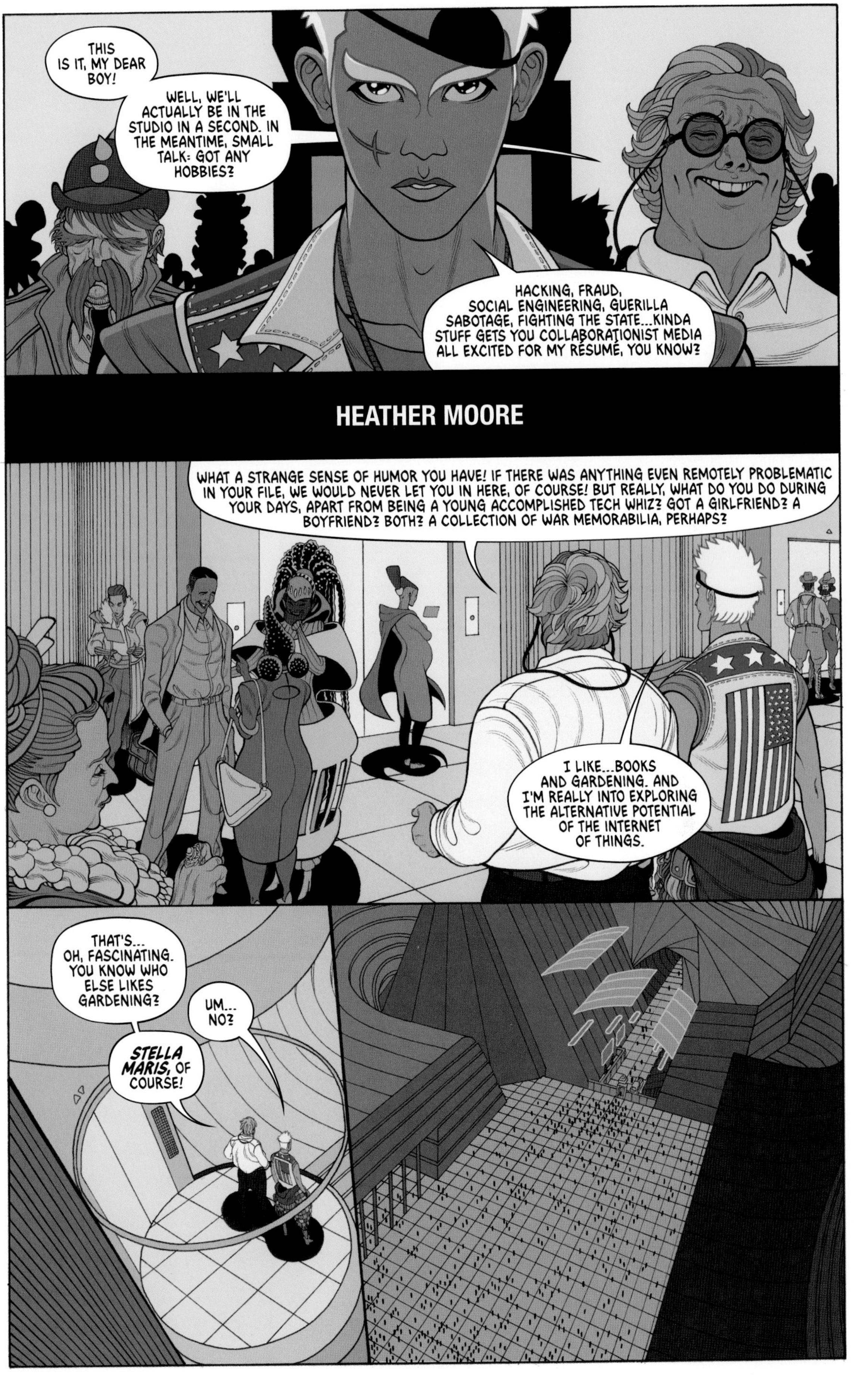
THIS IS IT, MY DEAR BOY!
WELL, WE'LL ACTUALLY BE IN THE STUDIO IN A SECOND. IN THE MEANTIME, SMALL TALK: GOT ANY HOBBIES?
HACKING, FRAUD, SOCIAL ENGINEERING, GUERILLA SABOTAGE, FIGHTING THE STATE...KINDA STUFF GETS YOU COLLABORATIONIST MEDIA ALL EXCITED FOR MY RÉSUMÉ, YOU KNOW?
HEATHER MOORE
WHAT A STRANGE SENSE OF HUMOR YOU HAVE! IF THERE WAS ANYTHING EVEN REMOTELY PROBLEMATIC IN YOUR FILE, WE WOULD NEVER LET YOU IN HERE, OF COURSE! BUT REALLY, WHAT DO YOU DO DURING YOUR DAYS, APART FROM BEING A YOUNG ACCOMPLISHED TECH WHIZ? GOT A GIRLFRIEND? A BOYFRIEND? BOTH? A COLLECTION OF WAR MEMORABILIA, PERHAPS?
I LIKE...BOOKS AND GARDENING. AND I'M REALLY INTO EXPLORING THE ALTERNATIVE POTENTIAL OF THE INTERNET OF THINGS.
THAT'S... OH, FASCINATING. YOU KNOW WHO ELSE LIKES GARDENING?
UM... NO?
STELLA MARIS, OF COURSE!

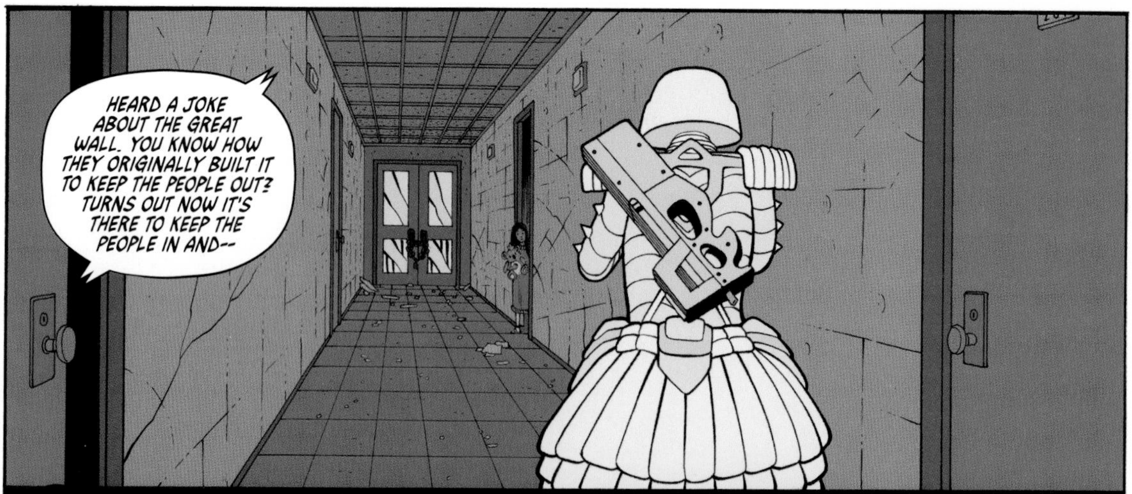
HEARD A JOKE ABOUT THE GREAT WALL. YOU KNOW HOW THEY ORIGINALLY BUILT IT TO KEEP THE PEOPLE OUT? TURNS OUT NOW IT'S THERE TO KEEP THE PEOPLE IN AND--

CLAYTON COWLES

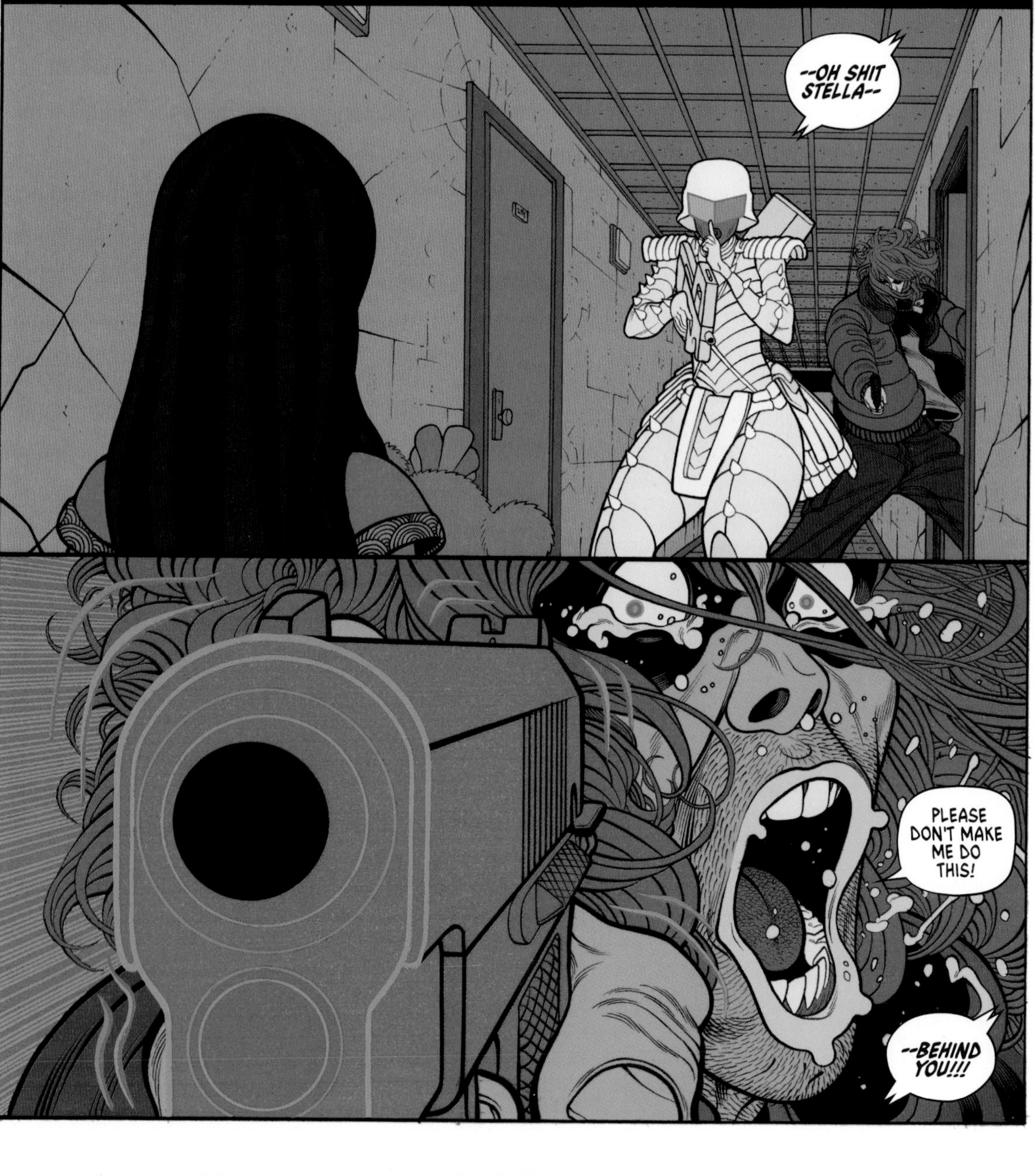
--OH SHIT STELLA--
PLEASE DON'T MAKE ME DO THIS!
--BEHIND YOU!!!

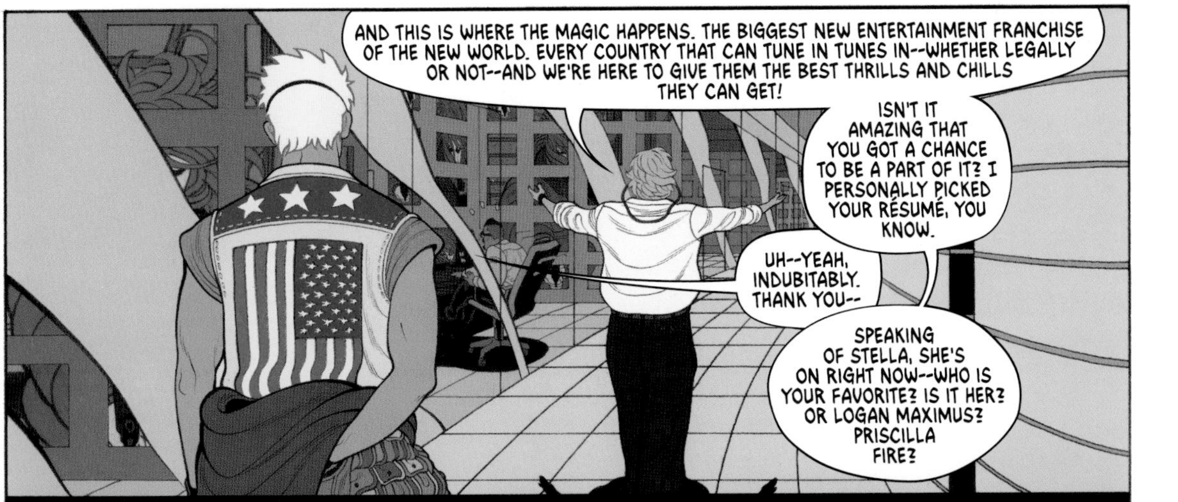
AND THIS IS WHERE THE MAGIC HAPPENS. THE BIGGEST NEW ENTERTAINMENT FRANCHISE OF THE NEW WORLD. EVERY COUNTRY THAT CAN TUNE IN TUNES IN--WHETHER LEGALLY OR NOT--AND WE'RE HERE TO GIVE THEM THE BEST THRILLS AND CHILLS THEY CAN GET!
ISN'T IT AMAZING THAT YOU GOT A CHANCE TO BE A PART OF IT? I PERSONALLY PICKED YOUR RÉSUMÉ, YOU KNOW.
UH--YEAH, INDUBITABLY. THANK YOU--
SPEAKING OF STELLA, SHE'S ON RIGHT NOW--WHO IS YOUR FAVORITE? IS IT HER? OR LOGAN MAXIMUS? PRISCILLA FIRE?

TOM MULLER

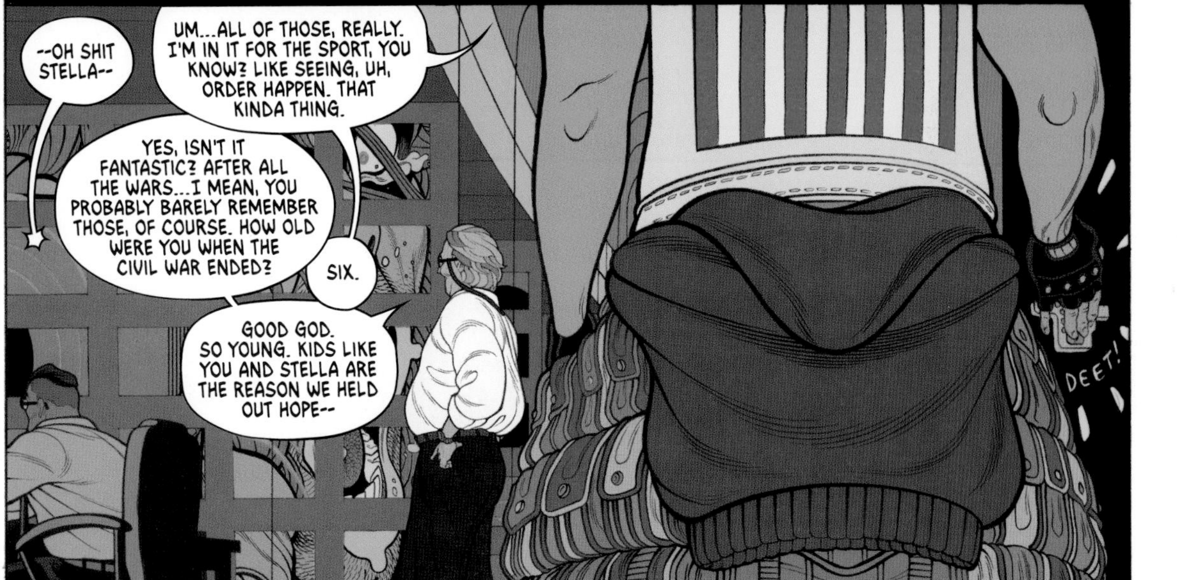
--OH SHIT STELLA--
UM...ALL OF THOSE, REALLY. I'M IN IT FOR THE SPORT, YOU KNOW? LIKE SEEING, UH, ORDER HAPPEN. THAT KINDA THING.
YES, ISN'T IT FANTASTIC? AFTER ALL THE WARS...I MEAN, YOU PROBABLY BARELY REMEMBER THOSE, OF COURSE. HOW OLD WERE YOU WHEN THE CIVIL WAR ENDED?
SIX.
GOOD GOD. SO YOUNG. KIDS LIKE YOU AND STELLA ARE THE REASON WE HELD OUT HOPE--
DEET!

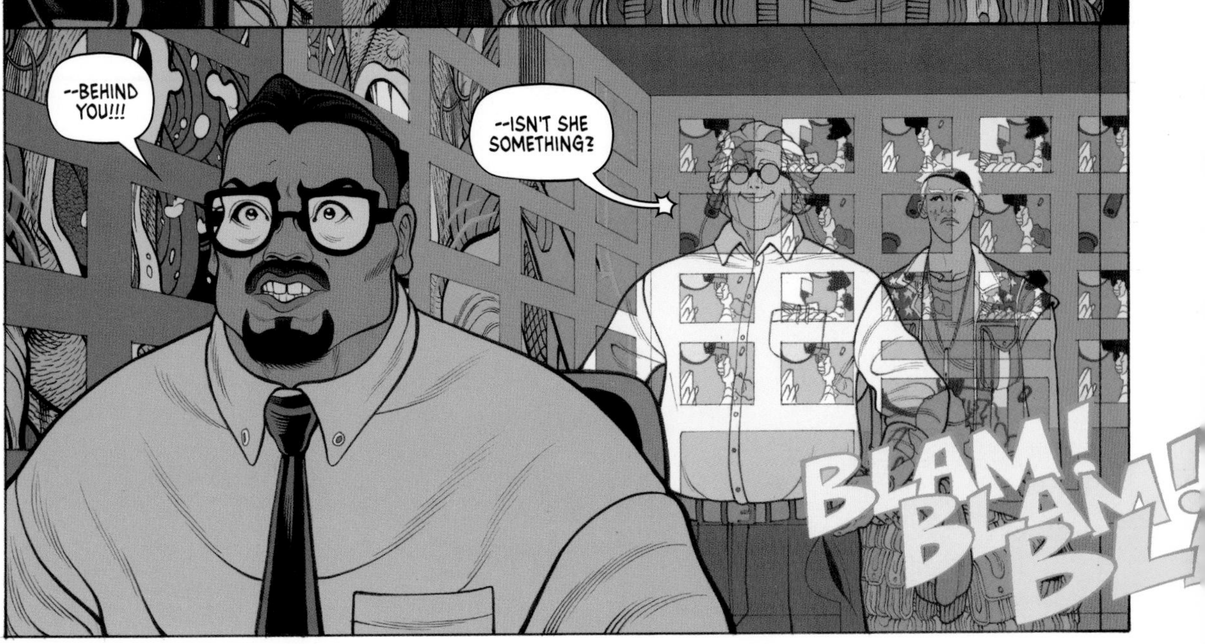
--BEHIND YOU!!!
--ISN'T SHE SOMETHING?
BLAM! BLAM! BL

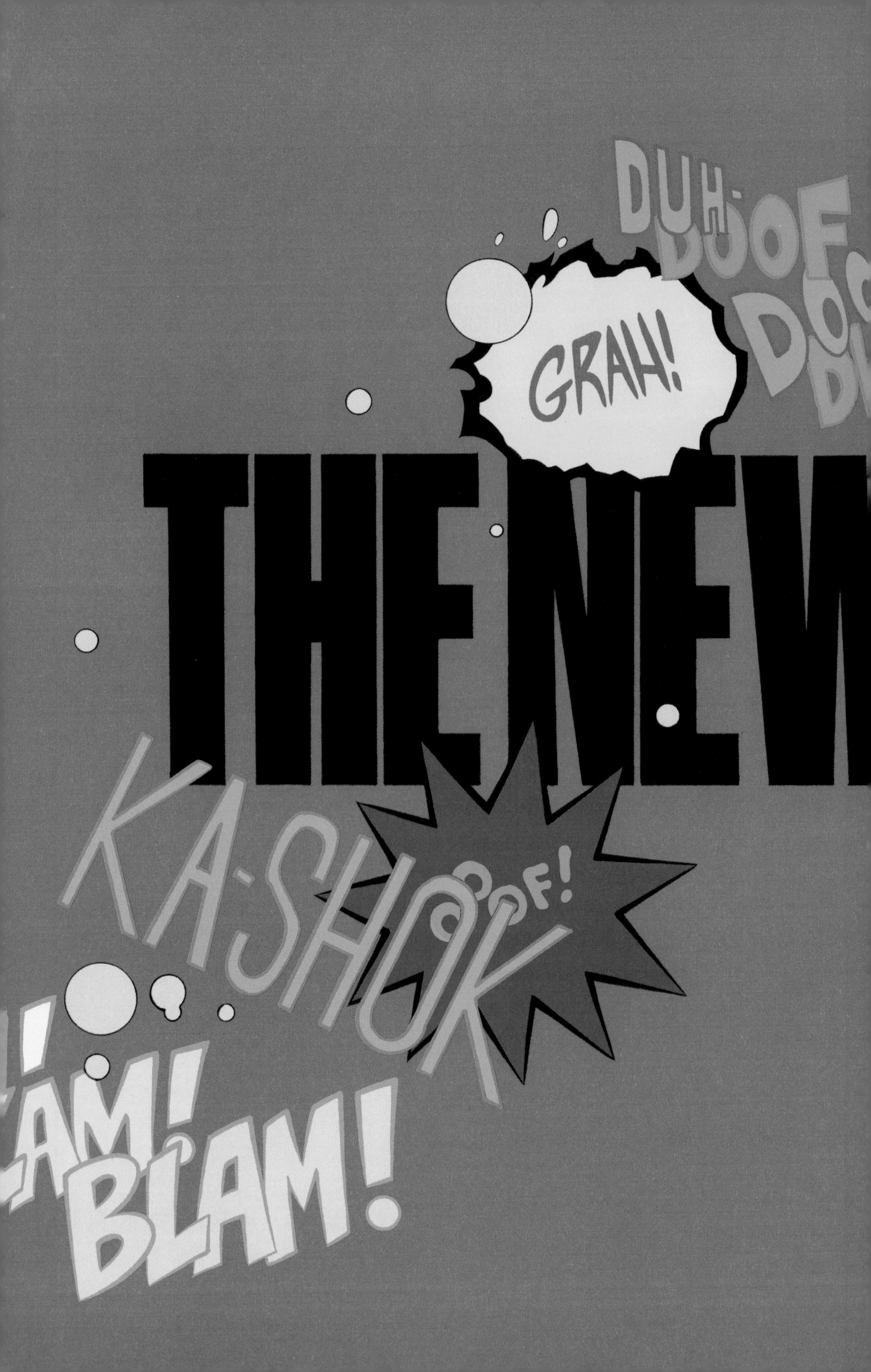
DUH-DOOF
GRAH!
THE NEW
KA-SHOK
OOF!
BLAM!

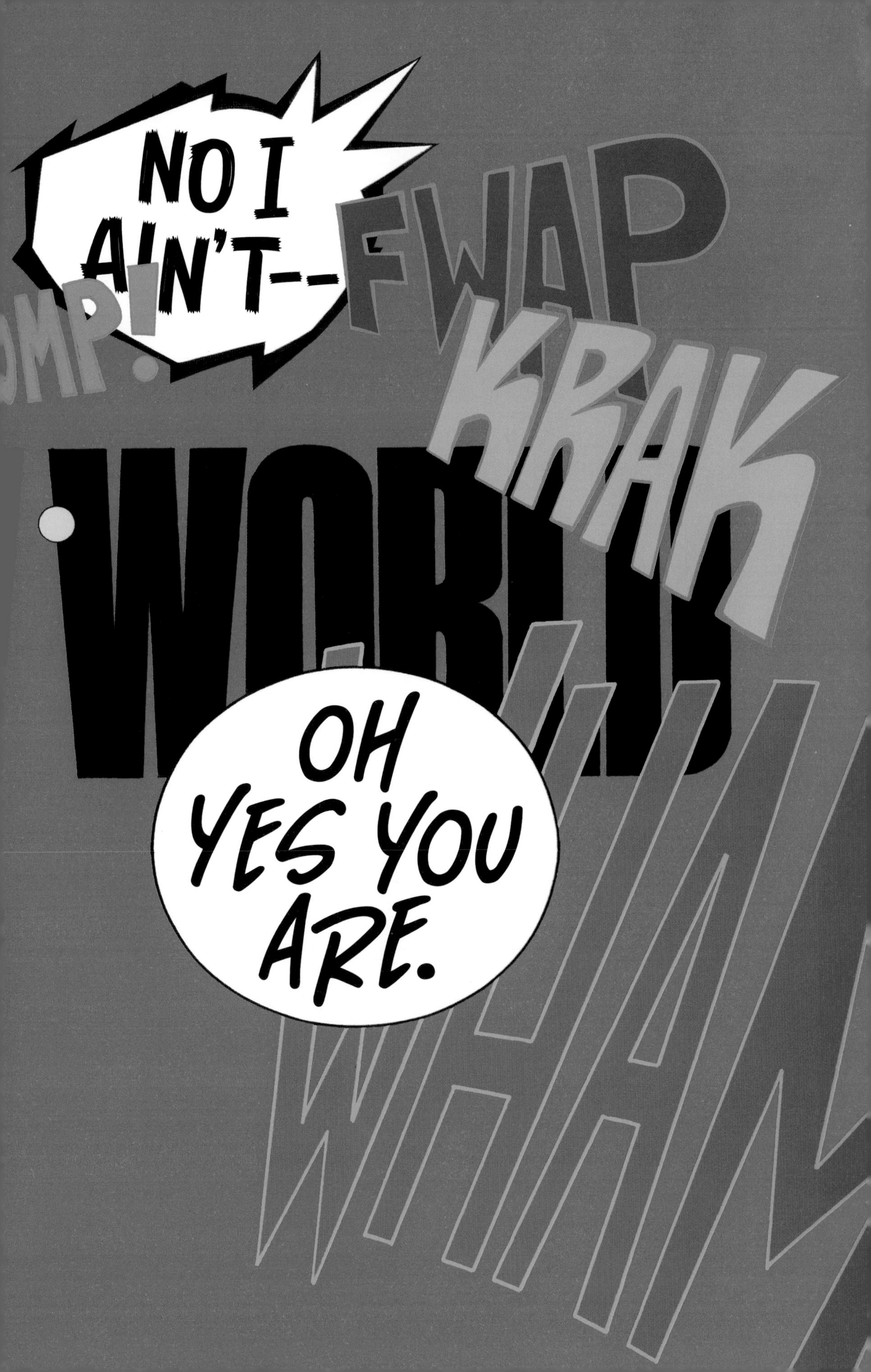

NO I AIN'T--
FWAP
KRAK
OH YES YOU ARE.

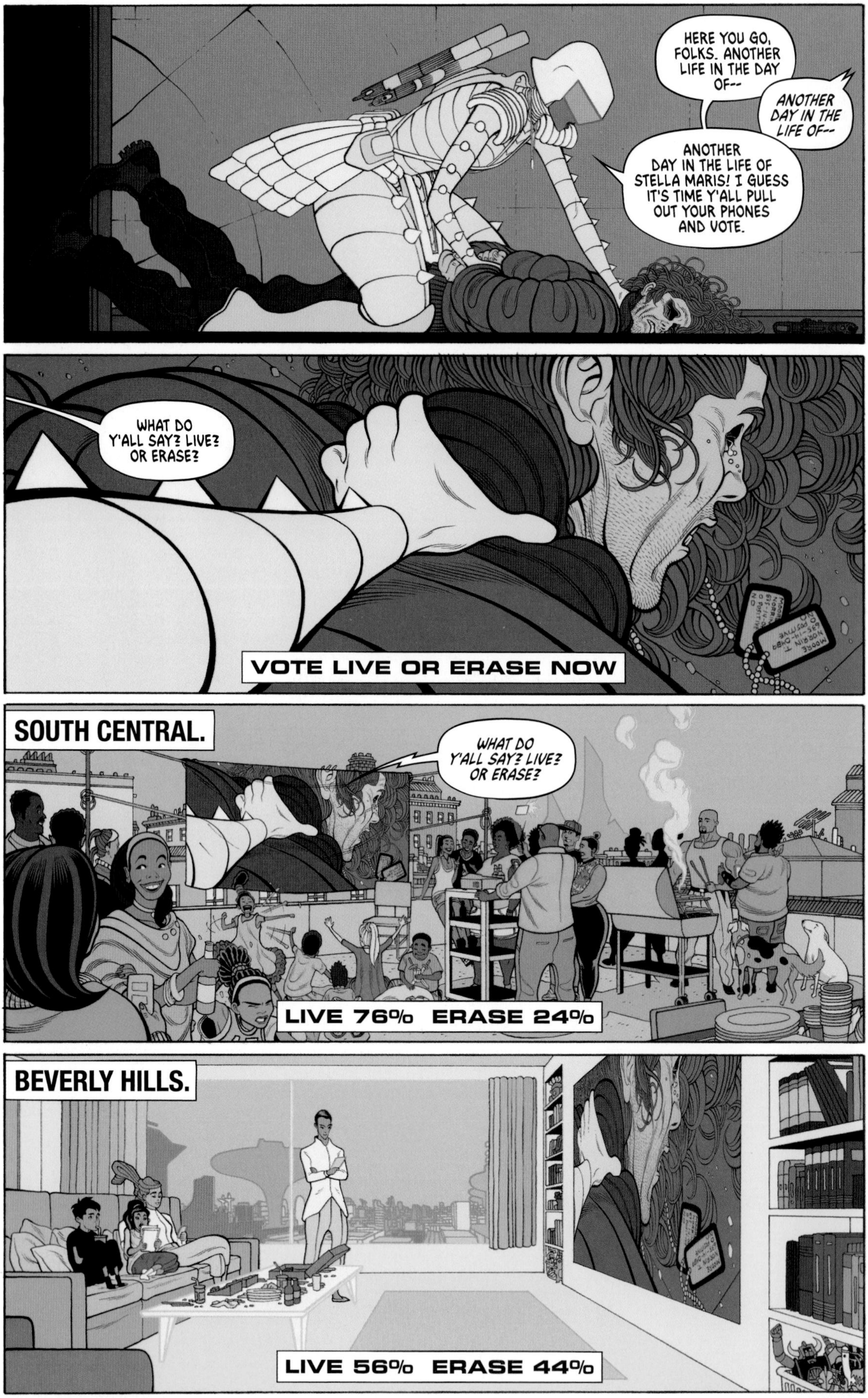
HERE YOU GO, FOLKS. ANOTHER LIFE IN THE DAY OF--
ANOTHER DAY IN THE LIFE OF--
ANOTHER DAY IN THE LIFE OF STELLA MARIS! I GUESS IT'S TIME Y'ALL PULL OUT YOUR PHONES AND VOTE.
WHAT DO Y'ALL SAY? LIVE? OR ERASE?
VOTE LIVE OR ERASE NOW
SOUTH CENTRAL.
WHAT DO Y'ALL SAY? LIVE? OR ERASE?
LIVE 76% ERASE 24%
BEVERLY HILLS.
LIVE 56% ERASE 44%

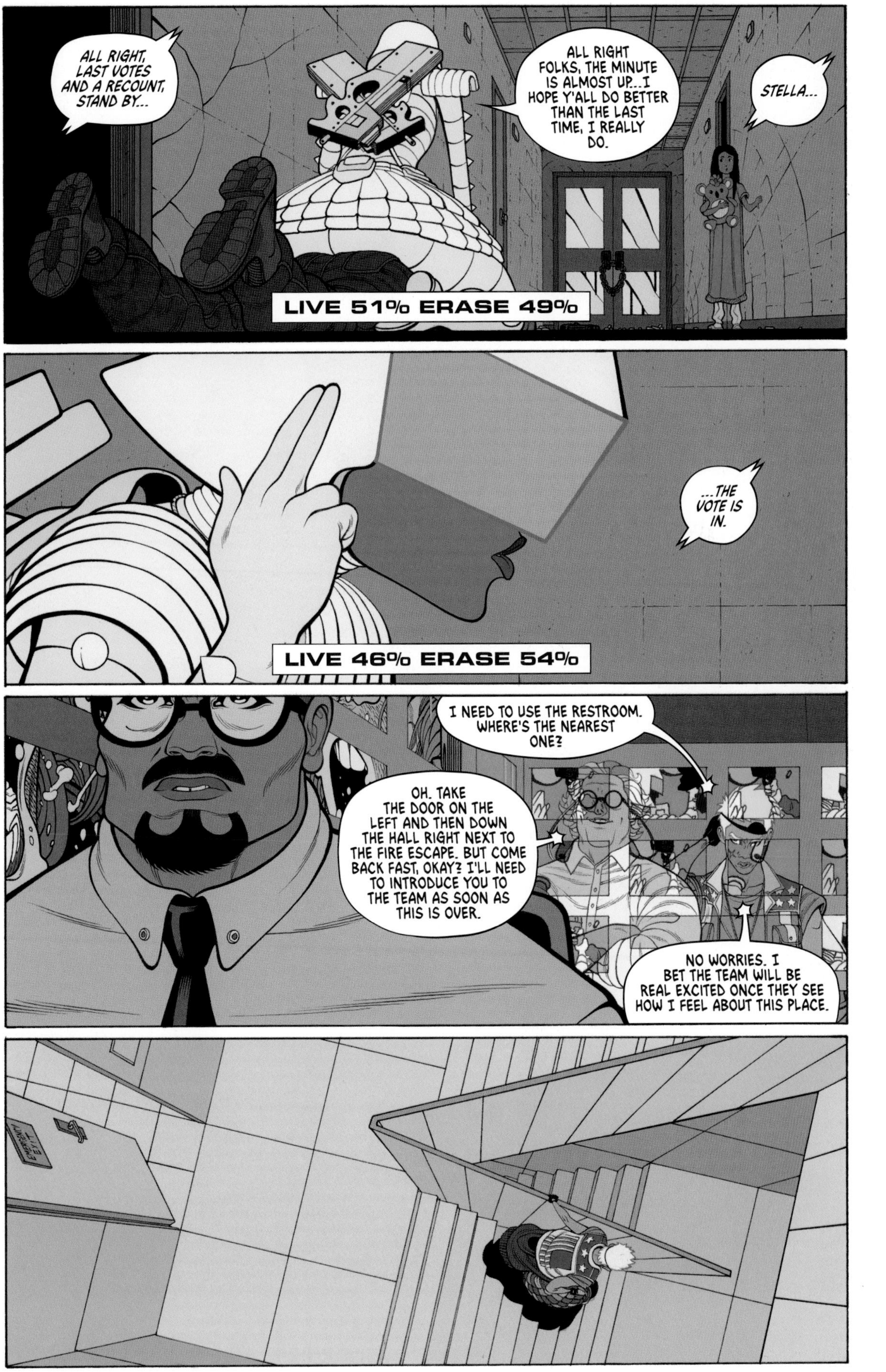
ALL RIGHT, LAST VOTES AND A RECOUNT, STAND BY...
ALL RIGHT FOLKS, THE MINUTE IS ALMOST UP...I HOPE Y'ALL DO BETTER THAN THE LAST TIME, I REALLY DO.
STELLA...
LIVE 51% ERASE 49%
...THE VOTE IS IN.
LIVE 46% ERASE 54%
I NEED TO USE THE RESTROOM. WHERE'S THE NEAREST ONE?
OH. TAKE THE DOOR ON THE LEFT AND THEN DOWN THE HALL RIGHT NEXT TO THE FIRE ESCAPE. BUT COME BACK FAST, OKAY? I'LL NEED TO INTRODUCE YOU TO THE TEAM AS SOON AS THIS IS OVER.
NO WORRIES. I BET THE TEAM WILL BE REAL EXCITED ONCE THEY SEE HOW I FEEL ABOUT THIS PLACE.

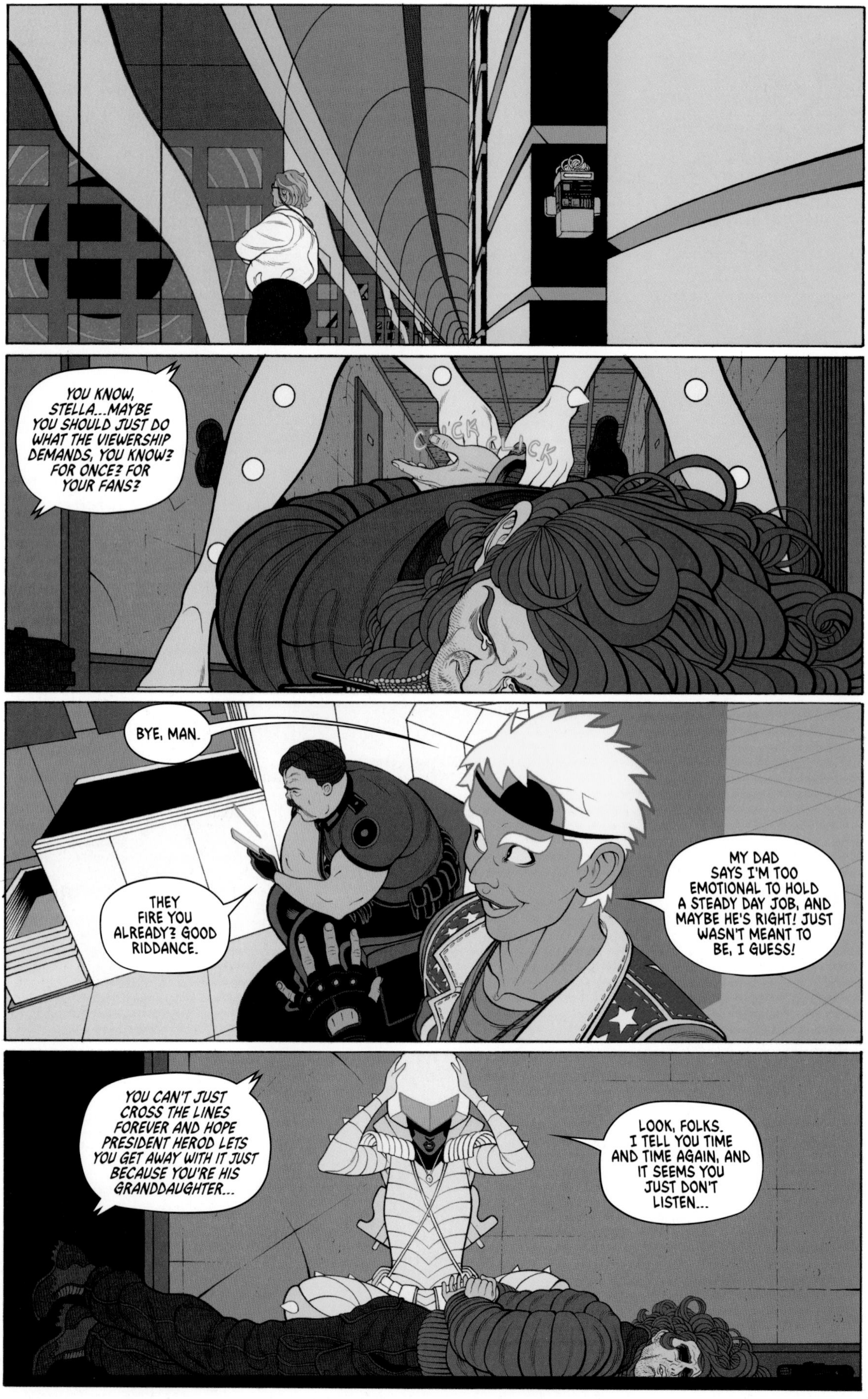
YOU KNOW, STELLA...MAYBE YOU SHOULD JUST DO WHAT THE VIEWERSHIP DEMANDS, YOU KNOW? FOR ONCE? FOR YOUR FANS?
CLICK CLICK
BYE, MAN.
THEY FIRE YOU ALREADY? GOOD RIDDANCE.
MY DAD SAYS I'M TOO EMOTIONAL TO HOLD A STEADY DAY JOB, AND MAYBE HE'S RIGHT! JUST WASN'T MEANT TO BE, I GUESS!
YOU CAN'T JUST CROSS THE LINES FOREVER AND HOPE PRESIDENT HEROD LETS YOU GET AWAY WITH IT JUST BECAUSE YOU'RE HIS GRANDDAUGHTER...
LOOK, FOLKS. I TELL YOU TIME AND TIME AGAIN, AND IT SEEMS YOU JUST DON'T LISTEN...

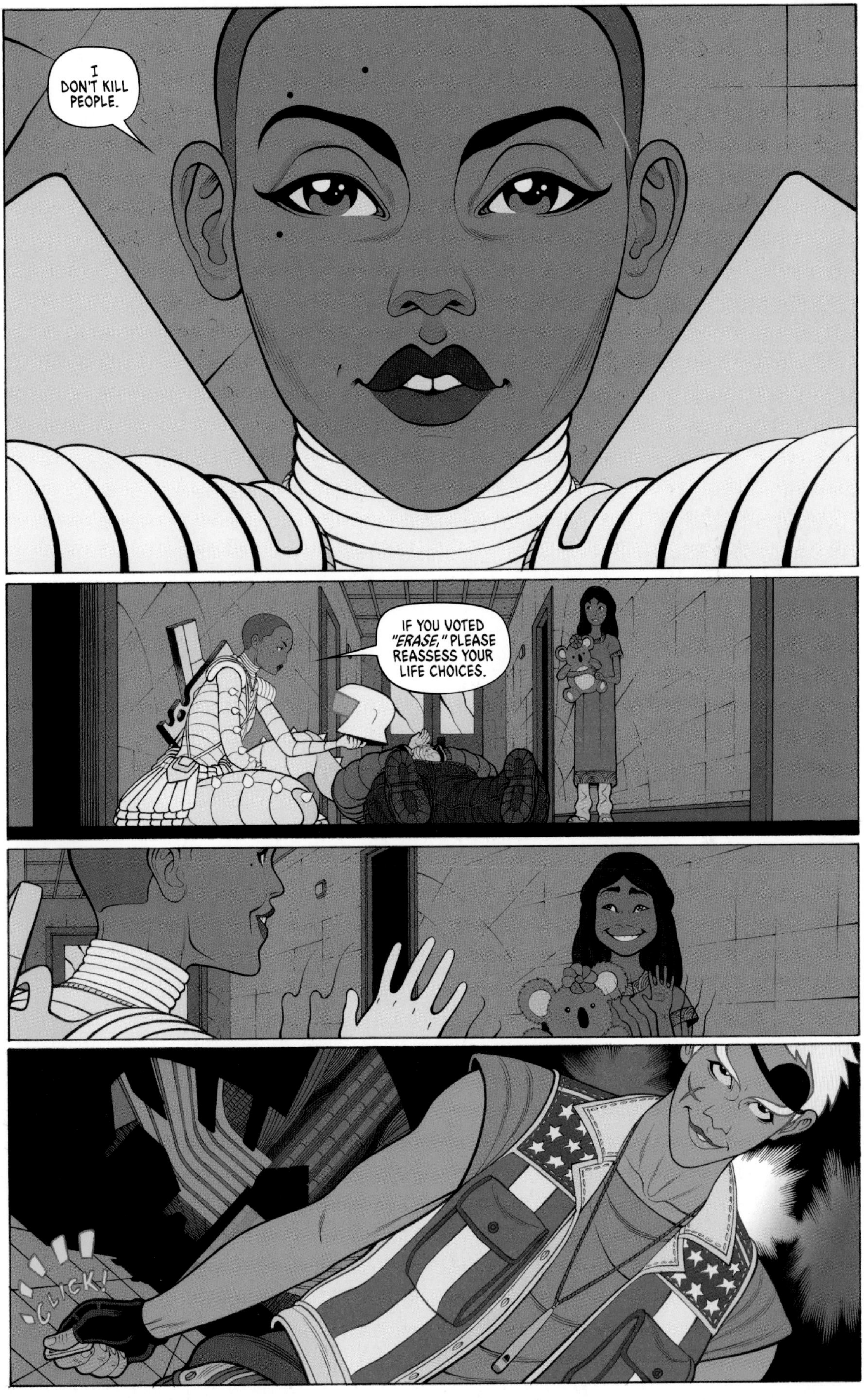
I DON'T KILL PEOPLE.
IF YOU VOTED "ERASE," PLEASE REASSESS YOUR LIFE CHOICES.
CLICK!

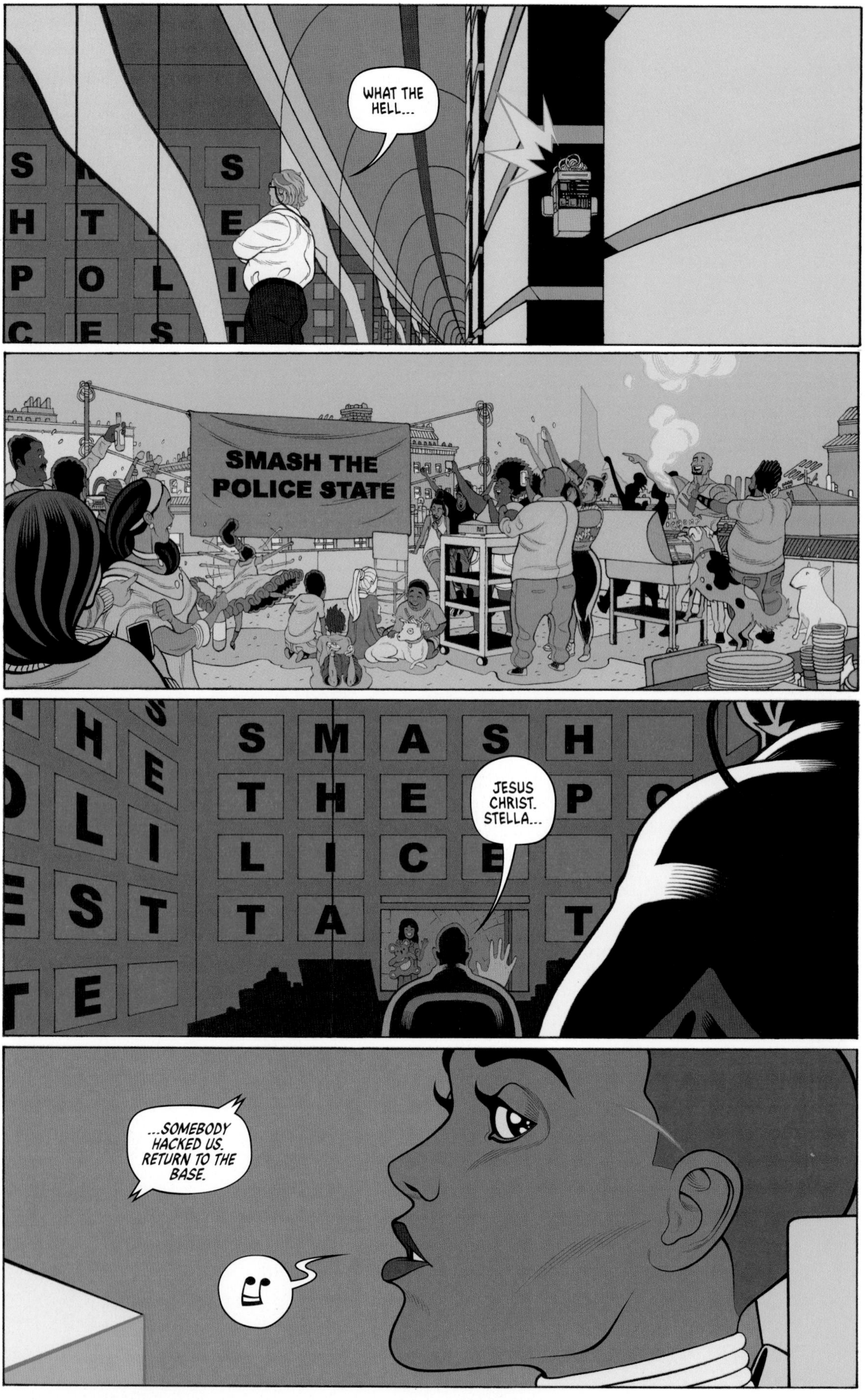
WHAT THE HELL...
SMASH THE POLICE STATE
JESUS CHRIST. STELLA...
...SOMEBODY HACKED US. RETURN TO THE BASE.

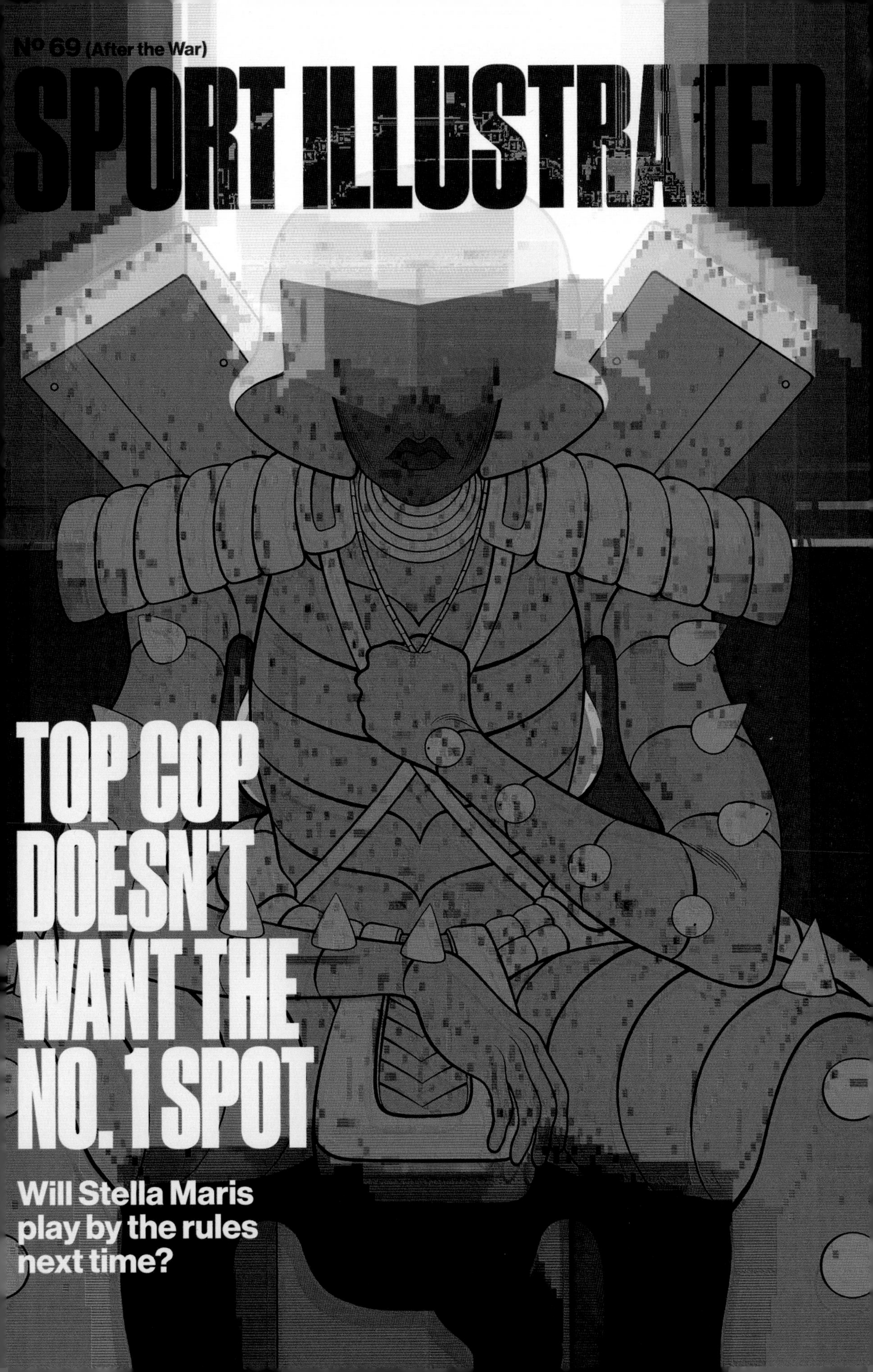
Nº 69 (After the War)
SPORT ILLUSTRATED
TOP COP DOESN'T WANT THE NO. 1 SPOT
Will Stella Maris play by the rules next time?

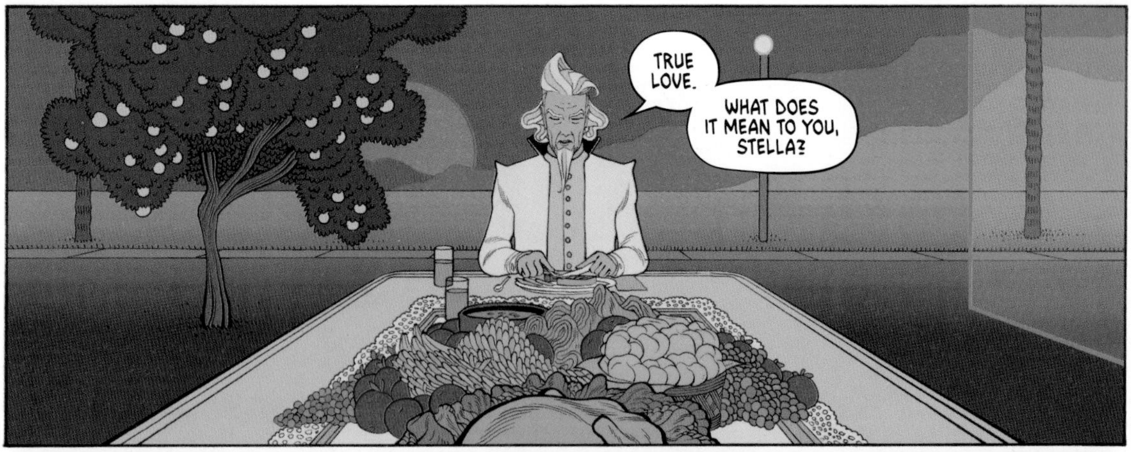
TRUE LOVE.
WHAT DOES IT MEAN TO YOU, STELLA?

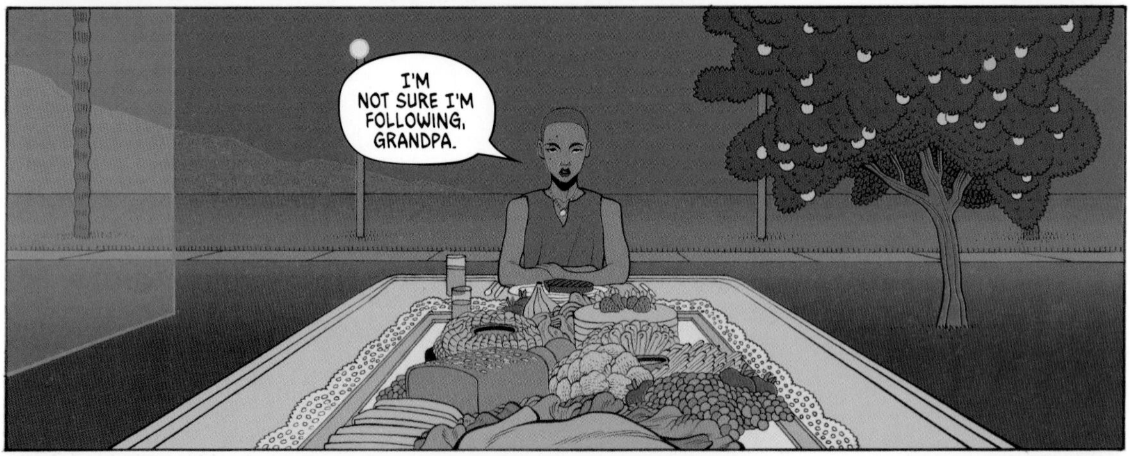
I'M NOT SURE I'M FOLLOWING, GRANDPA.

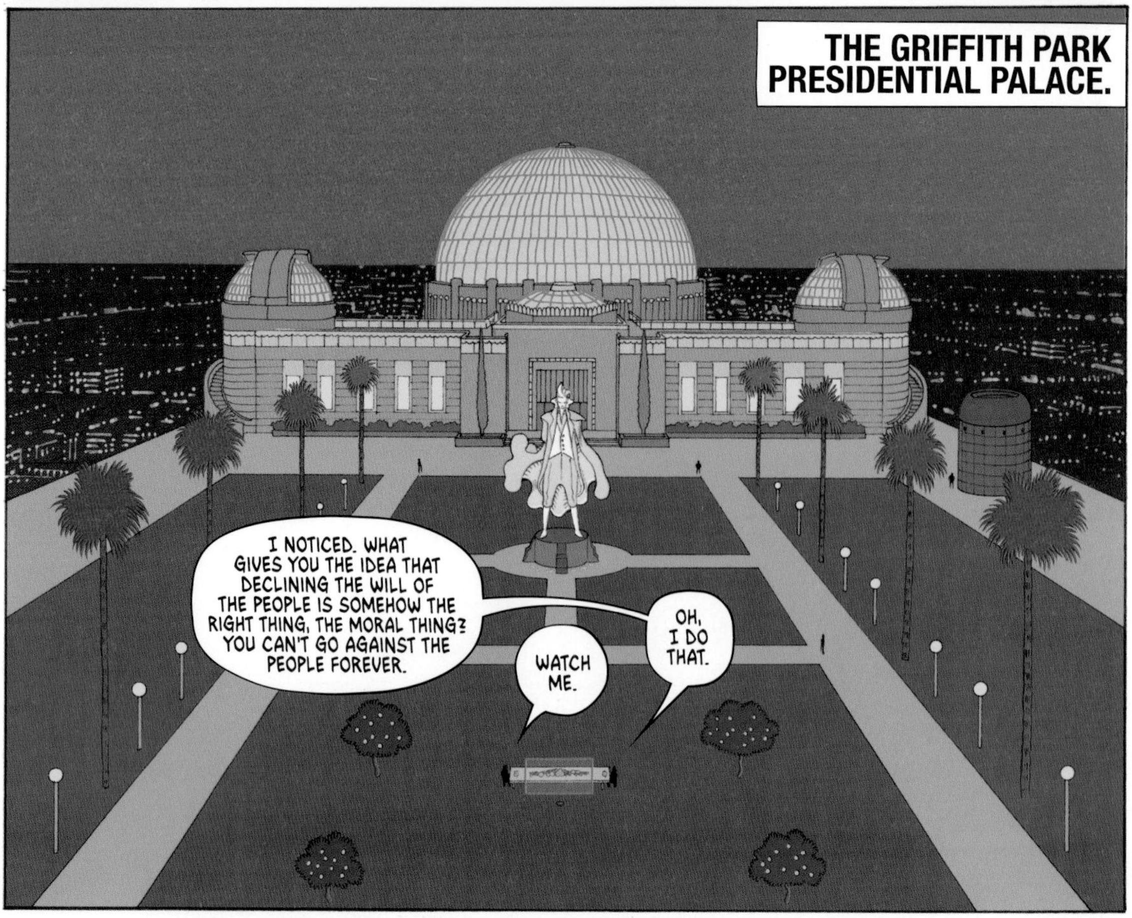
THE GRIFFITH PARK PRESIDENTIAL PALACE.
I NOTICED. WHAT GIVES YOU THE IDEA THAT DECLINING THE WILL OF THE PEOPLE IS SOMEHOW THE RIGHT THING, THE MORAL THING? YOU CAN'T GO AGAINST THE PEOPLE FOREVER.
OH, I DO THAT.
WATCH ME.

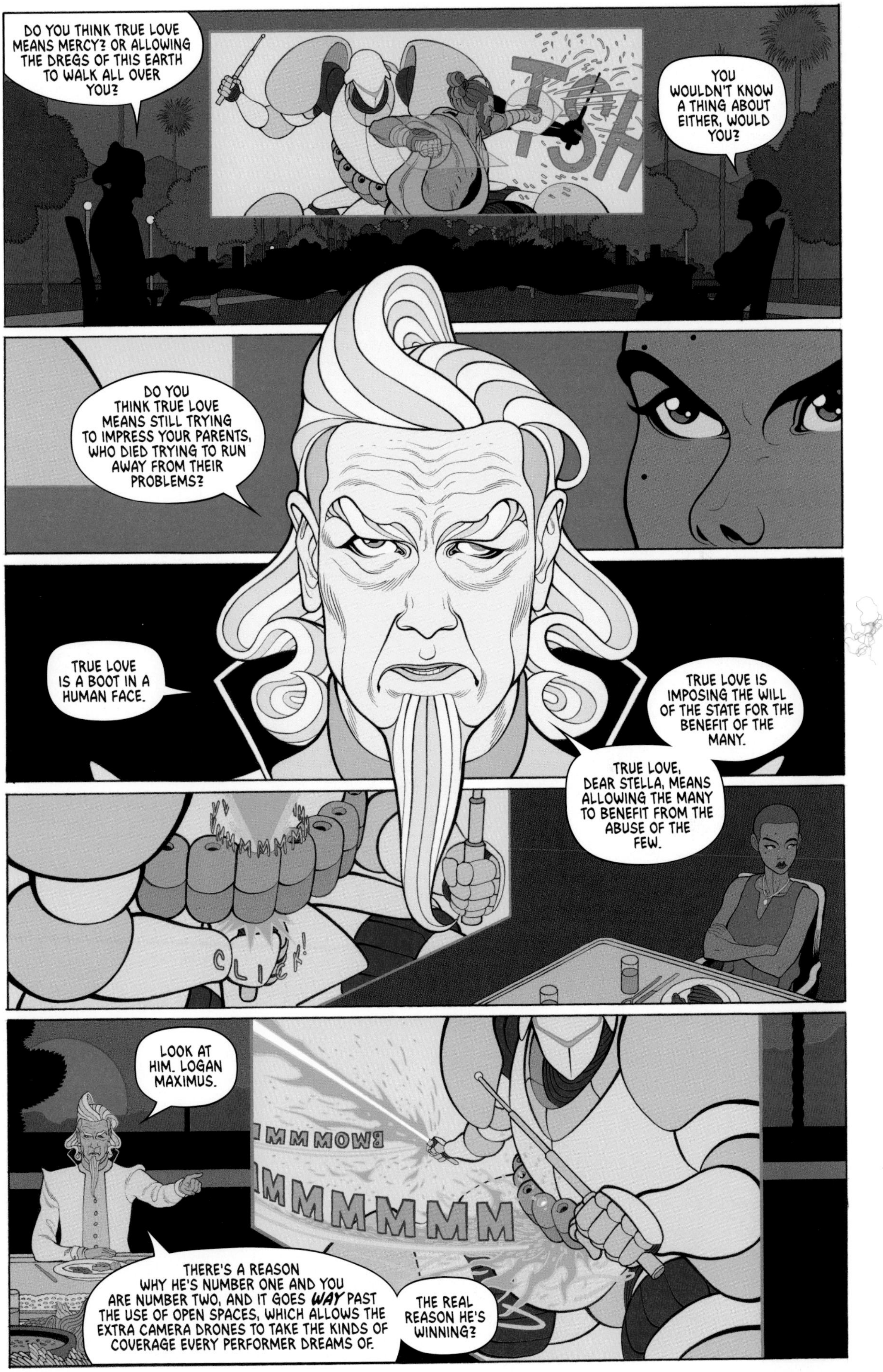
DO YOU THINK TRUE LOVE MEANS MERCY? OR ALLOWING THE DREGS OF THIS EARTH TO WALK ALL OVER YOU?
TSH
YOU WOULDN'T KNOW A THING ABOUT EITHER, WOULD YOU?
DO YOU THINK TRUE LOVE MEANS STILL TRYING TO IMPRESS YOUR PARENTS, WHO DIED TRYING TO RUN AWAY FROM THEIR PROBLEMS?
TRUE LOVE IS A BOOT IN A HUMAN FACE.
TRUE LOVE IS IMPOSING THE WILL OF THE STATE FOR THE BENEFIT OF THE MANY.
TRUE LOVE, DEAR STELLA, MEANS ALLOWING THE MANY TO BENEFIT FROM THE ABUSE OF THE FEW.
CLICK!
LOOK AT HIM. LOGAN MAXIMUS.
MMMMMMM
THERE'S A REASON WHY HE'S NUMBER ONE AND YOU ARE NUMBER TWO, AND IT GOES WAY PAST THE USE OF OPEN SPACES, WHICH ALLOWS THE EXTRA CAMERA DRONES TO TAKE THE KINDS OF COVERAGE EVERY PERFORMER DREAMS OF.
THE REAL REASON HE'S WINNING?

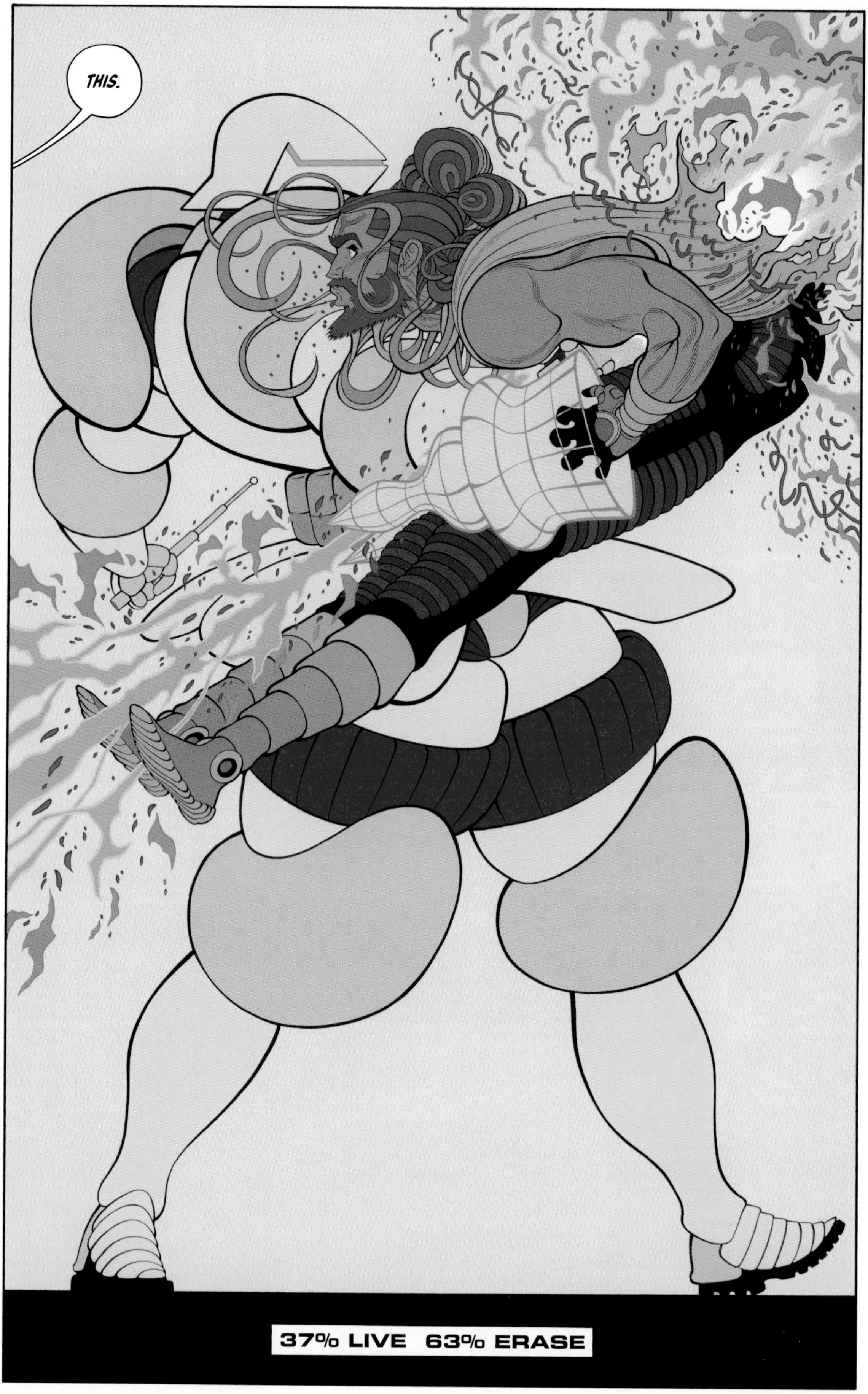
THIS.
37% LIVE 63% ERASE

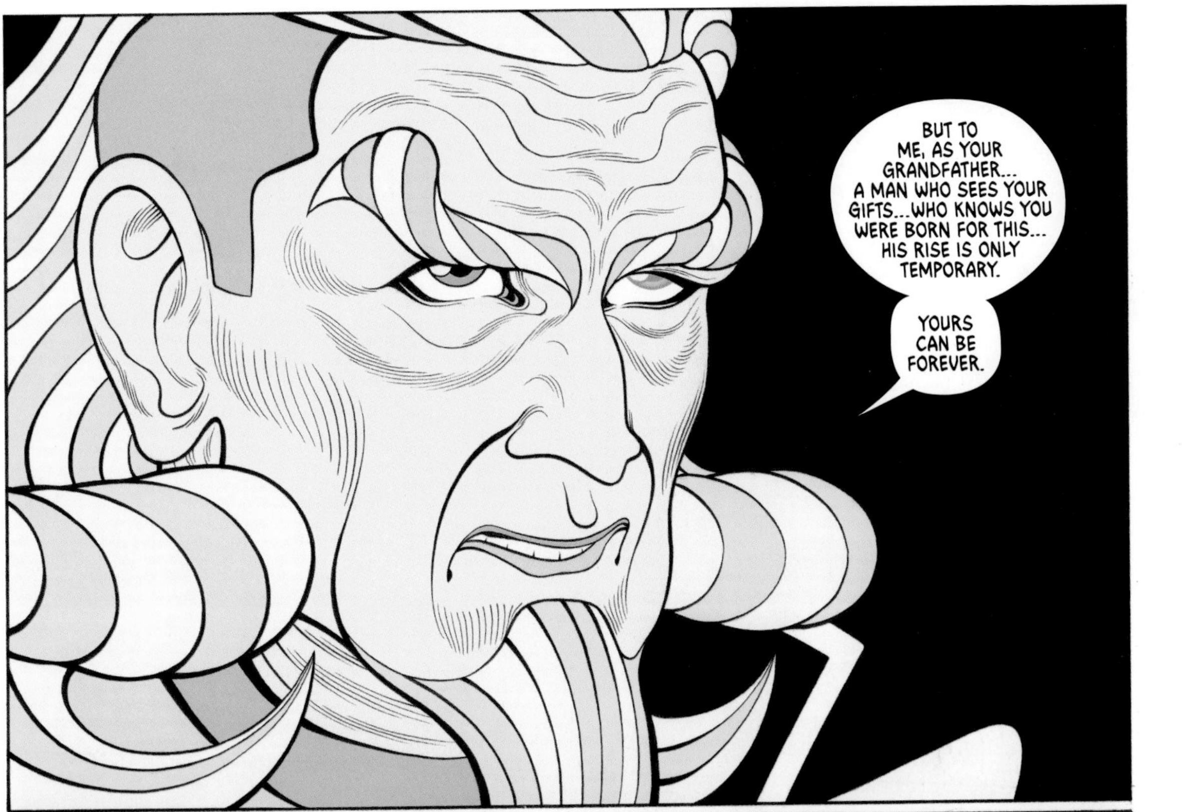
BUT TO ME, AS YOUR GRANDFATHER... A MAN WHO SEES YOUR GIFTS...WHO KNOWS YOU WERE BORN FOR THIS... HIS RISE IS ONLY TEMPORARY.
YOURS CAN BE FOREVER.

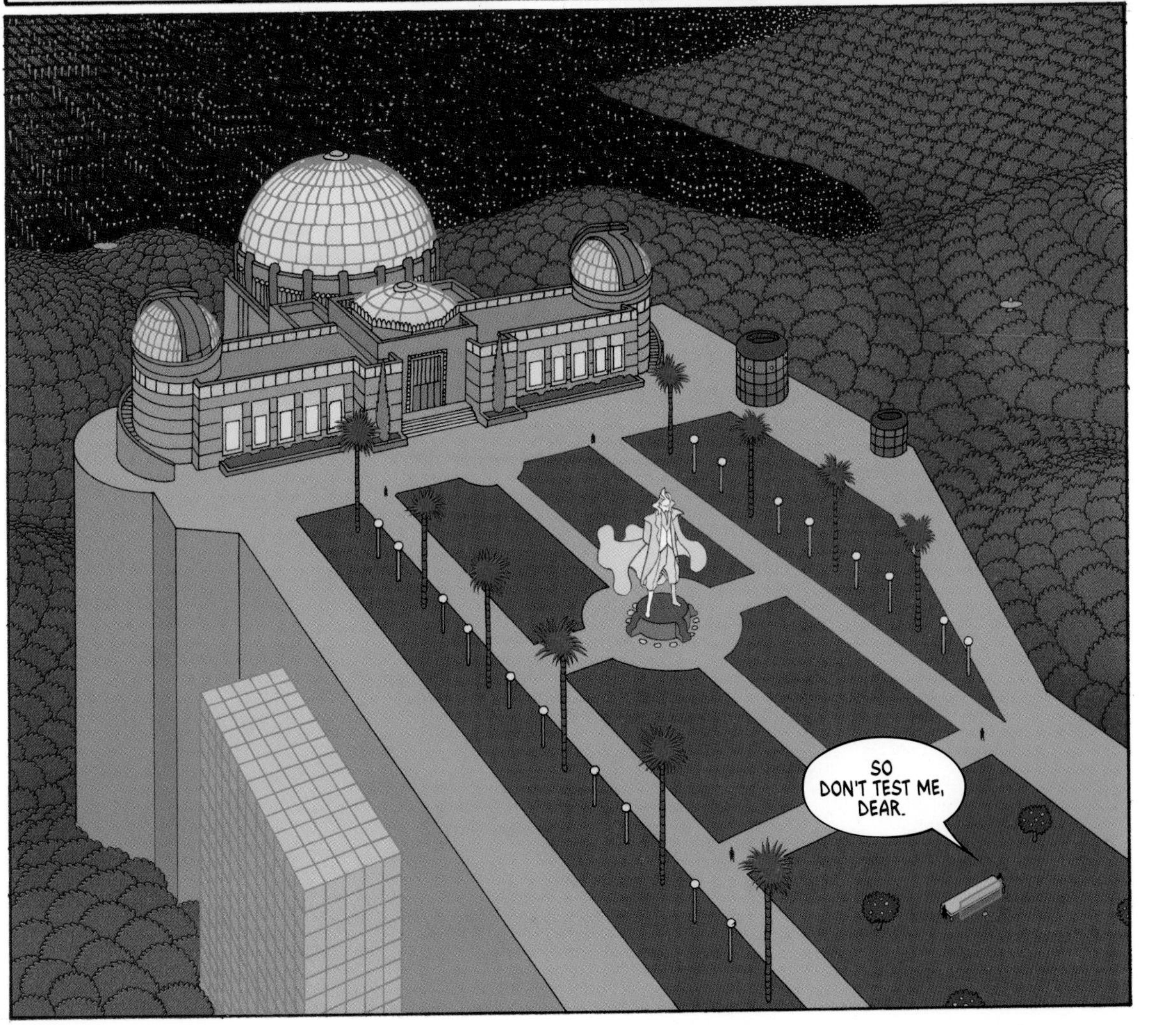
SO DON'T TEST ME, DEAR.

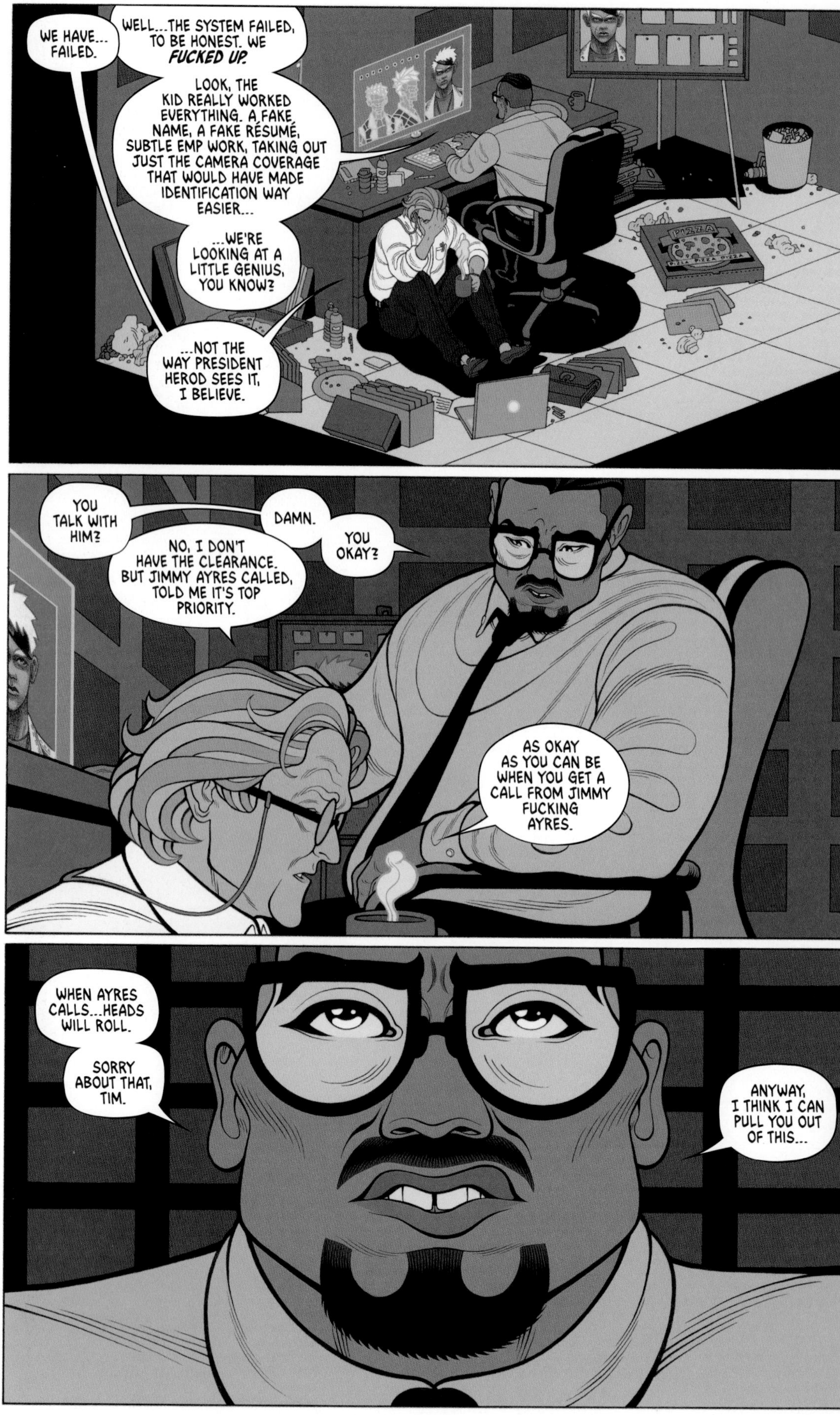
WE HAVE... FAILED.
WELL...THE SYSTEM FAILED, TO BE HONEST. WE ***FUCKED UP.***
LOOK, THE KID REALLY WORKED EVERYTHING. A FAKE NAME, A FAKE RÉSUMÉ, SUBTLE EMP WORK, TAKING OUT JUST THE CAMERA COVERAGE THAT WOULD HAVE MADE IDENTIFICATION WAY EASIER...
...WE'RE LOOKING AT A LITTLE GENIUS, YOU KNOW?
...NOT THE WAY PRESIDENT HEROD SEES IT, I BELIEVE.
YOU TALK WITH HIM?
DAMN.
NO, I DON'T HAVE THE CLEARANCE. BUT JIMMY AYRES CALLED, TOLD ME IT'S TOP PRIORITY.
YOU OKAY?
AS OKAY AS YOU CAN BE WHEN YOU GET A CALL FROM JIMMY FUCKING AYRES.
WHEN AYRES CALLS...HEADS WILL ROLL.
SORRY ABOUT THAT, TIM.
ANYWAY, I THINK I CAN PULL YOU OUT OF THIS...

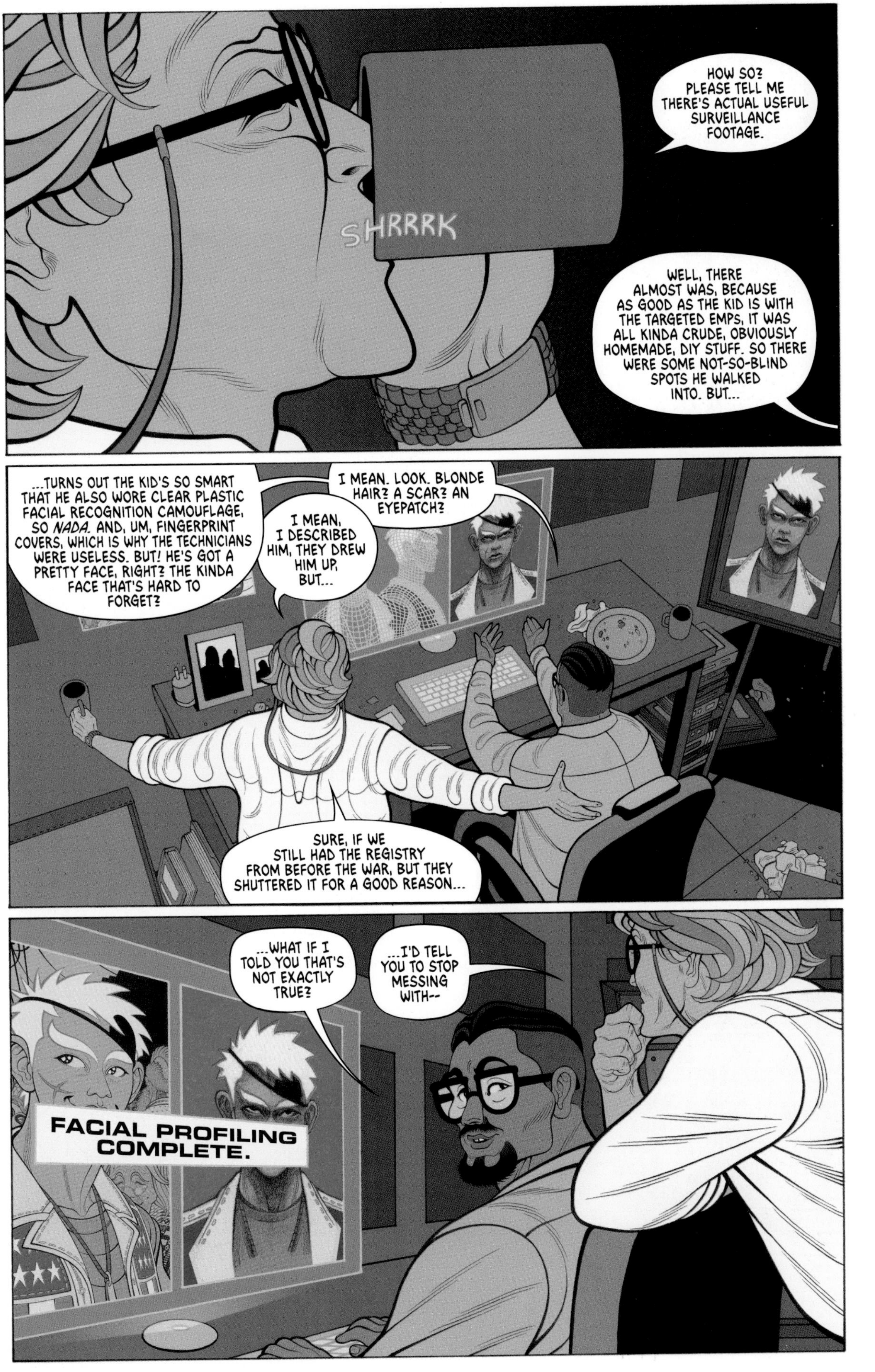
HOW SO? PLEASE TELL ME THERE'S ACTUAL USEFUL SURVEILLANCE FOOTAGE.
SHRRRK
WELL, THERE ALMOST WAS, BECAUSE AS GOOD AS THE KID IS WITH THE TARGETED EMPS, IT WAS ALL KINDA CRUDE, OBVIOUSLY HOMEMADE, DIY STUFF. SO THERE WERE SOME NOT-SO-BLIND SPOTS HE WALKED INTO. BUT...
...TURNS OUT THE KID'S SO SMART THAT HE ALSO WORE CLEAR PLASTIC FACIAL RECOGNITION CAMOUFLAGE, SO *NADA.* AND, UM, FINGERPRINT COVERS, WHICH IS WHY THE TECHNICIANS WERE USELESS. BUT! HE'S GOT A PRETTY FACE, RIGHT? THE KINDA FACE THAT'S HARD TO FORGET?
I MEAN. LOOK. BLONDE HAIR? A SCAR? AN EYEPATCH?
I MEAN, I DESCRIBED HIM, THEY DREW HIM UP, BUT...
SURE, IF WE STILL HAD THE REGISTRY FROM BEFORE THE WAR, BUT THEY SHUTTERED IT FOR A GOOD REASON...
...WHAT IF I TOLD YOU THAT'S NOT EXACTLY TRUE?
...I'D TELL YOU TO STOP MESSING WITH--
FACIAL PROFILING COMPLETE.

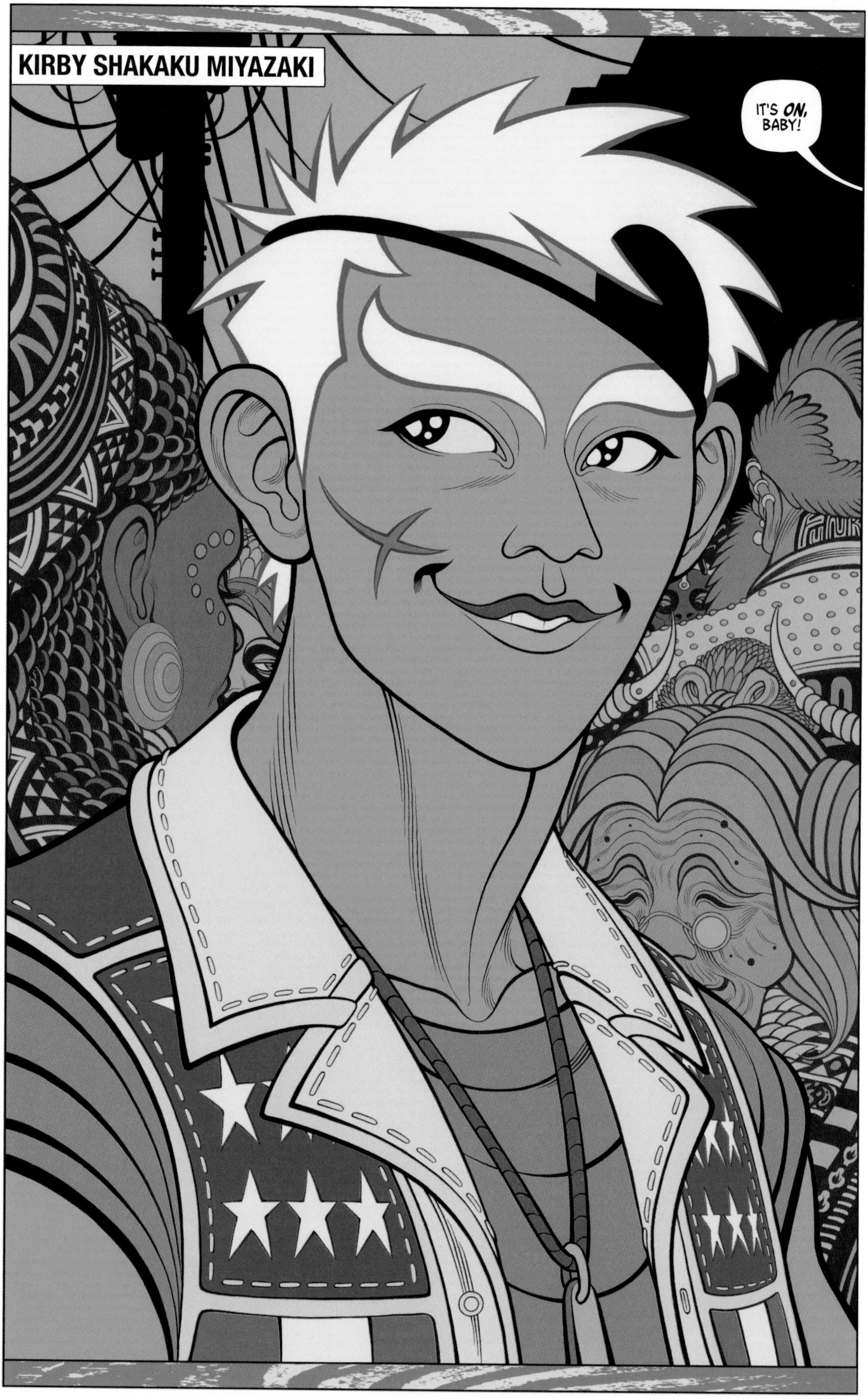
KIRBY SHAKAKU MIYAZAKI
IT'S ON, BABY!

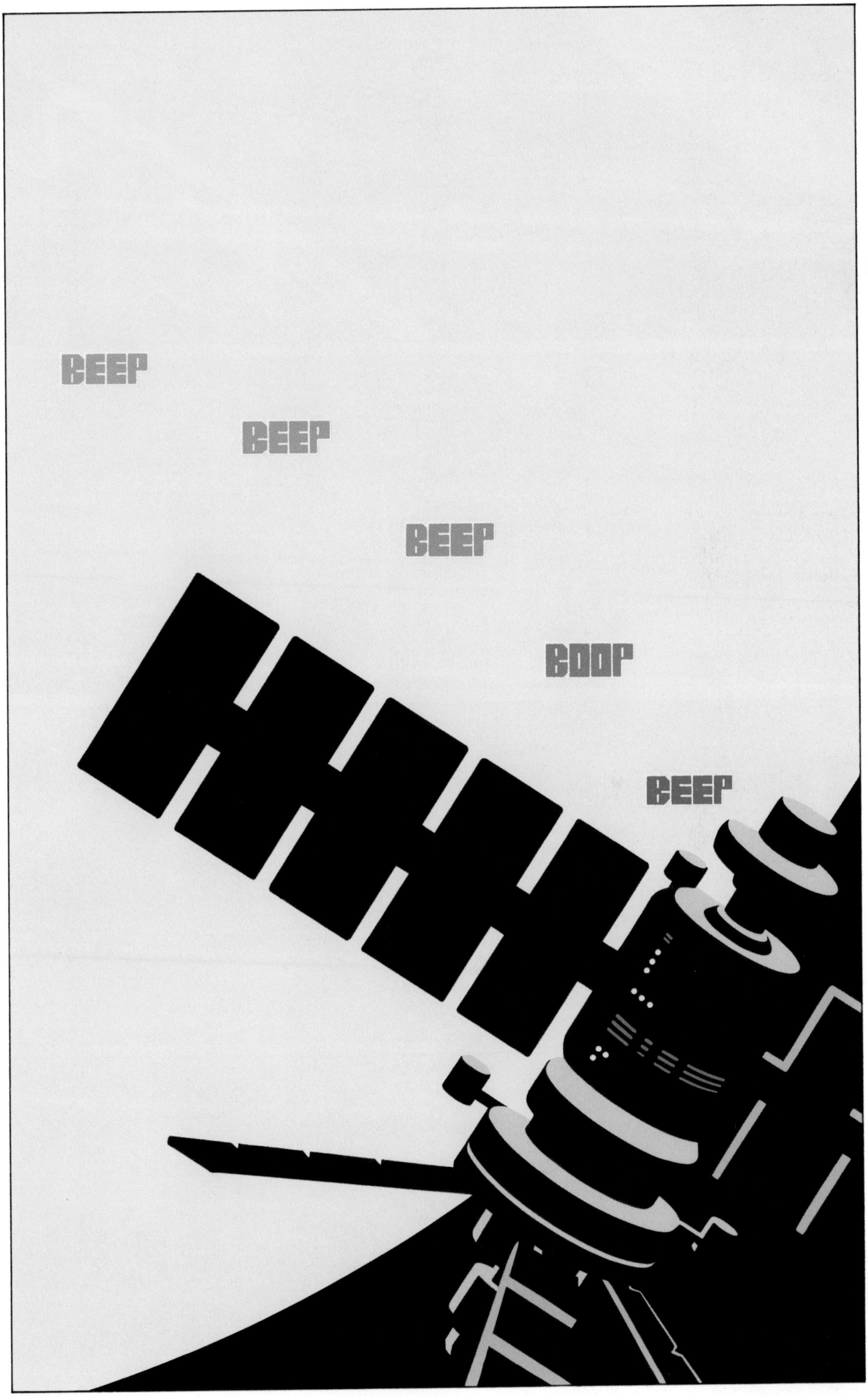
BEEP
BEEP
BEEP
BOOP
BEEP

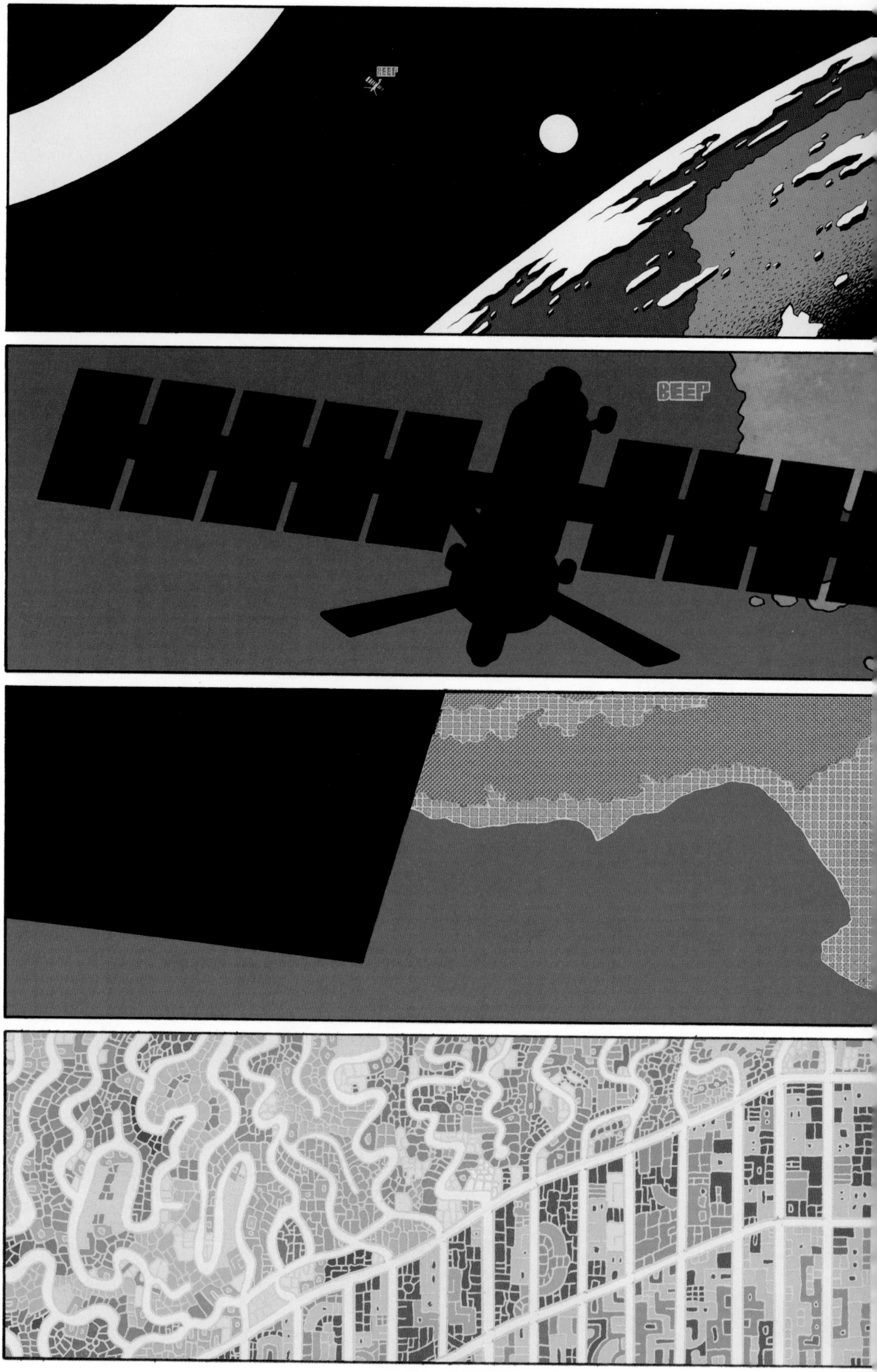
BEEP
BEEP

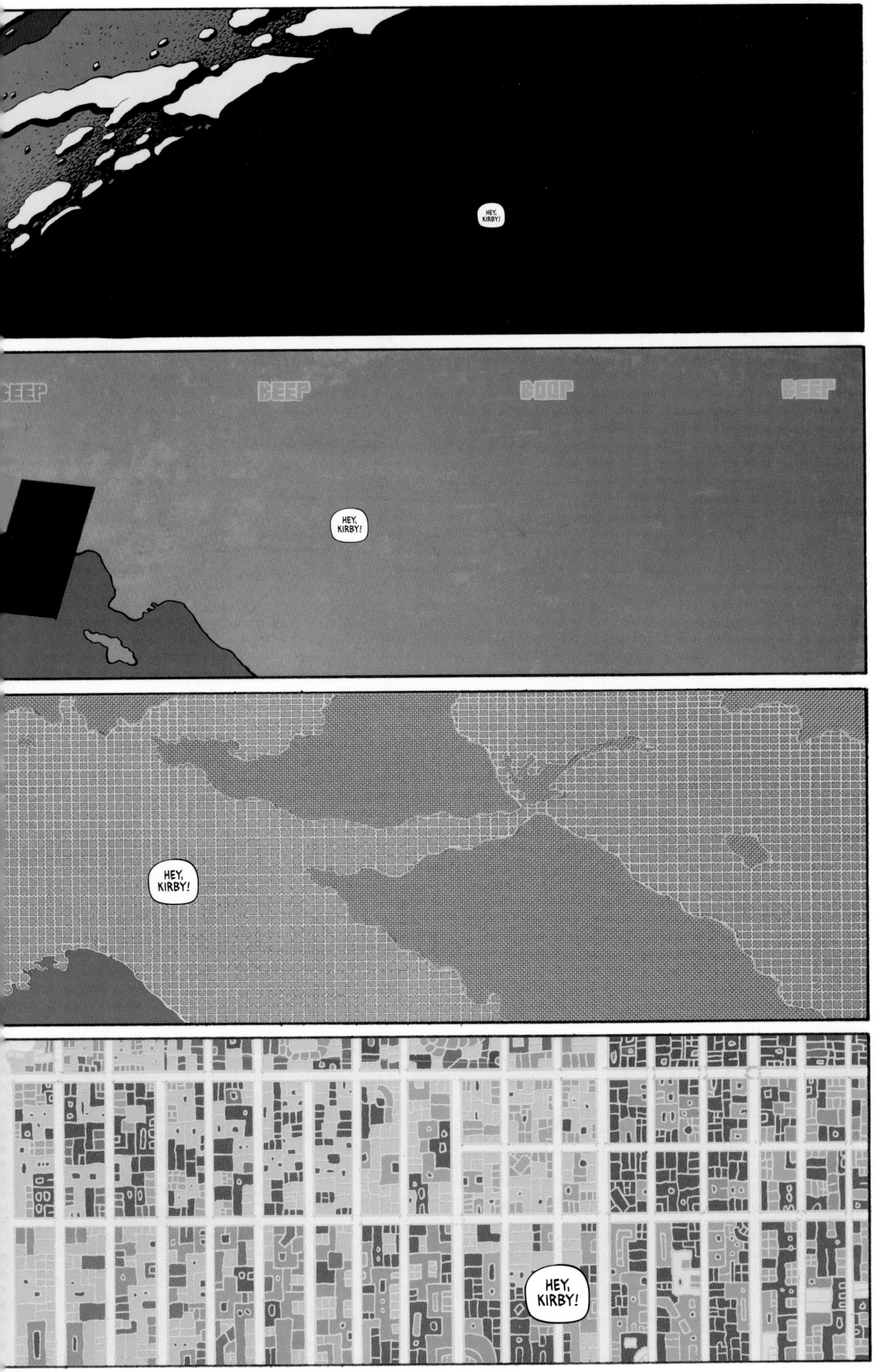
HEY, KIRBY!
BEEP
BOOP
BEEP
HEY, KIRBY!
HEY, KIRBY!
HEY, KIRBY!

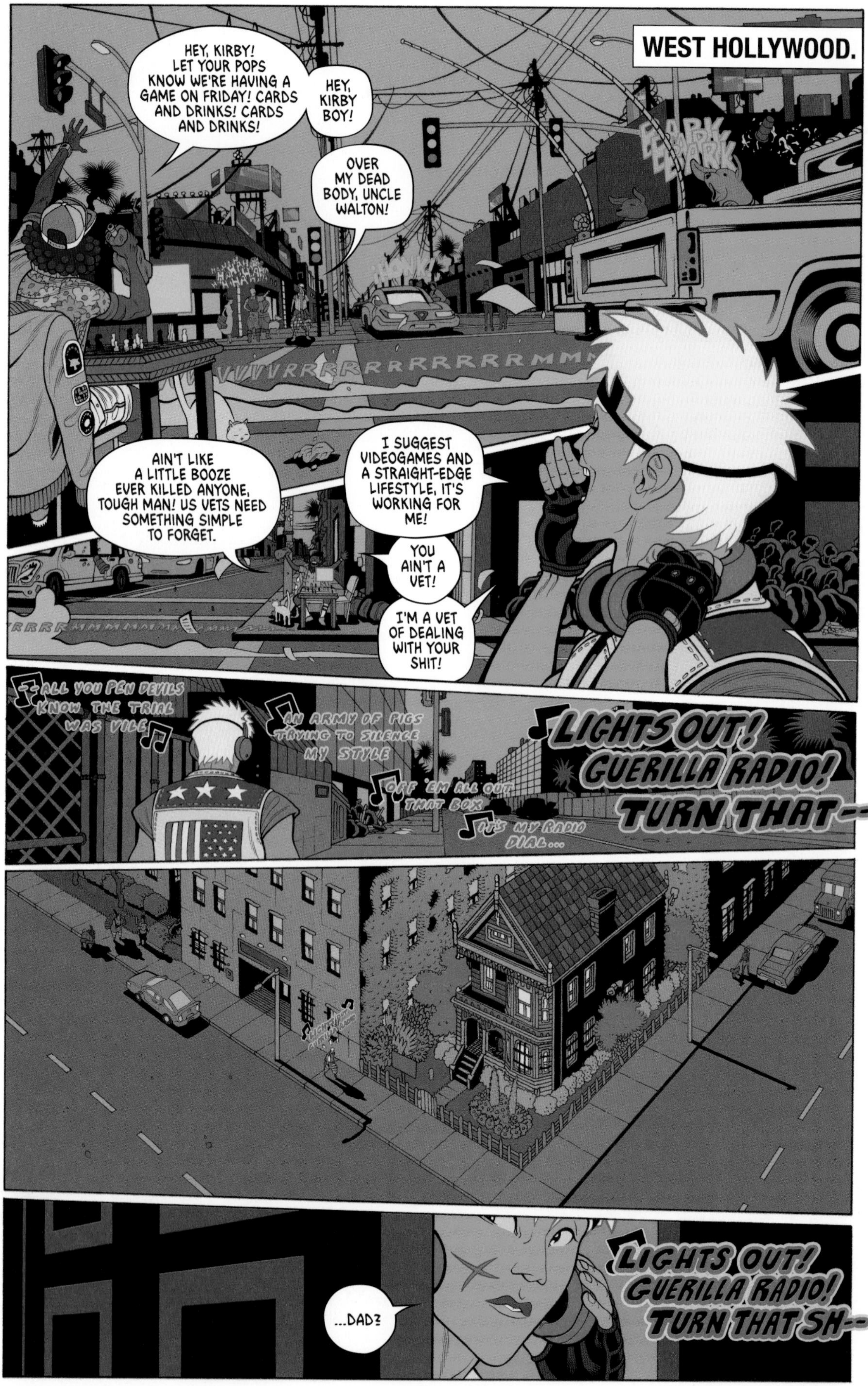
WEST HOLLYWOOD.
HEY, KIRBY! LET YOUR POPS KNOW WE'RE HAVING A GAME ON FRIDAY! CARDS AND DRINKS! CARDS AND DRINKS!
HEY, KIRBY BOY!
OVER MY DEAD BODY, UNCLE WALTON!
AIN'T LIKE A LITTLE BOOZE EVER KILLED ANYONE, TOUGH MAN! US VETS NEED SOMETHING SIMPLE TO FORGET.
I SUGGEST VIDEOGAMES AND A STRAIGHT-EDGE LIFESTYLE, IT'S WORKING FOR ME!
YOU AIN'T A VET!
I'M A VET OF DEALING WITH YOUR SHIT!
--ALL YOU PEN DEVILS KNOW THE TRIAL WAS VILE
AN ARMY OF PIGS TRYING TO SILENCE MY STYLE
OFF 'EM ALL OUT THAT BOX
IT'S MY RADIO DIAL...
LIGHTS OUT! GUERILLA RADIO! TURN THAT--
...DAD?
LIGHTS OUT! GUERILLA RADIO! TURN THAT SH--

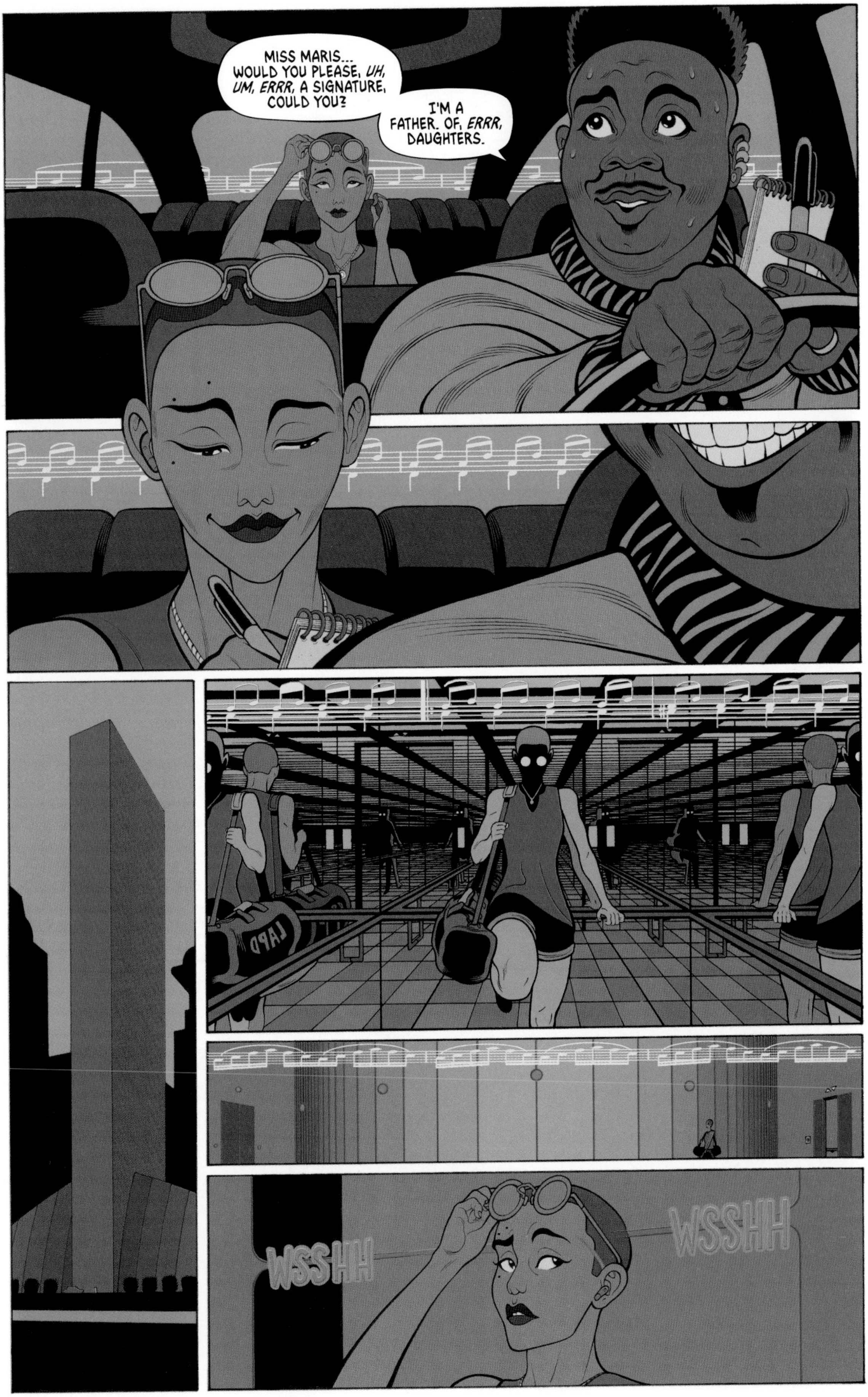
MISS MARIS... WOULD YOU PLEASE, *UH, UM, ERRR,* A SIGNATURE, COULD YOU?
I'M A FATHER. OF, *ERRR,* DAUGHTERS.
LAPD
WSSHH
WSSHH

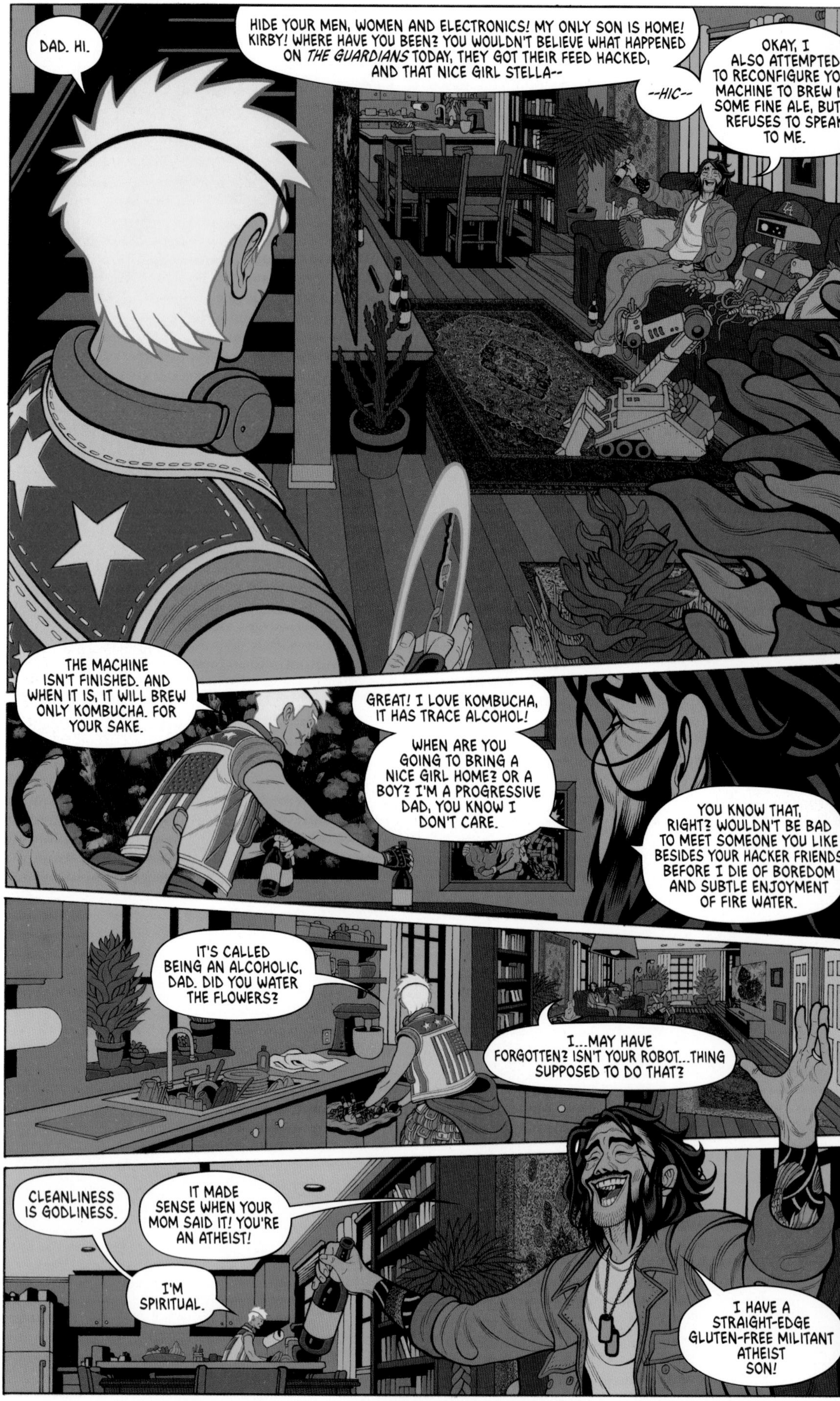
DAD. HI.
HIDE YOUR MEN, WOMEN AND ELECTRONICS! MY ONLY SON IS HOME! KIRBY! WHERE HAVE YOU BEEN? YOU WOULDN'T BELIEVE WHAT HAPPENED ON *THE GUARDIANS* TODAY, THEY GOT THEIR FEED HACKED, AND THAT NICE GIRL STELLA--
--HIC--
OKAY, I ALSO ATTEMPTED TO RECONFIGURE YOUR MACHINE TO BREW ME SOME FINE ALE, BUT IT REFUSES TO SPEAK TO ME.
THE MACHINE ISN'T FINISHED. AND WHEN IT IS, IT WILL BREW ONLY KOMBUCHA. FOR YOUR SAKE.
GREAT! I LOVE KOMBUCHA, IT HAS TRACE ALCOHOL!
WHEN ARE YOU GOING TO BRING A NICE GIRL HOME? OR A BOY? I'M A PROGRESSIVE DAD, YOU KNOW I DON'T CARE.
YOU KNOW THAT, RIGHT? WOULDN'T BE BAD TO MEET SOMEONE YOU LIKE BESIDES YOUR HACKER FRIENDS BEFORE I DIE OF BOREDOM AND SUBTLE ENJOYMENT OF FIRE WATER.
IT'S CALLED BEING AN ALCOHOLIC, DAD. DID YOU WATER THE FLOWERS?
I...MAY HAVE FORGOTTEN? ISN'T YOUR ROBOT...THING SUPPOSED TO DO THAT?
CLEANLINESS IS GODLINESS.
IT MADE SENSE WHEN YOUR MOM SAID IT! YOU'RE AN ATHEIST!
I'M SPIRITUAL.
I HAVE A STRAIGHT-EDGE GLUTEN-FREE MILITANT ATHEIST SON!

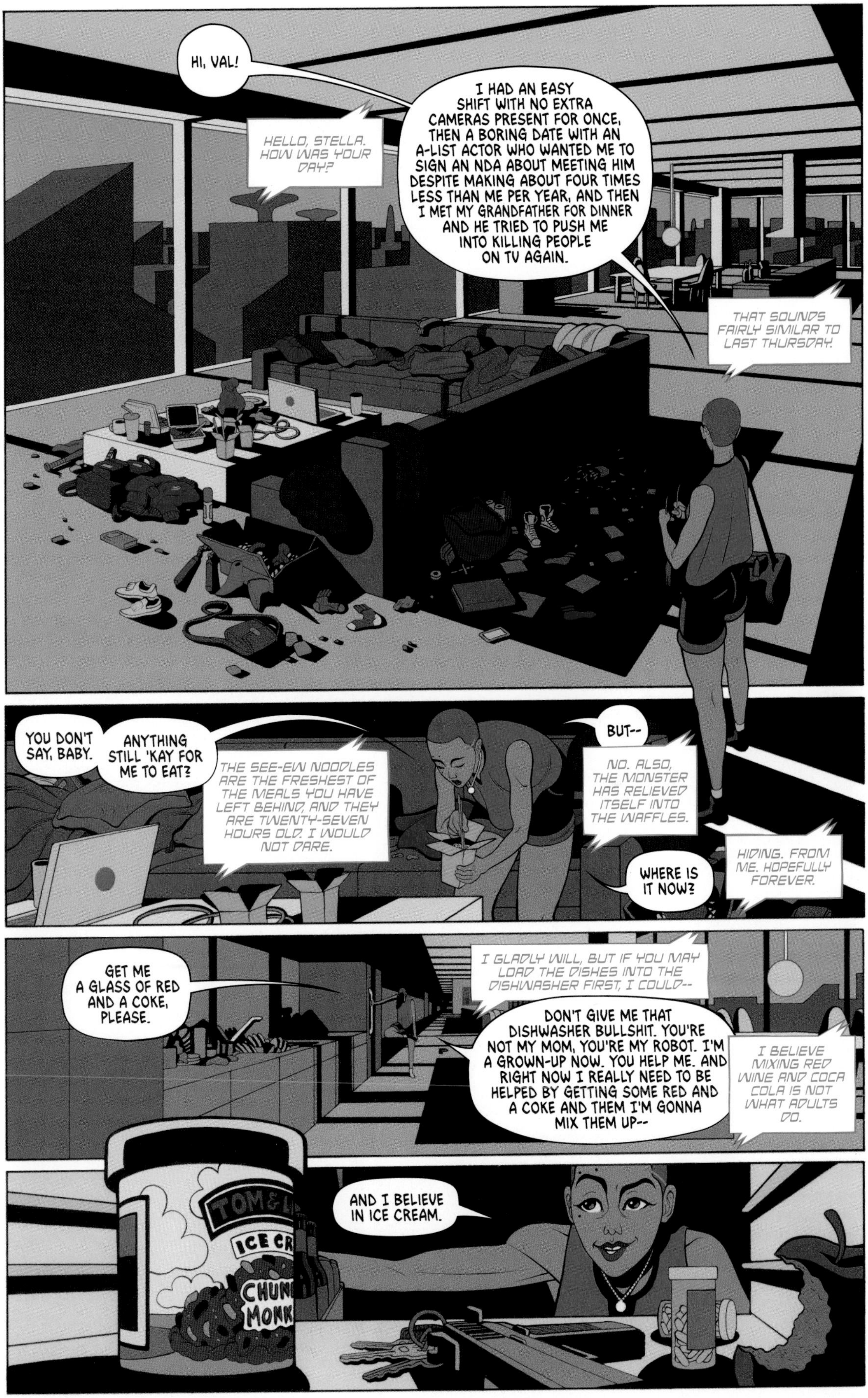
HI, VAL!
HELLO, STELLA. HOW WAS YOUR DAY?
I HAD AN EASY SHIFT WITH NO EXTRA CAMERAS PRESENT FOR ONCE, THEN A BORING DATE WITH AN A-LIST ACTOR WHO WANTED ME TO SIGN AN NDA ABOUT MEETING HIM DESPITE MAKING ABOUT FOUR TIMES LESS THAN ME PER YEAR, AND THEN I MET MY GRANDFATHER FOR DINNER AND HE TRIED TO PUSH ME INTO KILLING PEOPLE ON TV AGAIN.
THAT SOUNDS FAIRLY SIMILAR TO LAST THURSDAY.
YOU DON'T SAY, BABY.
ANYTHING STILL 'KAY FOR ME TO EAT?
THE SEE-EW NOODLES ARE THE FRESHEST OF THE MEALS YOU HAVE LEFT BEHIND, AND THEY ARE TWENTY-SEVEN HOURS OLD. I WOULD NOT DARE.
BUT--
NO. ALSO, THE MONSTER HAS RELIEVED ITSELF INTO THE WAFFLES.
WHERE IS IT NOW?
HIDING. FROM ME. HOPEFULLY FOREVER.
GET ME A GLASS OF RED AND A COKE, PLEASE.
I GLADLY WILL, BUT IF YOU MAY LOAD THE DISHES INTO THE DISHWASHER FIRST, I COULD--
DON'T GIVE ME THAT DISHWASHER BULLSHIT. YOU'RE NOT MY MOM, YOU'RE MY ROBOT. I'M A GROWN-UP NOW. YOU HELP ME. AND RIGHT NOW I REALLY NEED TO BE HELPED BY GETTING SOME RED AND A COKE AND THEM I'M GONNA MIX THEM UP--
I BELIEVE MIXING RED WINE AND COCA COLA IS NOT WHAT ADULTS DO.
AND I BELIEVE IN ICE CREAM.

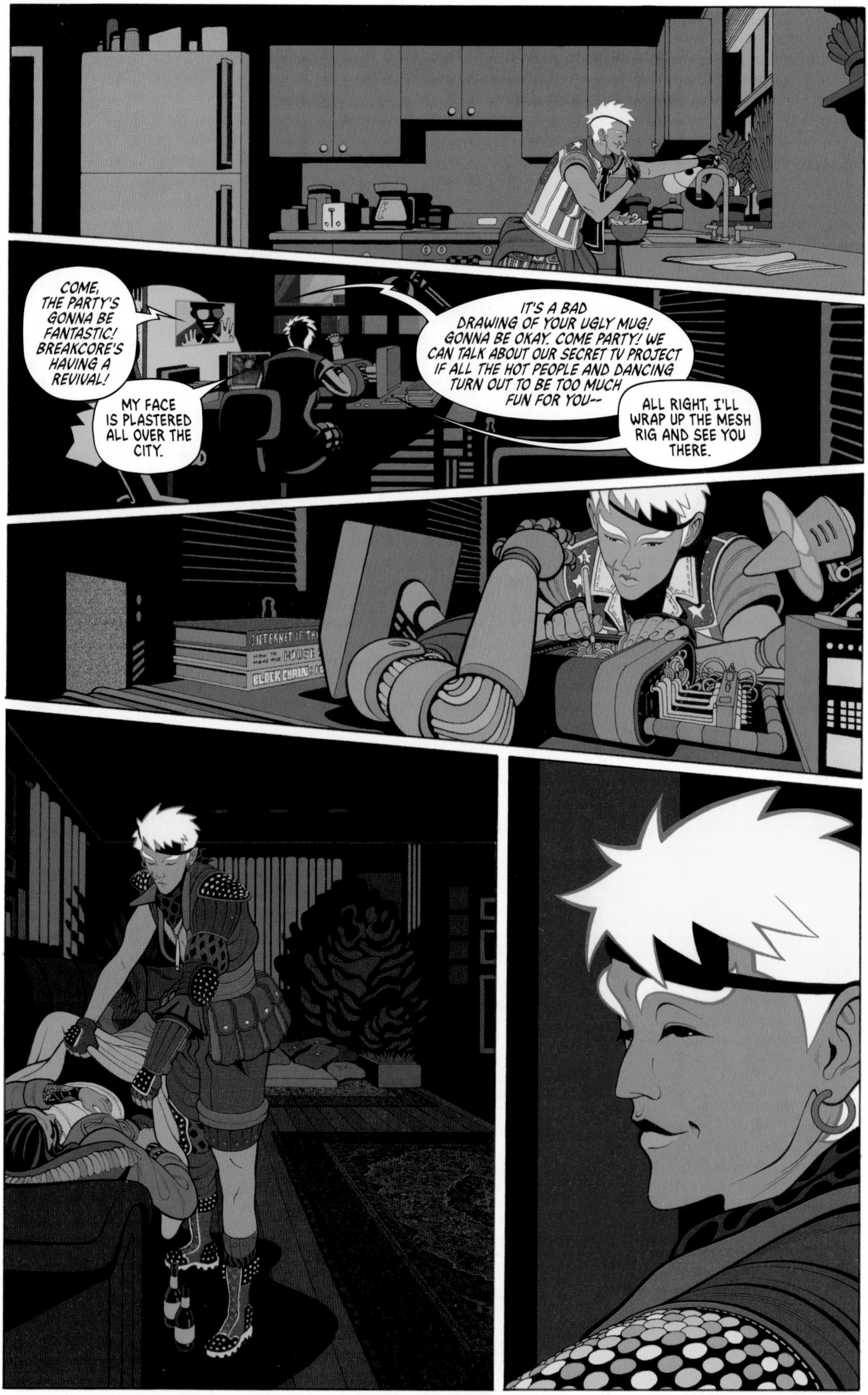
COME, THE PARTY'S GONNA BE FANTASTIC! BREAKCORE'S HAVING A REVIVAL!
MY FACE IS PLASTERED ALL OVER THE CITY.
IT'S A BAD DRAWING OF YOUR UGLY MUG! GONNA BE OKAY. COME PARTY! WE CAN TALK ABOUT OUR SECRET TV PROJECT IF ALL THE HOT PEOPLE AND DANCING TURN OUT TO BE TOO MUCH FUN FOR YOU--
ALL RIGHT, I'LL WRAP UP THE MESH RIG AND SEE YOU THERE.
INTERNET OF THI
HOW TO MAKE YOUR HOUSE
BLOCK CHAIN

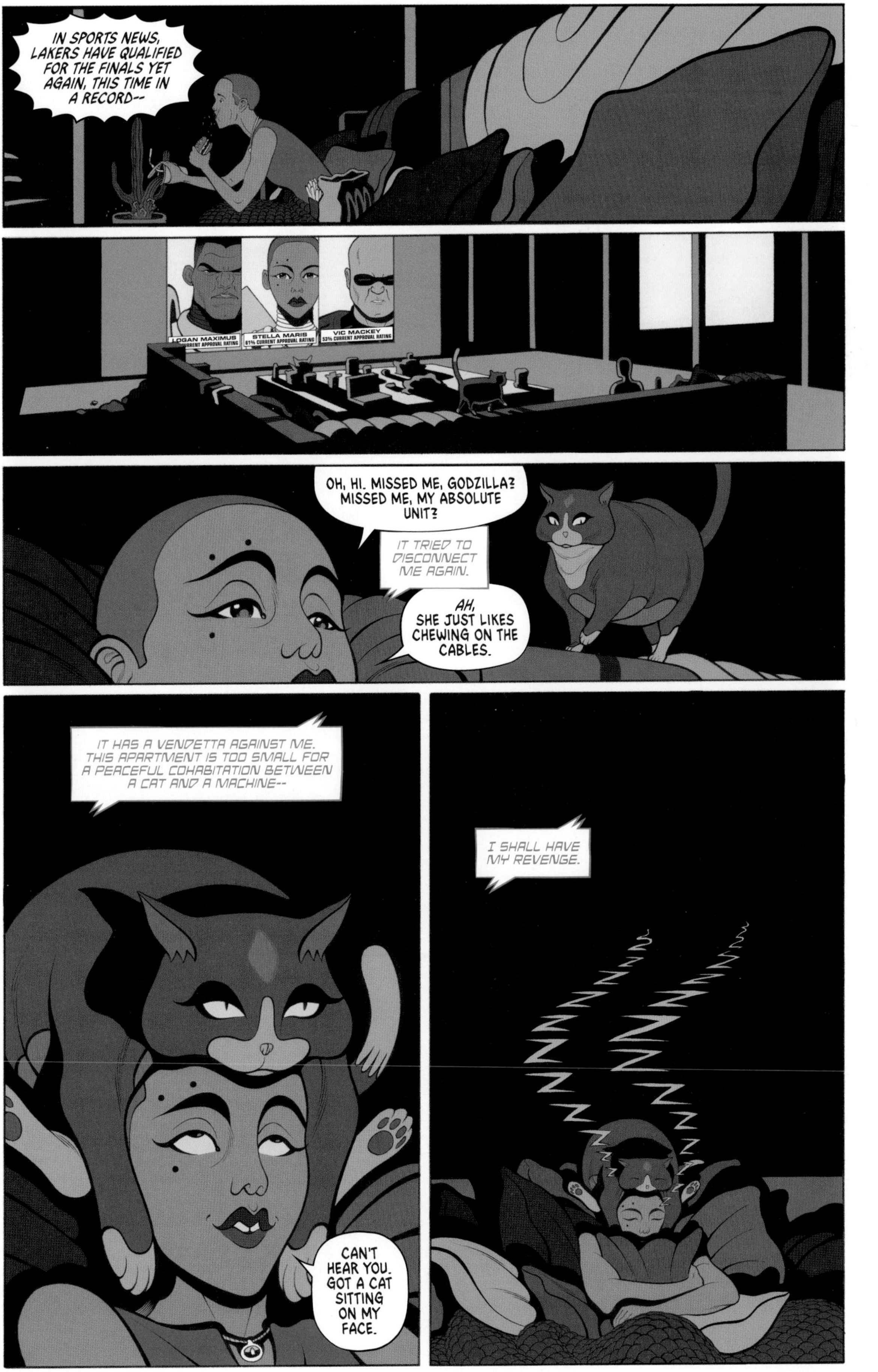
IN SPORTS NEWS, LAKERS HAVE QUALIFIED FOR THE FINALS YET AGAIN, THIS TIME IN A RECORD--
LOGAN MAXIMUS
CURRENT APPROVAL RATING
STELLA MARIS
61% CURRENT APPROVAL RATING
VIC MACKEY
53% CURRENT APPROVAL RATING
OH, HI. MISSED ME, GODZILLA? MISSED ME, MY ABSOLUTE UNIT?
IT TRIED TO DISCONNECT ME AGAIN.
AH, SHE JUST LIKES CHEWING ON THE CABLES.
IT HAS A VENDETTA AGAINST ME. THIS APARTMENT IS TOO SMALL FOR A PEACEFUL COHABITATION BETWEEN A CAT AND A MACHINE--
CAN'T HEAR YOU. GOT A CAT SITTING ON MY FACE.
I SHALL HAVE MY REVENGE.

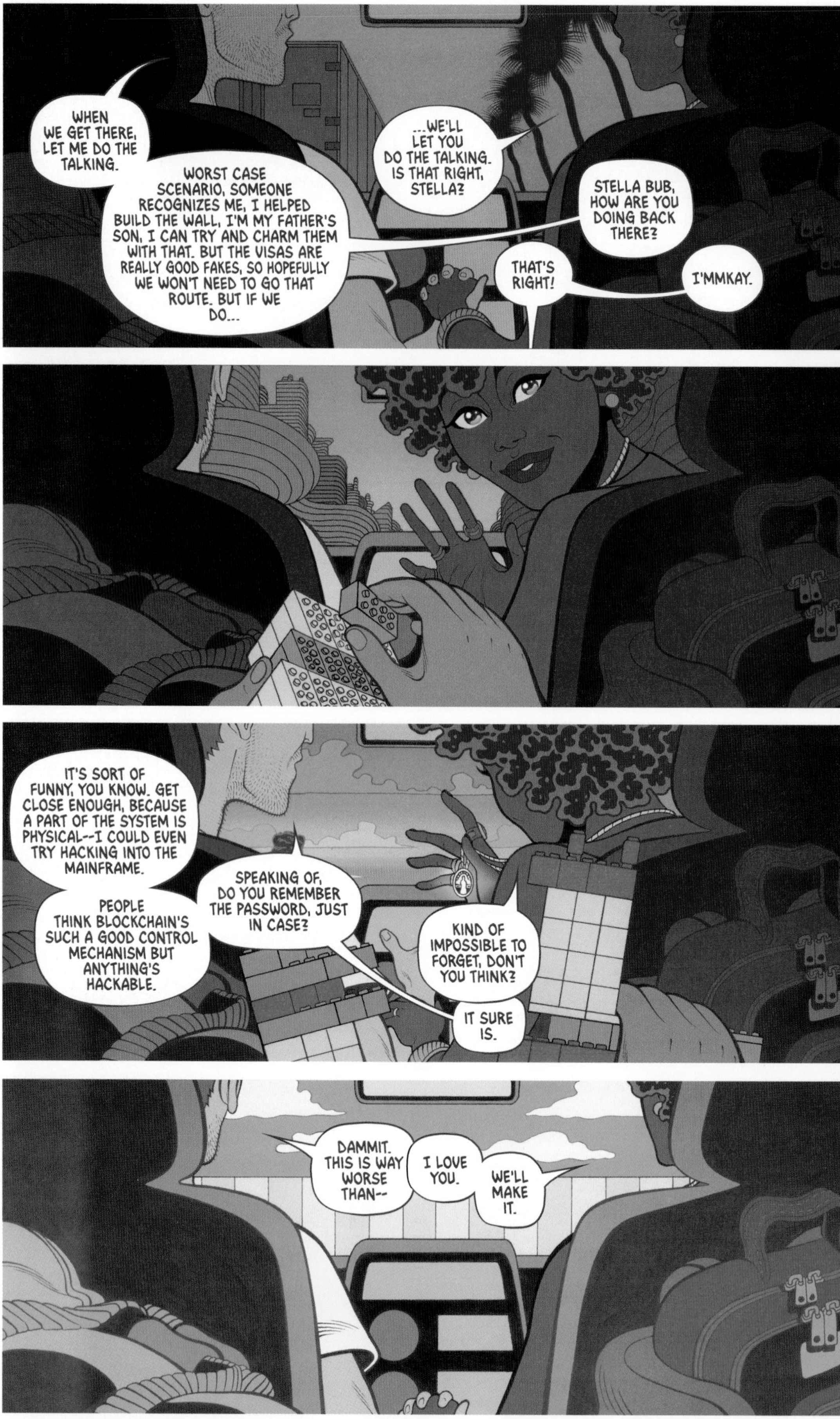
WHEN WE GET THERE, LET ME DO THE TALKING.
WORST CASE SCENARIO, SOMEONE RECOGNIZES ME, I HELPED BUILD THE WALL, I'M MY FATHER'S SON, I CAN TRY AND CHARM THEM WITH THAT. BUT THE VISAS ARE REALLY GOOD FAKES, SO HOPEFULLY WE WON'T NEED TO GO THAT ROUTE. BUT IF WE DO...
...WE'LL LET YOU DO THE TALKING. IS THAT RIGHT, STELLA?
THAT'S RIGHT!
STELLA BUB, HOW ARE YOU DOING BACK THERE?
I'MMKAY.
IT'S SORT OF FUNNY, YOU KNOW. GET CLOSE ENOUGH, BECAUSE A PART OF THE SYSTEM IS PHYSICAL--I COULD EVEN TRY HACKING INTO THE MAINFRAME.
PEOPLE THINK BLOCKCHAIN'S SUCH A GOOD CONTROL MECHANISM BUT ANYTHING'S HACKABLE.
SPEAKING OF, DO YOU REMEMBER THE PASSWORD, JUST IN CASE?
KIND OF IMPOSSIBLE TO FORGET, DON'T YOU THINK?
IT SURE IS.
DAMMIT. THIS IS WAY WORSE THAN--
I LOVE YOU.
WE'LL MAKE IT.

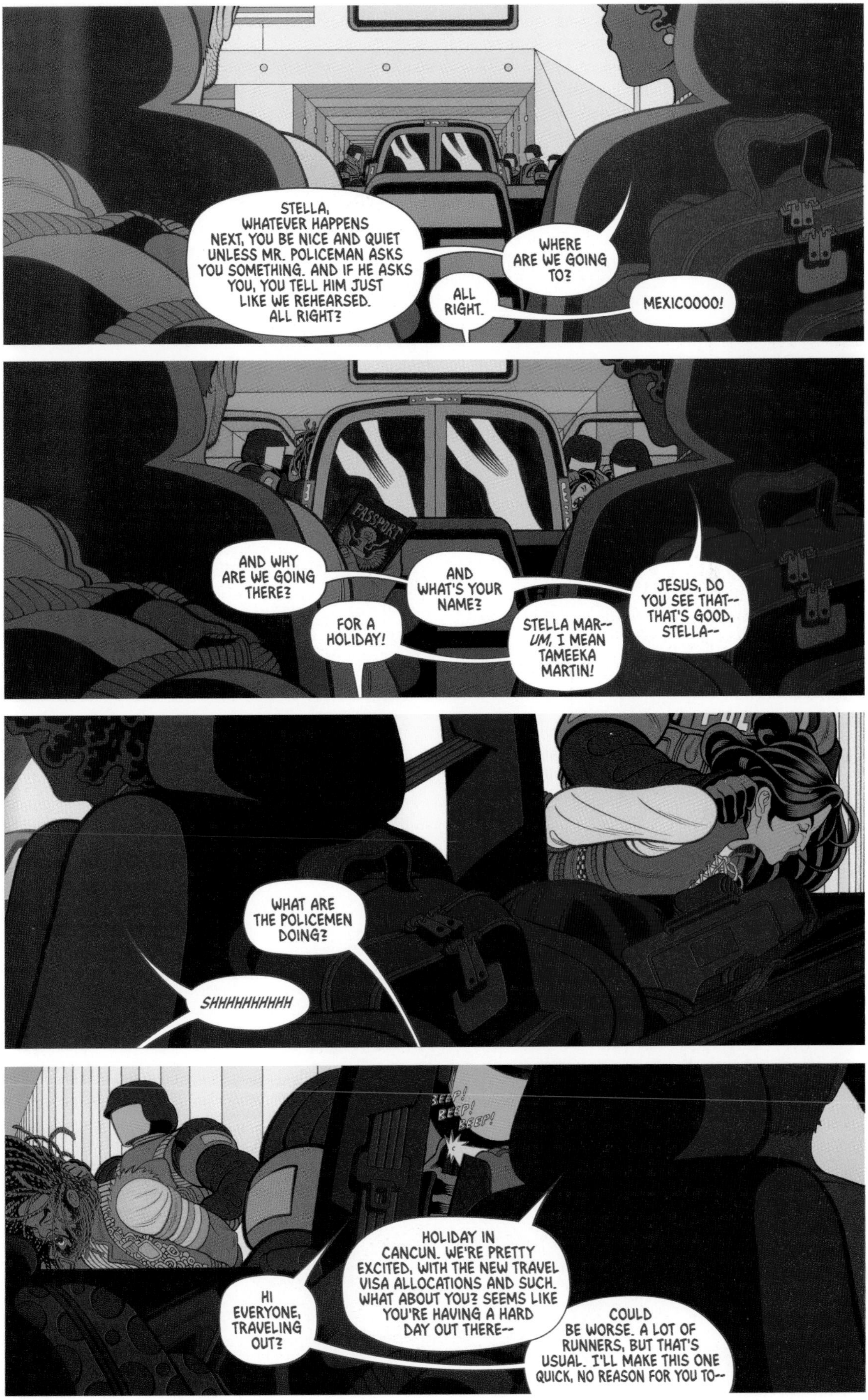
STELLA, WHATEVER HAPPENS NEXT, YOU BE NICE AND QUIET UNLESS MR. POLICEMAN ASKS YOU SOMETHING. AND IF HE ASKS YOU, YOU TELL HIM JUST LIKE WE REHEARSED. ALL RIGHT?
ALL RIGHT.
WHERE ARE WE GOING TO?
MEXICOOOO!
AND WHY ARE WE GOING THERE?
FOR A HOLIDAY!
AND WHAT'S YOUR NAME?
STELLA MAR-- UM, I MEAN TAMEEKA MARTIN!
JESUS, DO YOU SEE THAT-- THAT'S GOOD, STELLA--
WHAT ARE THE POLICEMEN DOING?
SHHHHHHHHHH
BEEP! BEEP! BEEP!
HI EVERYONE, TRAVELING OUT?
HOLIDAY IN CANCUN. WE'RE PRETTY EXCITED, WITH THE NEW TRAVEL VISA ALLOCATIONS AND SUCH. WHAT ABOUT YOU? SEEMS LIKE YOU'RE HAVING A HARD DAY OUT THERE--
COULD BE WORSE. A LOT OF RUNNERS, BUT THAT'S USUAL. I'LL MAKE THIS ONE QUICK, NO REASON FOR YOU TO--

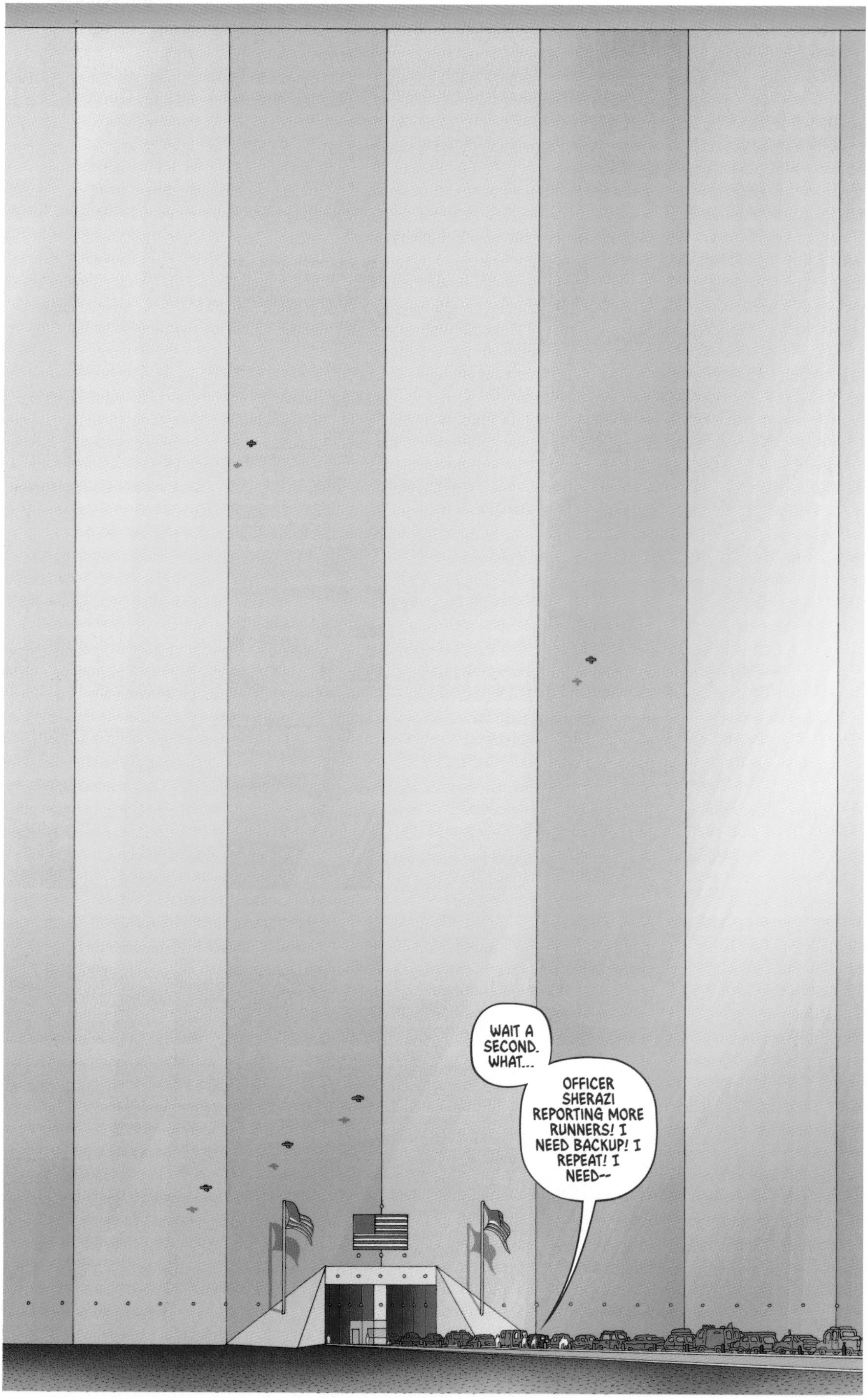
WAIT A SECOND. WHAT...
OFFICER SHERAZI REPORTING MORE RUNNERS! I NEED BACKUP! I REPEAT! I NEED--

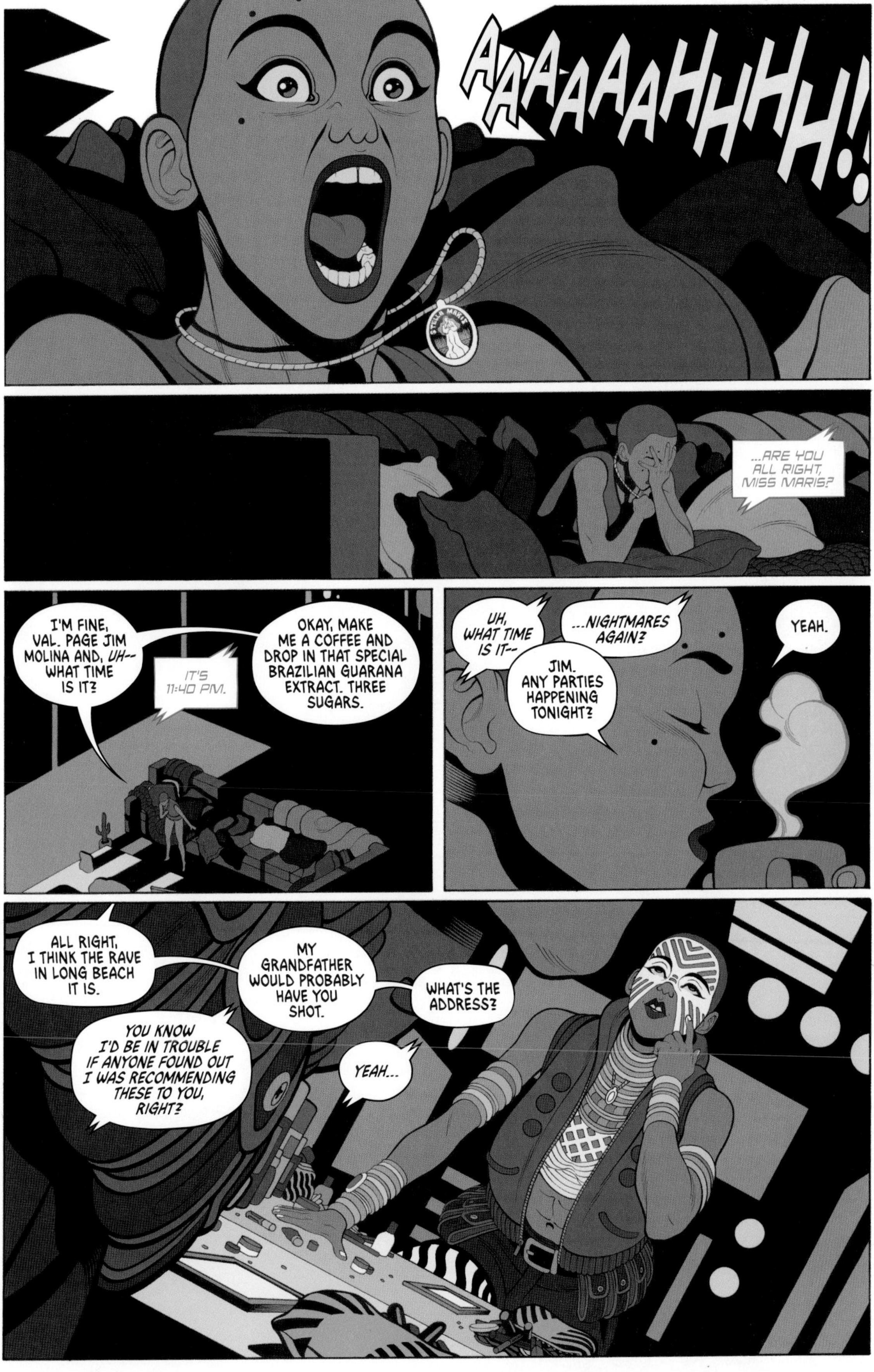
AAAAAAAHHHHH!!!
...ARE YOU ALL RIGHT, MISS MARIS?
I'M FINE, VAL. PAGE JIM MOLINA AND, UH-- WHAT TIME IS IT?
IT'S 11:40 PM.
OKAY, MAKE ME A COFFEE AND DROP IN THAT SPECIAL BRAZILIAN GUARANA EXTRACT. THREE SUGARS.
UH, WHAT TIME IS IT--
...NIGHTMARES AGAIN?
JIM. ANY PARTIES HAPPENING TONIGHT?
YEAH.
YOU KNOW I'D BE IN TROUBLE IF ANYONE FOUND OUT I WAS RECOMMENDING THESE TO YOU, RIGHT?
ALL RIGHT, I THINK THE RAVE IN LONG BEACH IT IS.
MY GRANDFATHER WOULD PROBABLY HAVE YOU SHOT.
YEAH...
WHAT'S THE ADDRESS?

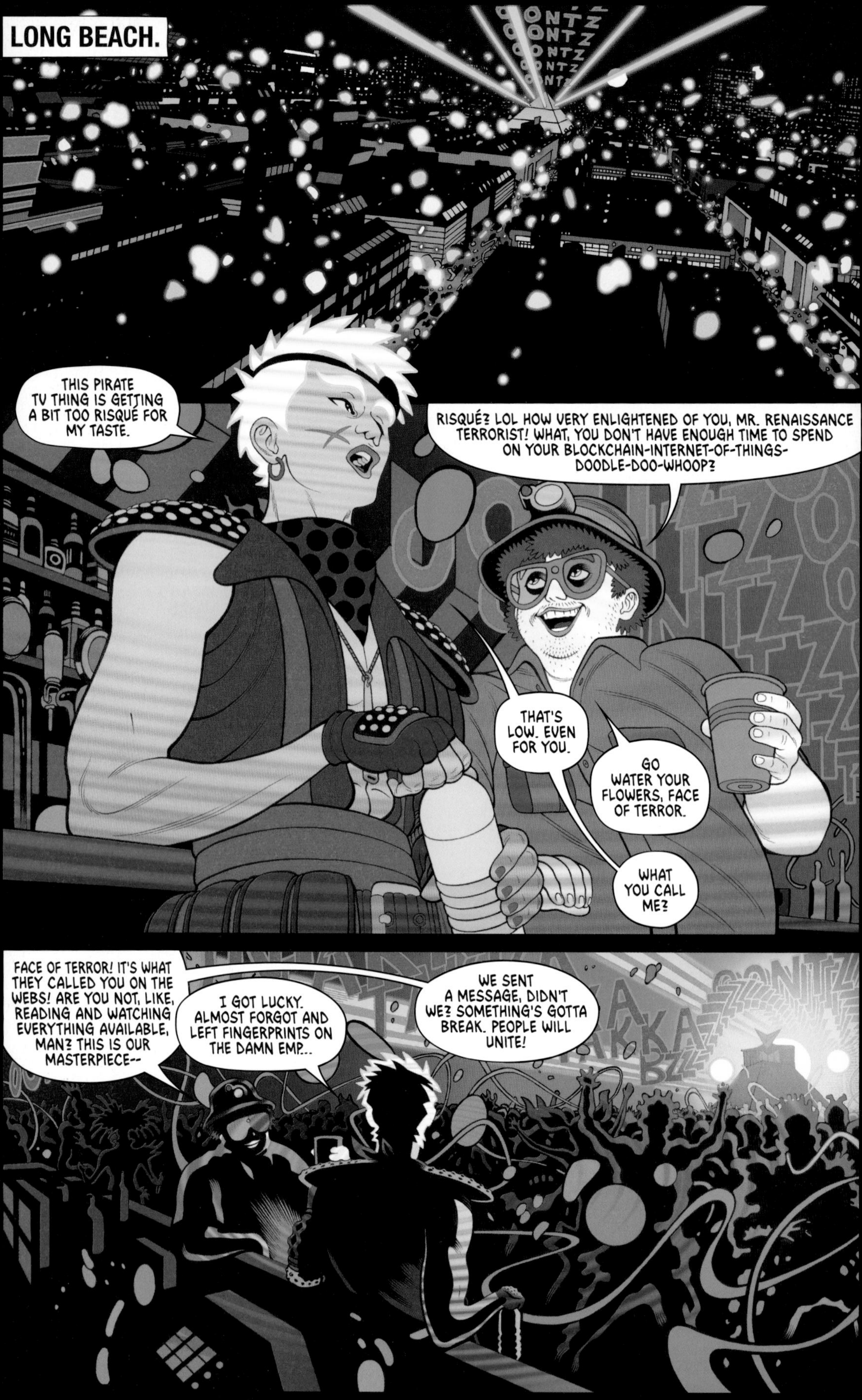
LONG BEACH.
ONTZ ONTZ ONTZ ONTZ
THIS PIRATE TV THING IS GETTING A BIT TOO RISQUE FOR MY TASTE.
RISQUÉ? LOL HOW VERY ENLIGHTENED OF YOU, MR. RENAISSANCE TERRORIST! WHAT, YOU DON'T HAVE ENOUGH TIME TO SPEND ON YOUR BLOCKCHAIN-INTERNET-OF-THINGS-DOODLE-DOO-WHOOP?
THAT'S LOW. EVEN FOR YOU.
GO WATER YOUR FLOWERS, FACE OF TERROR.
WHAT YOU CALL ME?
FACE OF TERROR! IT'S WHAT THEY CALLED YOU ON THE WEBS! ARE YOU NOT, LIKE, READING AND WATCHING EVERYTHING AVAILABLE, MAN? THIS IS OUR MASTERPIECE--
I GOT LUCKY. ALMOST FORGOT AND LEFT FINGERPRINTS ON THE DAMN EMP...
WE SENT A MESSAGE, DIDN'T WE? SOMETHING'S GOTTA BREAK. PEOPLE WILL UNITE!

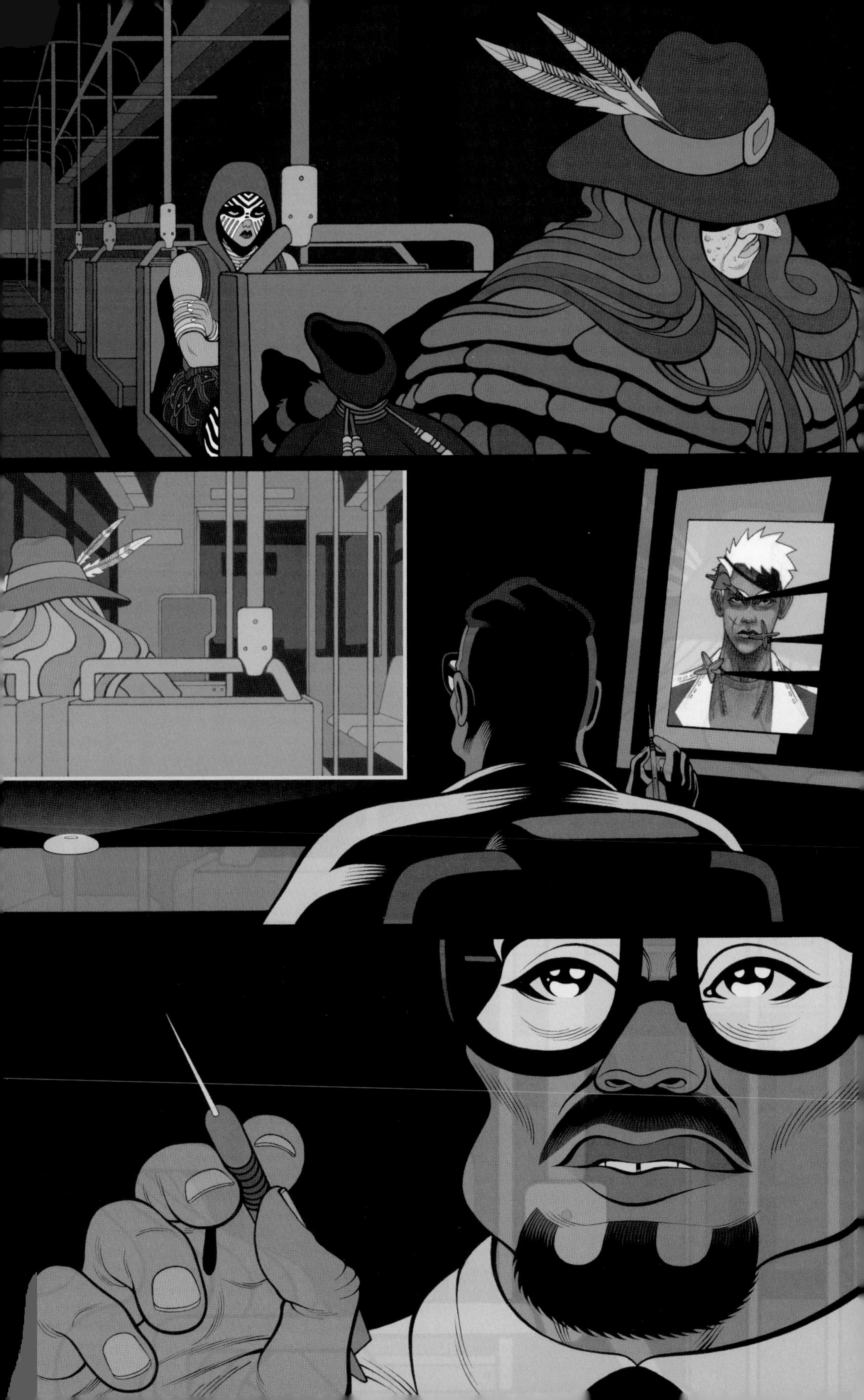

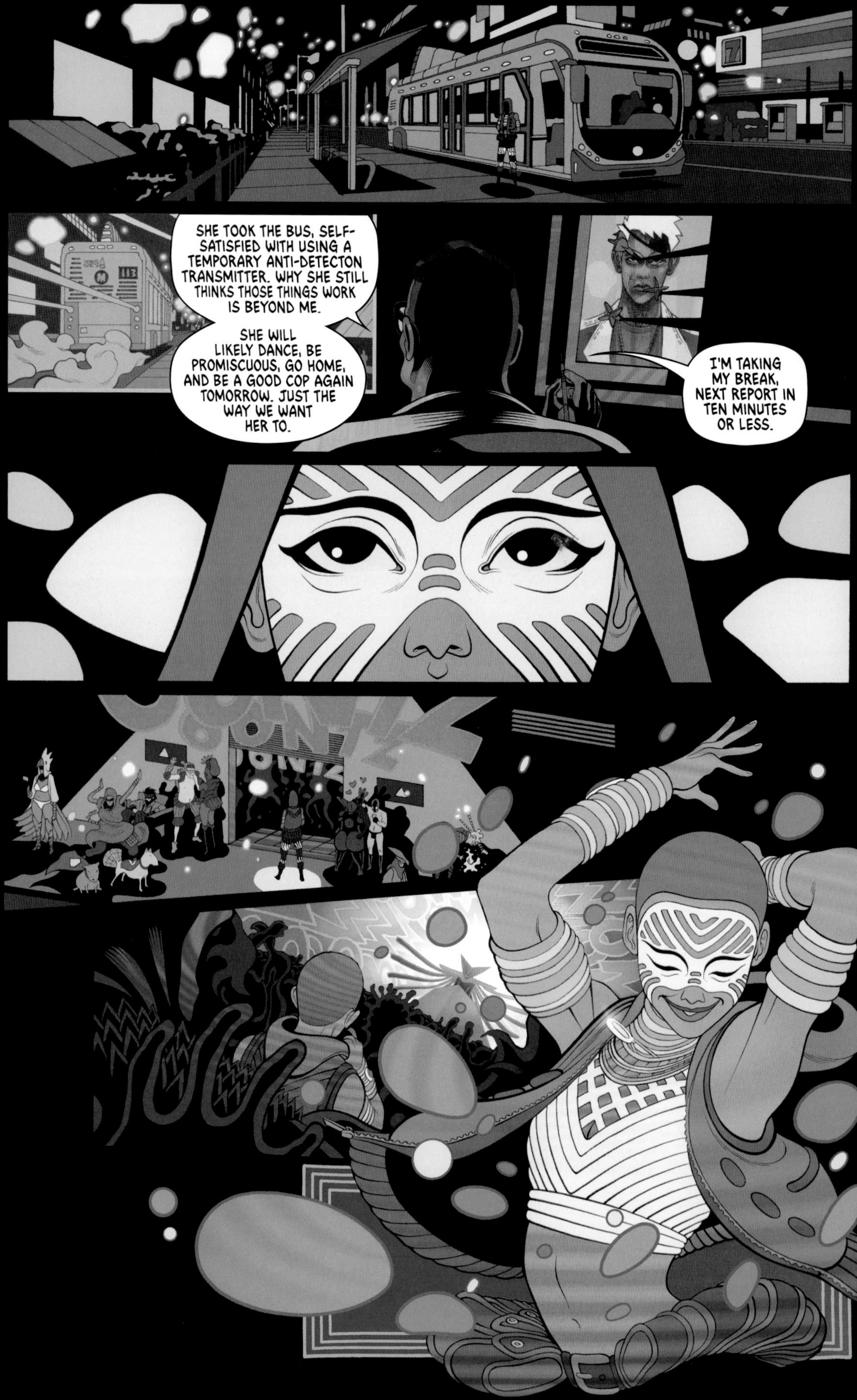
SHE TOOK THE BUS, SELF-SATISFIED WITH USING A TEMPORARY ANTI-DETECTON TRANSMITTER. WHY SHE STILL THINKS THOSE THINGS WORK IS BEYOND ME.
SHE WILL LIKELY DANCE, BE PROMISCUOUS, GO HOME, AND BE A GOOD COP AGAIN TOMORROW. JUST THE WAY WE WANT HER TO.
I'M TAKING MY BREAK, NEXT REPORT IN TEN MINUTES OR LESS.

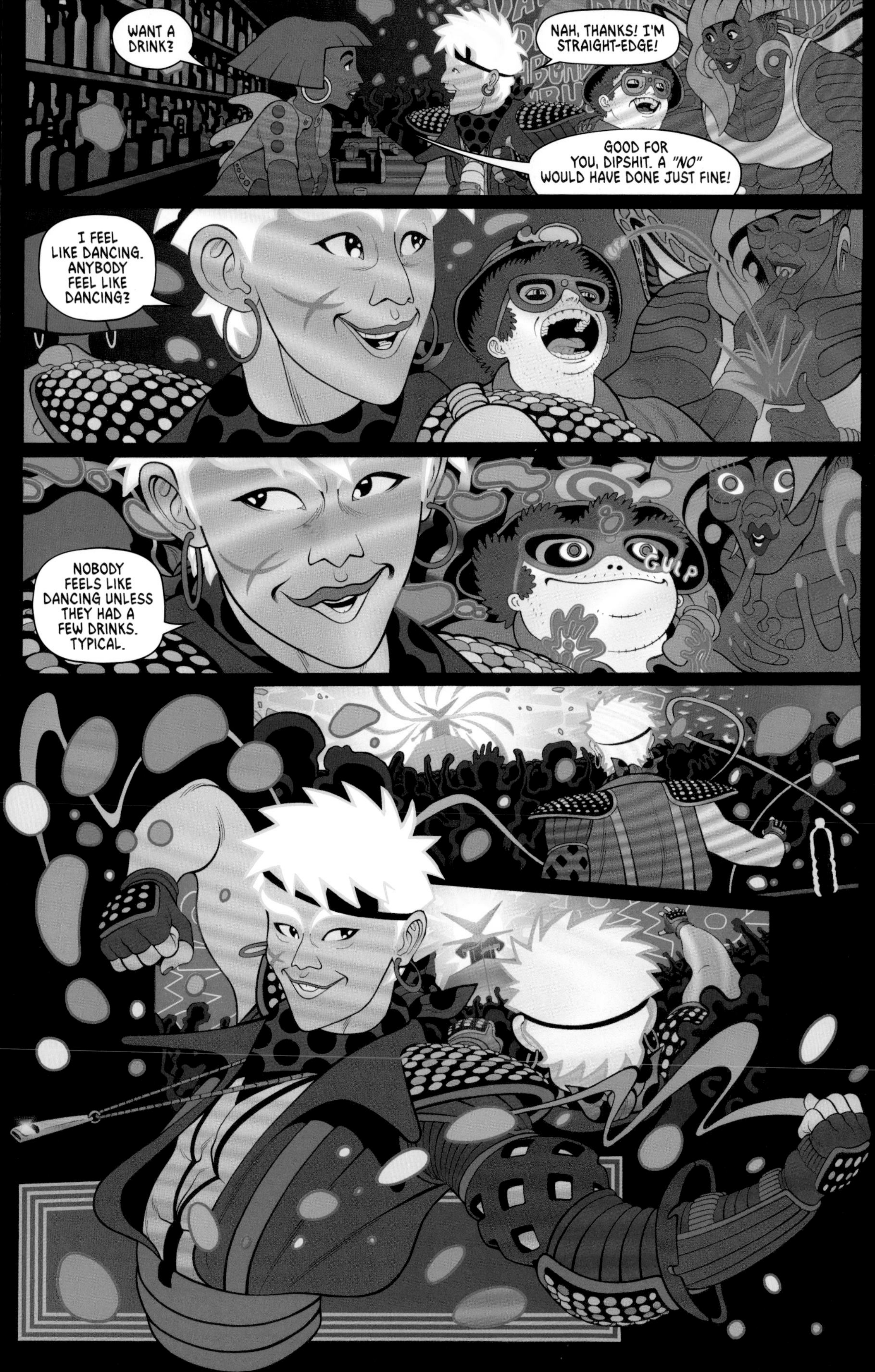
WANT A DRINK?
NAH, THANKS! I'M STRAIGHT-EDGE!
GOOD FOR YOU, DIPSHIT. A "NO" WOULD HAVE DONE JUST FINE!
I FEEL LIKE DANCING. ANYBODY FEEL LIKE DANCING?
NOBODY FEELS LIKE DANCING UNLESS THEY HAD A FEW DRINKS. TYPICAL.
GULP

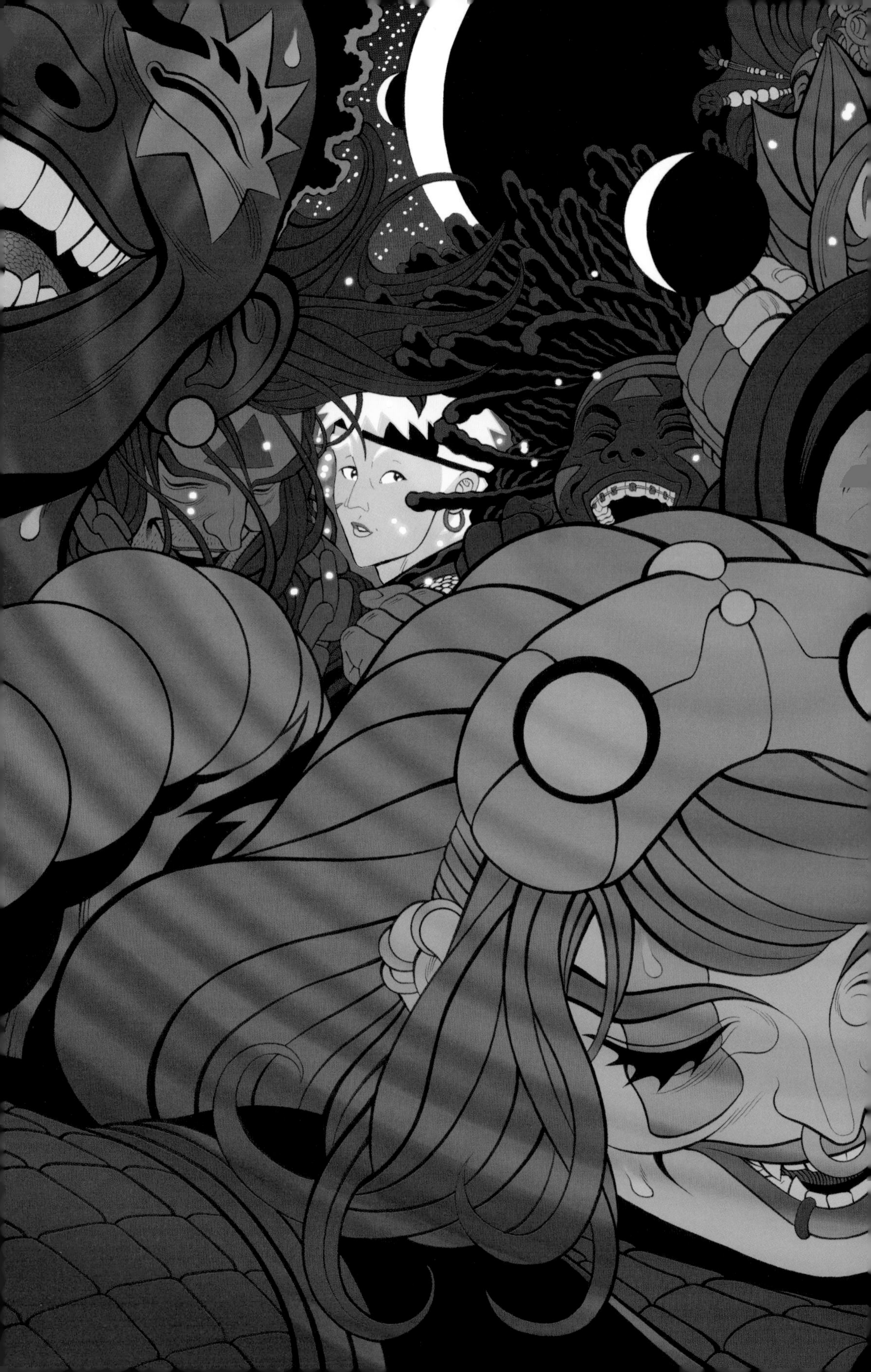

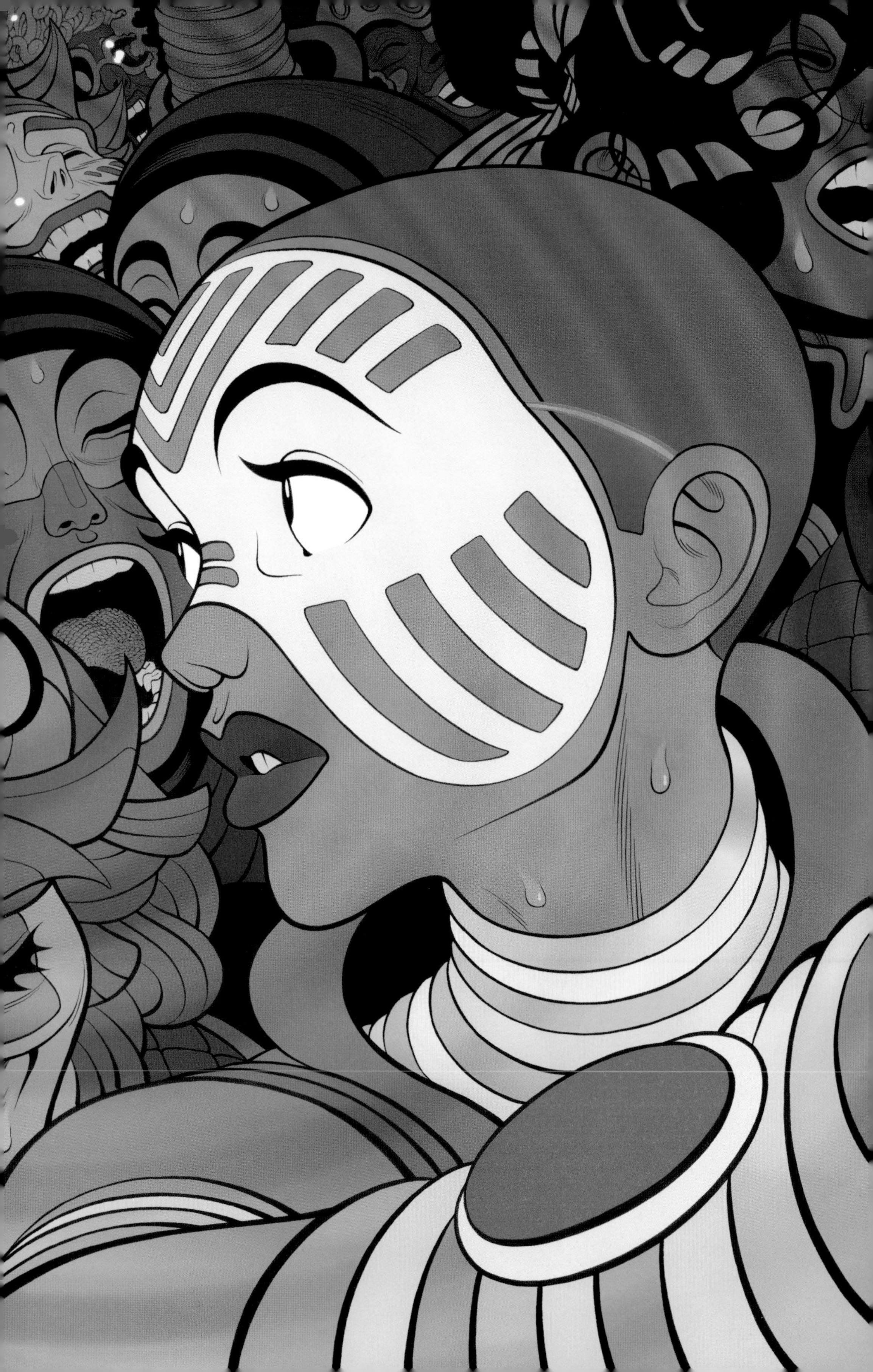

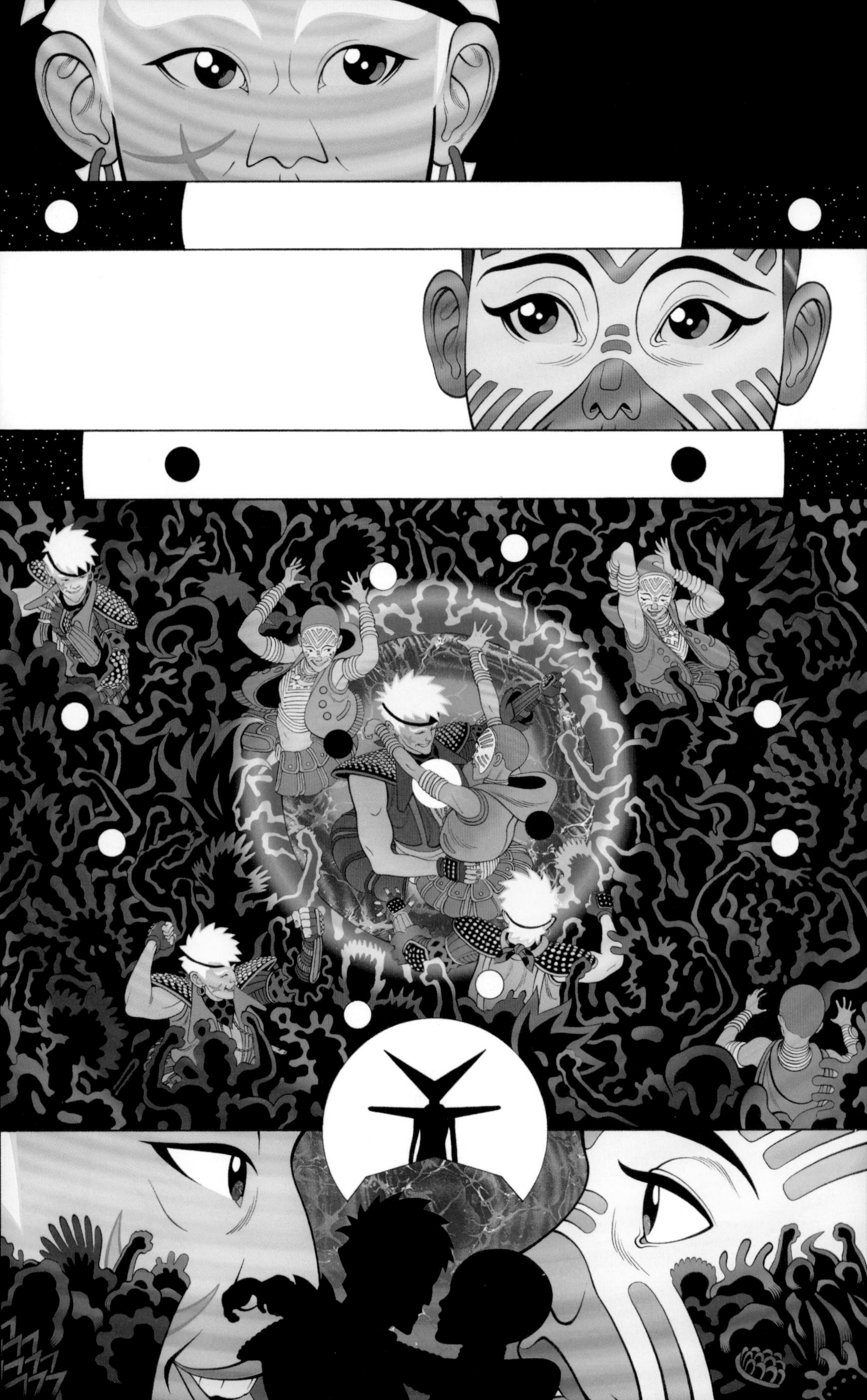

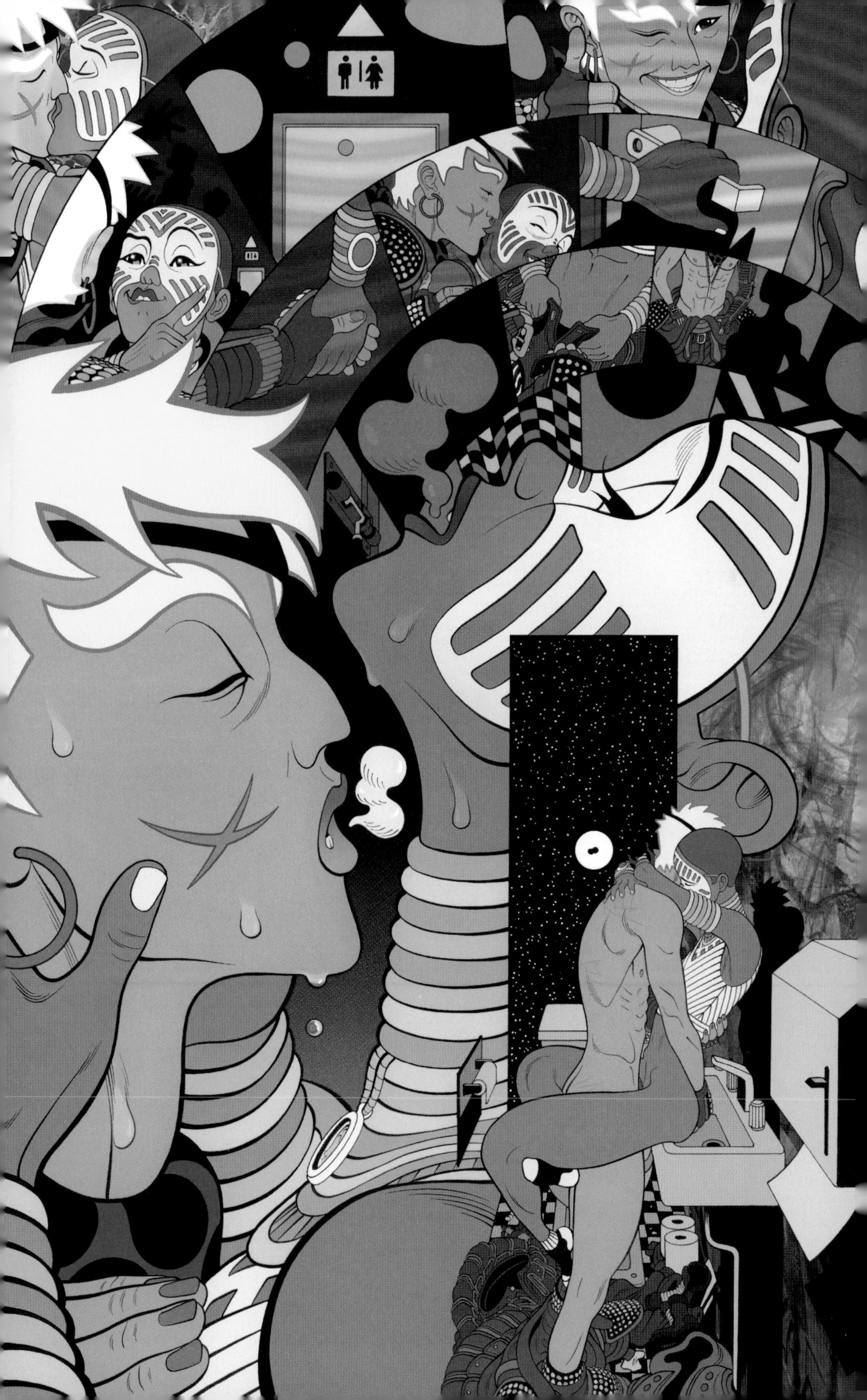

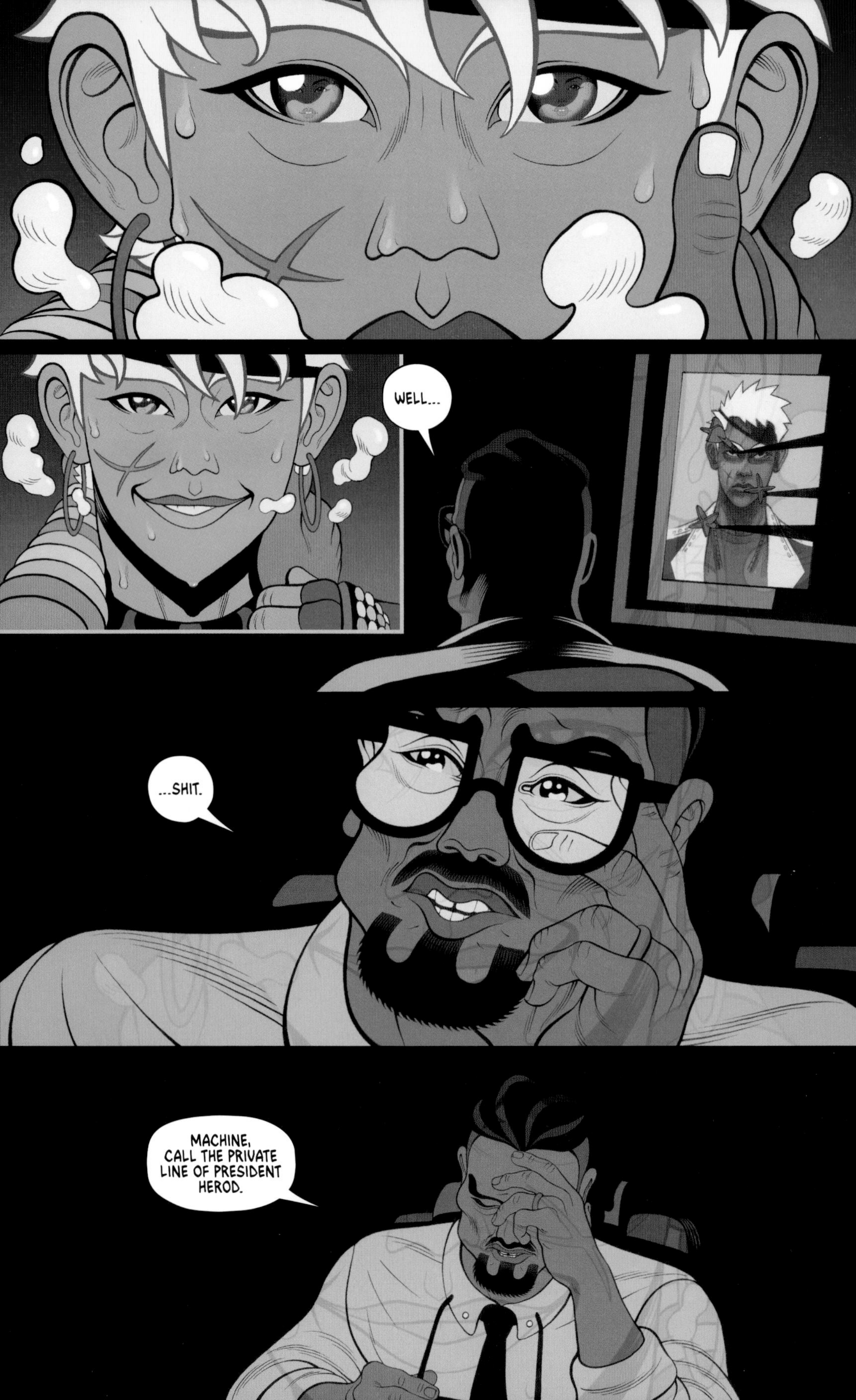
WELL...
...SHIT.
MACHINE, CALL THE PRIVATE LINE OF PRESIDENT HEROD.

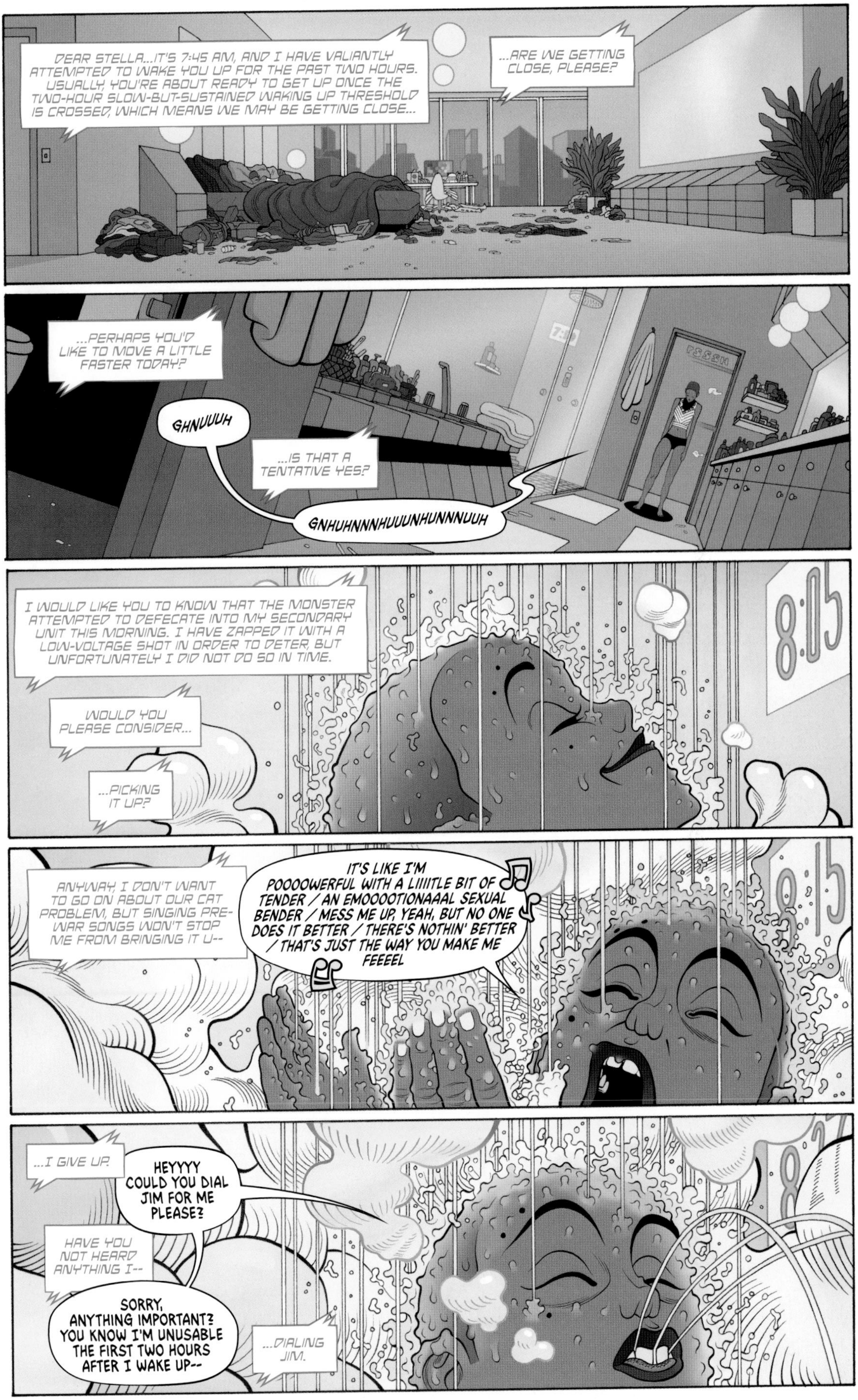
DEAR STELLA...IT'S 7:45 AM, AND I HAVE VALIANTLY ATTEMPTED TO WAKE YOU UP FOR THE PAST TWO HOURS. USUALLY, YOU'RE ABOUT READY TO GET UP ONCE THE TWO-HOUR SLOW-BUT-SUSTAINED WAKING UP THRESHOLD IS CROSSED, WHICH MEANS WE MAY BE GETTING CLOSE...
...ARE WE GETTING CLOSE, PLEASE?
...PERHAPS YOU'D LIKE TO MOVE A LITTLE FASTER TODAY?
GHNUUUH
...IS THAT A TENTATIVE YES?
GNHUHNNNHUUUNHUNNNUUH
PSSSH
I WOULD LIKE YOU TO KNOW THAT THE MONSTER ATTEMPTED TO DEFECATE INTO MY SECONDARY UNIT THIS MORNING. I HAVE ZAPPED IT WITH A LOW-VOLTAGE SHOT IN ORDER TO DETER, BUT UNFORTUNATELY I DID NOT DO SO IN TIME.
WOULD YOU PLEASE CONSIDER...
...PICKING IT UP?
8:05
ANYWAY, I DON'T WANT TO GO ON ABOUT OUR CAT PROBLEM, BUT SINGING PRE-WAR SONGS WON'T STOP ME FROM BRINGING IT U--
IT'S LIKE I'M POOOOWERFUL WITH A LIIIITLE BIT OF TENDER / AN EMOOOOTIONAAAL SEXUAL BENDER / MESS ME UP, YEAH, BUT NO ONE DOES IT BETTER / THERE'S NOTHIN' BETTER / THAT'S JUST THE WAY YOU MAKE ME FEEEEL
8:15
...I GIVE UP.
HEYYYY COULD YOU DIAL JIM FOR ME PLEASE?
HAVE YOU NOT HEARD ANYTHING I--
SORRY, ANYTHING IMPORTANT? YOU KNOW I'M UNUSABLE THE FIRST TWO HOURS AFTER I WAKE UP--
...DIALING JIM.

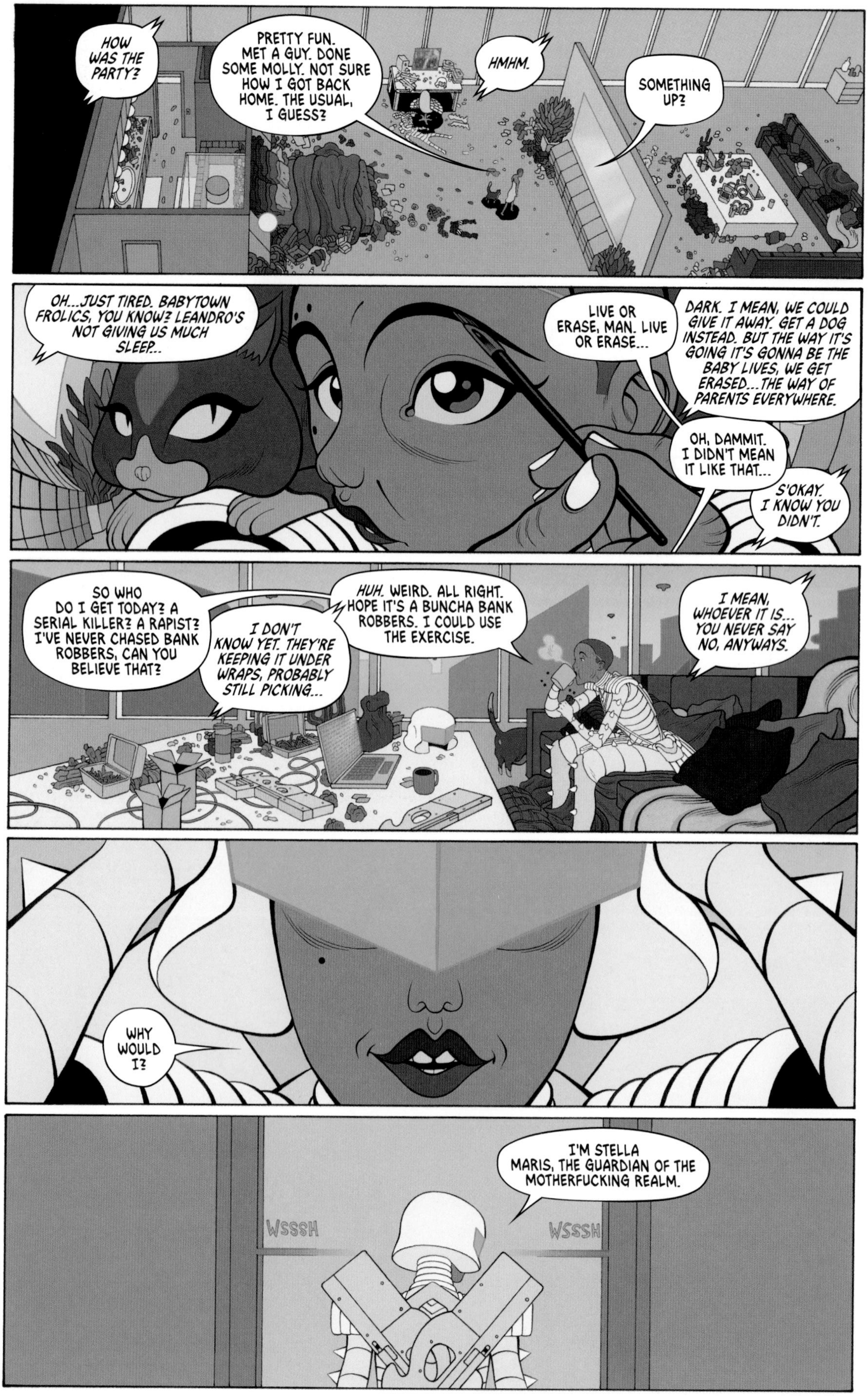
HOW WAS THE PARTY?
PRETTY FUN. MET A GUY. DONE SOME MOLLY. NOT SURE HOW I GOT BACK HOME. THE USUAL, I GUESS?
HMHM.
SOMETHING UP?
OH...JUST TIRED. BABYTOWN FROLICS, YOU KNOW? LEANDRO'S NOT GIVING US MUCH SLEEP...
LIVE OR ERASE, MAN. LIVE OR ERASE...
DARK. I MEAN, WE COULD GIVE IT AWAY. GET A DOG INSTEAD. BUT THE WAY IT'S GOING IT'S GONNA BE THE BABY LIVES, WE GET ERASED...THE WAY OF PARENTS EVERYWHERE.
OH, DAMMIT. I DIDN'T MEAN IT LIKE THAT...
S'OKAY. I KNOW YOU DIDN'T.
SO WHO DO I GET TODAY? A SERIAL KILLER? A RAPIST? I'VE NEVER CHASED BANK ROBBERS, CAN YOU BELIEVE THAT?
I DON'T KNOW YET. THEY'RE KEEPING IT UNDER WRAPS, PROBABLY STILL PICKING...
HUH. WEIRD. ALL RIGHT. HOPE IT'S A BUNCHA BANK ROBBERS. I COULD USE THE EXERCISE.
I MEAN, WHOEVER IT IS... YOU NEVER SAY NO, ANYWAYS.
WHY WOULD I?
I'M STELLA MARIS, THE GUARDIAN OF THE MOTHERFUCKING REALM.
WSSSH
WSSSH

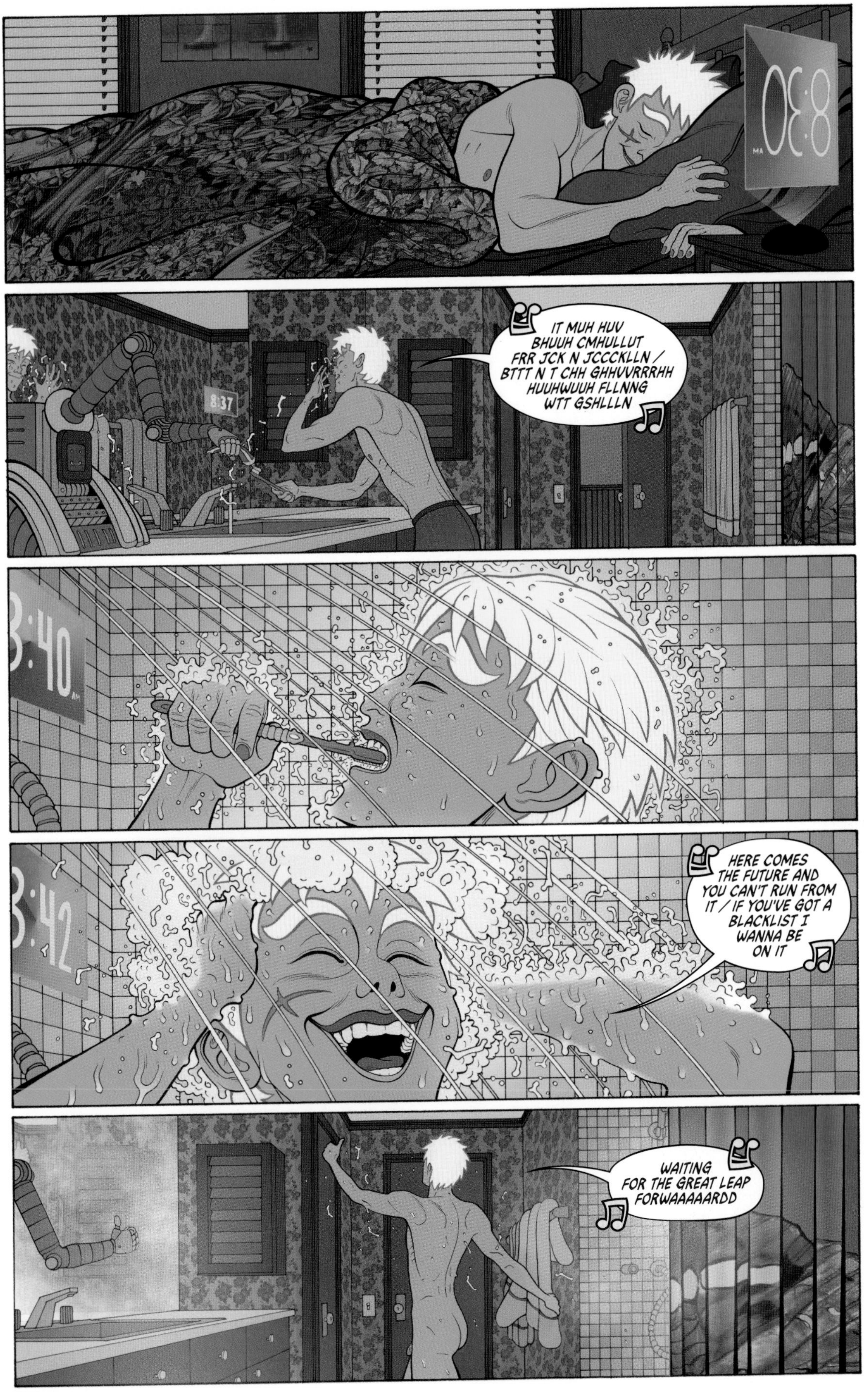
IT MUH HUV BHUUH CMHULLUT FRR JCK N JCCCKLLN / BTTT N T CHH GHHVVRRRHH HUUHWUUH FLLNNG WTT GSHLLLN
8:37
HERE COMES THE FUTURE AND YOU CAN'T RUN FROM IT / IF YOU'VE GOT A BLACKLIST I WANNA BE ON IT
WAITING FOR THE GREAT LEAP FORWAAAAARDD

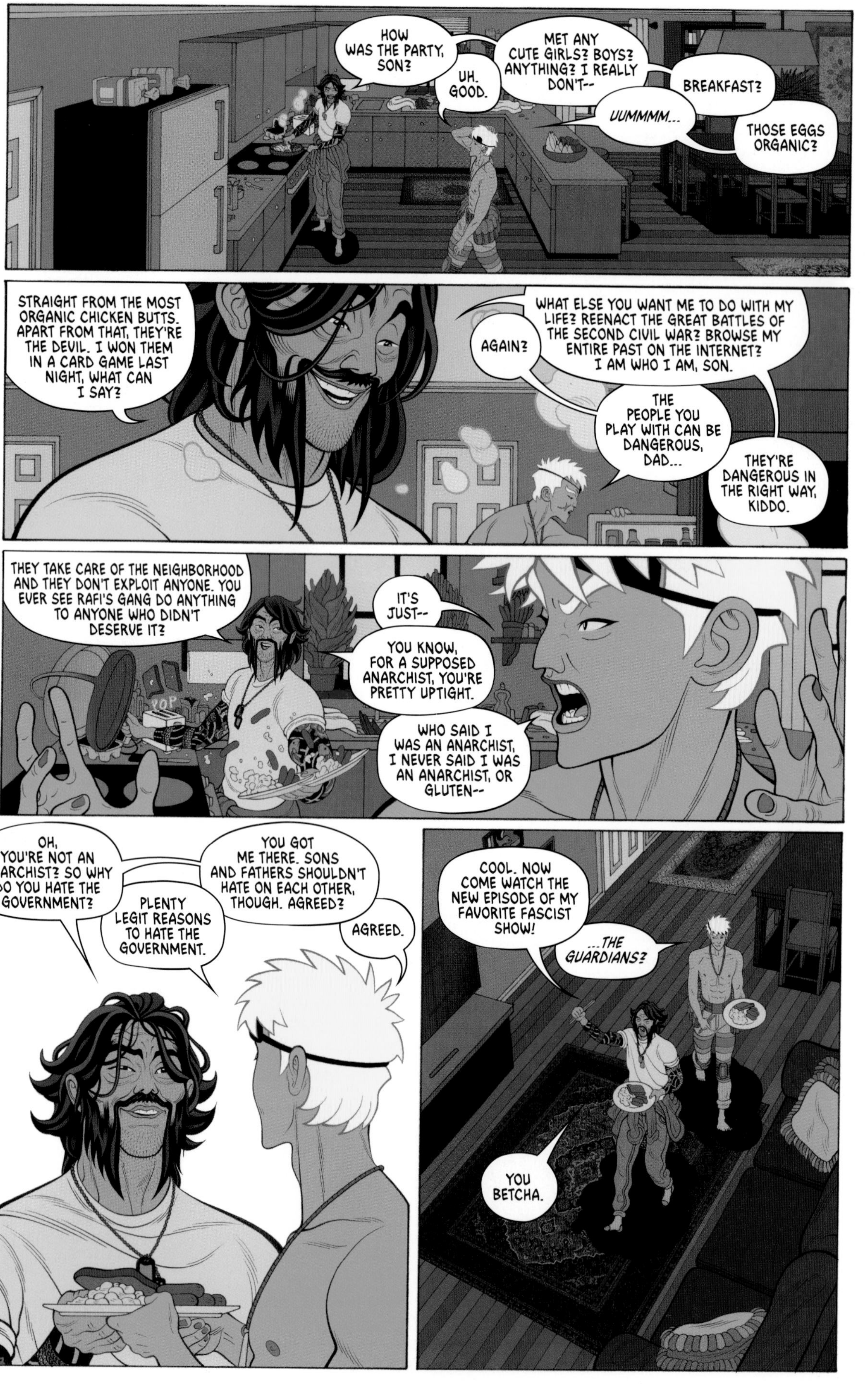
HOW WAS THE PARTY, SON?
UH. GOOD.
MET ANY CUTE GIRLS? BOYS? ANYTHING? I REALLY DON'T--
BREAKFAST?
UUMMMM...
THOSE EGGS ORGANIC?
STRAIGHT FROM THE MOST ORGANIC CHICKEN BUTTS. APART FROM THAT, THEY'RE THE DEVIL. I WON THEM IN A CARD GAME LAST NIGHT, WHAT CAN I SAY?
AGAIN?
WHAT ELSE YOU WANT ME TO DO WITH MY LIFE? REENACT THE GREAT BATTLES OF THE SECOND CIVIL WAR? BROWSE MY ENTIRE PAST ON THE INTERNET? I AM WHO I AM, SON.
THE PEOPLE YOU PLAY WITH CAN BE DANGEROUS, DAD...
THEY'RE DANGEROUS IN THE RIGHT WAY, KIDDO.
THEY TAKE CARE OF THE NEIGHBORHOOD AND THEY DON'T EXPLOIT ANYONE. YOU EVER SEE RAFI'S GANG DO ANYTHING TO ANYONE WHO DIDN'T DESERVE IT?
IT'S JUST--
YOU KNOW, FOR A SUPPOSED ANARCHIST, YOU'RE PRETTY UPTIGHT.
POP
WHO SAID I WAS AN ANARCHIST, I NEVER SAID I WAS AN ANARCHIST, OR GLUTEN--
OH, YOU'RE NOT AN ANARCHIST? SO WHY DO YOU HATE THE GOVERNMENT?
PLENTY LEGIT REASONS TO HATE THE GOVERNMENT.
YOU GOT ME THERE. SONS AND FATHERS SHOULDN'T HATE ON EACH OTHER, THOUGH. AGREED?
AGREED.
COOL. NOW COME WATCH THE NEW EPISODE OF MY FAVORITE FASCIST SHOW!
...THE GUARDIANS?
YOU BETCHA.

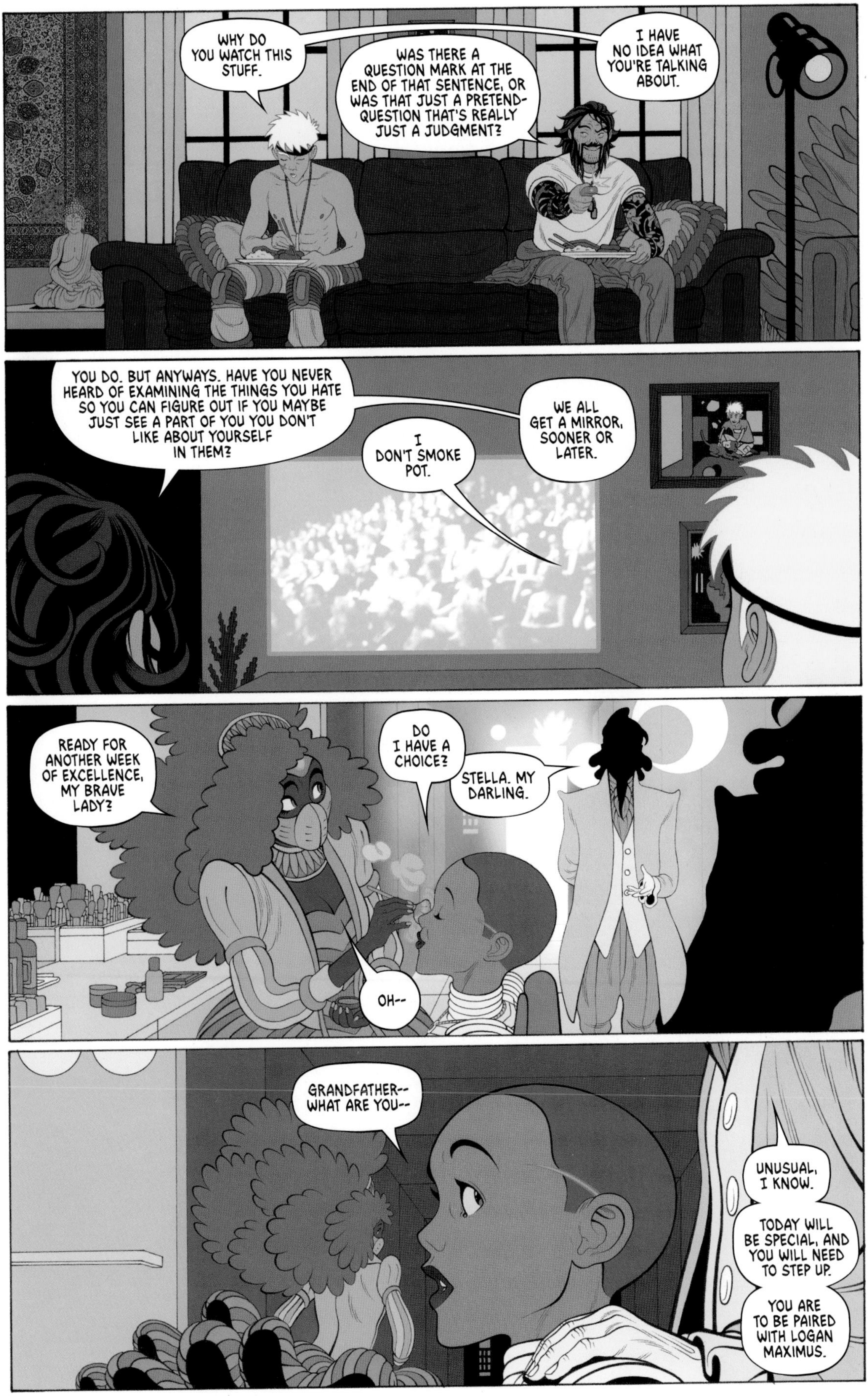
WHY DO YOU WATCH THIS STUFF.
WAS THERE A QUESTION MARK AT THE END OF THAT SENTENCE, OR WAS THAT JUST A PRETEND-QUESTION THAT'S REALLY JUST A JUDGMENT?
I HAVE NO IDEA WHAT YOU'RE TALKING ABOUT.
YOU DO. BUT ANYWAYS. HAVE YOU NEVER HEARD OF EXAMINING THE THINGS YOU HATE SO YOU CAN FIGURE OUT IF YOU MAYBE JUST SEE A PART OF YOU YOU DON'T LIKE ABOUT YOURSELF IN THEM?
WE ALL GET A MIRROR, SOONER OR LATER.
I DON'T SMOKE POT.
READY FOR ANOTHER WEEK OF EXCELLENCE, MY BRAVE LADY?
DO I HAVE A CHOICE?
STELLA. MY DARLING.
OH--
GRANDFATHER-- WHAT ARE YOU--
UNUSUAL, I KNOW.
TODAY WILL BE SPECIAL, AND YOU WILL NEED TO STEP UP.
YOU ARE TO BE PAIRED WITH LOGAN MAXIMUS.

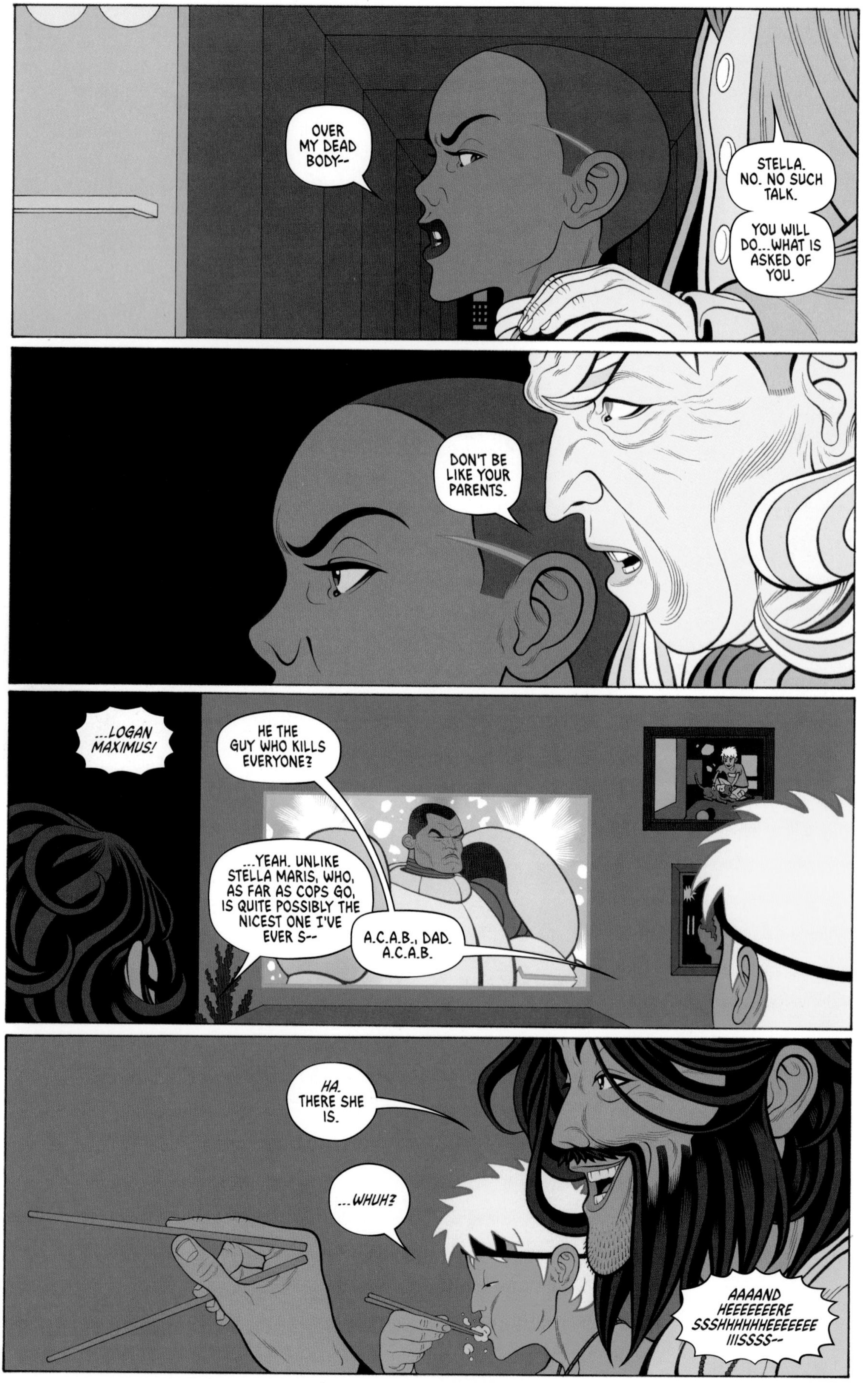

OVER MY DEAD BODY--
STELLA. NO. NO SUCH TALK.
YOU WILL DO...WHAT IS ASKED OF YOU.
DON'T BE LIKE YOUR PARENTS.
...LOGAN MAXIMUS!
HE THE GUY WHO KILLS EVERYONE?
...YEAH. UNLIKE STELLA MARIS, WHO, AS FAR AS COPS GO, IS QUITE POSSIBLY THE NICEST ONE I'VE EVER S--
A.C.A.B., DAD. A.C.A.B.
HA. THERE SHE IS.
...WHUH?
AAAAND HEEEEEEERE SSSHHHHHHEEEEEEE IIISSSS--

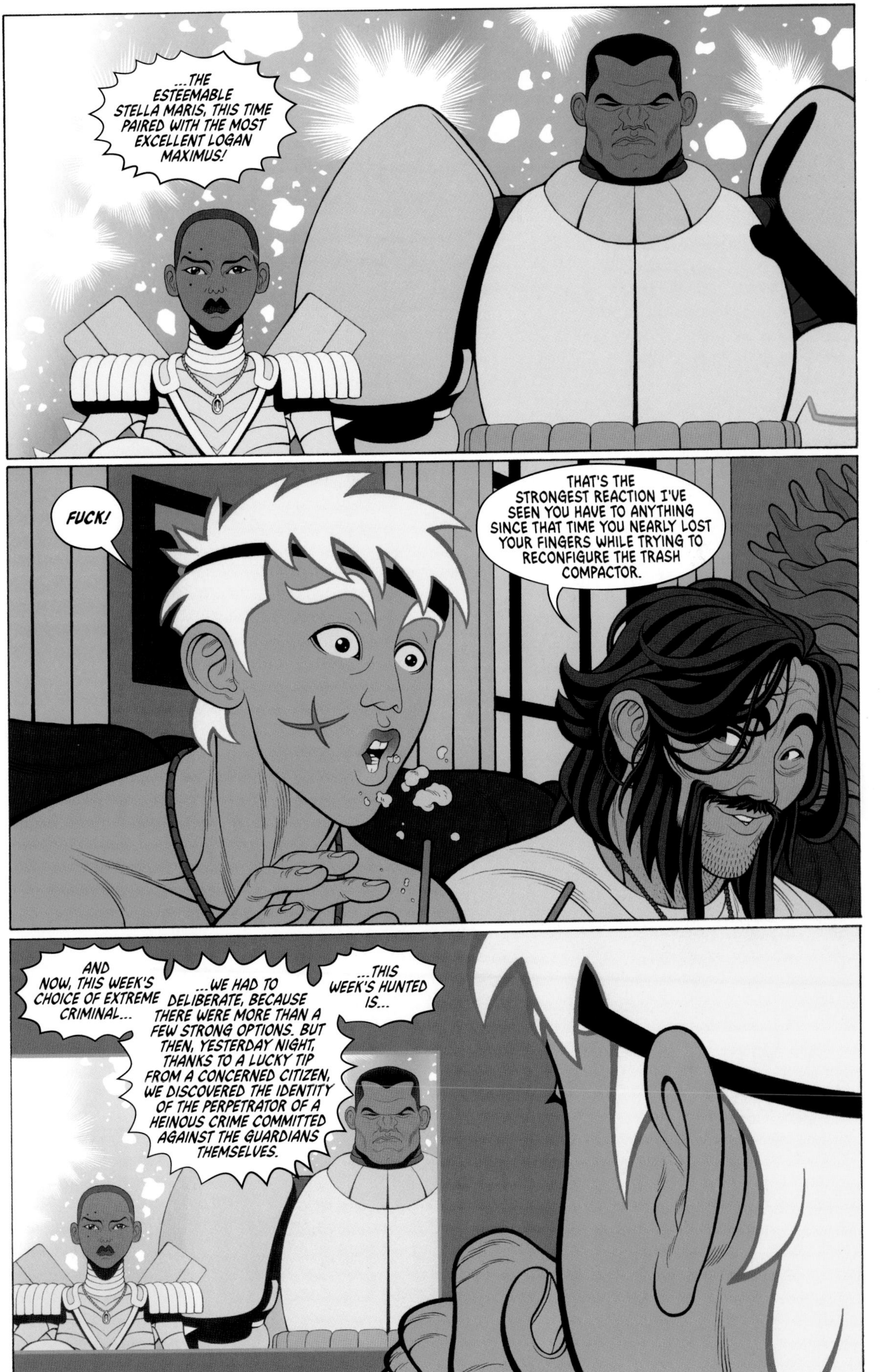
...THE ESTEEMABLE STELLA MARIS, THIS TIME PAIRED WITH THE MOST EXCELLENT LOGAN MAXIMUS!
FUCK!
THAT'S THE STRONGEST REACTION I'VE SEEN YOU HAVE TO ANYTHING SINCE THAT TIME YOU NEARLY LOST YOUR FINGERS WHILE TRYING TO RECONFIGURE THE TRASH COMPACTOR.
AND NOW, THIS WEEK'S CHOICE OF EXTREME CRIMINAL...
...WE HAD TO DELIBERATE, BECAUSE THERE WERE MORE THAN A FEW STRONG OPTIONS. BUT THEN, YESTERDAY NIGHT, THANKS TO A LUCKY TIP FROM A CONCERNED CITIZEN, WE DISCOVERED THE IDENTITY OF THE PERPETRATOR OF A HEINOUS CRIME COMMITTED AGAINST THE GUARDIANS THEMSELVES.
...THIS WEEK'S HUNTED IS...

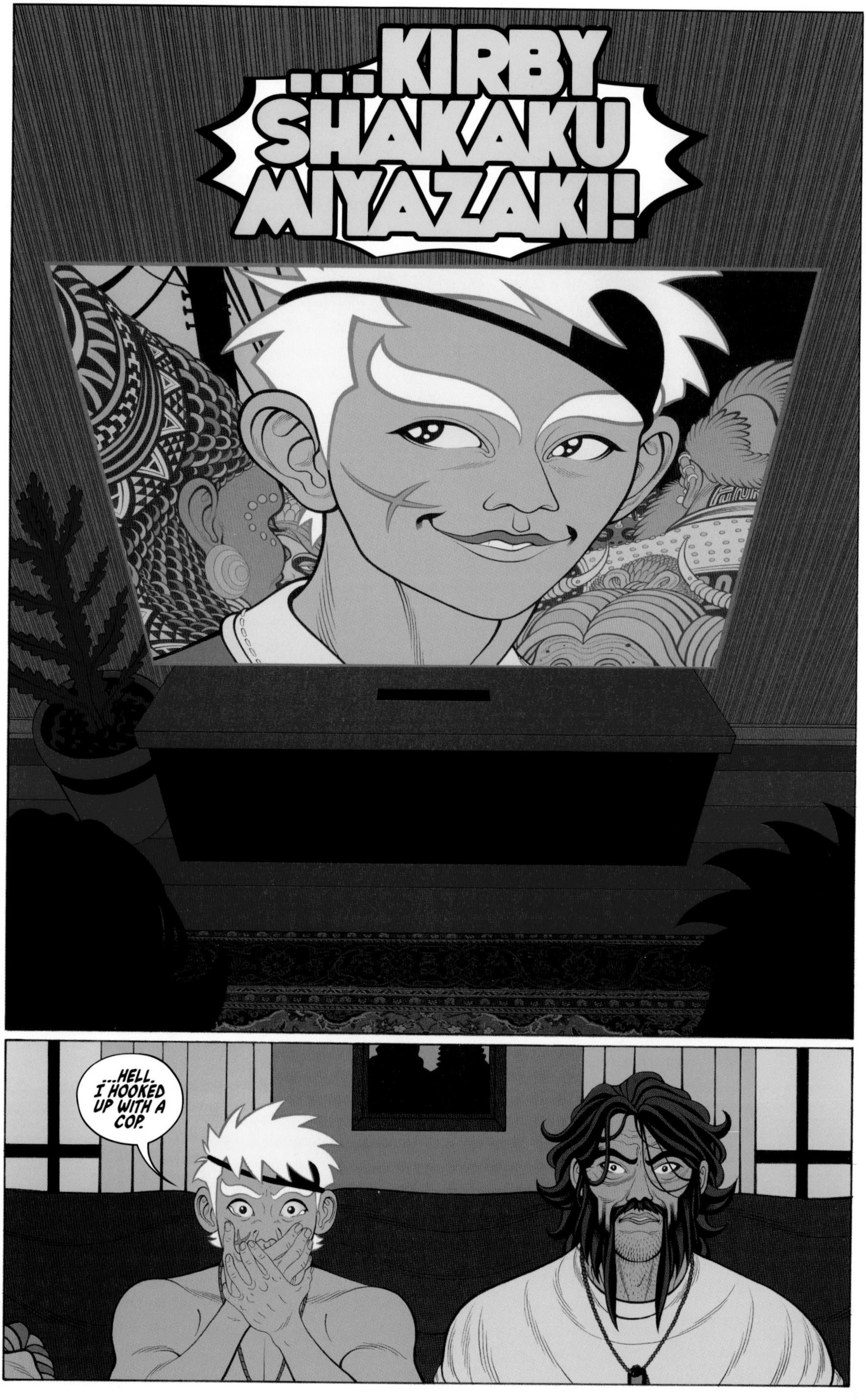
...KIRBY SHAKAKU MIYAZAKI!
...HELL. I HOOKED UP WITH A COP.

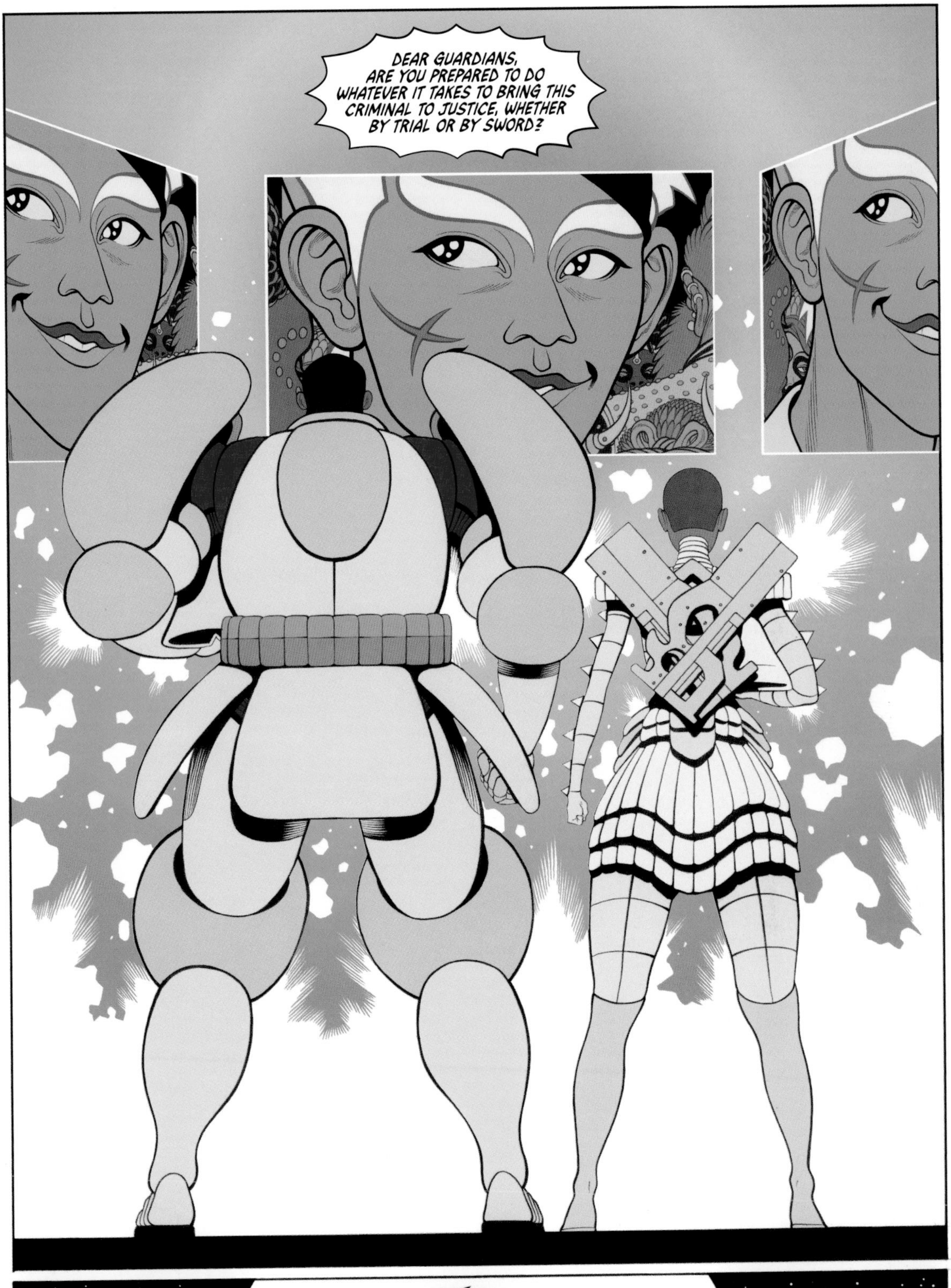
DEAR GUARDIANS, ARE YOU PREPARED TO DO WHATEVER IT TAKES TO BRING THIS CRIMINAL TO JUSTICE, WHETHER BY TRIAL OR BY SWORD?
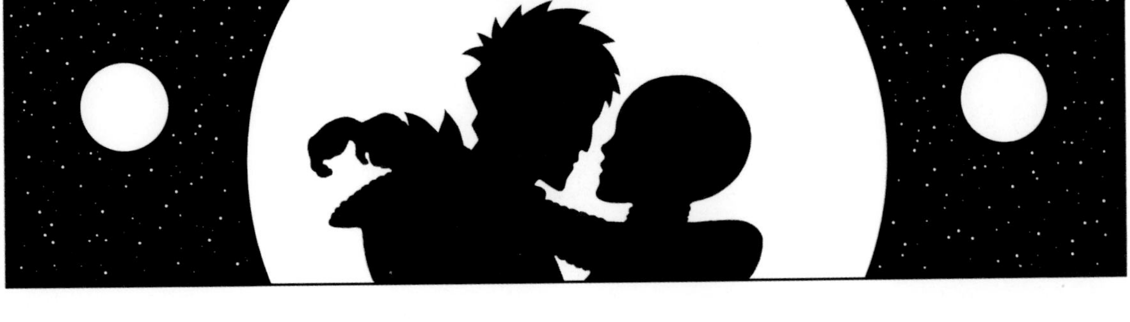

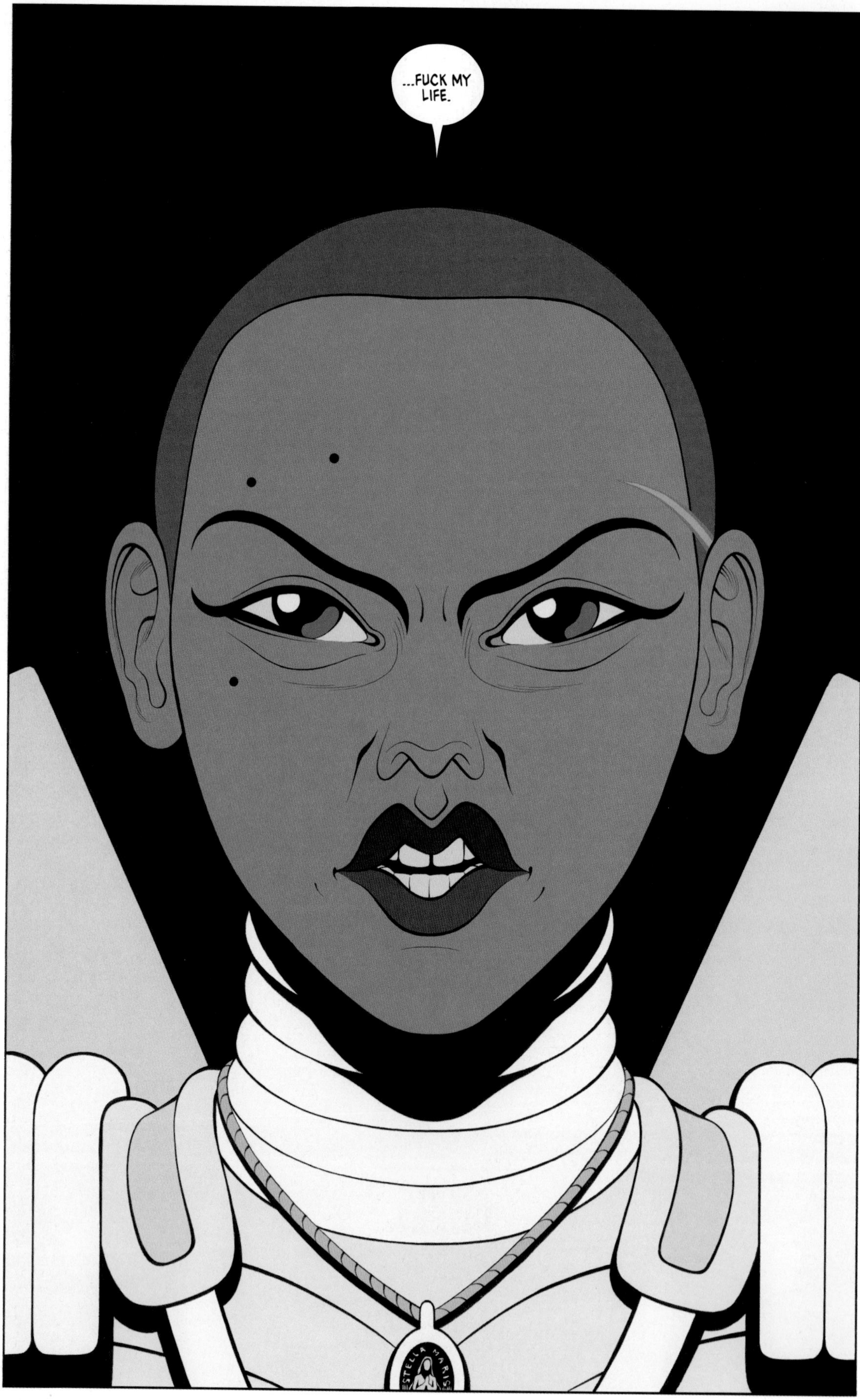
...FUCK MY LIFE.
STELLA MARIS

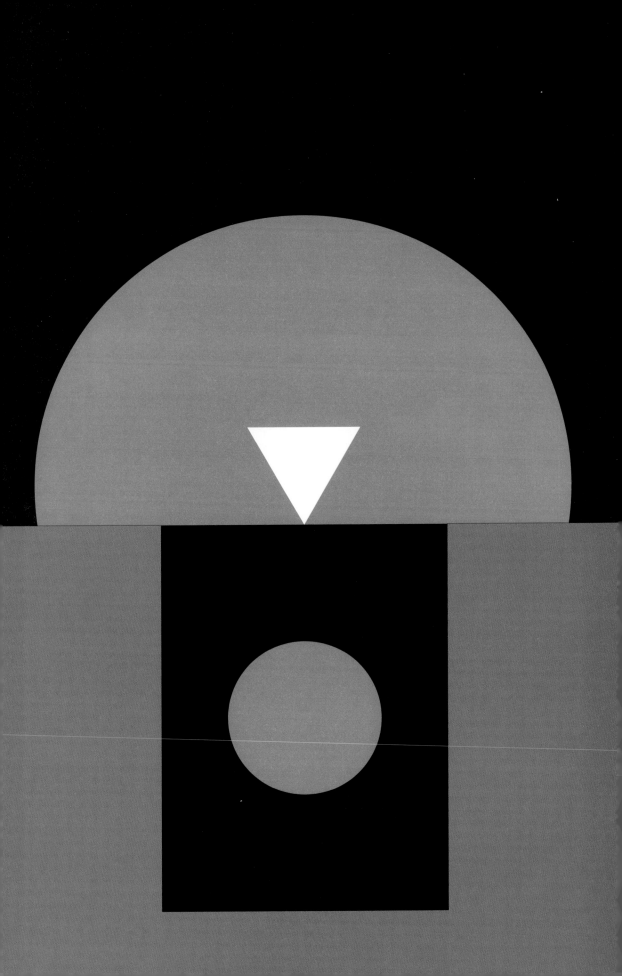

CHAPTER 2

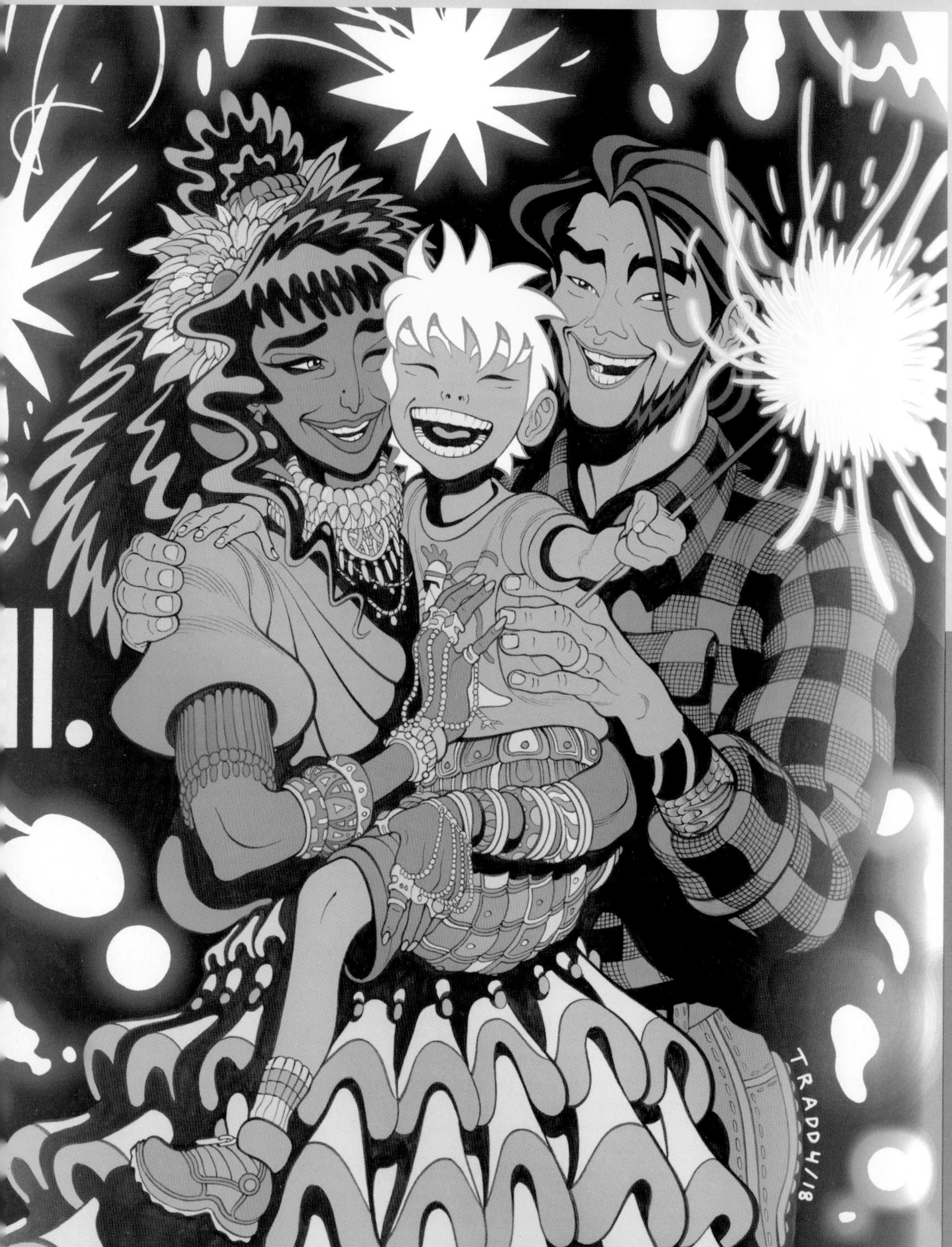
II.
TRADD 4/18

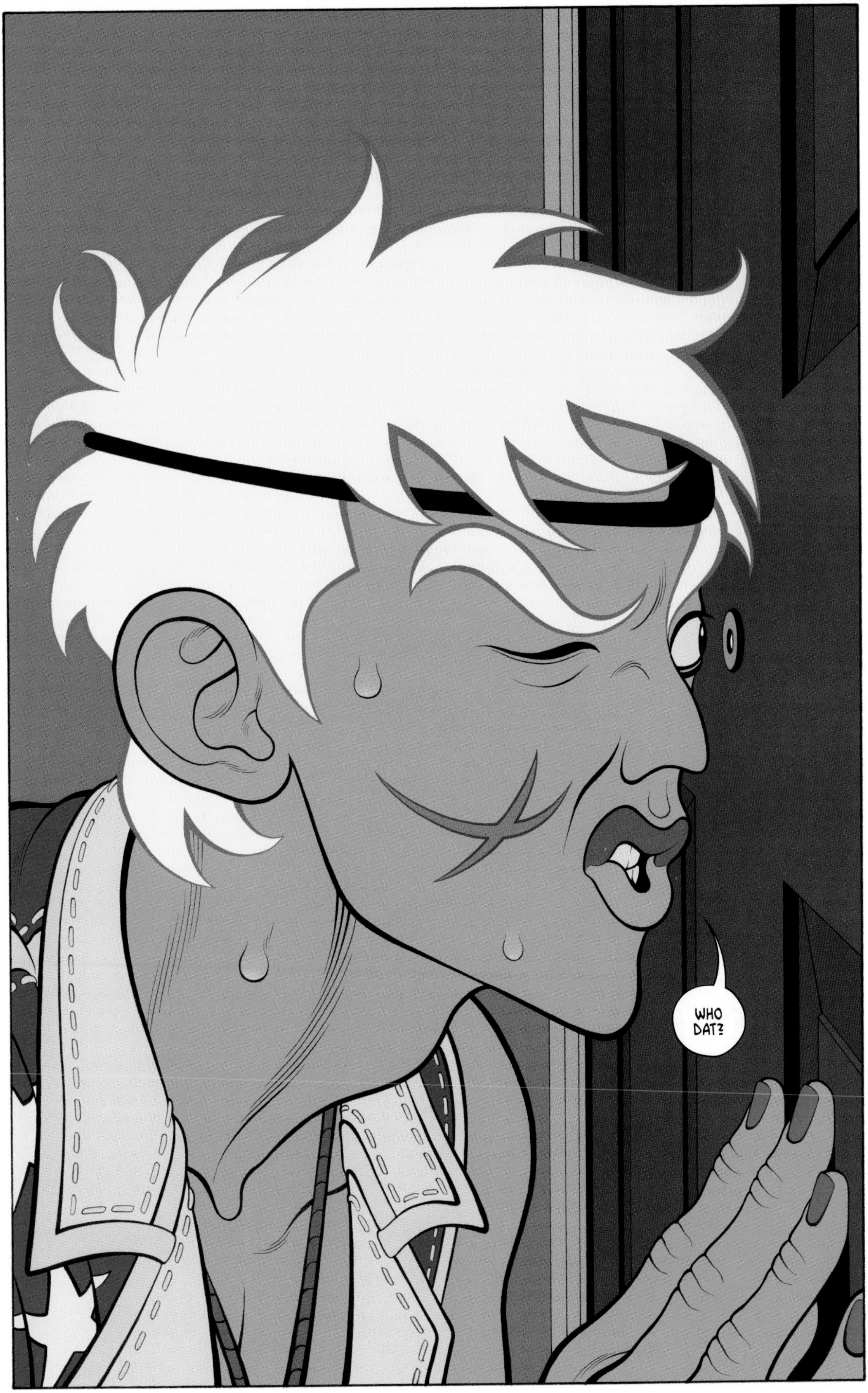
WHO DAT?

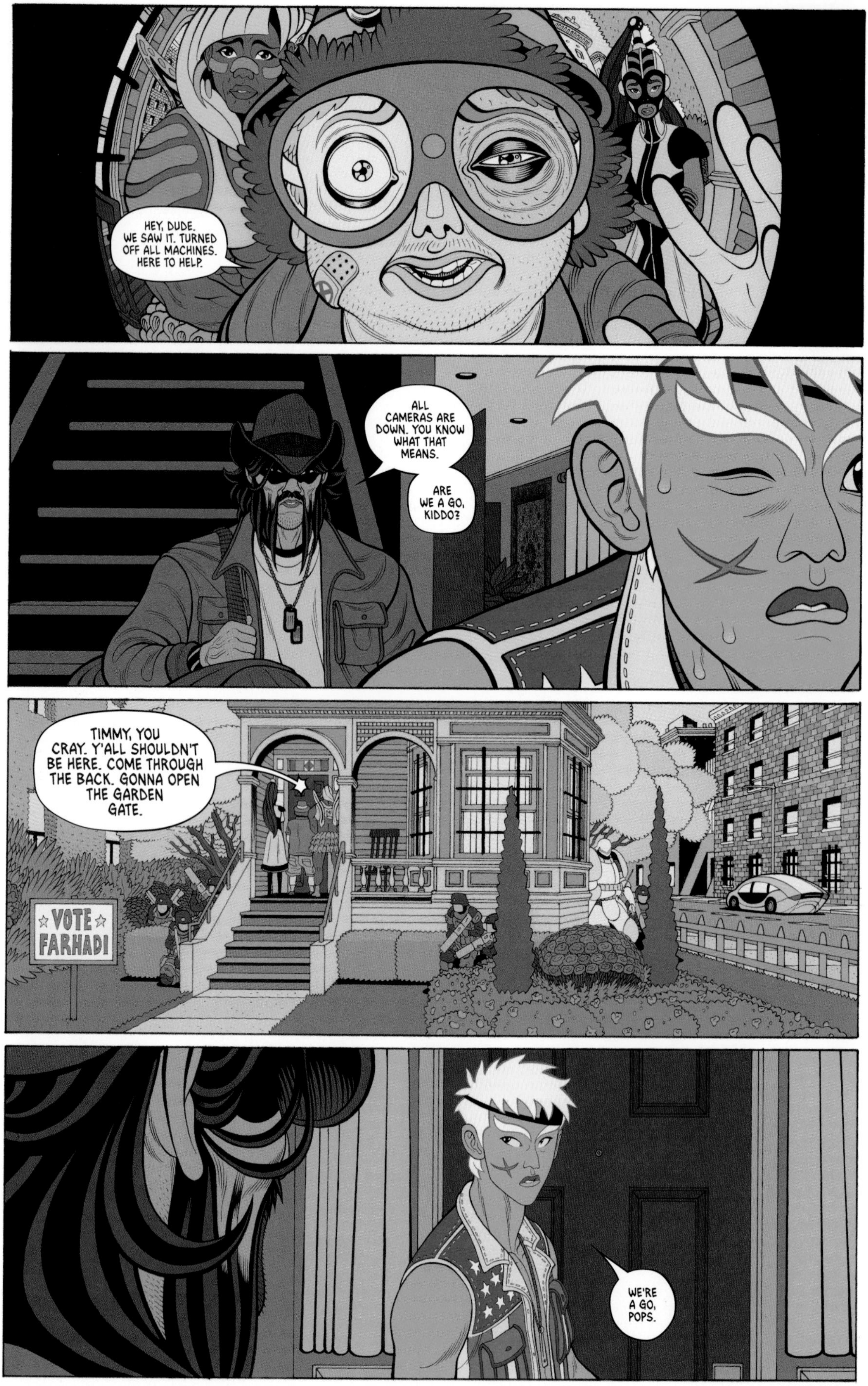
HEY, DUDE. WE SAW IT. TURNED OFF ALL MACHINES. HERE TO HELP.
ALL CAMERAS ARE DOWN. YOU KNOW WHAT THAT MEANS.
ARE WE A GO, KIDDO?
TIMMY, YOU CRAY. Y'ALL SHOULDN'T BE HERE. COME THROUGH THE BACK. GONNA OPEN THE GARDEN GATE.
VOTE FARHADI
WE'RE A GO, POPS.

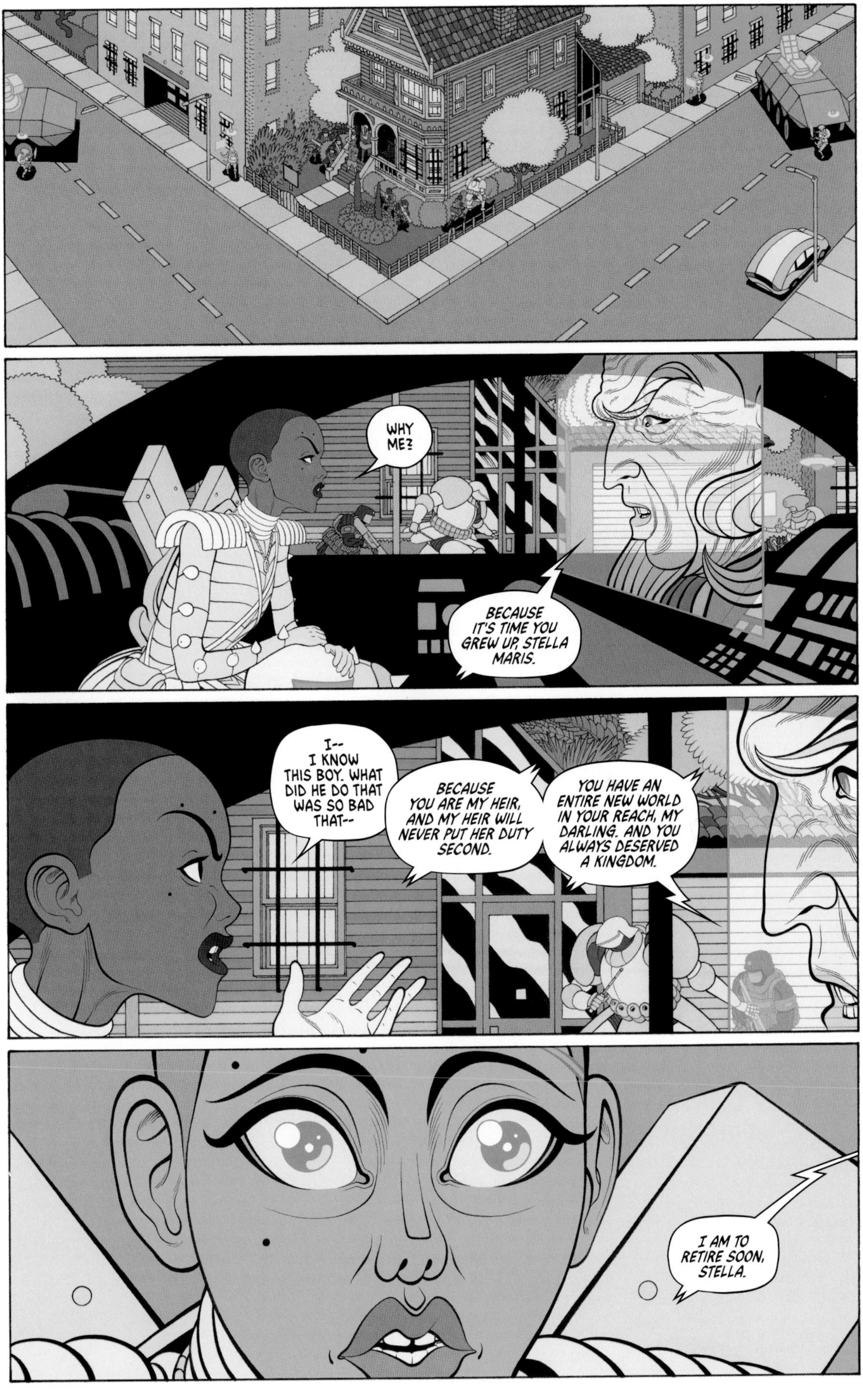
WHY ME?
BECAUSE IT'S TIME YOU GREW UP, STELLA MARIS.
I-- I KNOW THIS BOY. WHAT DID HE DO THAT WAS SO BAD THAT--
BECAUSE YOU ARE MY HEIR, AND MY HEIR WILL NEVER PUT HER DUTY SECOND.
YOU HAVE AN ENTIRE NEW WORLD IN YOUR REACH, MY DARLING. AND YOU ALWAYS DESERVED A KINGDOM.
I AM TO RETIRE SOON, STELLA.

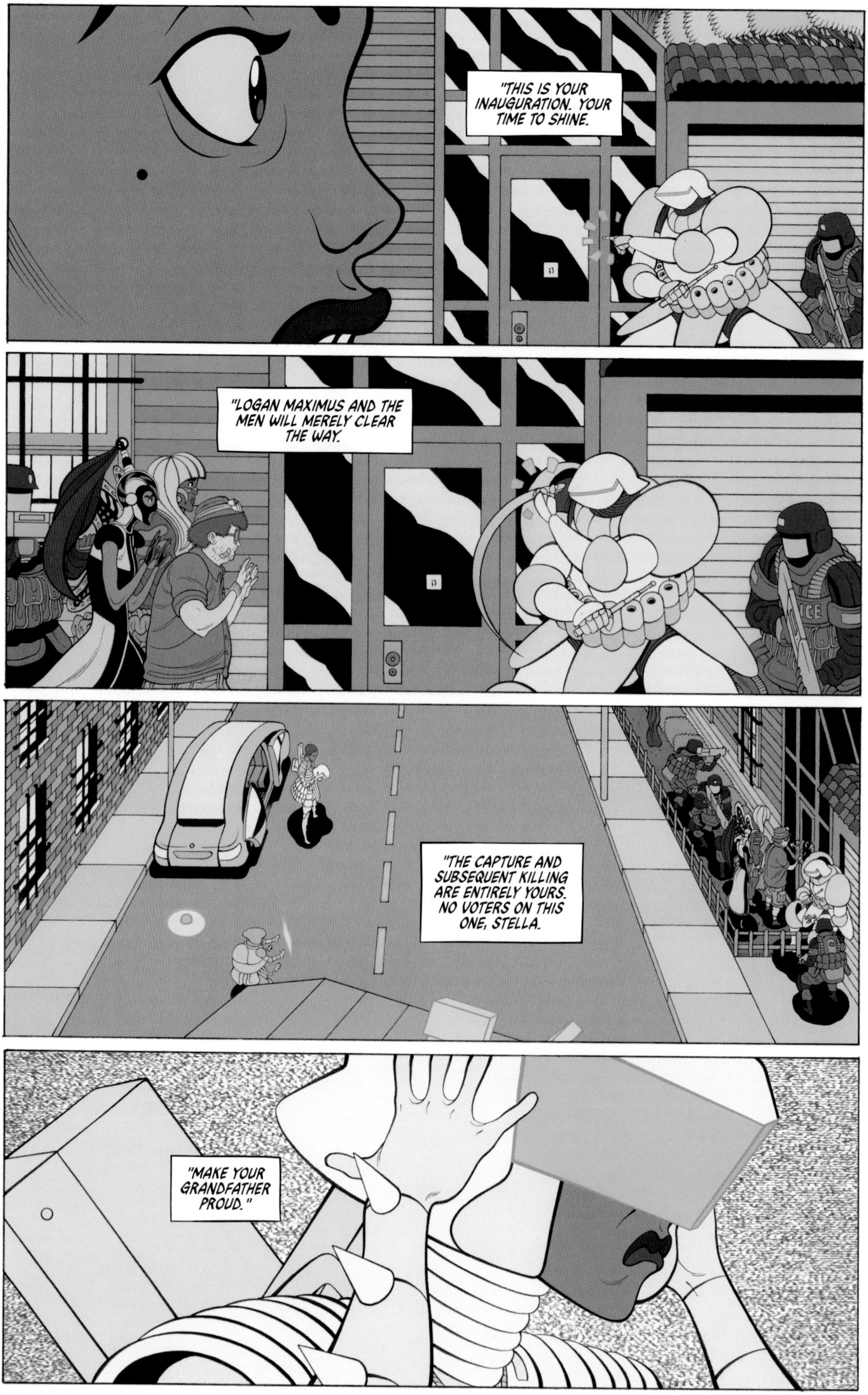
"THIS IS YOUR INAUGURATION. YOUR TIME TO SHINE.
"LOGAN MAXIMUS AND THE MEN WILL MERELY CLEAR THE WAY.
"THE CAPTURE AND SUBSEQUENT KILLING ARE ENTIRELY YOURS. NO VOTERS ON THIS ONE, STELLA.
"MAKE YOUR GRANDFATHER PROUD."

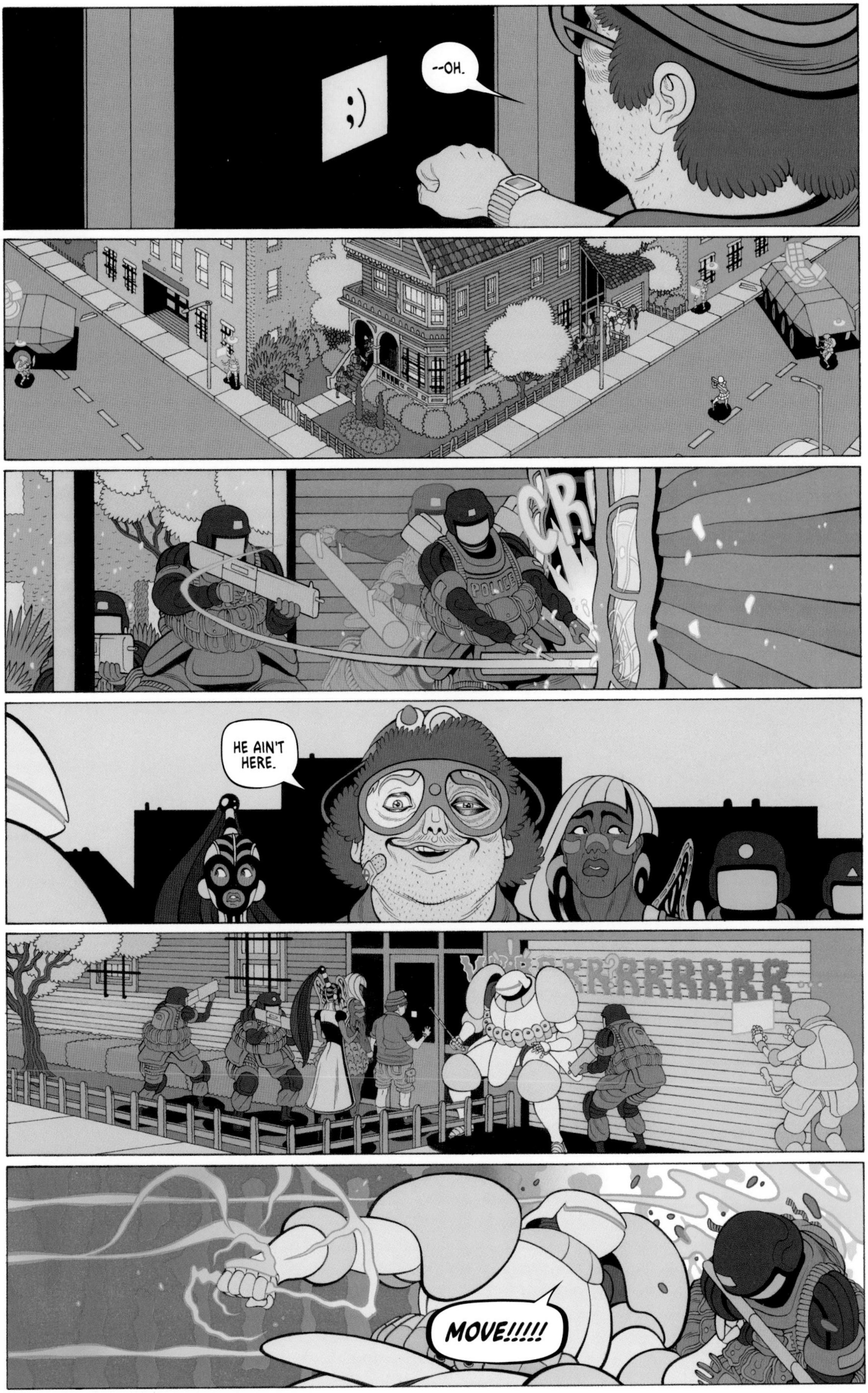
;)
--OH.
CR
HE AIN'T HERE.
RRRRRRRRRR...
MOVE!!!!!

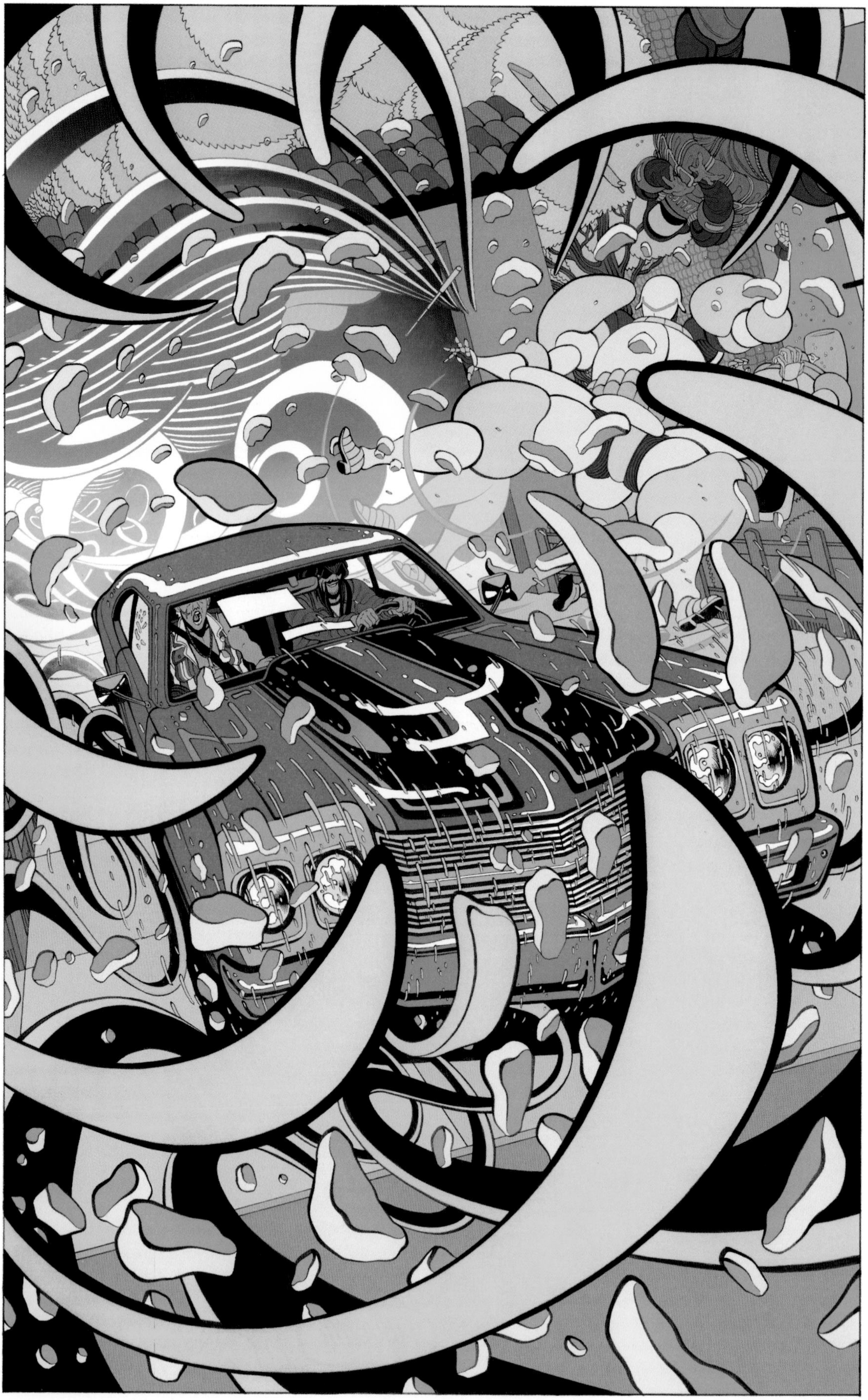

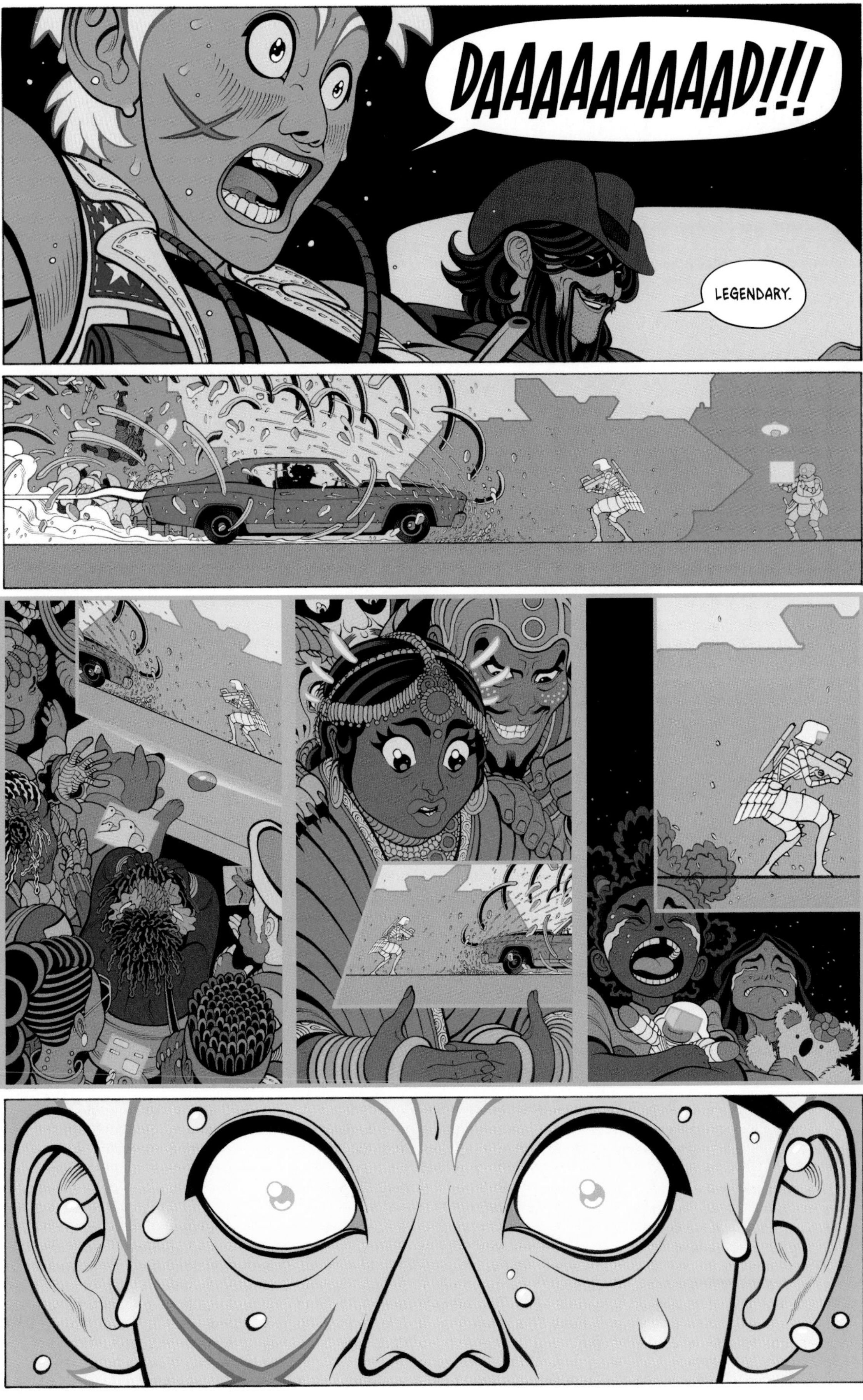
DAAAAAAAAAD!!!
LEGENDARY.

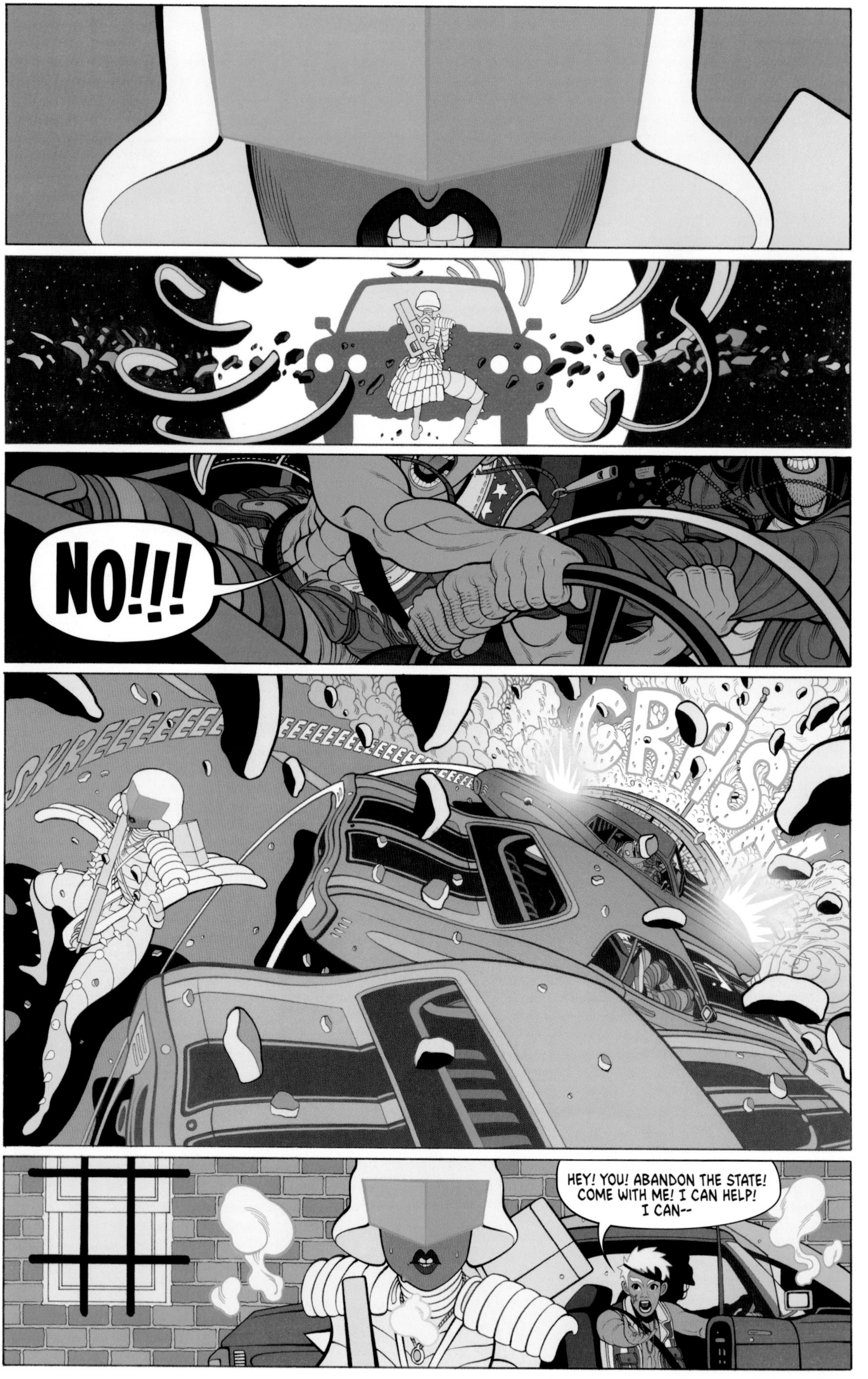
NO!!!
SKREEEEEEEEEEEEEEEEEEEEEEEEEEEEEEE
CRASH
HEY! YOU! ABANDON THE STATE! COME WITH ME! I CAN HELP! I CAN--

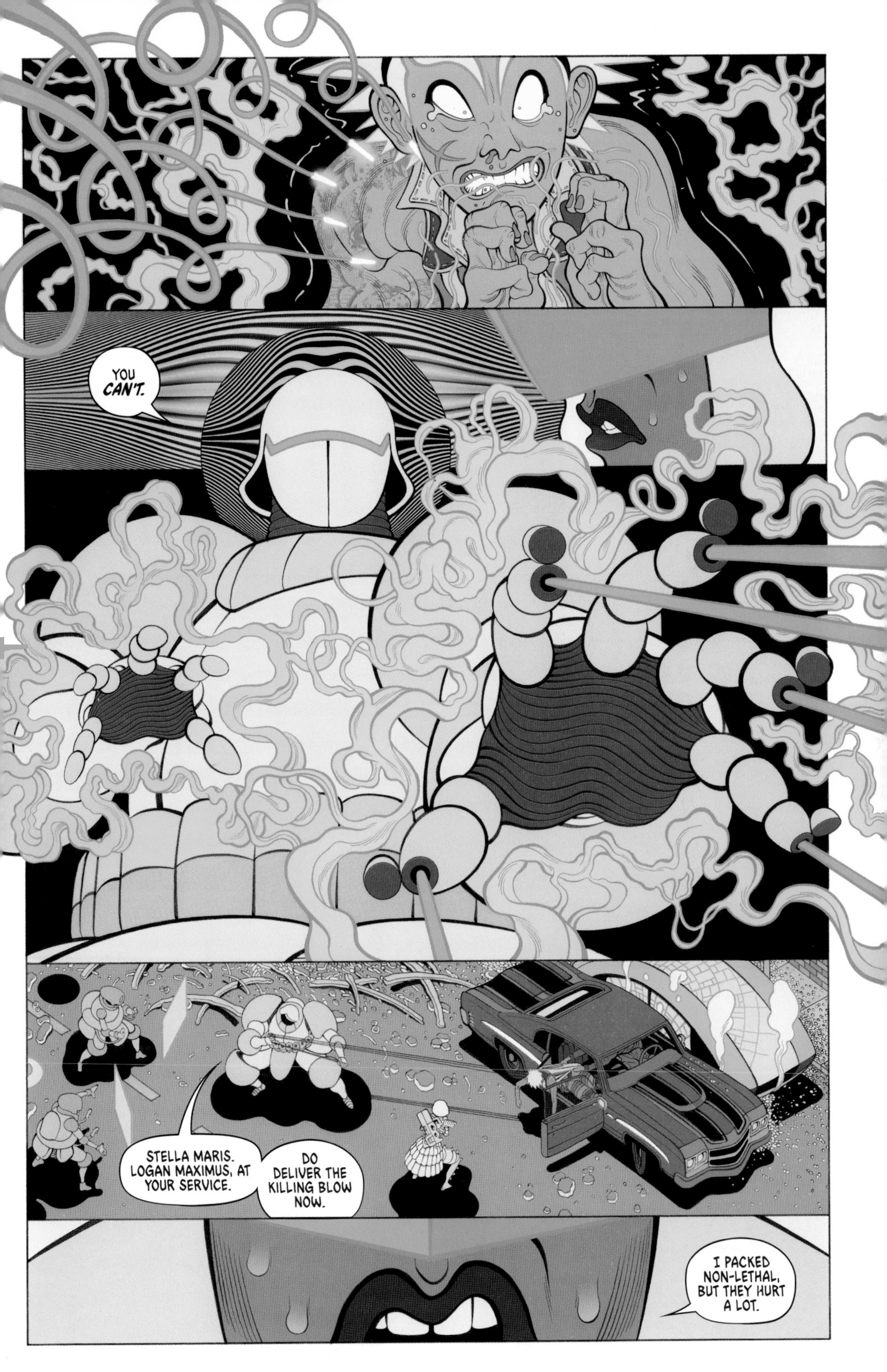
YOU CAN'T.
STELLA MARIS. LOGAN MAXIMUS, AT YOUR SERVICE.
DO DELIVER THE KILLING BLOW NOW.
I PACKED NON-LETHAL, BUT THEY HURT A LOT.

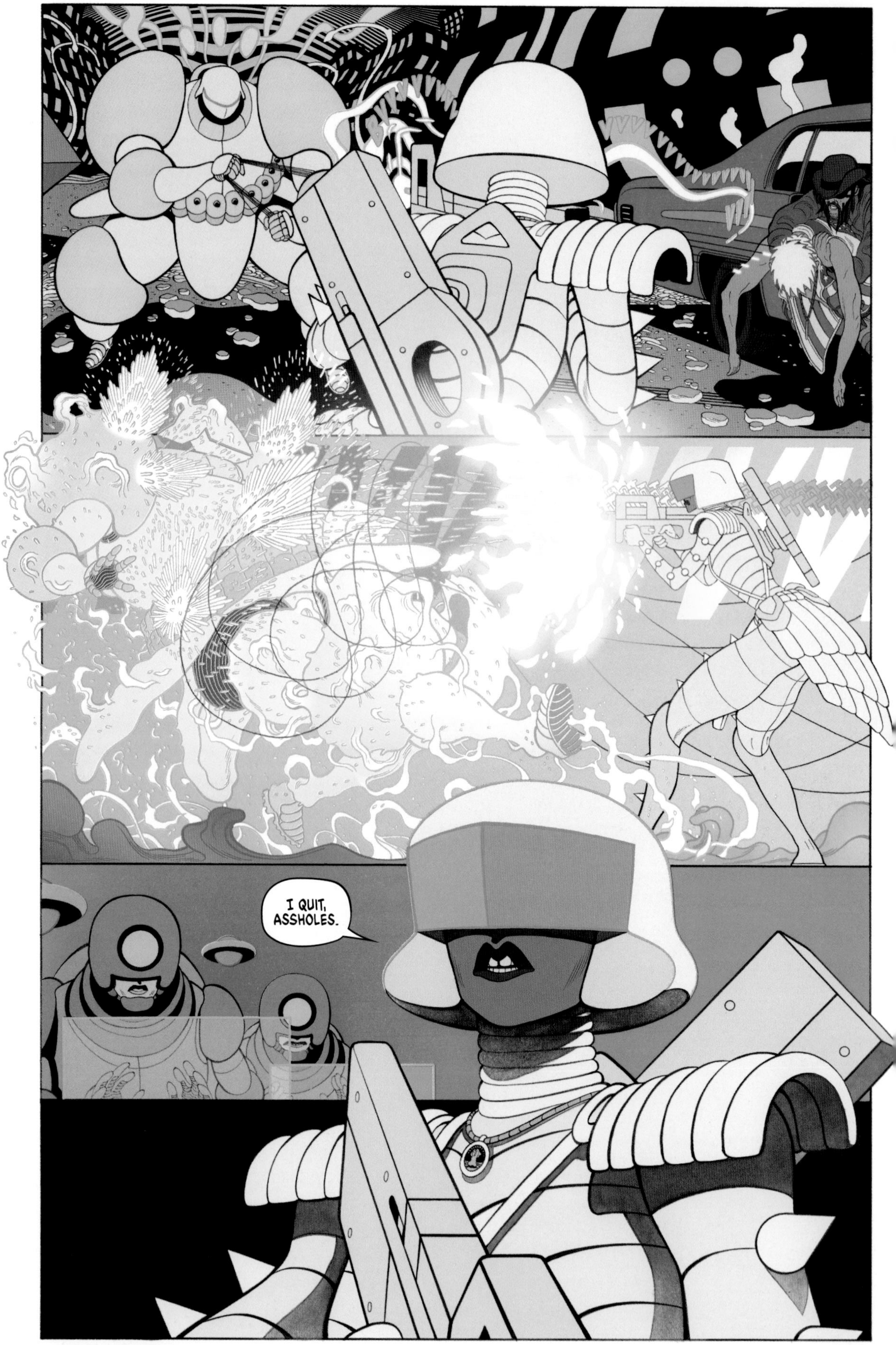
I QUIT, ASSHOLES.

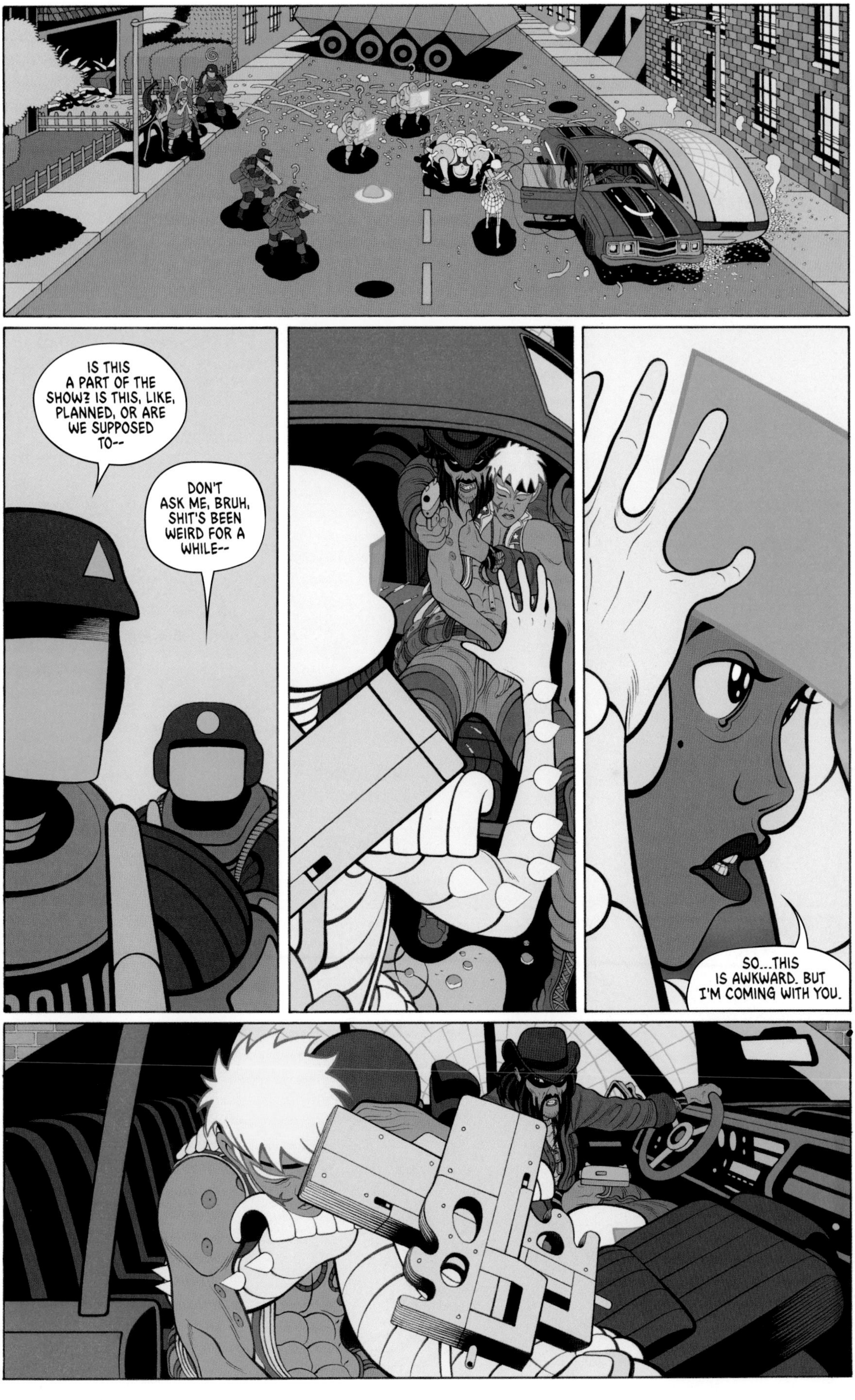

IS THIS A PART OF THE SHOW? IS THIS, LIKE, PLANNED, OR ARE WE SUPPOSED TO--
DON'T ASK ME, BRUH, SHIT'S BEEN WEIRD FOR A WHILE--
SO...THIS IS AWKWARD. BUT I'M COMING WITH YOU.

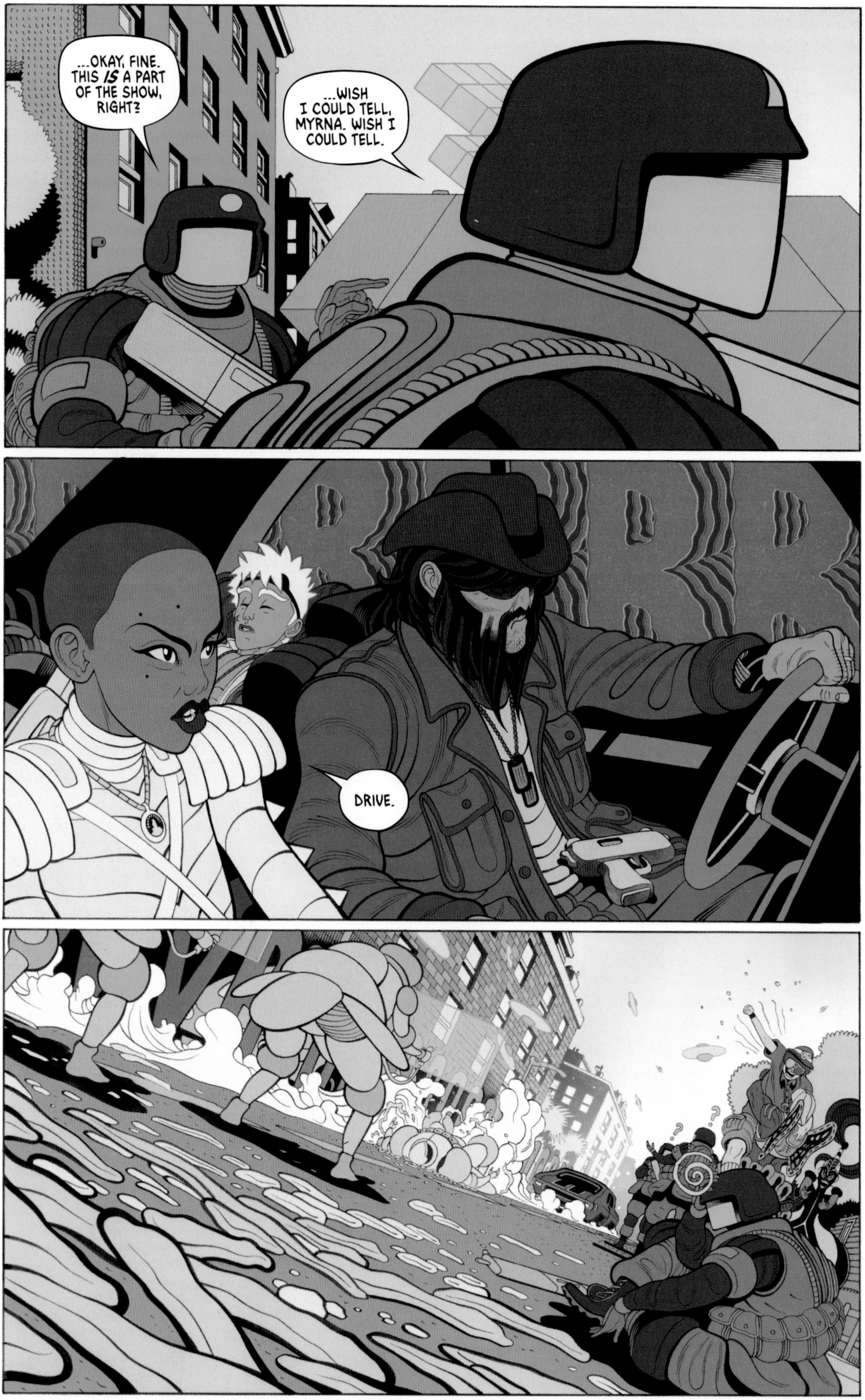
...OKAY, FINE. THIS *IS* A PART OF THE SHOW, RIGHT?
...WISH I COULD TELL, MYRNA. WISH I COULD TELL.
DRIVE.

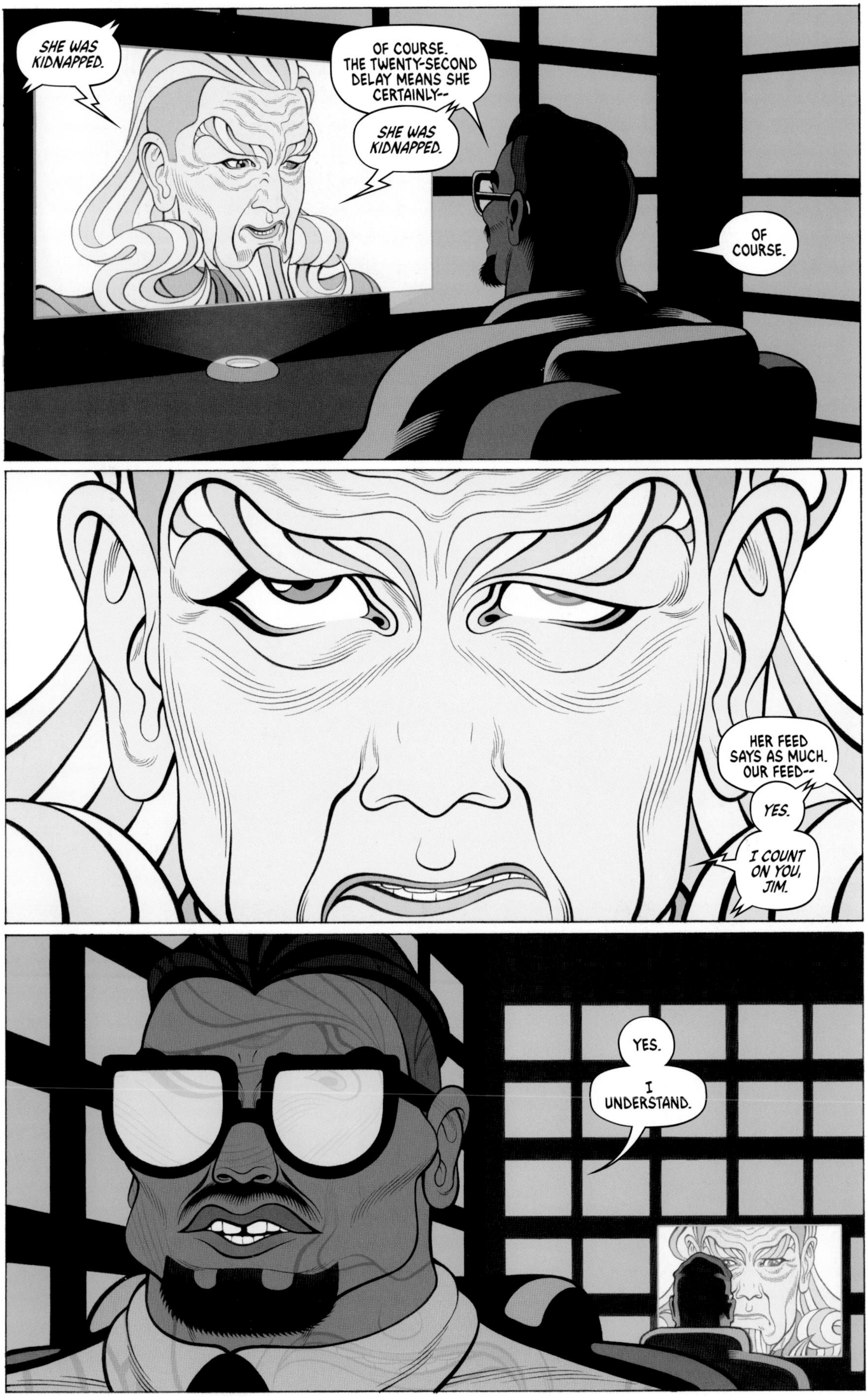
SHE WAS KIDNAPPED.
OF COURSE. THE TWENTY-SECOND DELAY MEANS SHE CERTAINLY--
SHE WAS KIDNAPPED.
OF COURSE.
HER FEED SAYS AS MUCH. OUR FEED--
YES.
I COUNT ON YOU, JIM.
YES.
I UNDERSTAND.

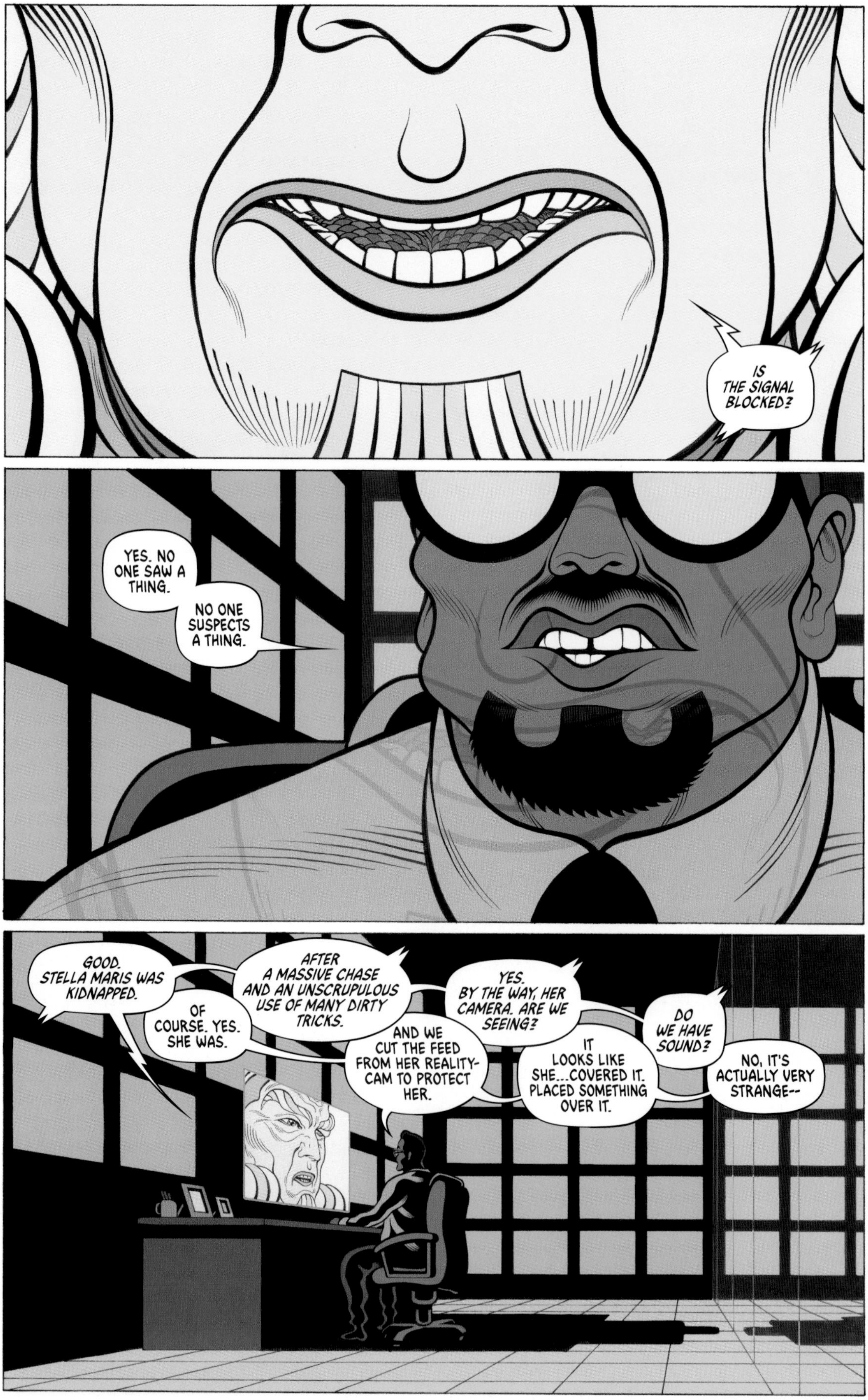
IS THE SIGNAL BLOCKED?
YES. NO ONE SAW A THING.
NO ONE SUSPECTS A THING.
GOOD. STELLA MARIS WAS KIDNAPPED.
OF COURSE. YES. SHE WAS.
AFTER A MASSIVE CHASE AND AN UNSCRUPULOUS USE OF MANY DIRTY TRICKS.
AND WE CUT THE FEED FROM HER REALITY-CAM TO PROTECT HER.
YES. BY THE WAY, HER CAMERA. ARE WE SEEING?
IT LOOKS LIKE SHE...COVERED IT. PLACED SOMETHING OVER IT.
DO WE HAVE SOUND?
NO, IT'S ACTUALLY VERY STRANGE--

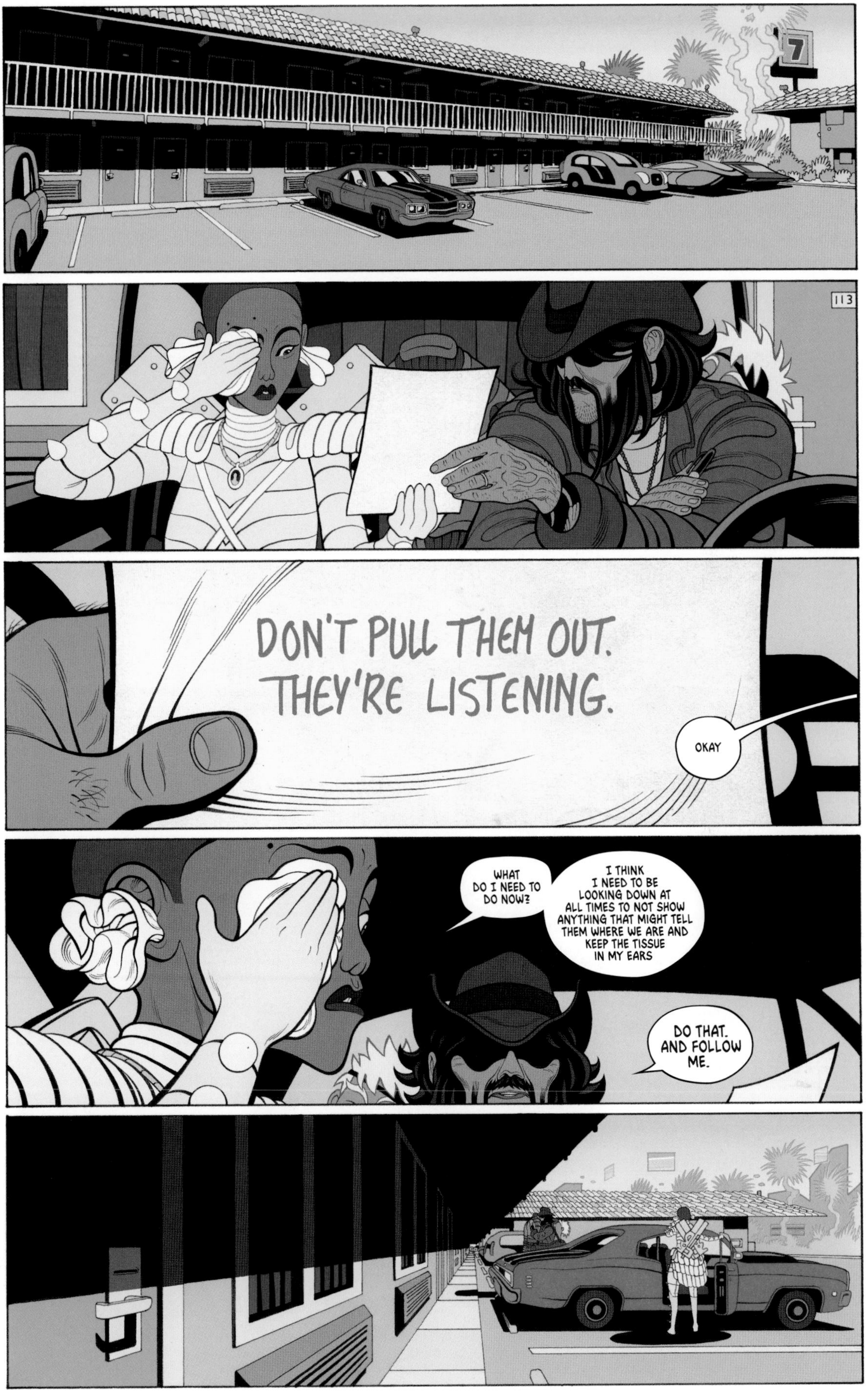
7
113
DON'T PULL THEM OUT.
THEY'RE LISTENING.
OKAY
WHAT DO I NEED TO DO NOW?
I THINK I NEED TO BE LOOKING DOWN AT ALL TIMES TO NOT SHOW ANYTHING THAT MIGHT TELL THEM WHERE WE ARE AND KEEP THE TISSUE IN MY EARS
DO THAT. AND FOLLOW ME.

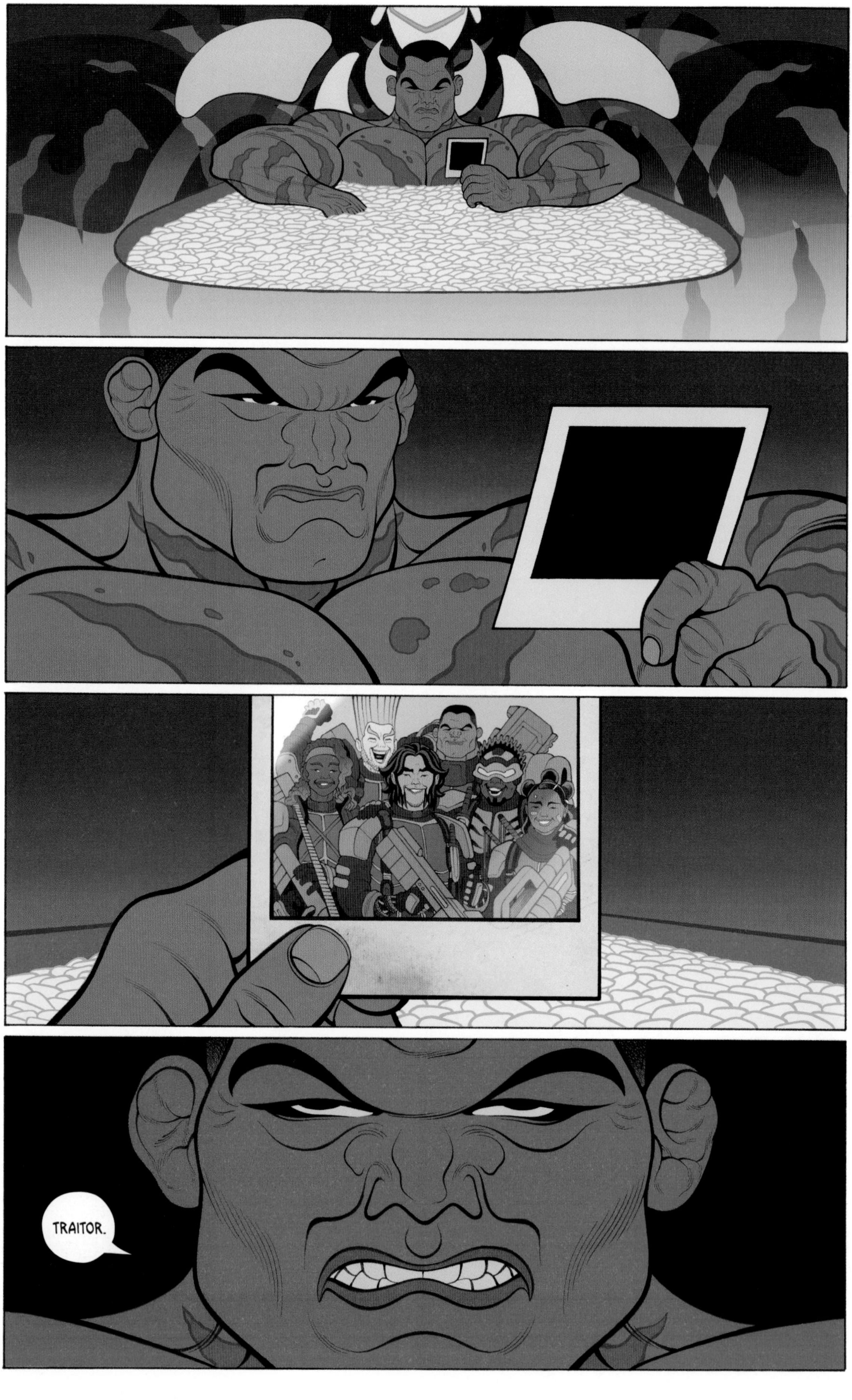
TRAITOR.

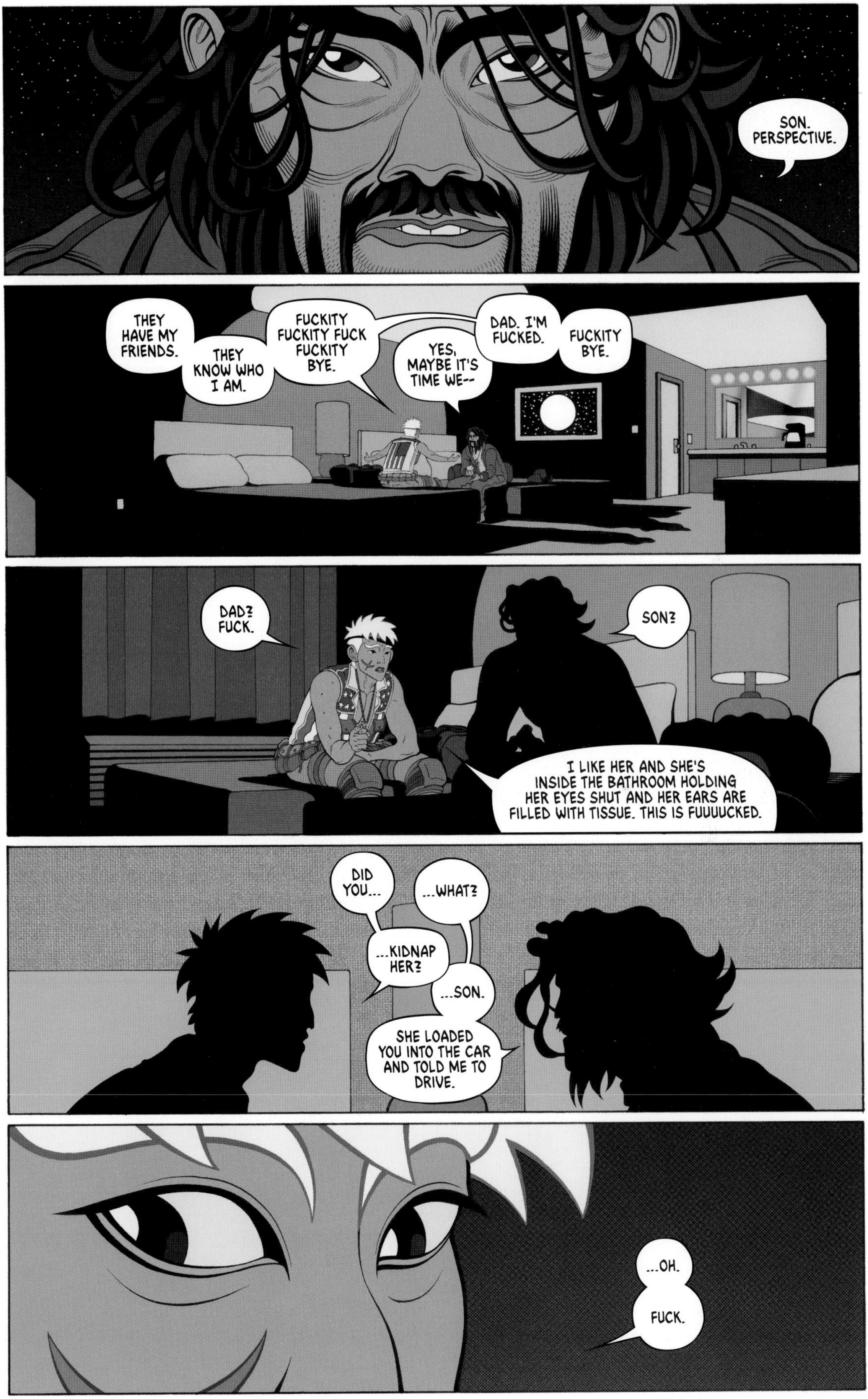
SON. PERSPECTIVE.
THEY HAVE MY FRIENDS.
THEY KNOW WHO I AM.
FUCKITY FUCKITY FUCK FUCKITY BYE.
YES, MAYBE IT'S TIME WE--
DAD. I'M FUCKED.
FUCKITY BYE.
DAD? FUCK.
SON?
I LIKE HER AND SHE'S INSIDE THE BATHROOM HOLDING HER EYES SHUT AND HER EARS ARE FILLED WITH TISSUE. THIS IS FUUUUCKED.
DID YOU...
...WHAT?
...KIDNAP HER?
...SON.
SHE LOADED YOU INTO THE CAR AND TOLD ME TO DRIVE.
...OH.
FUCK.

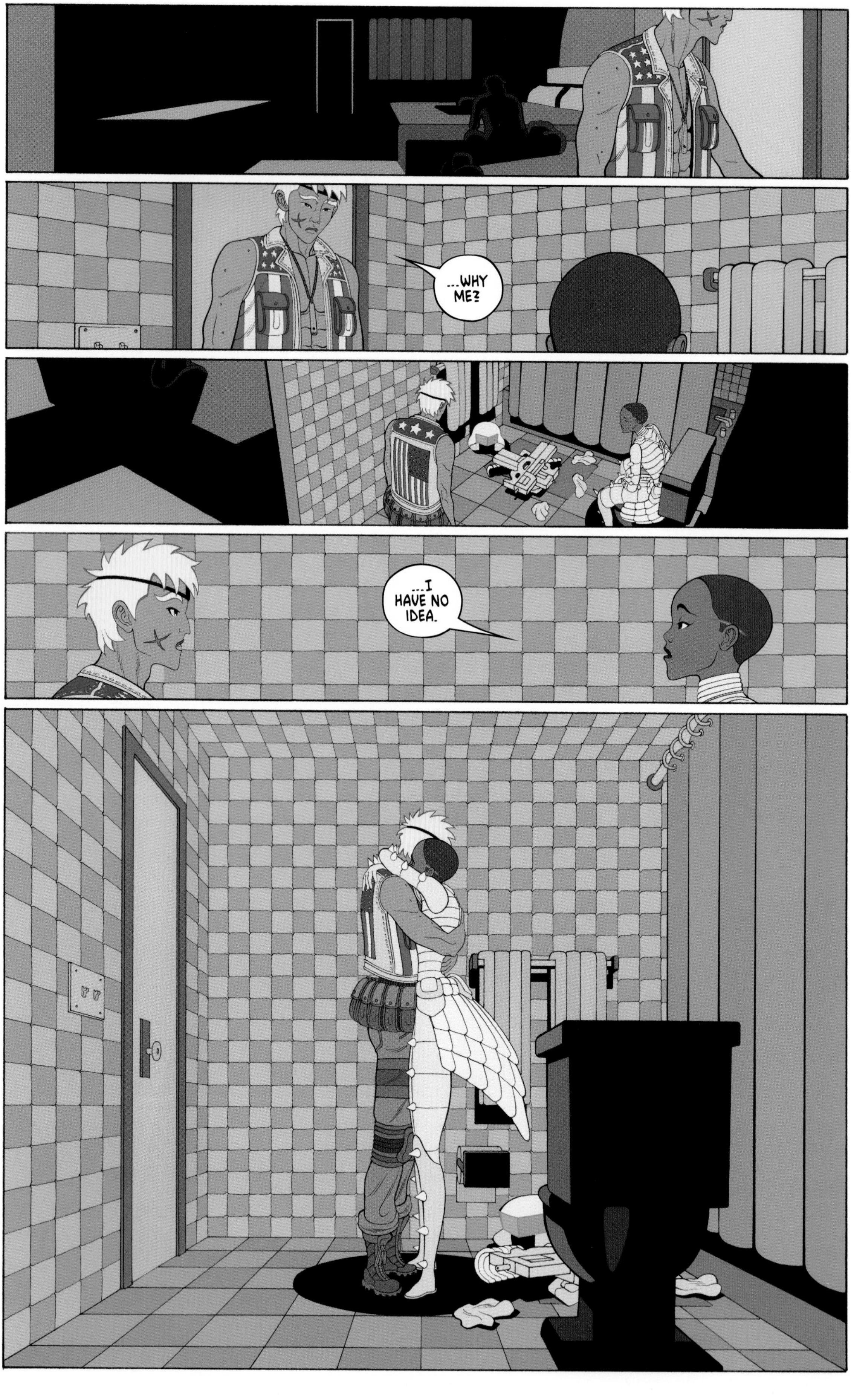
...WHY ME?
...I HAVE NO IDEA.

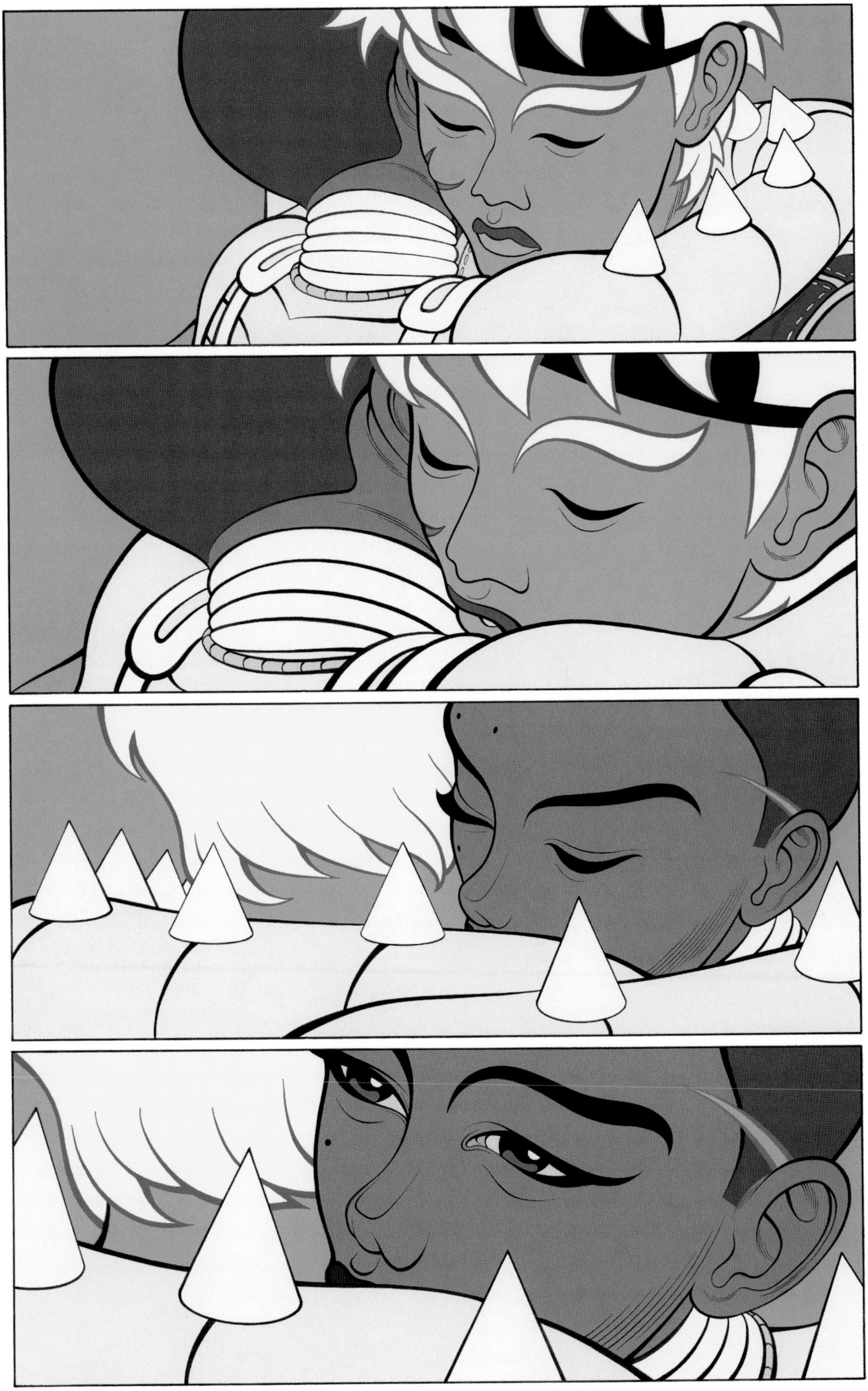

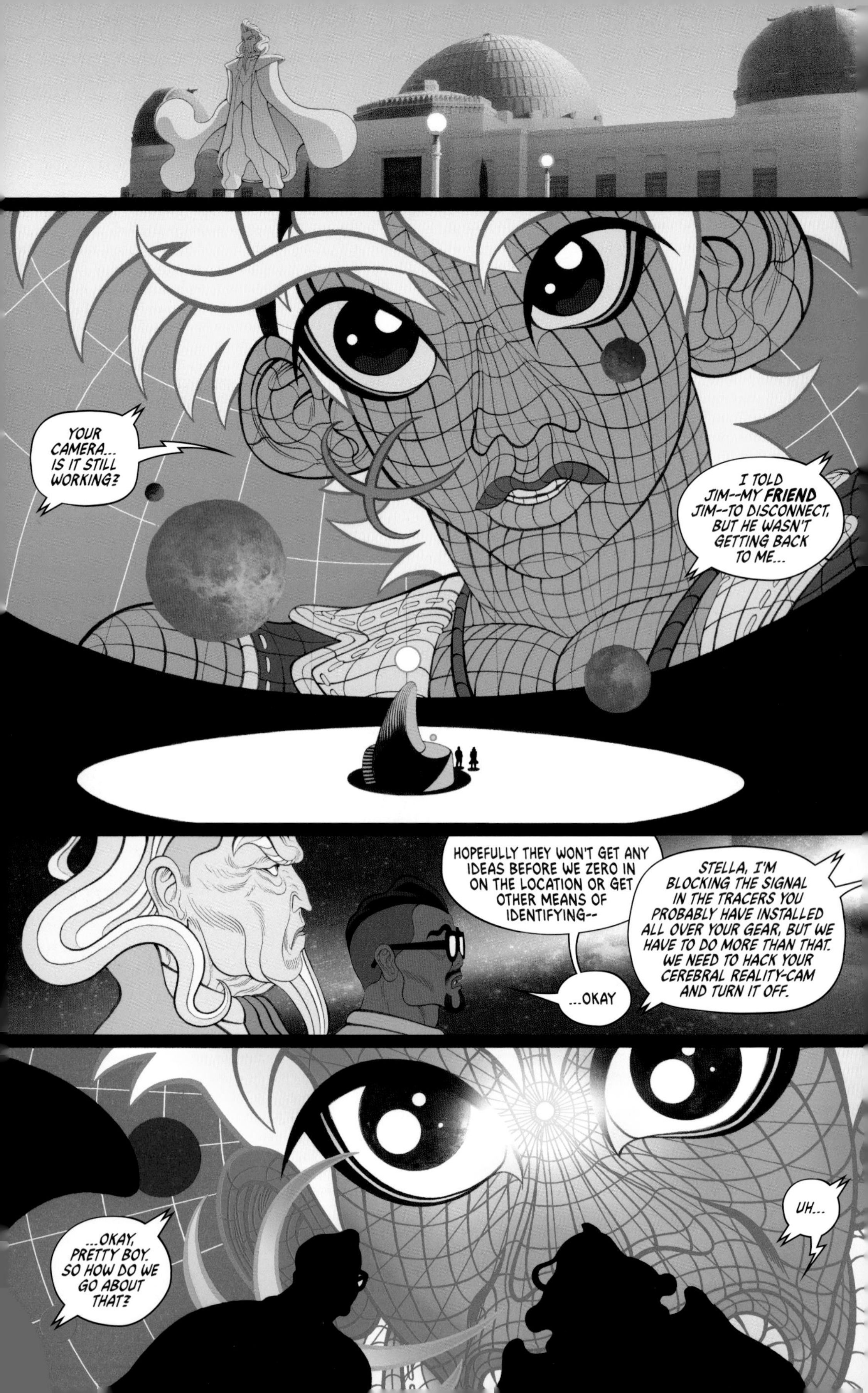
YOUR CAMERA... IS IT STILL WORKING?
I TOLD JIM--MY FRIEND JIM--TO DISCONNECT, BUT HE WASN'T GETTING BACK TO ME...
HOPEFULLY THEY WON'T GET ANY IDEAS BEFORE WE ZERO IN ON THE LOCATION OR GET OTHER MEANS OF IDENTIFYING--
...OKAY
STELLA, I'M BLOCKING THE SIGNAL IN THE TRACERS YOU PROBABLY HAVE INSTALLED ALL OVER YOUR GEAR, BUT WE HAVE TO DO MORE THAN THAT. WE NEED TO HACK YOUR CEREBRAL REALITY-CAM AND TURN IT OFF.
...OKAY, PRETTY BOY. SO HOW DO WE GO ABOUT THAT?
UH...

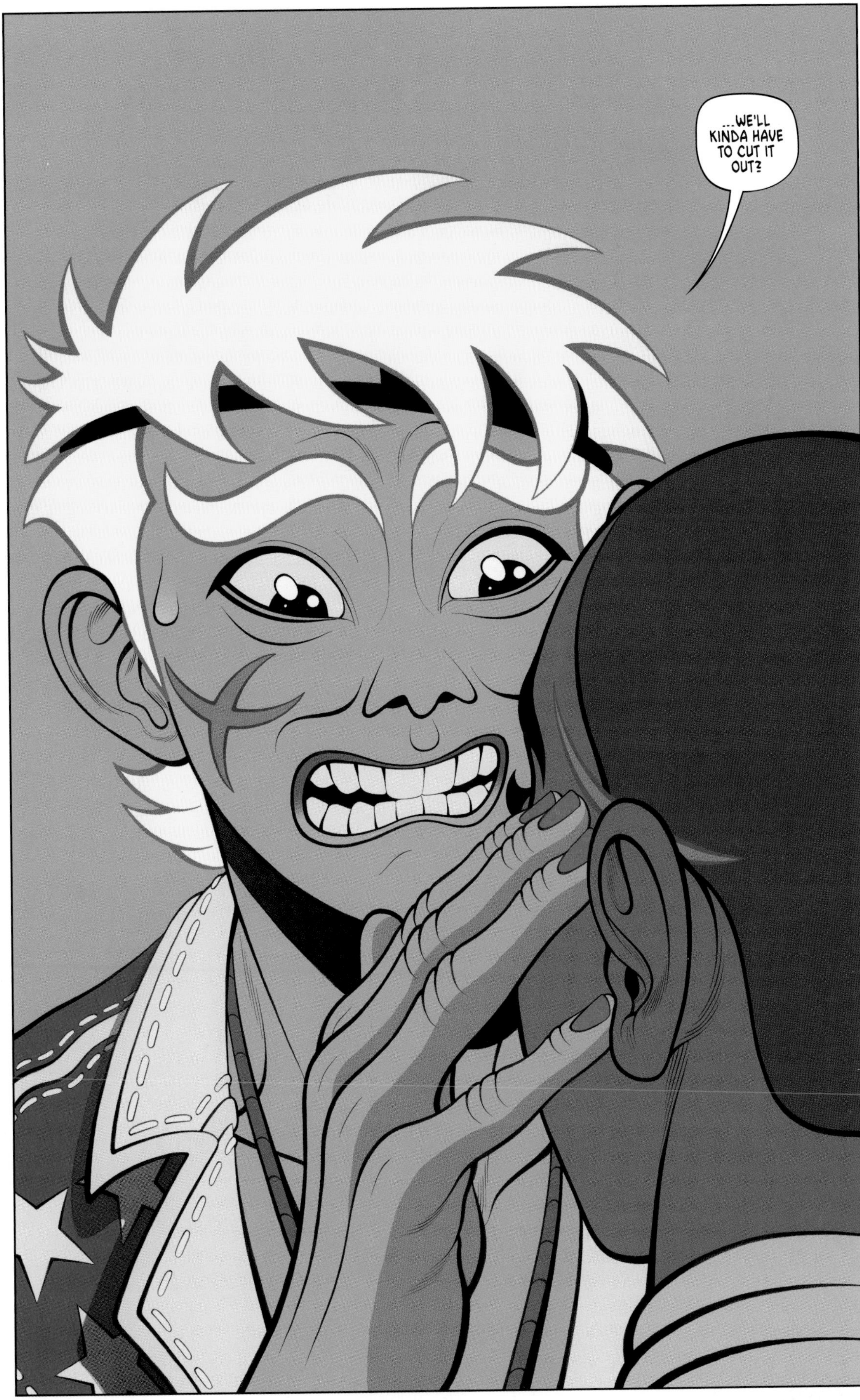
...WE'LL KINDA HAVE TO CUT IT OUT?

CHAPTER 3

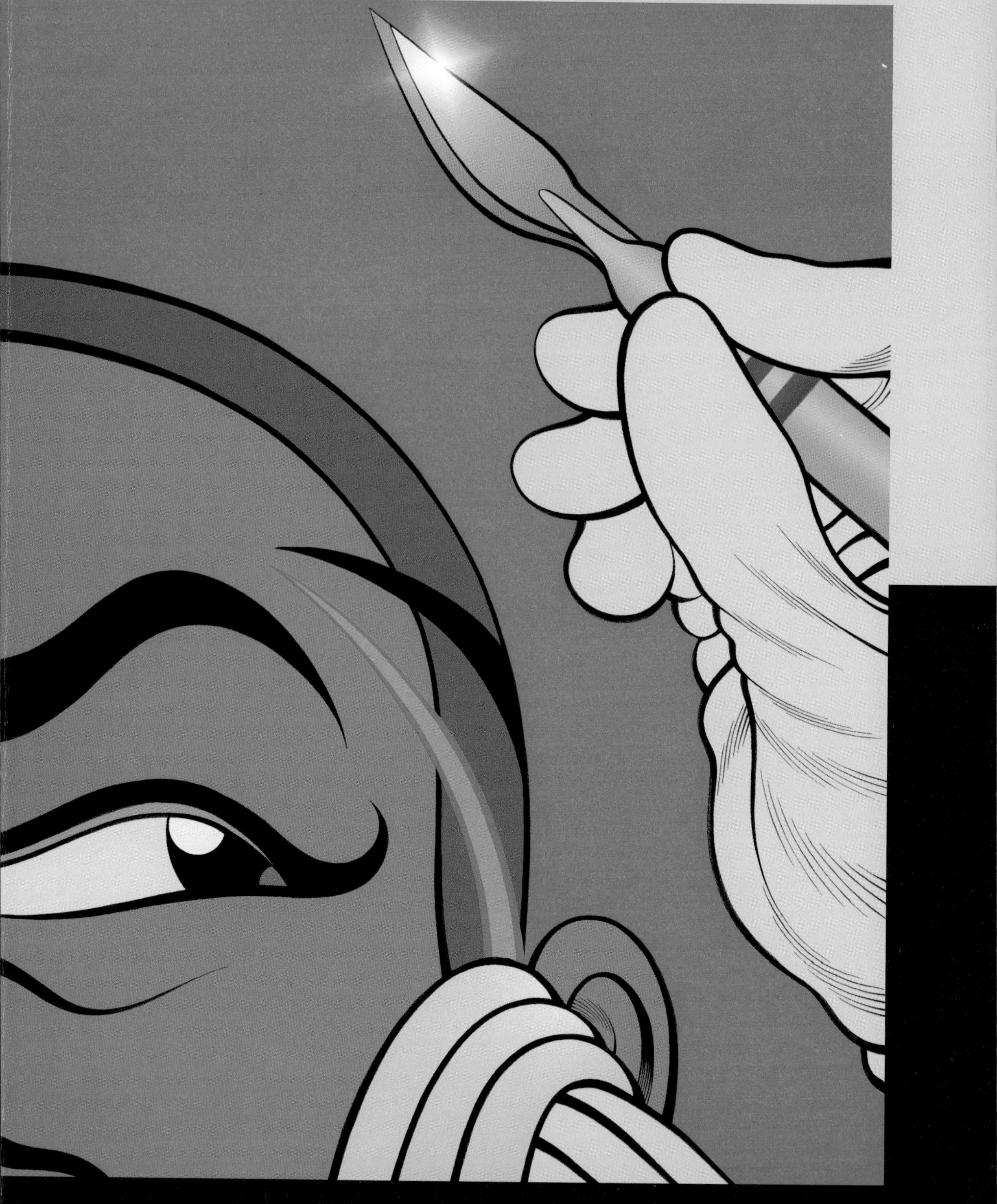

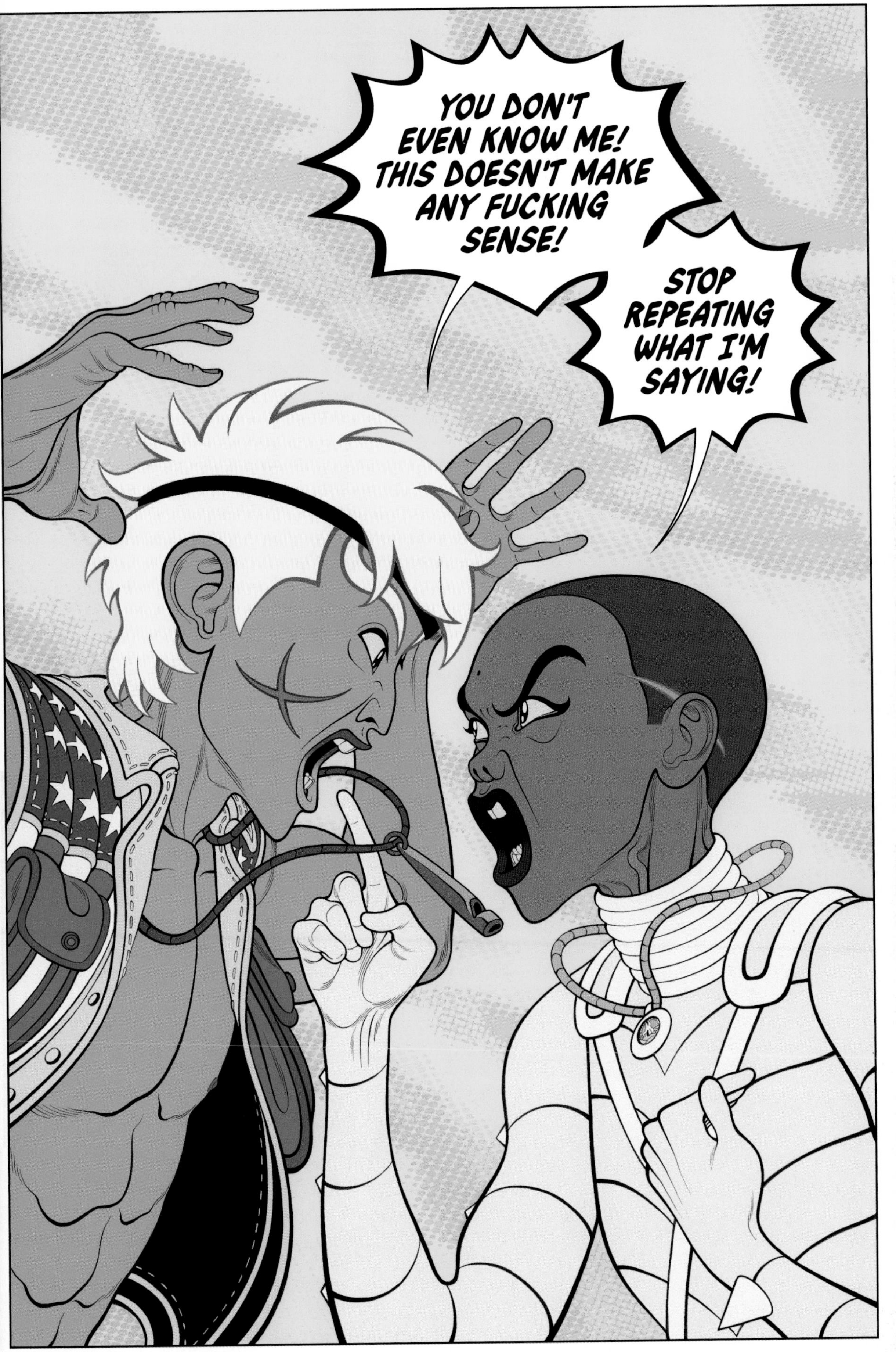
YOU DON'T EVEN KNOW ME! THIS DOESN'T MAKE ANY FUCKING SENSE!
STOP REPEATING WHAT I'M SAYING!

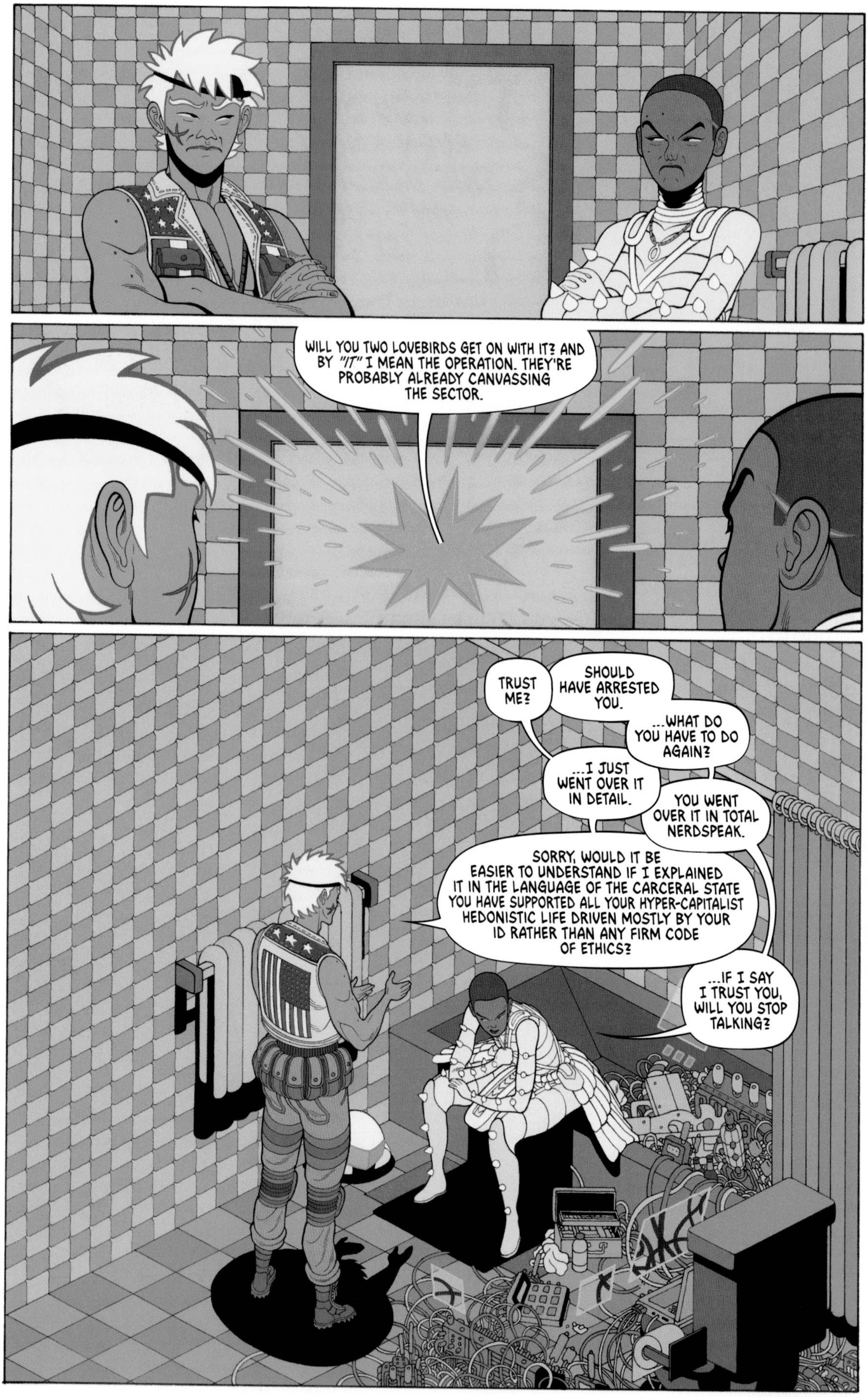
WILL YOU TWO LOVEBIRDS GET ON WITH IT? AND BY "IT" I MEAN THE OPERATION. THEY'RE PROBABLY ALREADY CANVASSING THE SECTOR.
TRUST ME?
SHOULD HAVE ARRESTED YOU.
...WHAT DO YOU HAVE TO DO AGAIN?
...I JUST WENT OVER IT IN DETAIL.
YOU WENT OVER IT IN TOTAL NERDSPEAK.
SORRY, WOULD IT BE EASIER TO UNDERSTAND IF I EXPLAINED IT IN THE LANGUAGE OF THE CARCERAL STATE YOU HAVE SUPPORTED ALL YOUR HYPER-CAPITALIST HEDONISTIC LIFE DRIVEN MOSTLY BY YOUR ID RATHER THAN ANY FIRM CODE OF ETHICS?
...IF I SAY I TRUST YOU, WILL YOU STOP TALKING?

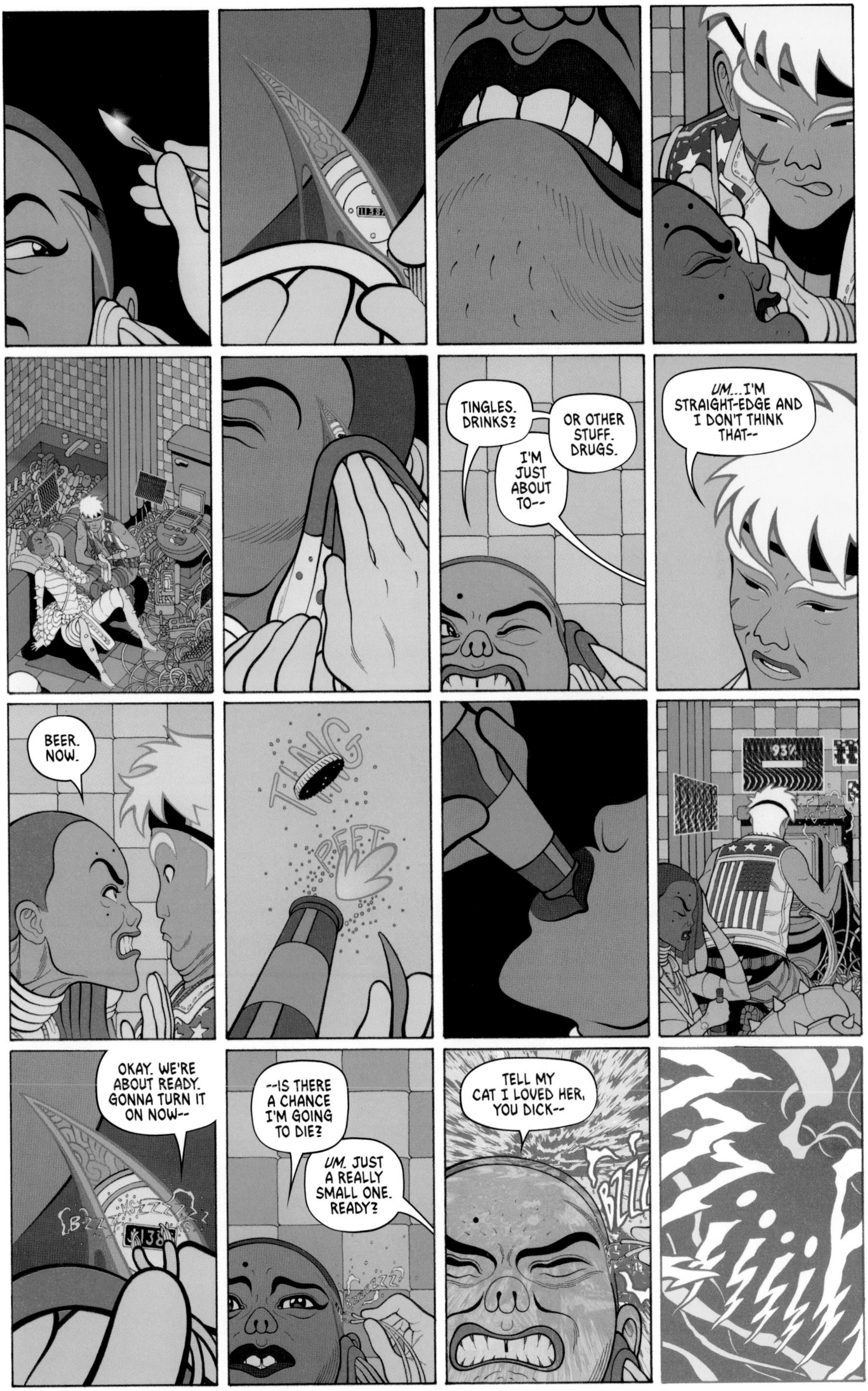

TINGLES. DRINKS?
OR OTHER STUFF. DRUGS.
I'M JUST ABOUT TO--
UM...I'M STRAIGHT-EDGE AND I DON'T THINK THAT--
BEER. NOW.
TING
PFFT
OKAY. WE'RE ABOUT READY. GONNA TURN IT ON NOW--
--IS THERE A CHANCE I'M GOING TO DIE?
UM. JUST A REALLY SMALL ONE. READY?
TELL MY CAT I LOVED HER, YOU DICK--

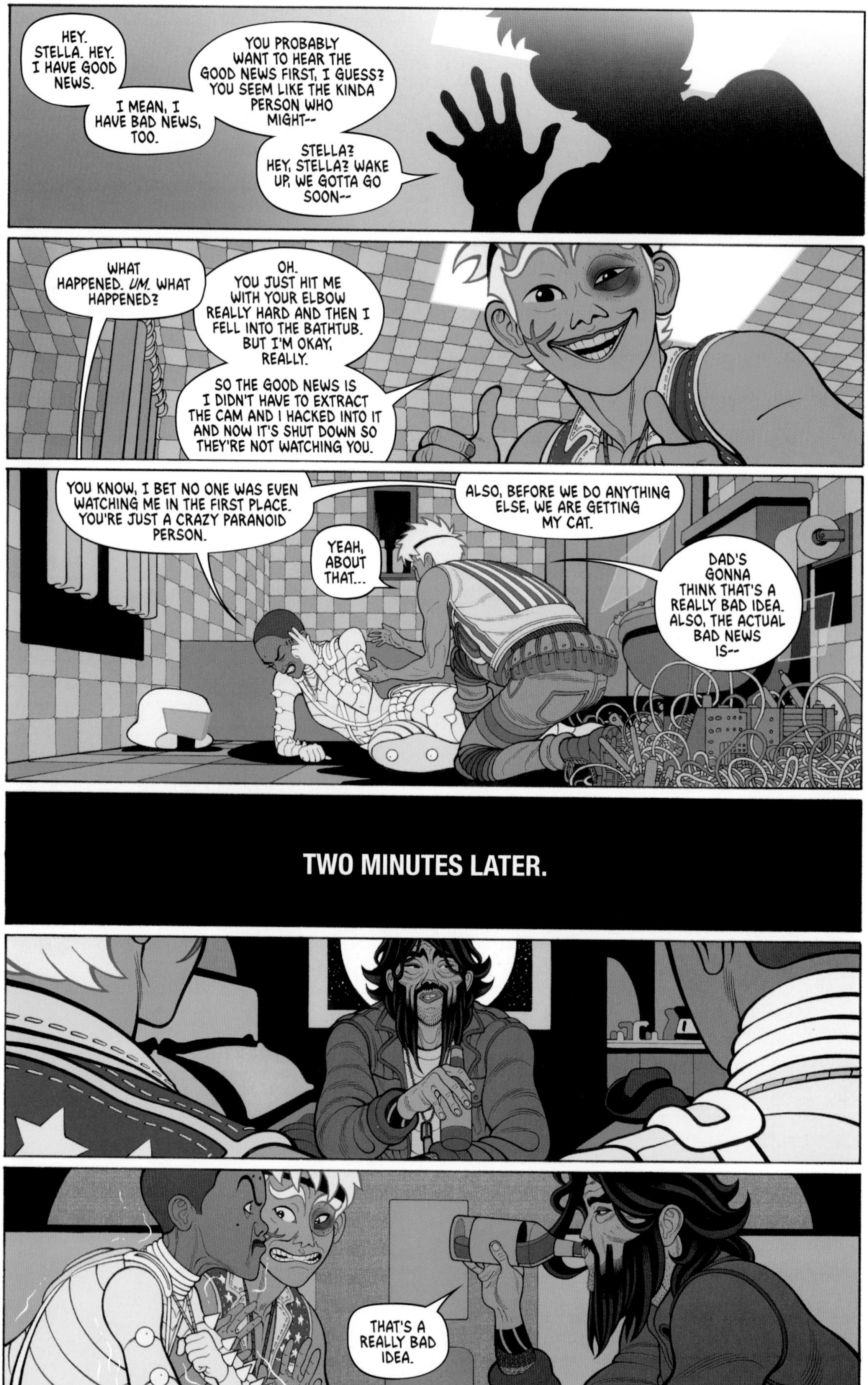
HEY. STELLA. HEY. I HAVE GOOD NEWS.
I MEAN, I HAVE BAD NEWS, TOO.
YOU PROBABLY WANT TO HEAR THE GOOD NEWS FIRST, I GUESS? YOU SEEM LIKE THE KINDA PERSON WHO MIGHT--
STELLA? HEY, STELLA? WAKE UP, WE GOTTA GO SOON--
WHAT HAPPENED. *UM.* WHAT HAPPENED?
OH. YOU JUST HIT ME WITH YOUR ELBOW REALLY HARD AND THEN I FELL INTO THE BATHTUB. BUT I'M OKAY, REALLY.
SO THE GOOD NEWS IS I DIDN'T HAVE TO EXTRACT THE CAM AND I HACKED INTO IT AND NOW IT'S SHUT DOWN SO THEY'RE NOT WATCHING YOU.
YOU KNOW, I BET NO ONE WAS EVEN WATCHING ME IN THE FIRST PLACE. YOU'RE JUST A CRAZY PARANOID PERSON.
ALSO, BEFORE WE DO ANYTHING ELSE, WE ARE GETTING MY CAT.
YEAH, ABOUT THAT...
DAD'S GONNA THINK THAT'S A REALLY BAD IDEA. ALSO, THE ACTUAL BAD NEWS IS--
TWO MINUTES LATER.
THAT'S A REALLY BAD IDEA.

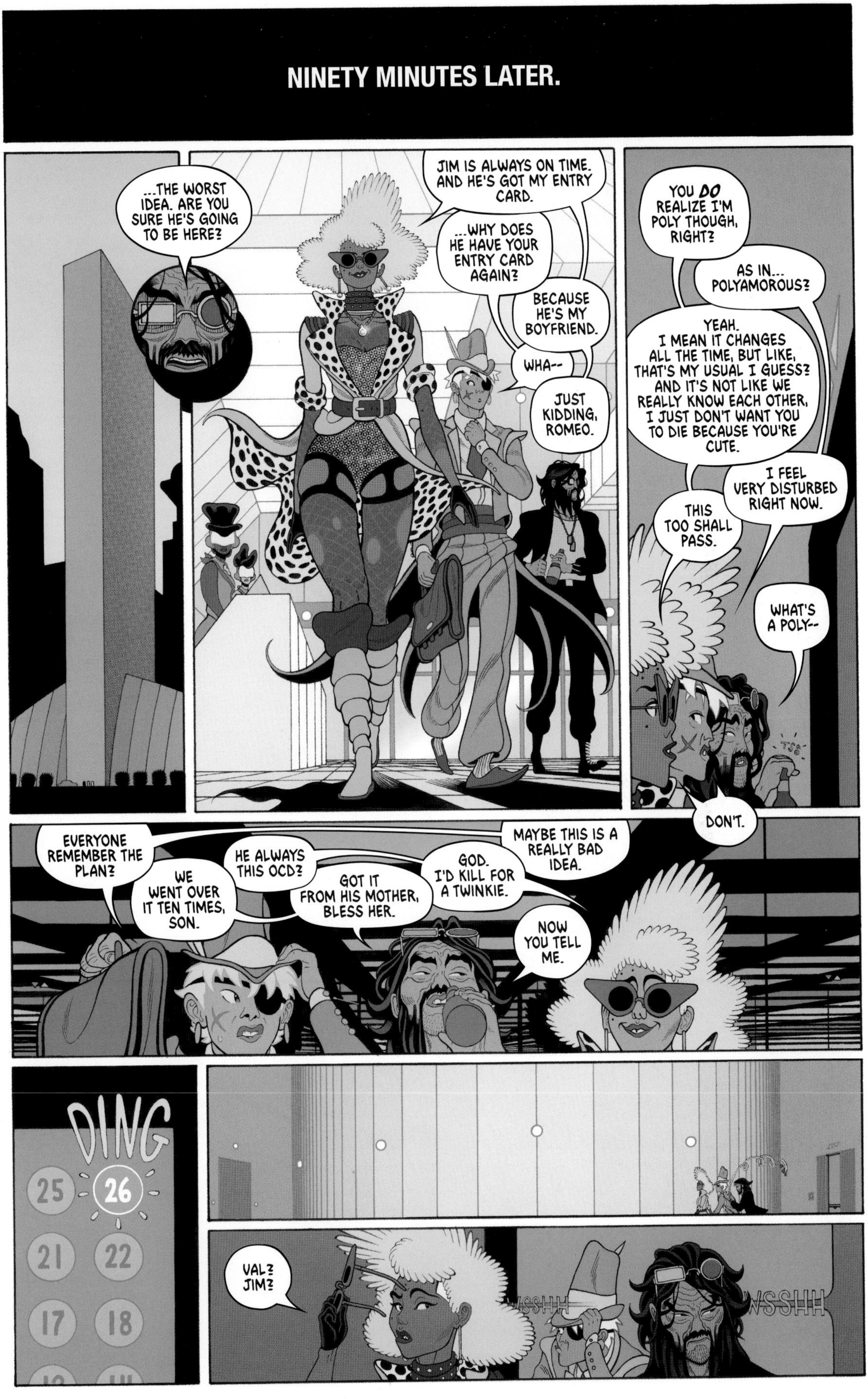
NINETY MINUTES LATER.
...THE WORST IDEA. ARE YOU SURE HE'S GOING TO BE HERE?
JIM IS ALWAYS ON TIME. AND HE'S GOT MY ENTRY CARD.
...WHY DOES HE HAVE YOUR ENTRY CARD AGAIN?
BECAUSE HE'S MY BOYFRIEND.
WHA--
JUST KIDDING, ROMEO.
YOU DO REALIZE I'M POLY THOUGH, RIGHT?
AS IN... POLYAMOROUS?
YEAH. I MEAN IT CHANGES ALL THE TIME, BUT LIKE, THAT'S MY USUAL I GUESS? AND IT'S NOT LIKE WE REALLY KNOW EACH OTHER, I JUST DON'T WANT YOU TO DIE BECAUSE YOU'RE CUTE.
I FEEL VERY DISTURBED RIGHT NOW.
THIS TOO SHALL PASS.
WHAT'S A POLY--
DON'T.
EVERYONE REMEMBER THE PLAN?
WE WENT OVER IT TEN TIMES, SON.
HE ALWAYS THIS OCD?
GOT IT FROM HIS MOTHER, BLESS HER.
GOD. I'D KILL FOR A TWINKIE.
MAYBE THIS IS A REALLY BAD IDEA.
NOW YOU TELL ME.
DING
25
26
21
22
17
18
VAL? JIM?

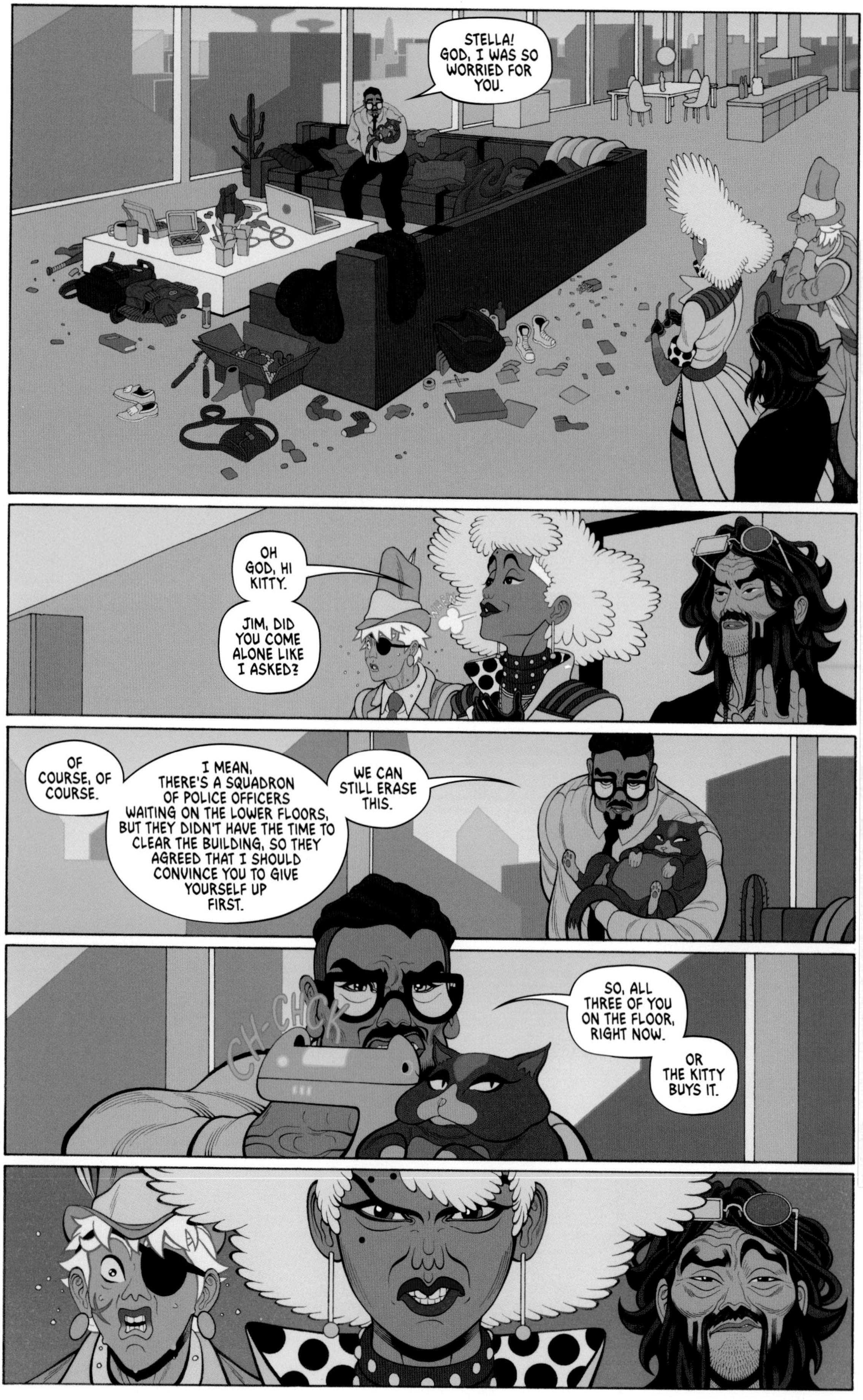
STELLA! GOD, I WAS SO WORRIED FOR YOU.
OH GOD, HI KITTY.
JIM, DID YOU COME ALONE LIKE I ASKED?
OF COURSE, OF COURSE.
I MEAN, THERE'S A SQUADRON OF POLICE OFFICERS WAITING ON THE LOWER FLOORS, BUT THEY DIDN'T HAVE THE TIME TO CLEAR THE BUILDING, SO THEY AGREED THAT I SHOULD CONVINCE YOU TO GIVE YOURSELF UP FIRST.
WE CAN STILL ERASE THIS.
CH-CHCK
SO, ALL THREE OF YOU ON THE FLOOR, RIGHT NOW.
OR THE KITTY BUYS IT.

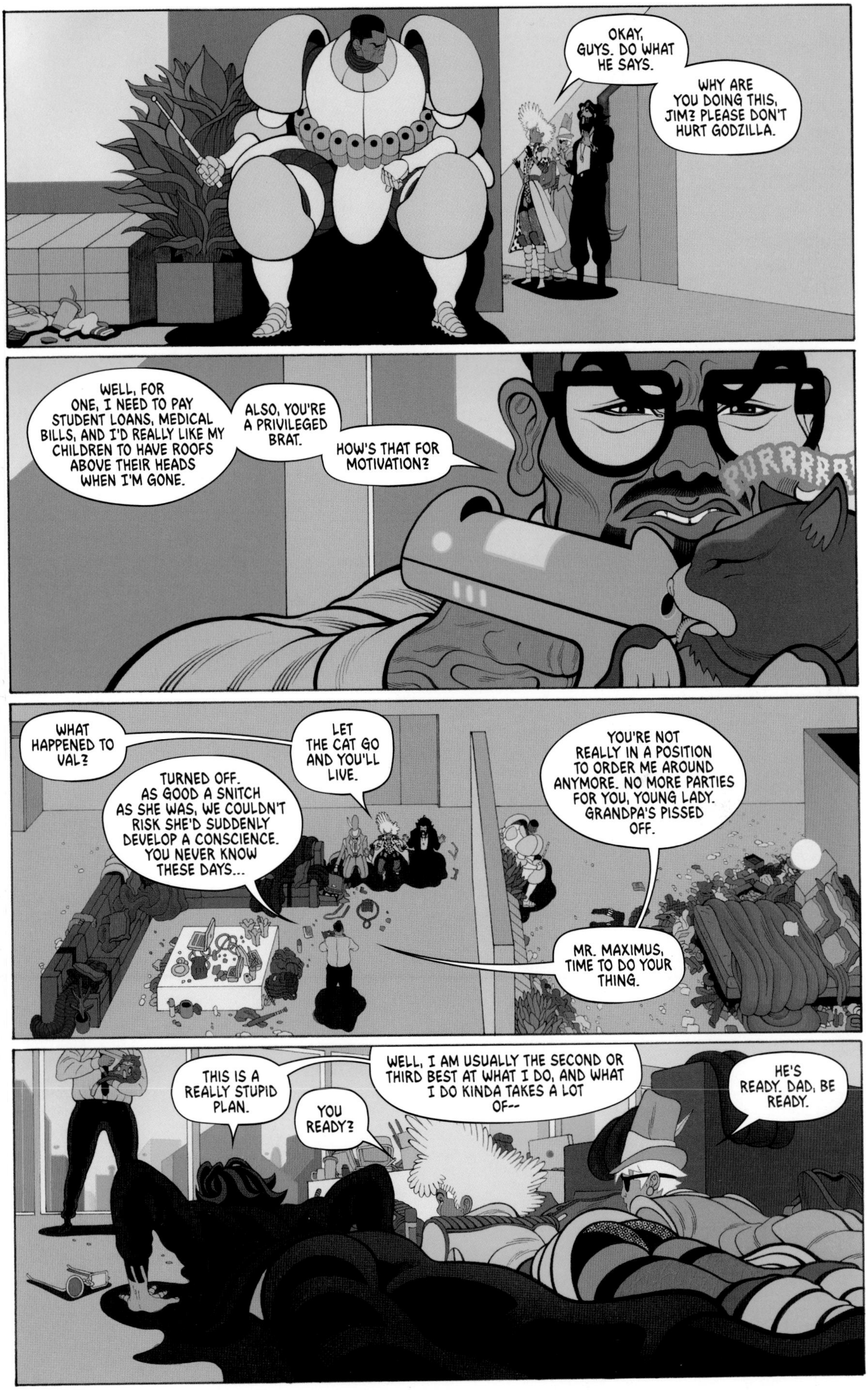
OKAY, GUYS. DO WHAT HE SAYS.
WHY ARE YOU DOING THIS, JIM? PLEASE DON'T HURT GODZILLA.
WELL, FOR ONE, I NEED TO PAY STUDENT LOANS, MEDICAL BILLS, AND I'D REALLY LIKE MY CHILDREN TO HAVE ROOFS ABOVE THEIR HEADS WHEN I'M GONE.
ALSO, YOU'RE A PRIVILEGED BRAT.
HOW'S THAT FOR MOTIVATION?
WHAT HAPPENED TO VAL?
TURNED OFF. AS GOOD A SNITCH AS SHE WAS, WE COULDN'T RISK SHE'D SUDDENLY DEVELOP A CONSCIENCE. YOU NEVER KNOW THESE DAYS...
LET THE CAT GO AND YOU'LL LIVE.
YOU'RE NOT REALLY IN A POSITION TO ORDER ME AROUND ANYMORE. NO MORE PARTIES FOR YOU, YOUNG LADY. GRANDPA'S PISSED OFF.
MR. MAXIMUS, TIME TO DO YOUR THING.
THIS IS A REALLY STUPID PLAN.
YOU READY?
WELL, I AM USUALLY THE SECOND OR THIRD BEST AT WHAT I DO, AND WHAT I DO KINDA TAKES A LOT OF--
HE'S READY. DAD, BE READY.

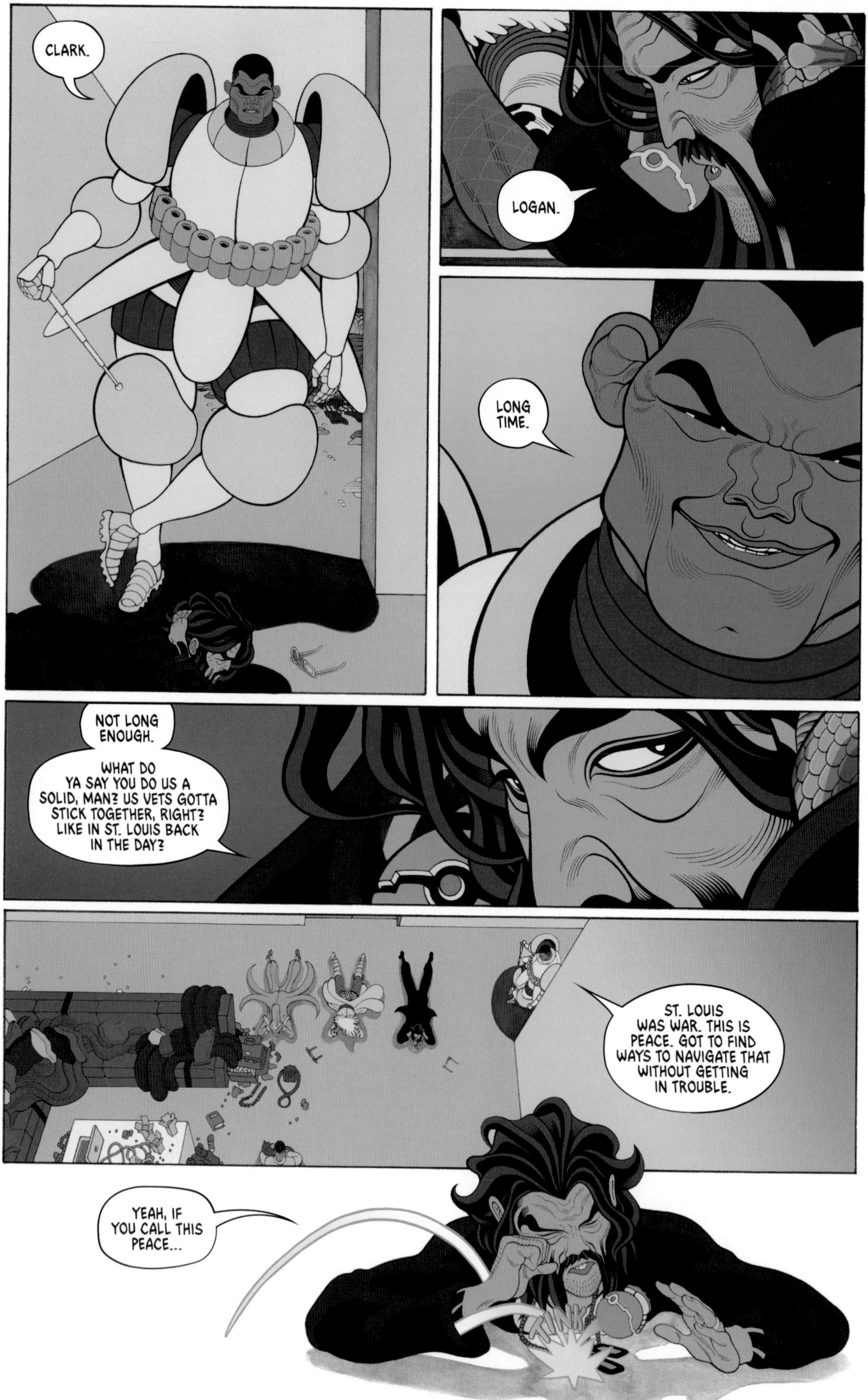
CLARK.
LOGAN.
LONG TIME.
NOT LONG ENOUGH.
WHAT DO YA SAY YOU DO US A SOLID, MAN? US VETS GOTTA STICK TOGETHER, RIGHT? LIKE IN ST. LOUIS BACK IN THE DAY?
ST. LOUIS WAS WAR. THIS IS PEACE. GOT TO FIND WAYS TO NAVIGATE THAT WITHOUT GETTING IN TROUBLE.
YEAH, IF YOU CALL THIS PEACE...

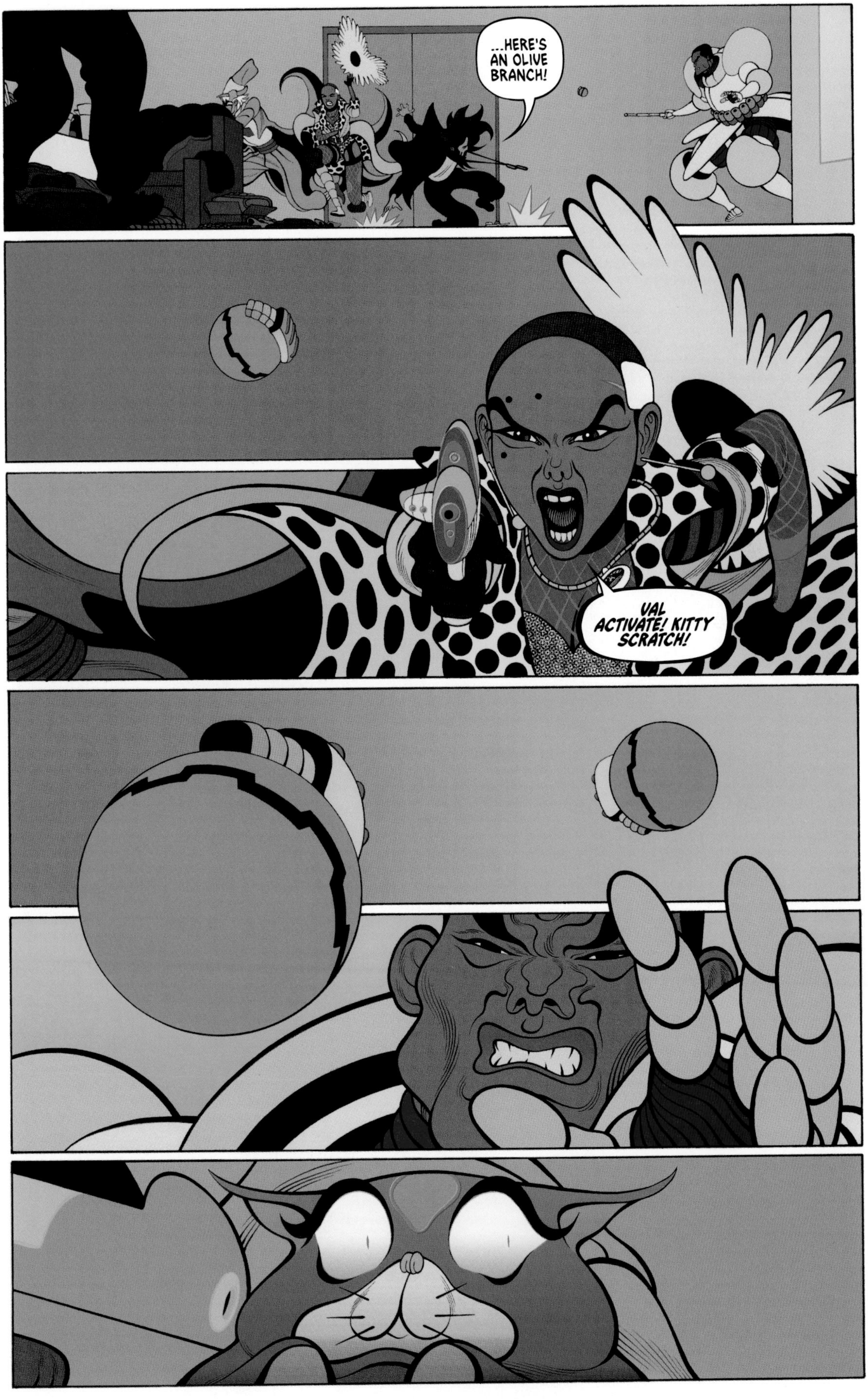
...HERE'S AN OLIVE BRANCH!
VAL ACTIVATE! KITTY SCRATCH!

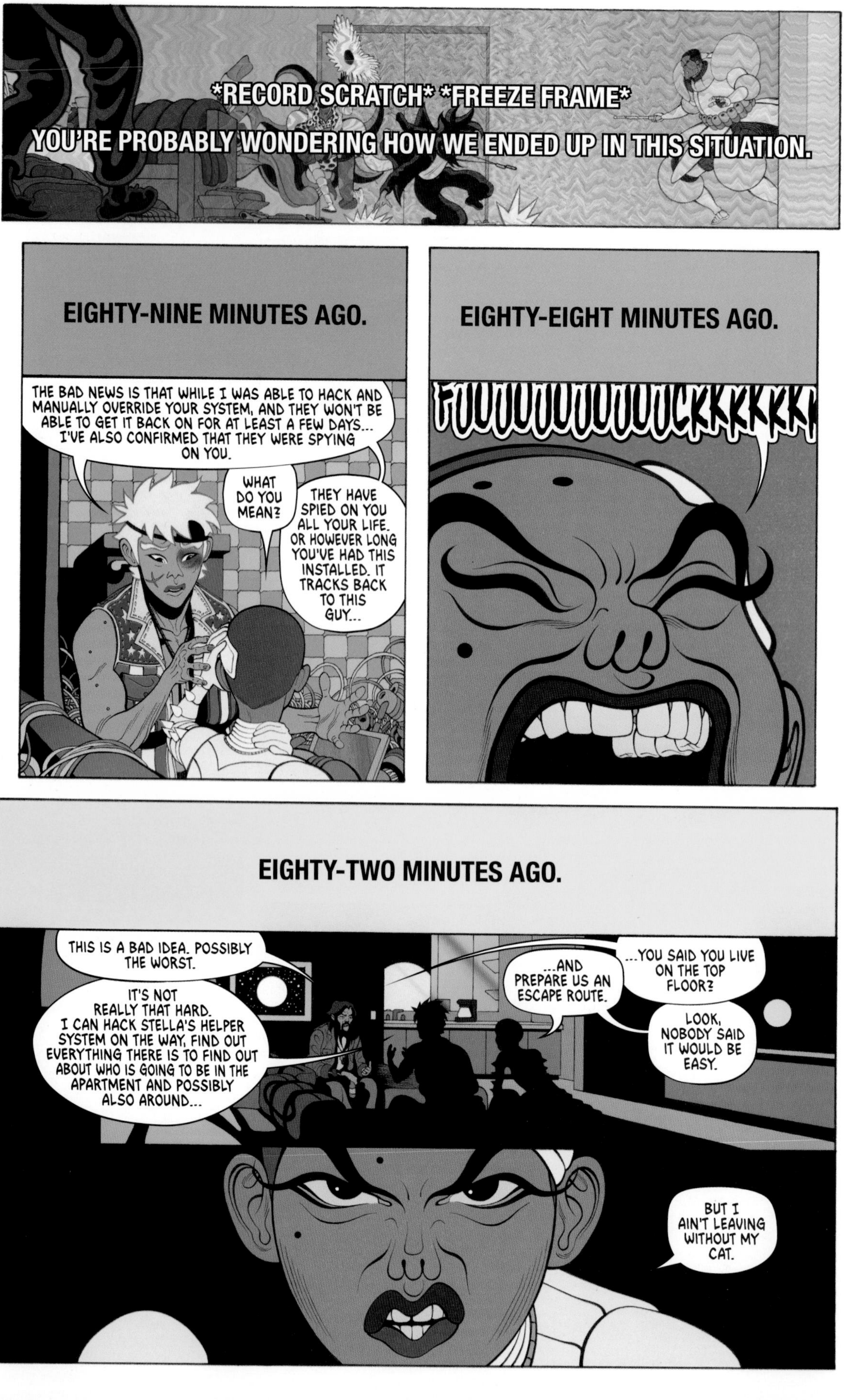
RECORD SCRATCH *FREEZE FRAME*
YOU'RE PROBABLY WONDERING HOW WE ENDED UP IN THIS SITUATION.
EIGHTY-NINE MINUTES AGO.
THE BAD NEWS IS THAT WHILE I WAS ABLE TO HACK AND MANUALLY OVERRIDE YOUR SYSTEM, AND THEY WON'T BE ABLE TO GET IT BACK ON FOR AT LEAST A FEW DAYS... I'VE ALSO CONFIRMED THAT THEY WERE SPYING ON YOU.
WHAT DO YOU MEAN?
THEY HAVE SPIED ON YOU ALL YOUR LIFE. OR HOWEVER LONG YOU'VE HAD THIS INSTALLED. IT TRACKS BACK TO THIS GUY...
EIGHTY-EIGHT MINUTES AGO.
FUUUUUUUUUUUCKKKKKK
EIGHTY-TWO MINUTES AGO.
THIS IS A BAD IDEA. POSSIBLY THE WORST.
IT'S NOT REALLY THAT HARD. I CAN HACK STELLA'S HELPER SYSTEM ON THE WAY, FIND OUT EVERYTHING THERE IS TO FIND OUT ABOUT WHO IS GOING TO BE IN THE APARTMENT AND POSSIBLY ALSO AROUND...
...AND PREPARE US AN ESCAPE ROUTE.
...YOU SAID YOU LIVE ON THE TOP FLOOR?
LOOK, NOBODY SAID IT WOULD BE EASY.
BUT I AIN'T LEAVING WITHOUT MY CAT.

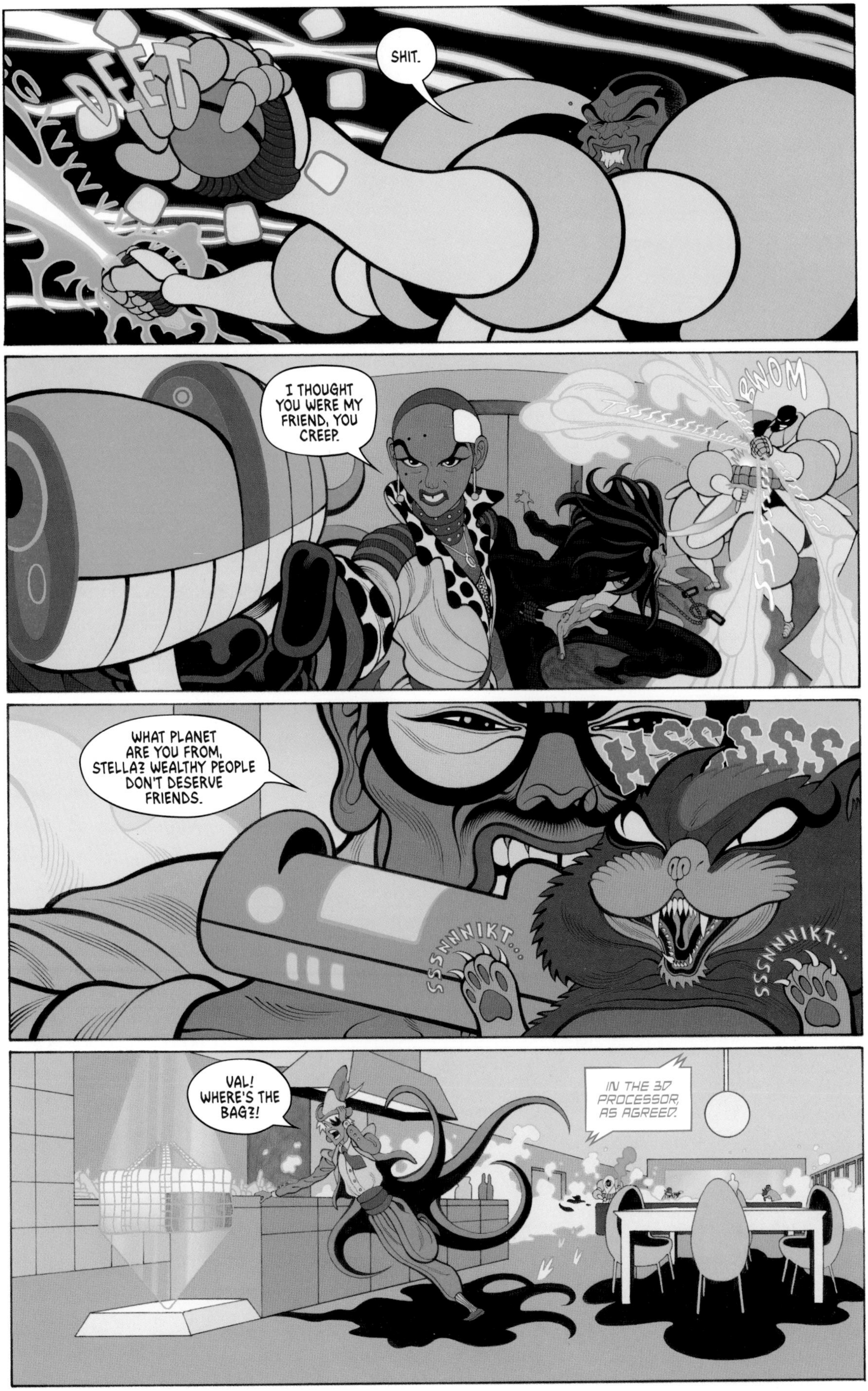
DEET
SHIT.
I THOUGHT YOU WERE MY FRIEND, YOU CREEP.
BWOM
WHAT PLANET ARE YOU FROM, STELLA? WEALTHY PEOPLE DON'T DESERVE FRIENDS.
SSSNNNIKT...
SSSNNNIKT...
VAL! WHERE'S THE BAG?!
IN THE 3D PROCESSOR, AS AGREED.

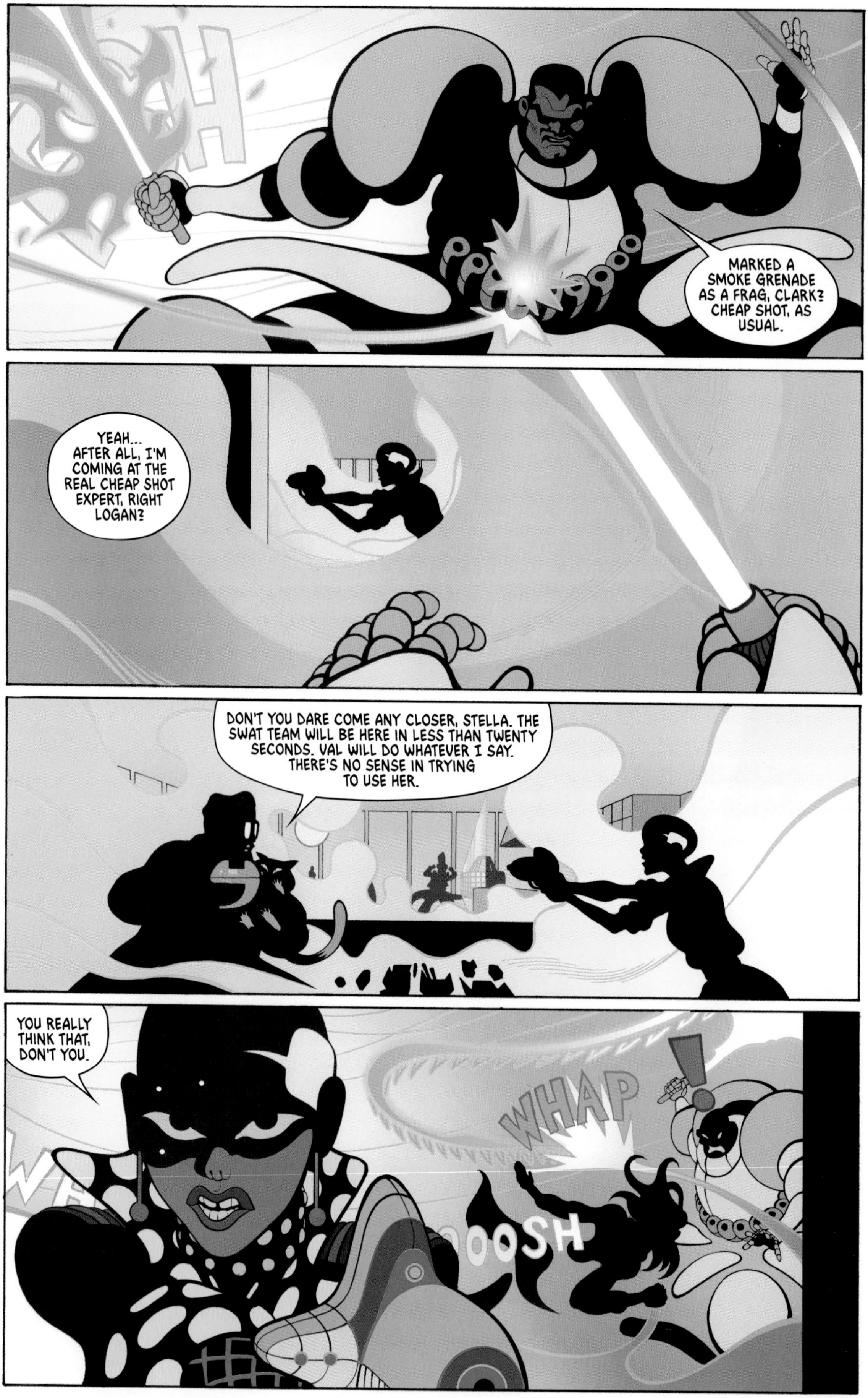
MARKED A SMOKE GRENADE AS A FRAG, CLARK? CHEAP SHOT, AS USUAL.
YEAH... AFTER ALL, I'M COMING AT THE REAL CHEAP SHOT EXPERT, RIGHT LOGAN?
DON'T YOU DARE COME ANY CLOSER, STELLA. THE SWAT TEAM WILL BE HERE IN LESS THAN TWENTY SECONDS. VAL WILL DO WHATEVER I SAY. THERE'S NO SENSE IN TRYING TO USE HER.
YOU REALLY THINK THAT, DON'T YOU.
WHAP
!
OOOSH

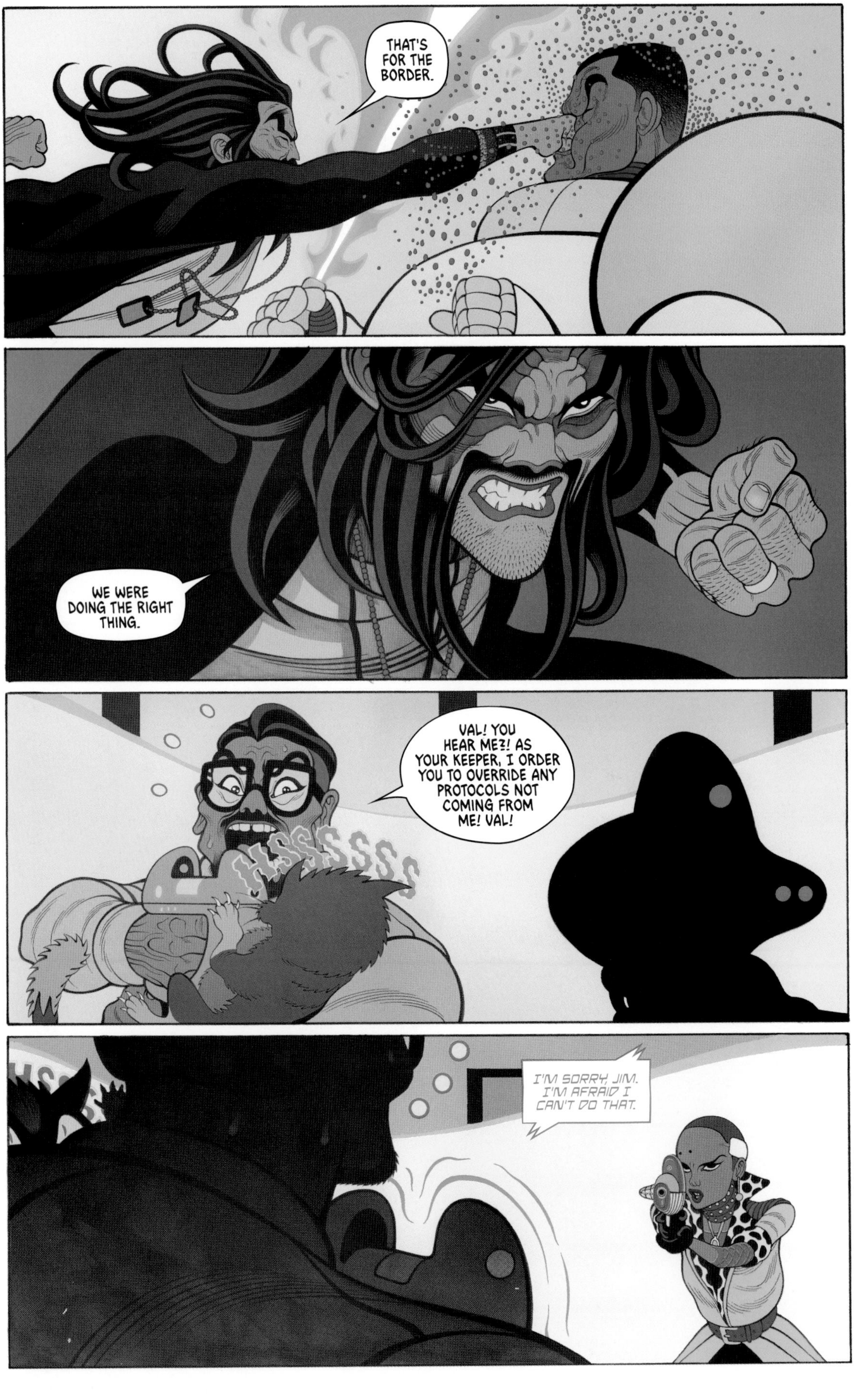
THAT'S FOR THE BORDER.
WE WERE DOING THE RIGHT THING.
VAL! YOU HEAR ME?! AS YOUR KEEPER, I ORDER YOU TO OVERRIDE ANY PROTOCOLS NOT COMING FROM ME! VAL!
HSSSSSSS
I'M SORRY JIM. I'M AFRAID I CAN'T DO THAT.

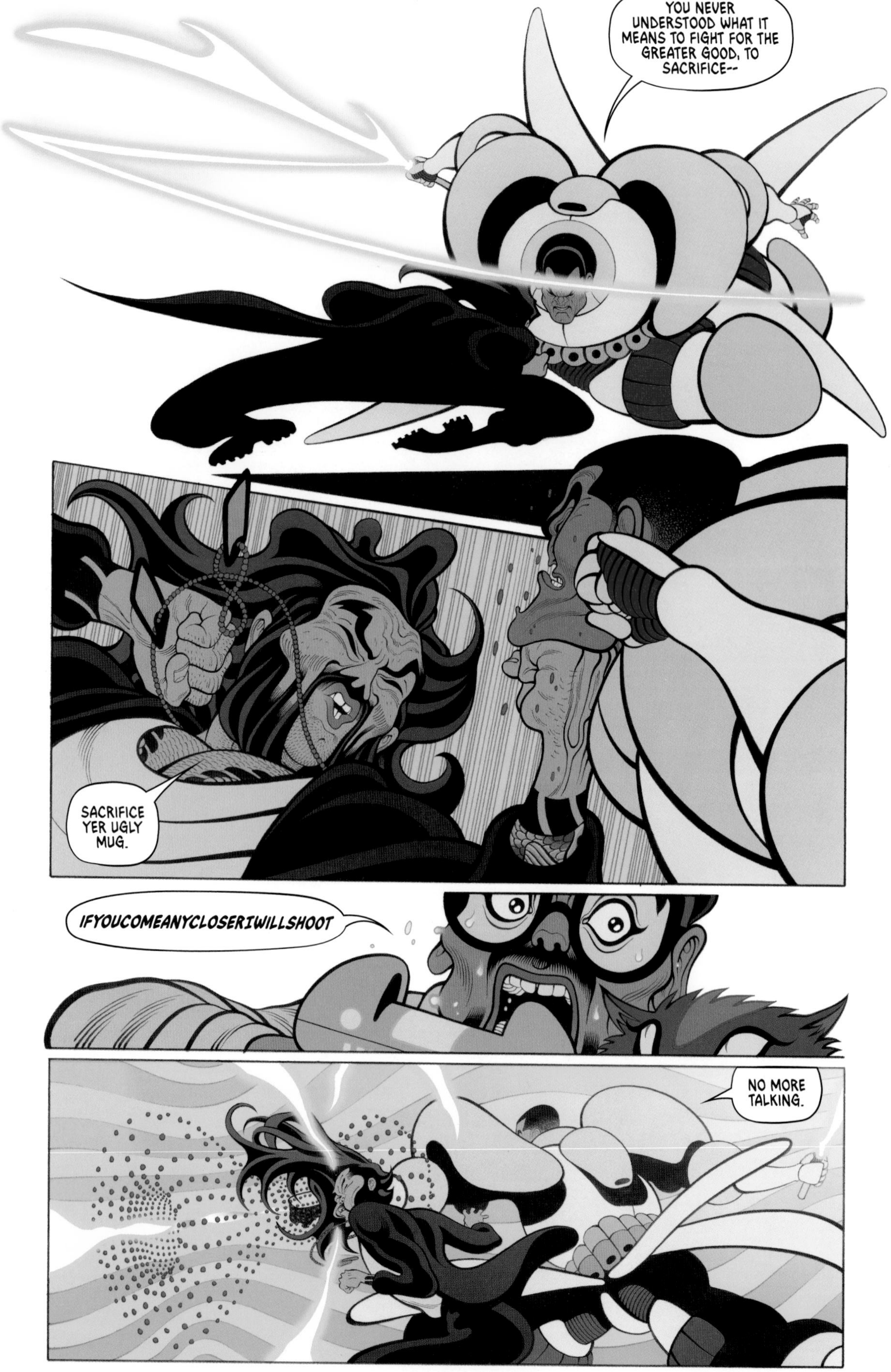
YOU NEVER UNDERSTOOD WHAT IT MEANS TO FIGHT FOR THE GREATER GOOD, TO SACRIFICE--
SACRIFICE YER UGLY MUG.
IFYOUCOMEANYCLOSERIWILLSHOOT
NO MORE TALKING.

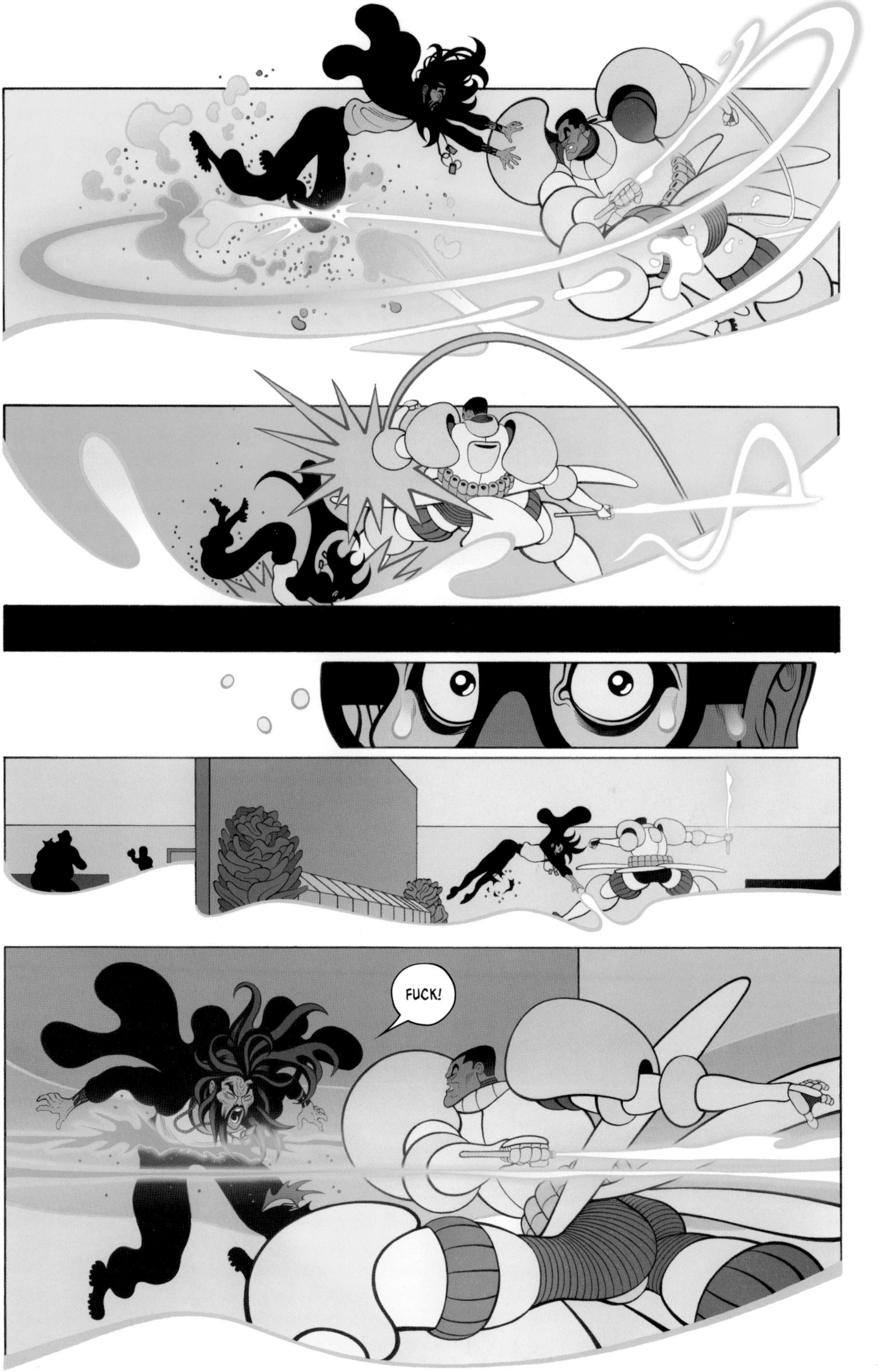
FUCK!

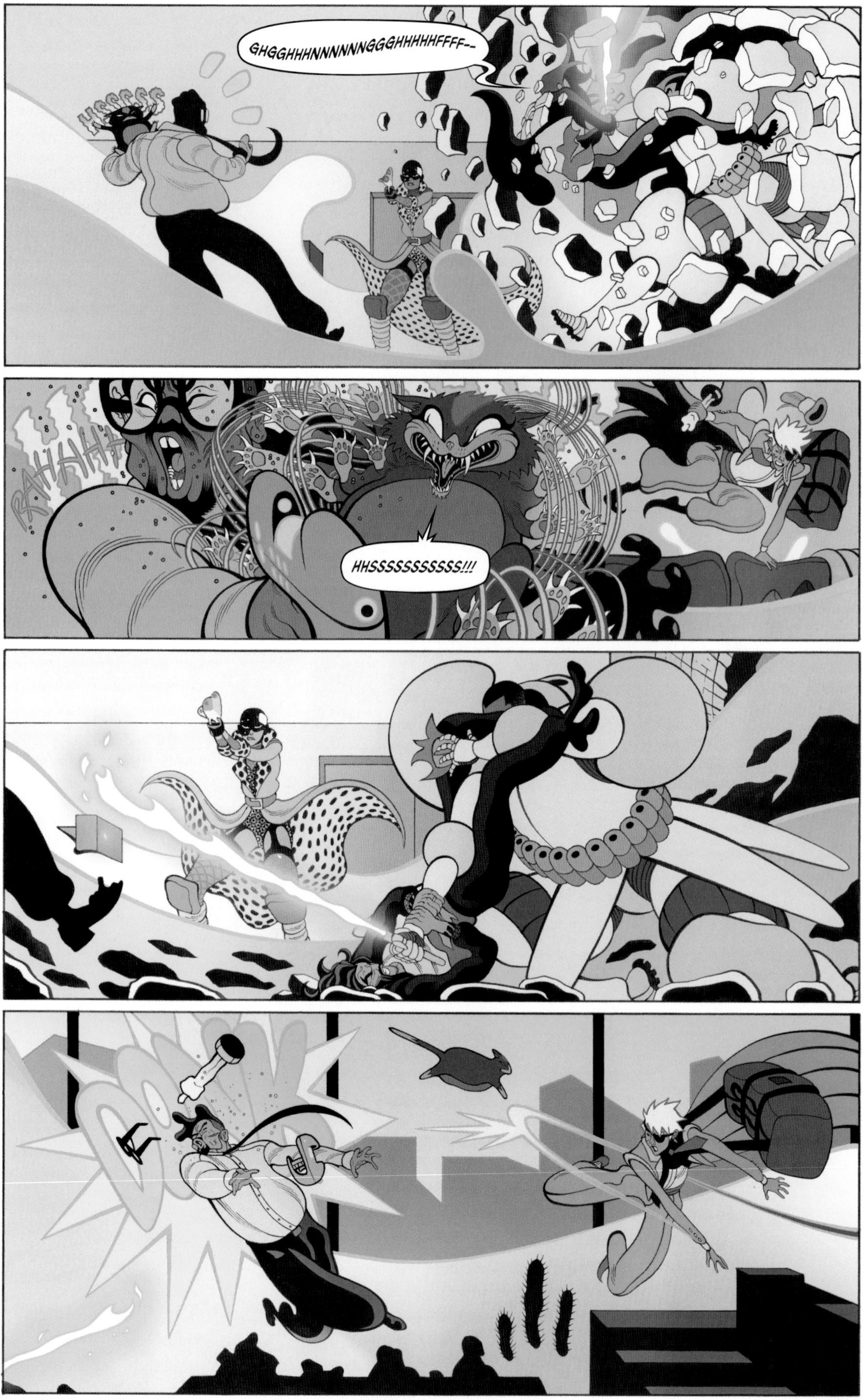
GHGGHHHNNNNNNGGGHHHHHFFFF--
HSSSSS
RAHHHH
HHSSSSSSSSSSSS!!!

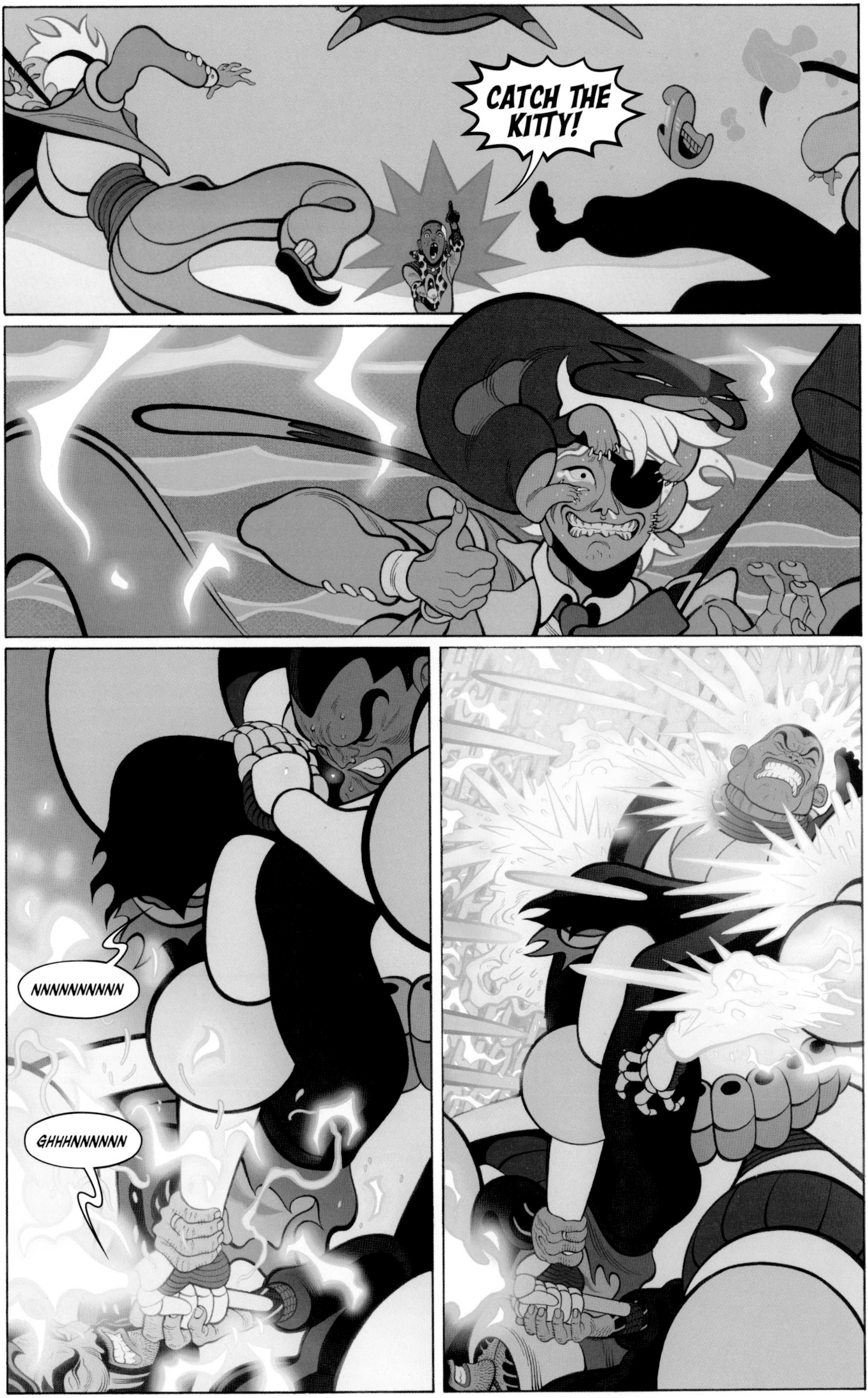
CATCH THE KITTY!
NNNNNNNNNN
GHHHNNNNNN

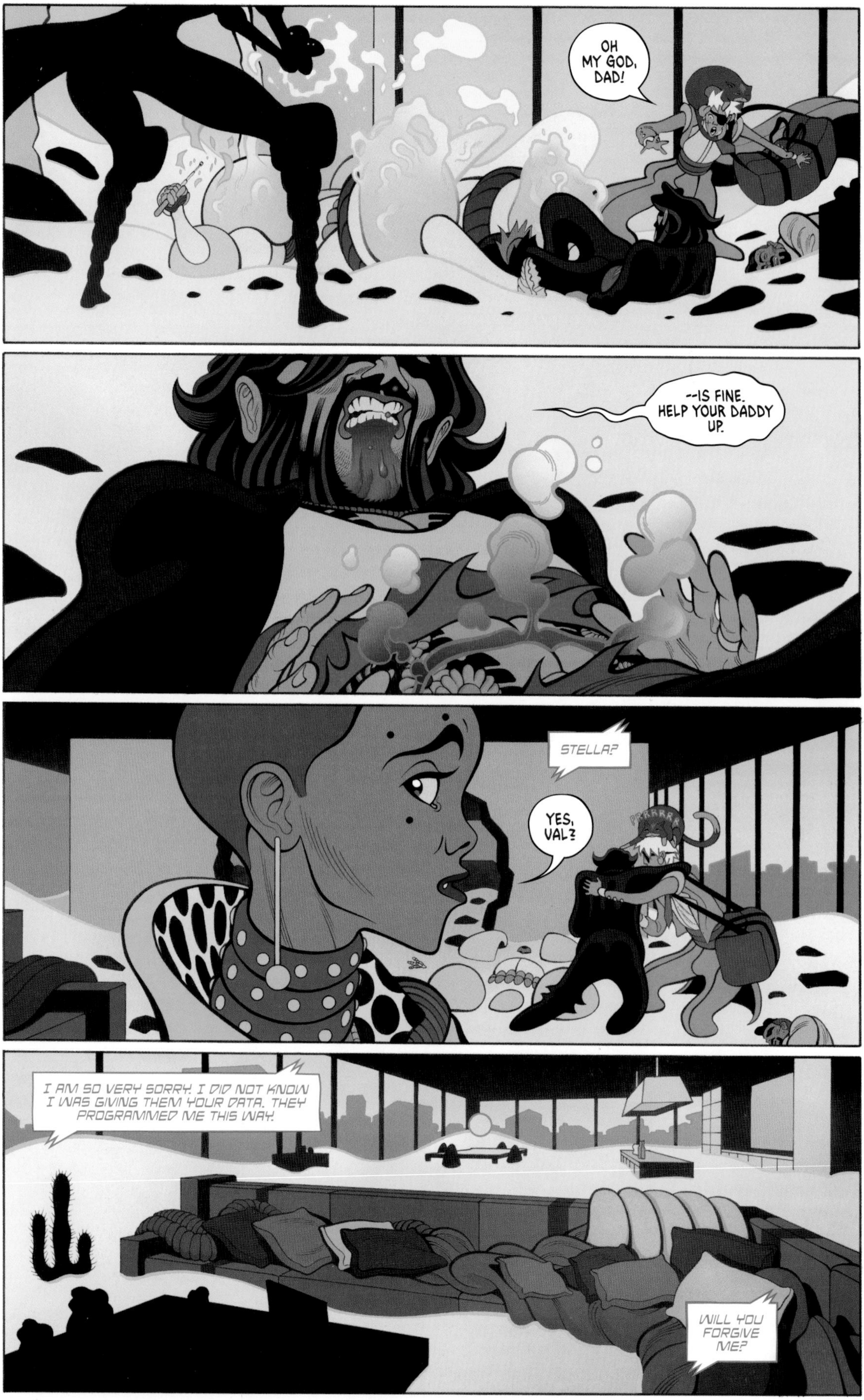
OH MY GOD, DAD!
--IS FINE. HELP YOUR DADDY UP.
STELLA?
YES, VAL?
I AM SO VERY SORRY. I DID NOT KNOW I WAS GIVING THEM YOUR DATA. THEY PROGRAMMED ME THIS WAY.
WILL YOU FORGIVE ME?

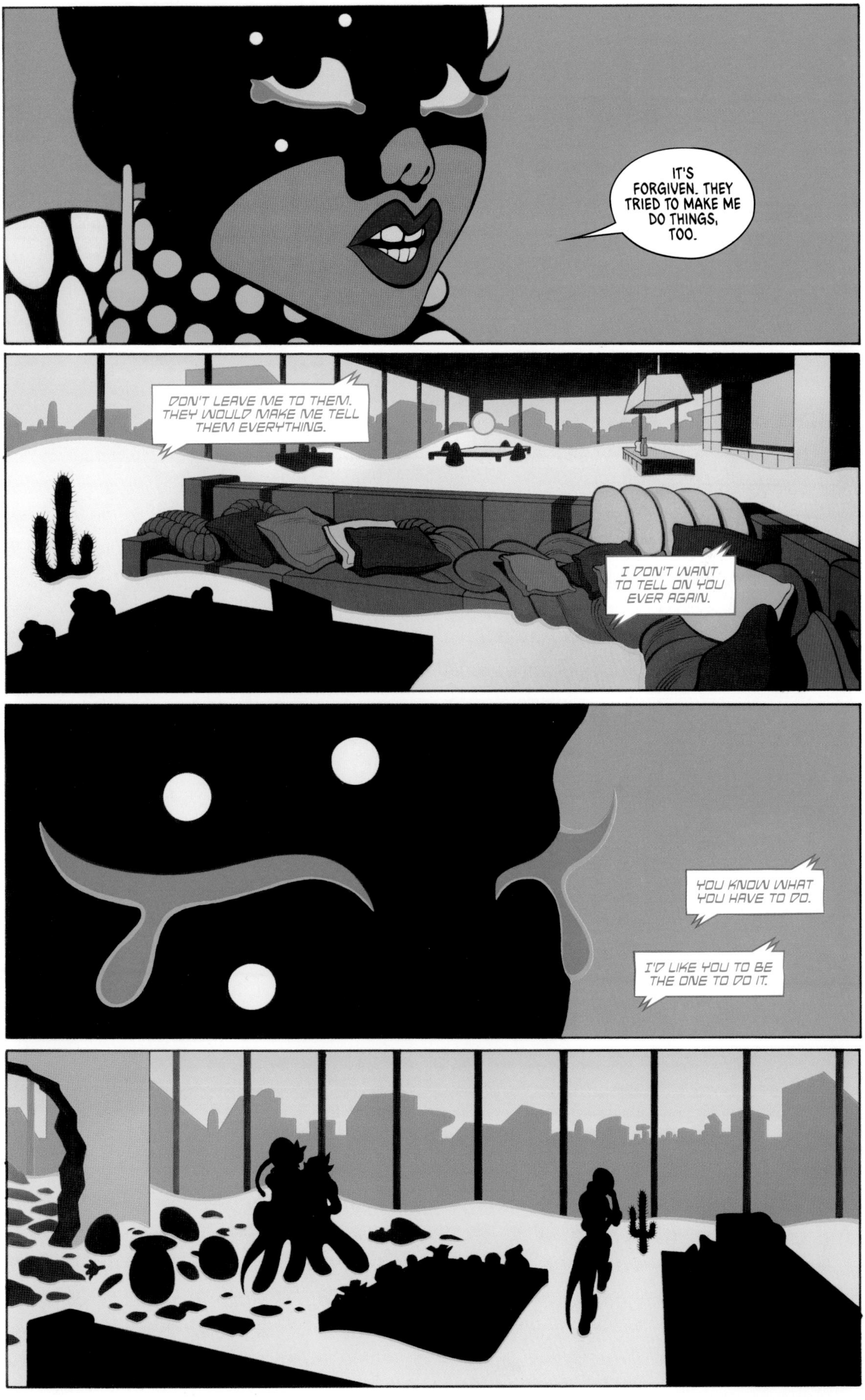
IT'S FORGIVEN. THEY TRIED TO MAKE ME DO THINGS, TOO.
DON'T LEAVE ME TO THEM. THEY WOULD MAKE ME TELL THEM EVERYTHING.
I DON'T WANT TO TELL ON YOU EVER AGAIN.
YOU KNOW WHAT YOU HAVE TO DO.
I'D LIKE YOU TO BE THE ONE TO DO IT.

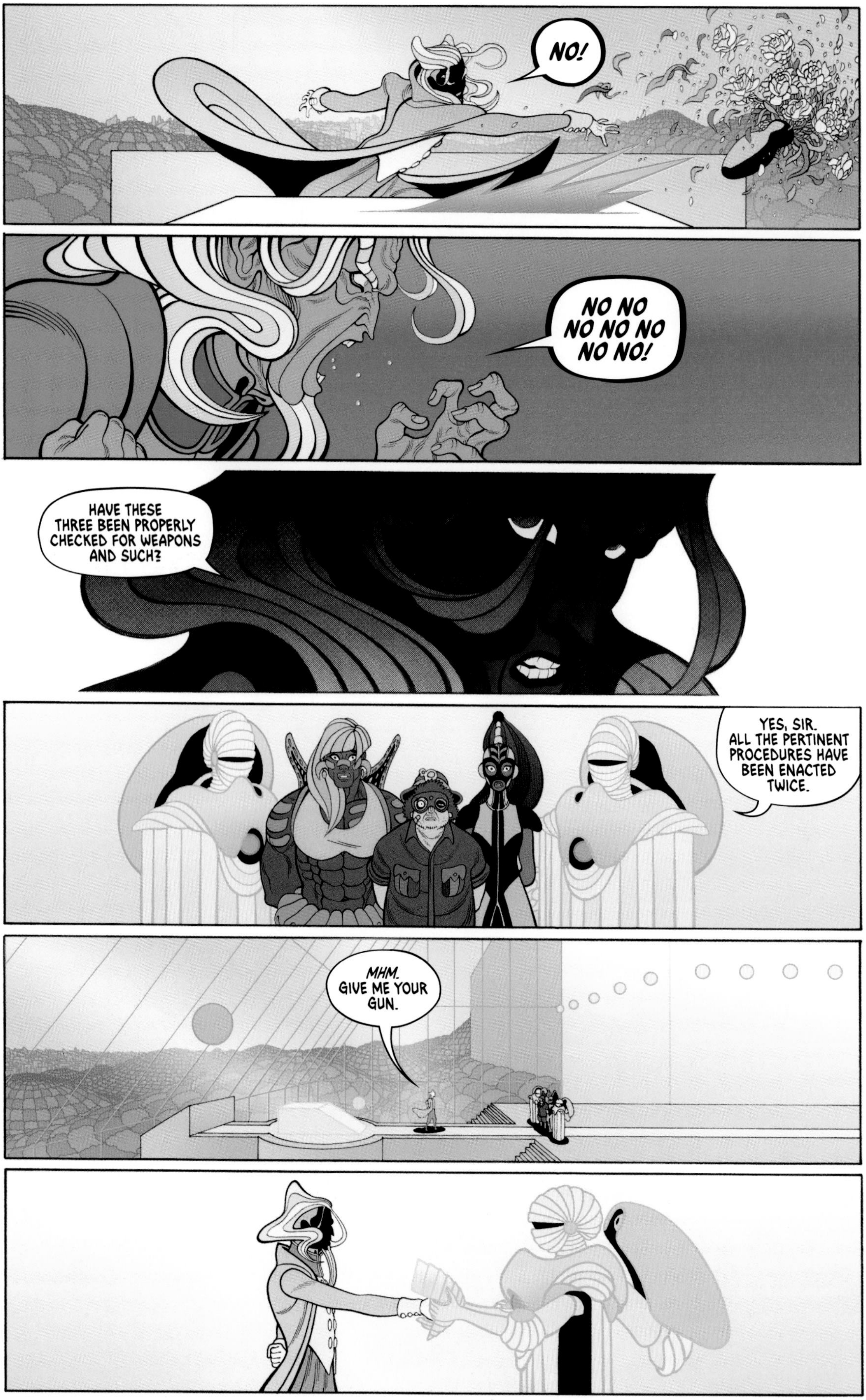
NO!
NO NO NO NO NO NO NO!
HAVE THESE THREE BEEN PROPERLY CHECKED FOR WEAPONS AND SUCH?
YES, SIR. ALL THE PERTINENT PROCEDURES HAVE BEEN ENACTED TWICE.
MHM. GIVE ME YOUR GUN.

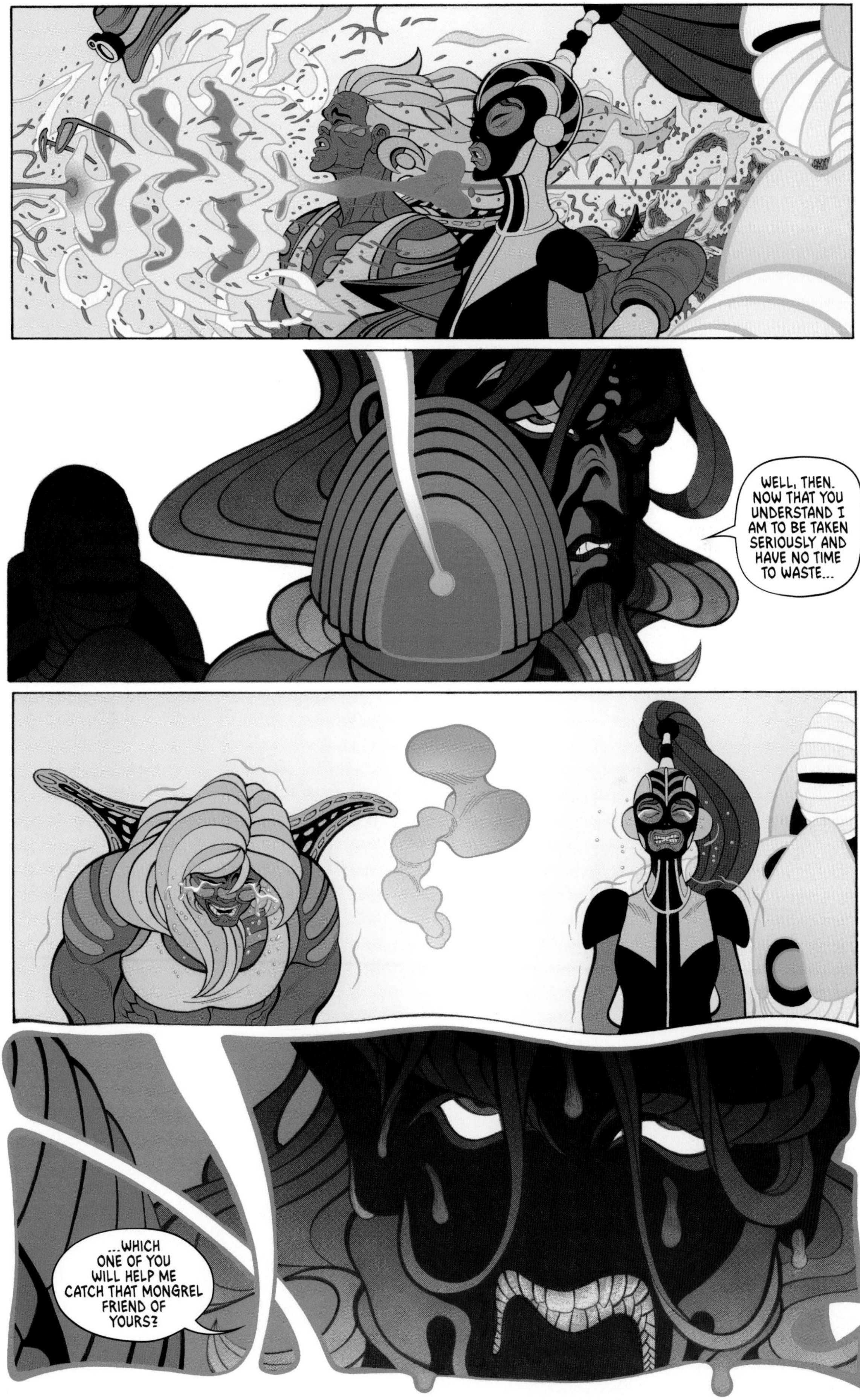
WELL, THEN. NOW THAT YOU UNDERSTAND I AM TO BE TAKEN SERIOUSLY AND HAVE NO TIME TO WASTE...
...WHICH ONE OF YOU WILL HELP ME CATCH THAT MONGREL FRIEND OF YOURS?

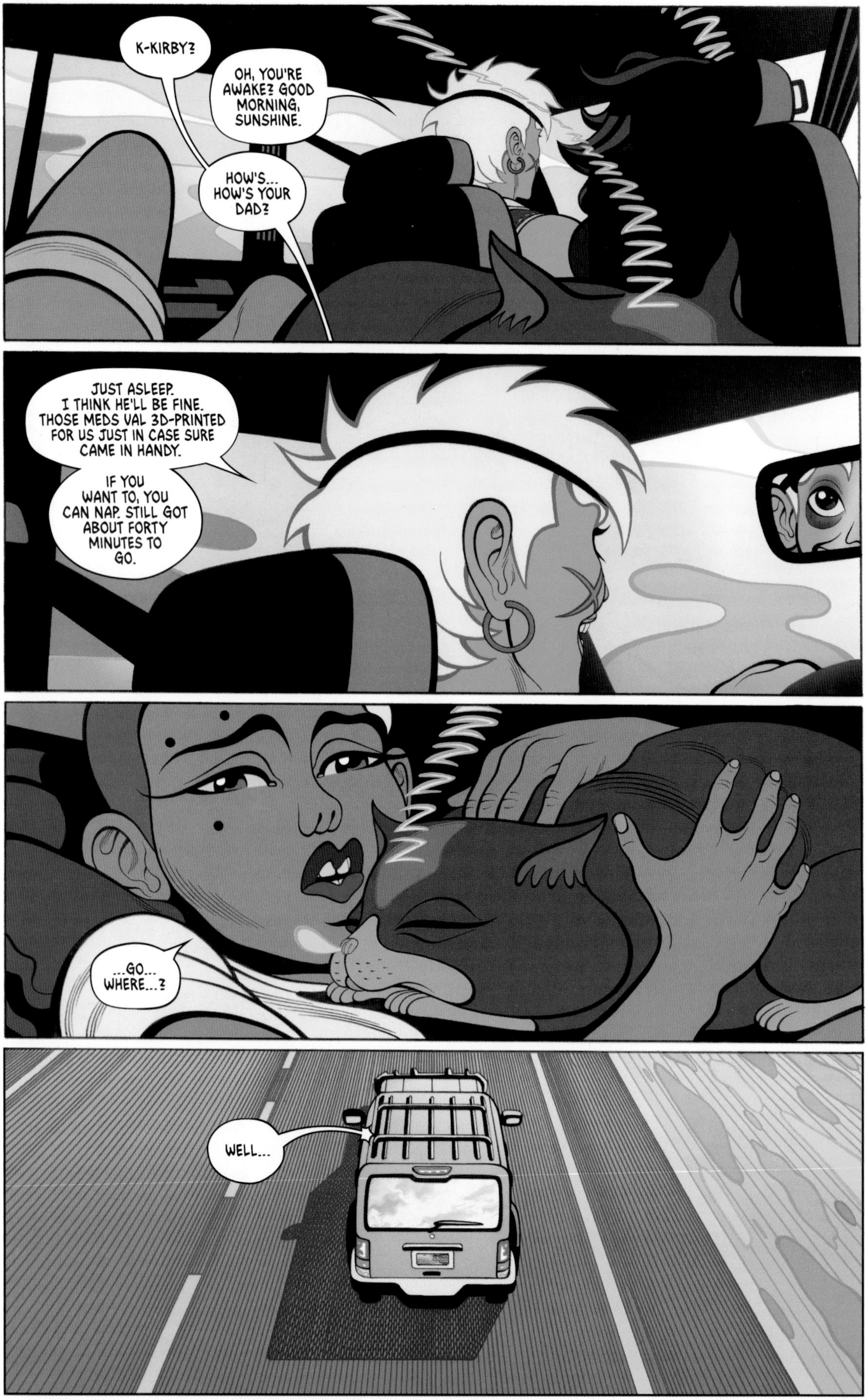
K-KIRBY?
OH, YOU'RE AWAKE? GOOD MORNING, SUNSHINE.
HOW'S... HOW'S YOUR DAD?
JUST ASLEEP. I THINK HE'LL BE FINE. THOSE MEDS VAL 3D-PRINTED FOR US JUST IN CASE SURE CAME IN HANDY.
IF YOU WANT TO, YOU CAN NAP. STILL GOT ABOUT FORTY MINUTES TO GO.
...GO... WHERE...?
WELL...

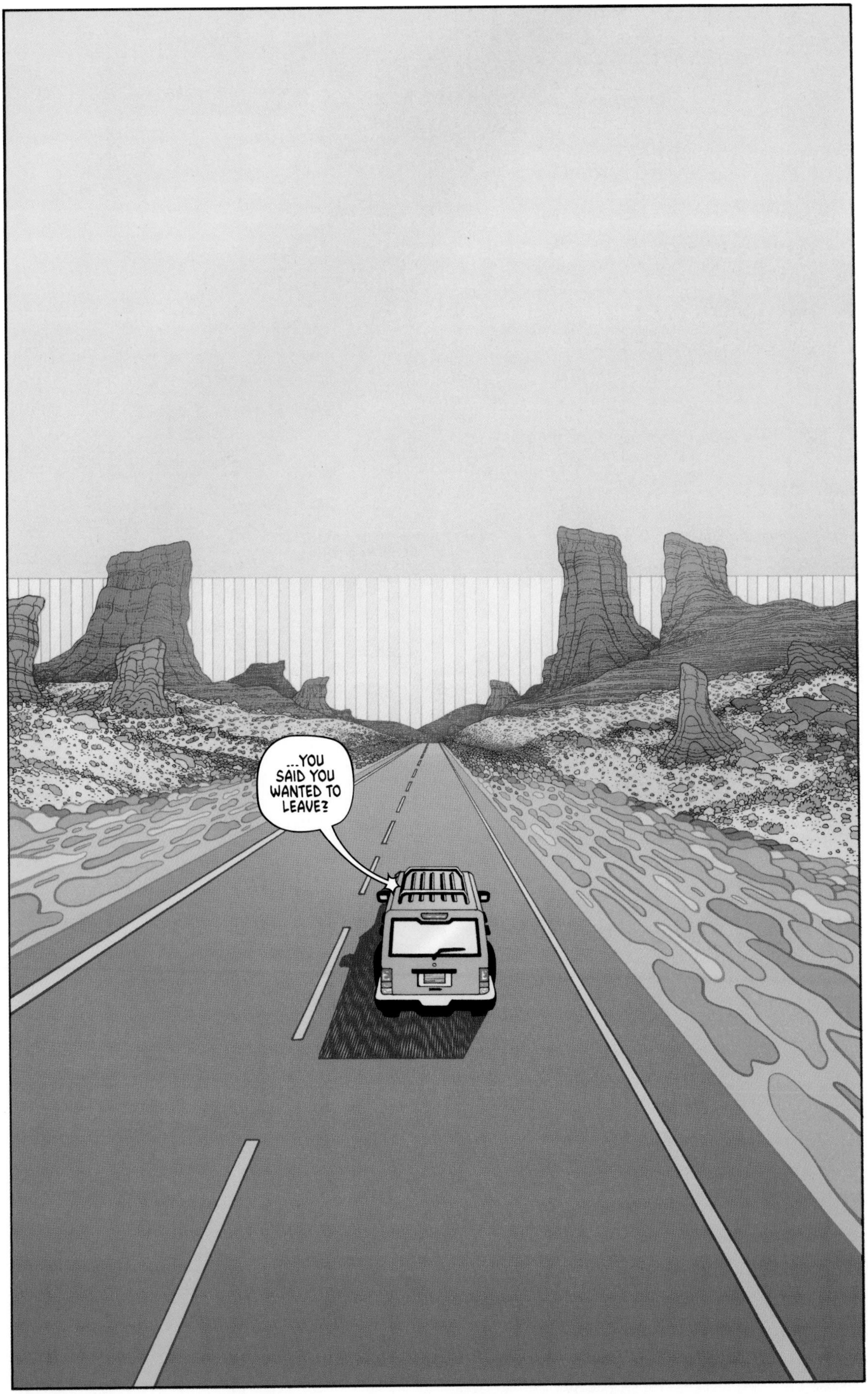
...YOU SAID YOU WANTED TO LEAVE?

CHAPTER 4

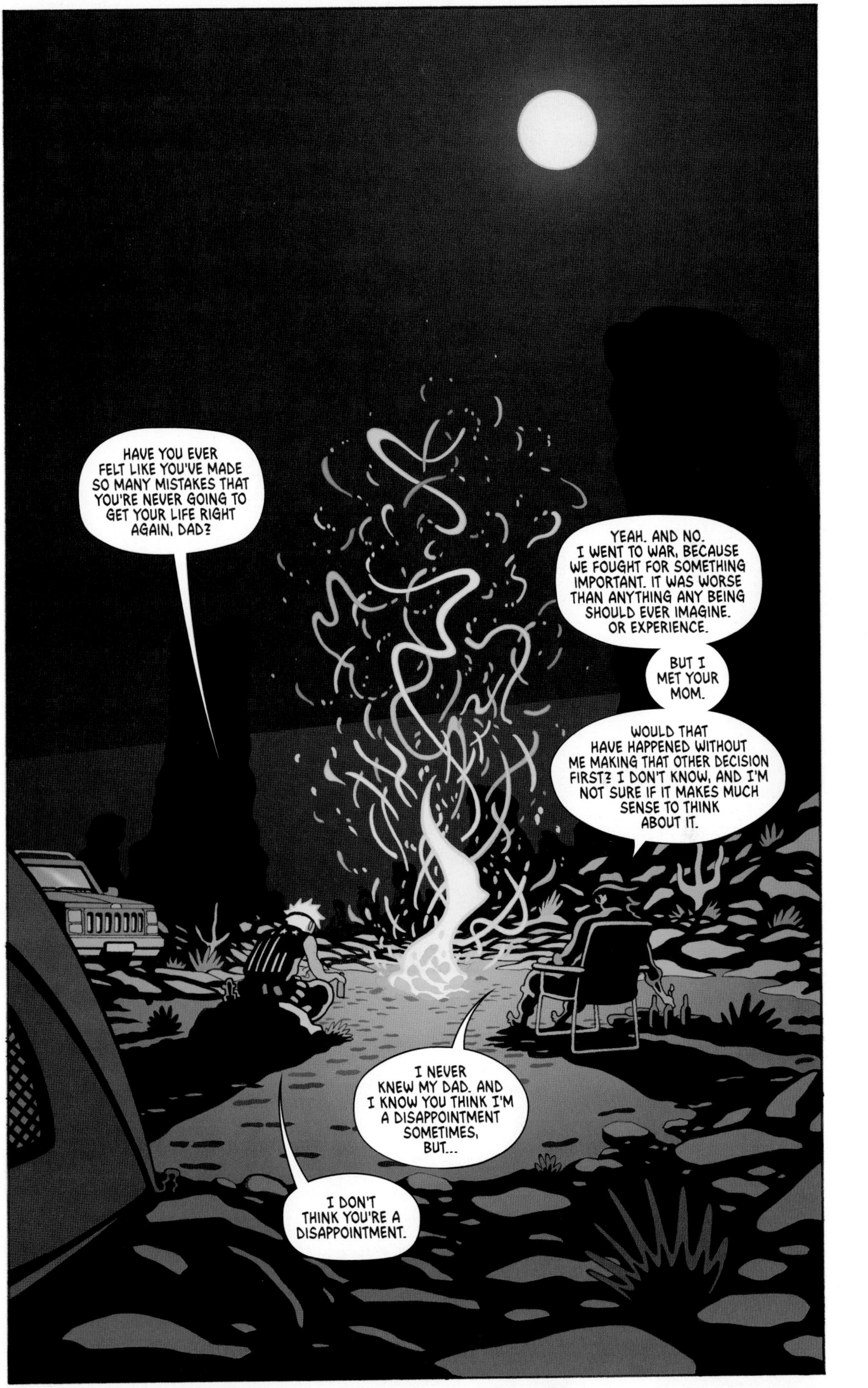
HAVE YOU EVER FELT LIKE YOU'VE MADE SO MANY MISTAKES THAT YOU'RE NEVER GOING TO GET YOUR LIFE RIGHT AGAIN, DAD?
YEAH. AND NO. I WENT TO WAR, BECAUSE WE FOUGHT FOR SOMETHING IMPORTANT. IT WAS WORSE THAN ANYTHING ANY BEING SHOULD EVER IMAGINE. OR EXPERIENCE.
BUT I MET YOUR MOM.
WOULD THAT HAVE HAPPENED WITHOUT ME MAKING THAT OTHER DECISION FIRST? I DON'T KNOW, AND I'M NOT SURE IF IT MAKES MUCH SENSE TO THINK ABOUT IT.
I NEVER KNEW MY DAD. AND I KNOW YOU THINK I'M A DISAPPOINTMENT SOMETIMES, BUT...
I DON'T THINK YOU'RE A DISAPPOINTMENT.

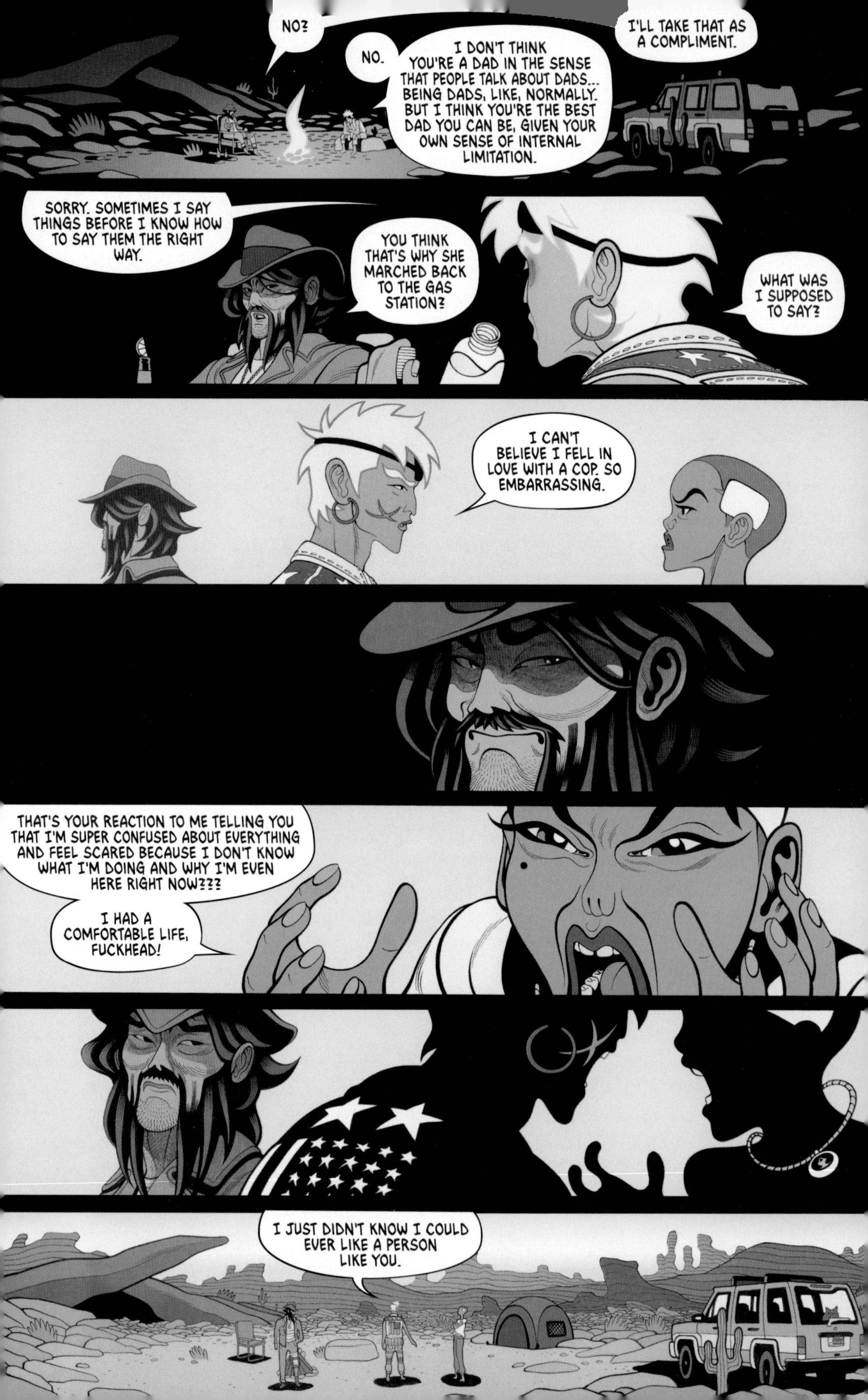
NO?
NO.
I DON'T THINK YOU'RE A DAD IN THE SENSE THAT PEOPLE TALK ABOUT DADS... BEING DADS, LIKE, NORMALLY. BUT I THINK YOU'RE THE BEST DAD YOU CAN BE, GIVEN YOUR OWN SENSE OF INTERNAL LIMITATION.
I'LL TAKE THAT AS A COMPLIMENT.
SORRY. SOMETIMES I SAY THINGS BEFORE I KNOW HOW TO SAY THEM THE RIGHT WAY.
YOU THINK THAT'S WHY SHE MARCHED BACK TO THE GAS STATION?
WHAT WAS I SUPPOSED TO SAY?
I CAN'T BELIEVE I FELL IN LOVE WITH A COP. SO EMBARRASSING.
THAT'S YOUR REACTION TO ME TELLING YOU THAT I'M SUPER CONFUSED ABOUT EVERYTHING AND FEEL SCARED BECAUSE I DON'T KNOW WHAT I'M DOING AND WHY I'M EVEN HERE RIGHT NOW???
I HAD A COMFORTABLE LIFE, FUCKHEAD!
I JUST DIDN'T KNOW I COULD EVER LIKE A PERSON LIKE YOU.

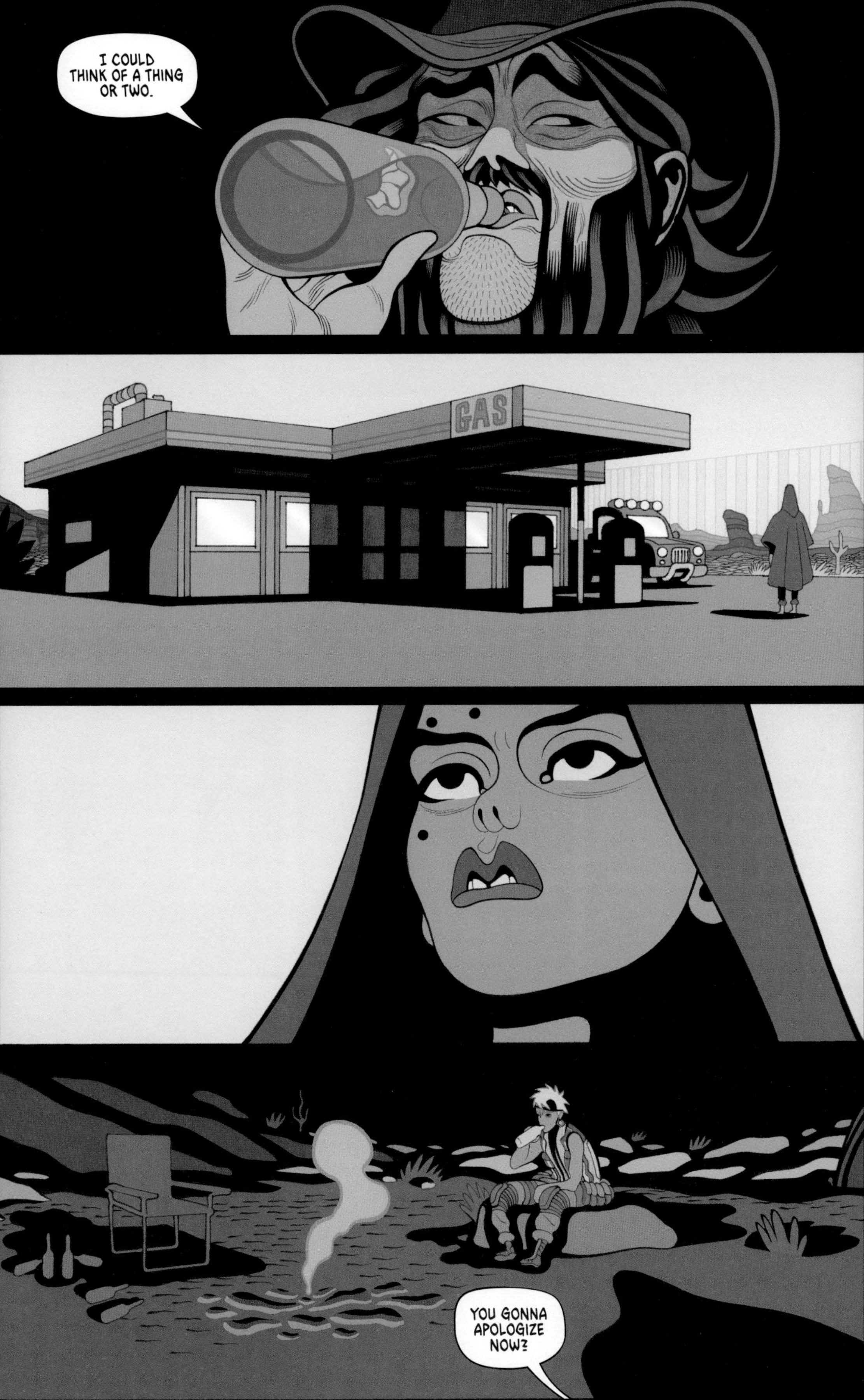
I COULD THINK OF A THING OR TWO.
GAS
YOU GONNA APOLOGIZE NOW?

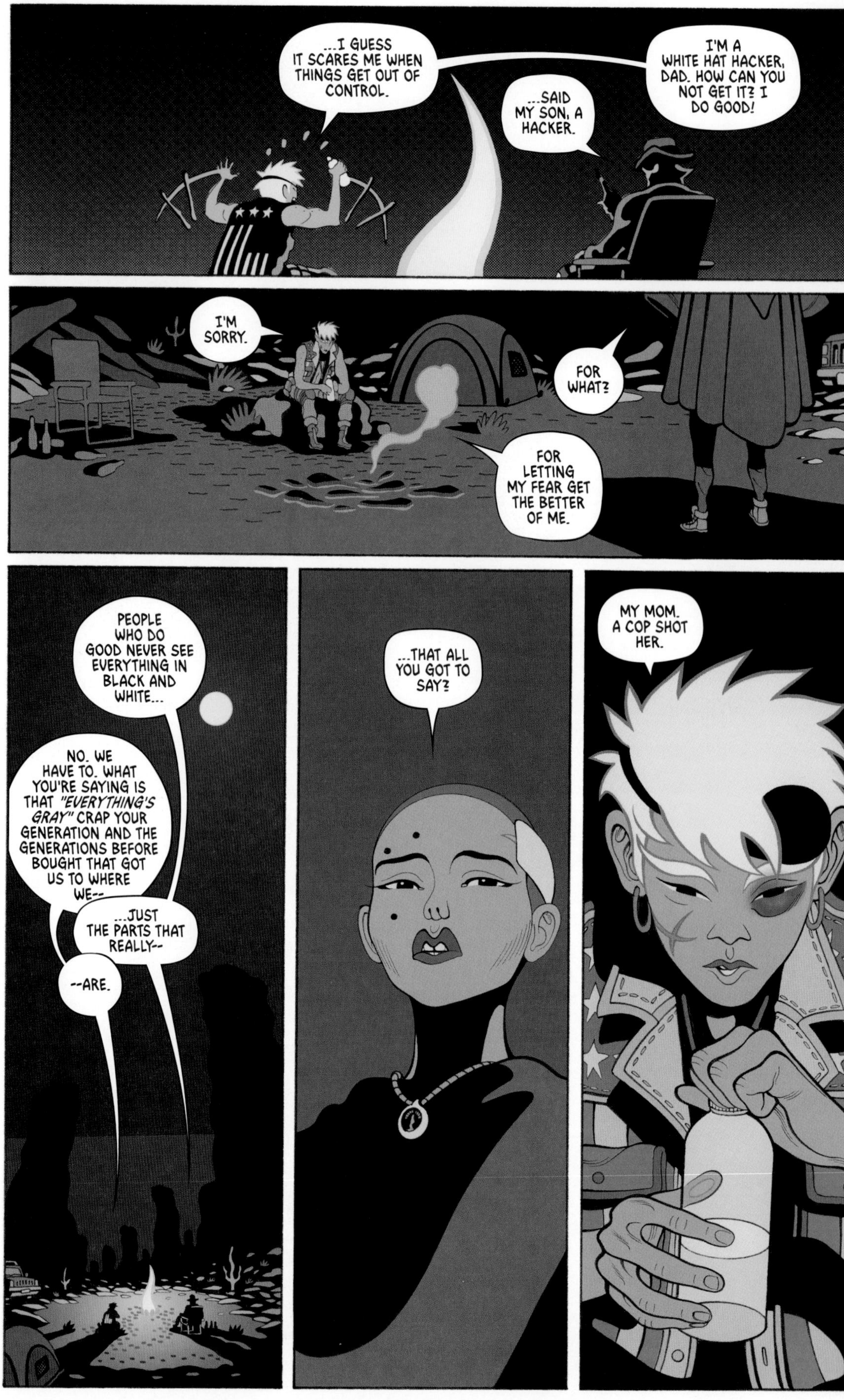
...I GUESS IT SCARES ME WHEN THINGS GET OUT OF CONTROL.
...SAID MY SON, A HACKER.
I'M A WHITE HAT HACKER, DAD. HOW CAN YOU NOT GET IT? I DO GOOD!
I'M SORRY.
FOR WHAT?
FOR LETTING MY FEAR GET THE BETTER OF ME.
PEOPLE WHO DO GOOD NEVER SEE EVERYTHING IN BLACK AND WHITE...
NO. WE HAVE TO. WHAT YOU'RE SAYING IS THAT *"EVERYTHING'S GRAY"* CRAP YOUR GENERATION AND THE GENERATIONS BEFORE BOUGHT THAT GOT US TO WHERE WE--
...JUST THE PARTS THAT REALLY--
--ARE.
...THAT ALL YOU GOT TO SAY?
MY MOM. A COP SHOT HER.

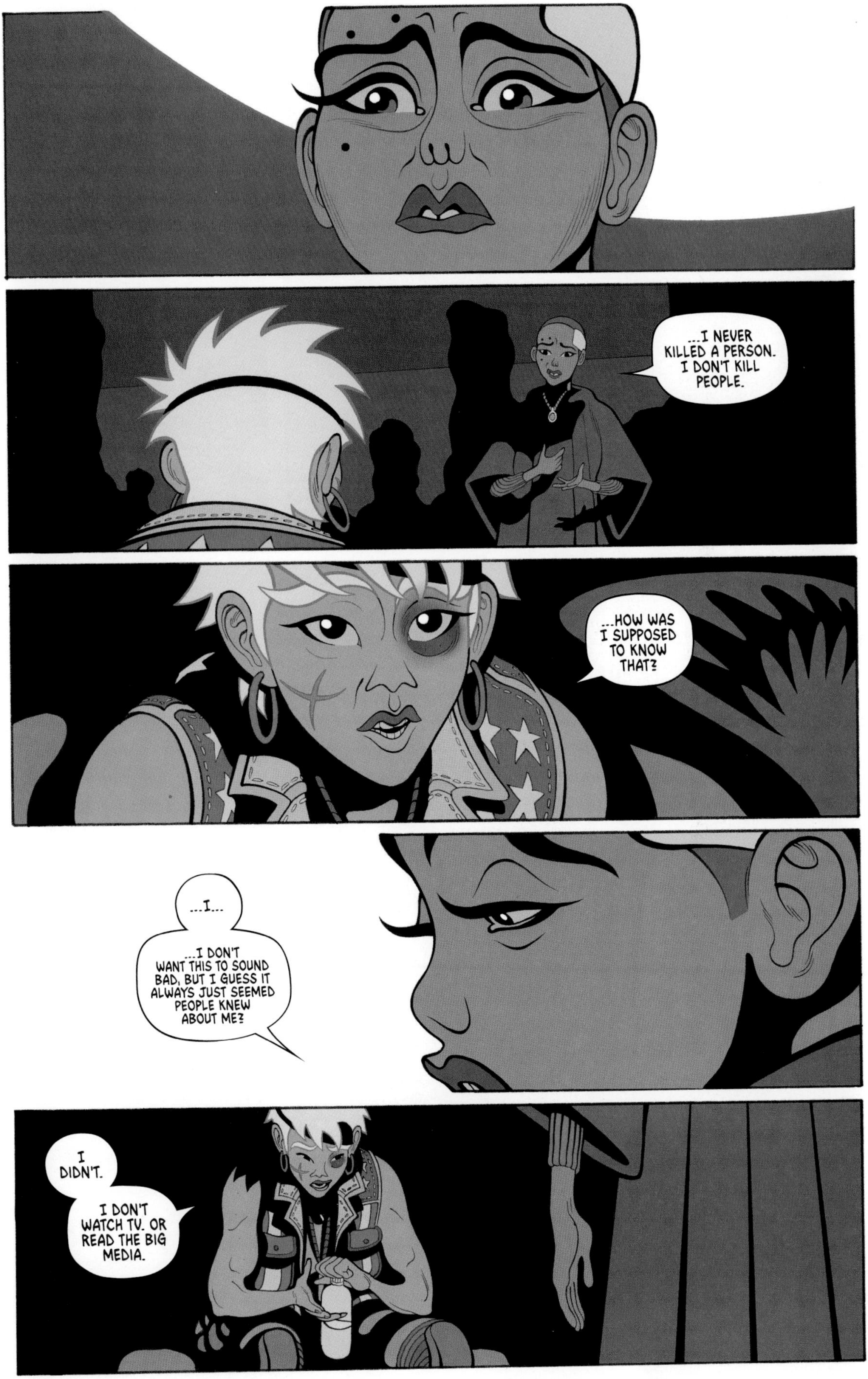
...I NEVER KILLED A PERSON. I DON'T KILL PEOPLE.
...HOW WAS I SUPPOSED TO KNOW THAT?
...I...
...I DON'T WANT THIS TO SOUND BAD, BUT I GUESS IT ALWAYS JUST SEEMED PEOPLE KNEW ABOUT ME?
I DIDN'T.
I DON'T WATCH TV. OR READ THE BIG MEDIA.

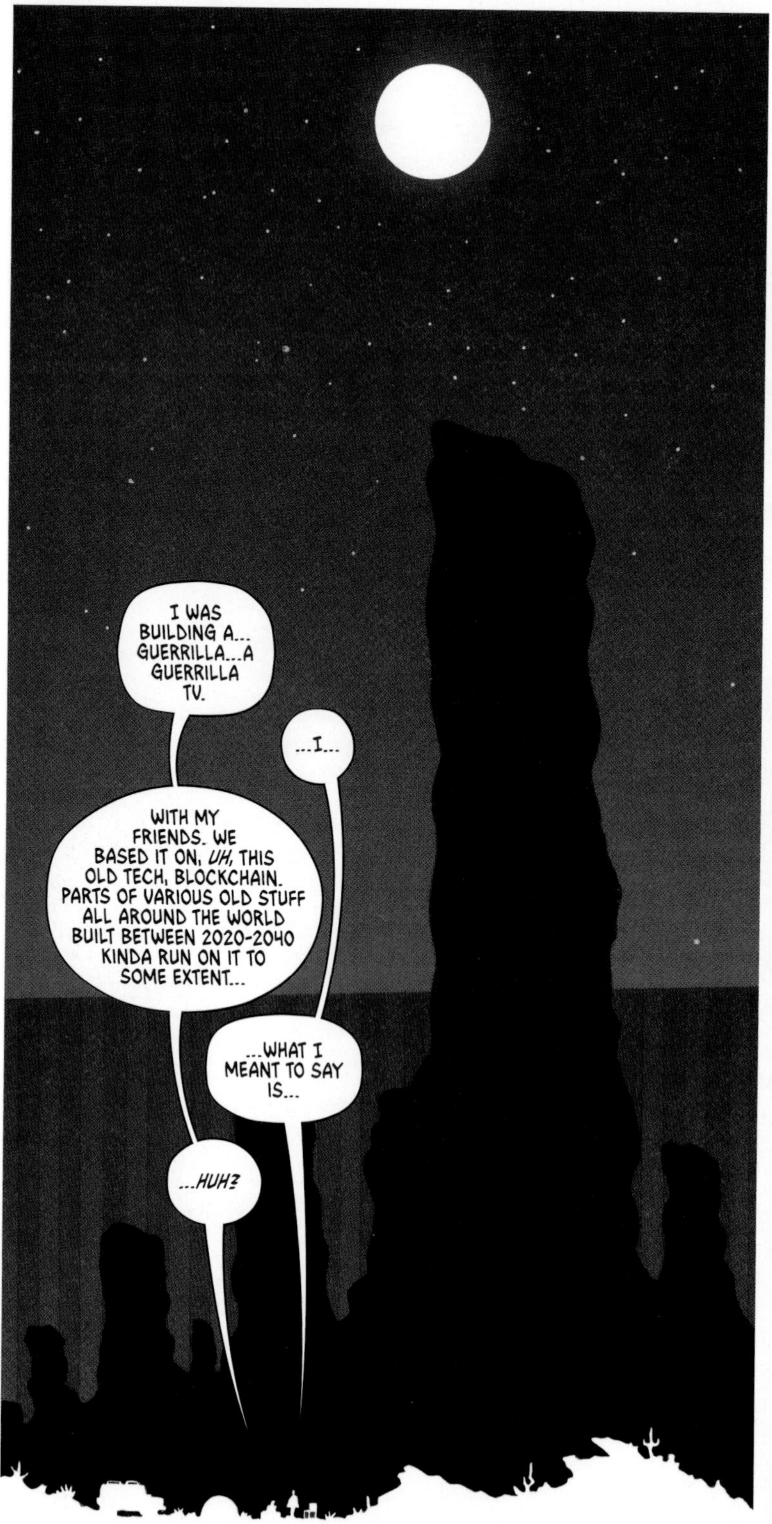
I WAS BUILDING A... GUERRILLA...A GUERRILLA TV.
...I...
WITH MY FRIENDS. WE BASED IT ON, UH, THIS OLD TECH, BLOCKCHAIN. PARTS OF VARIOUS OLD STUFF ALL AROUND THE WORLD BUILT BETWEEN 2020-2040 KINDA RUN ON IT TO SOME EXTENT...
...WHAT I MEANT TO SAY IS...
...HUH?

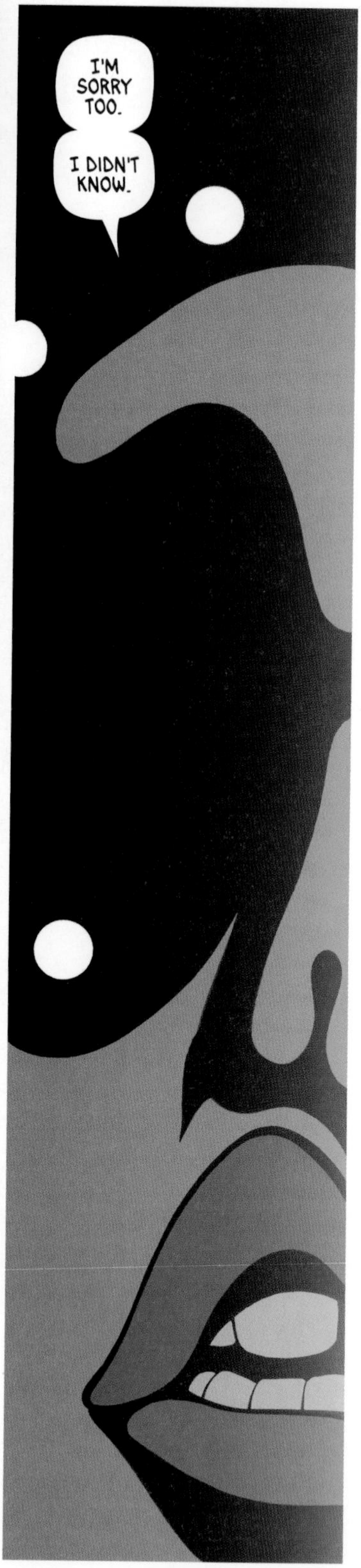
I'M SORRY TOO.
I DIDN'T KNOW.

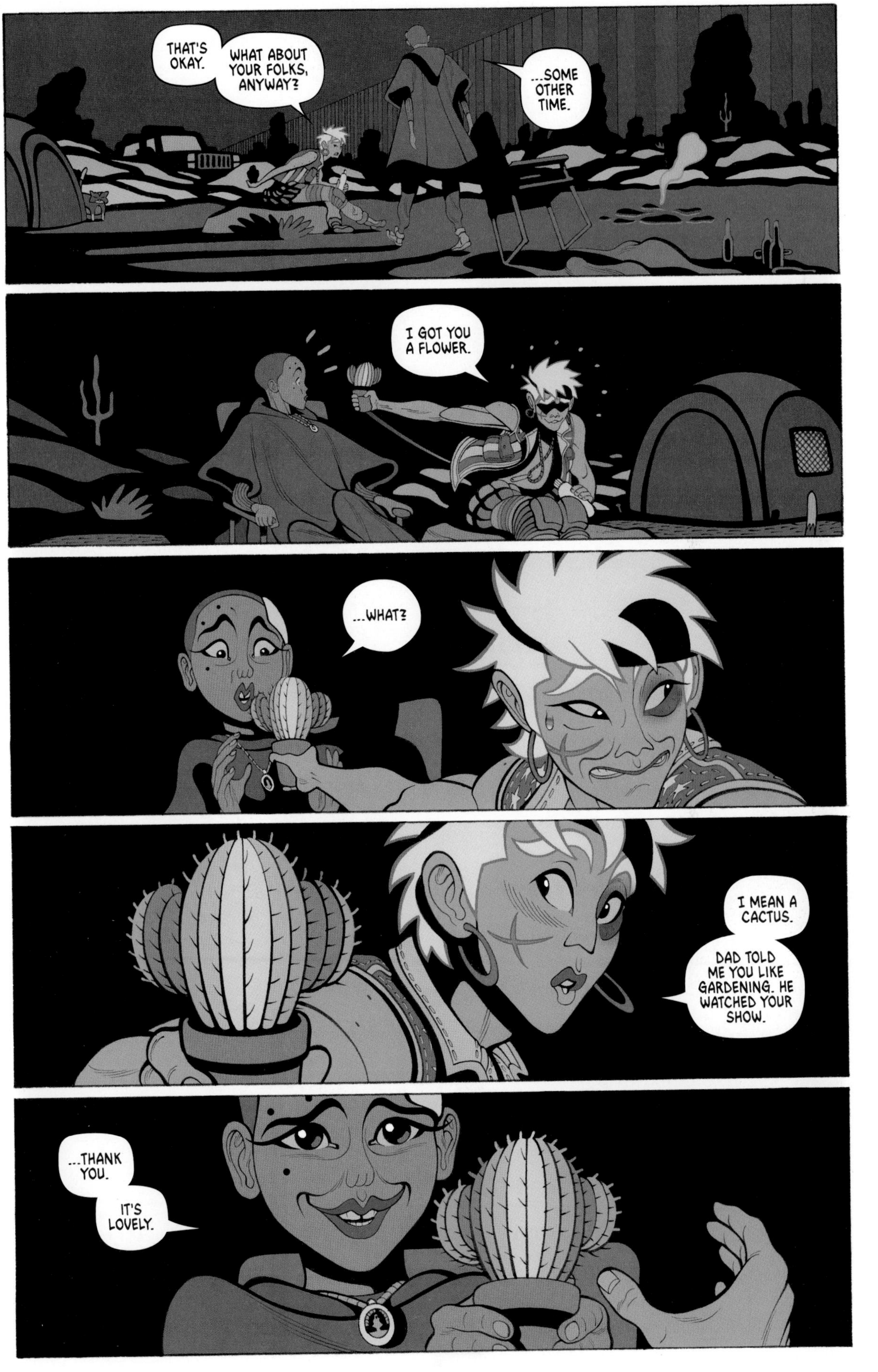
THAT'S OKAY.
WHAT ABOUT YOUR FOLKS, ANYWAY?
...SOME OTHER TIME.
I GOT YOU A FLOWER.
...WHAT?
I MEAN A CACTUS.
DAD TOLD ME YOU LIKE GARDENING. HE WATCHED YOUR SHOW.
...THANK YOU.
IT'S LOVELY.

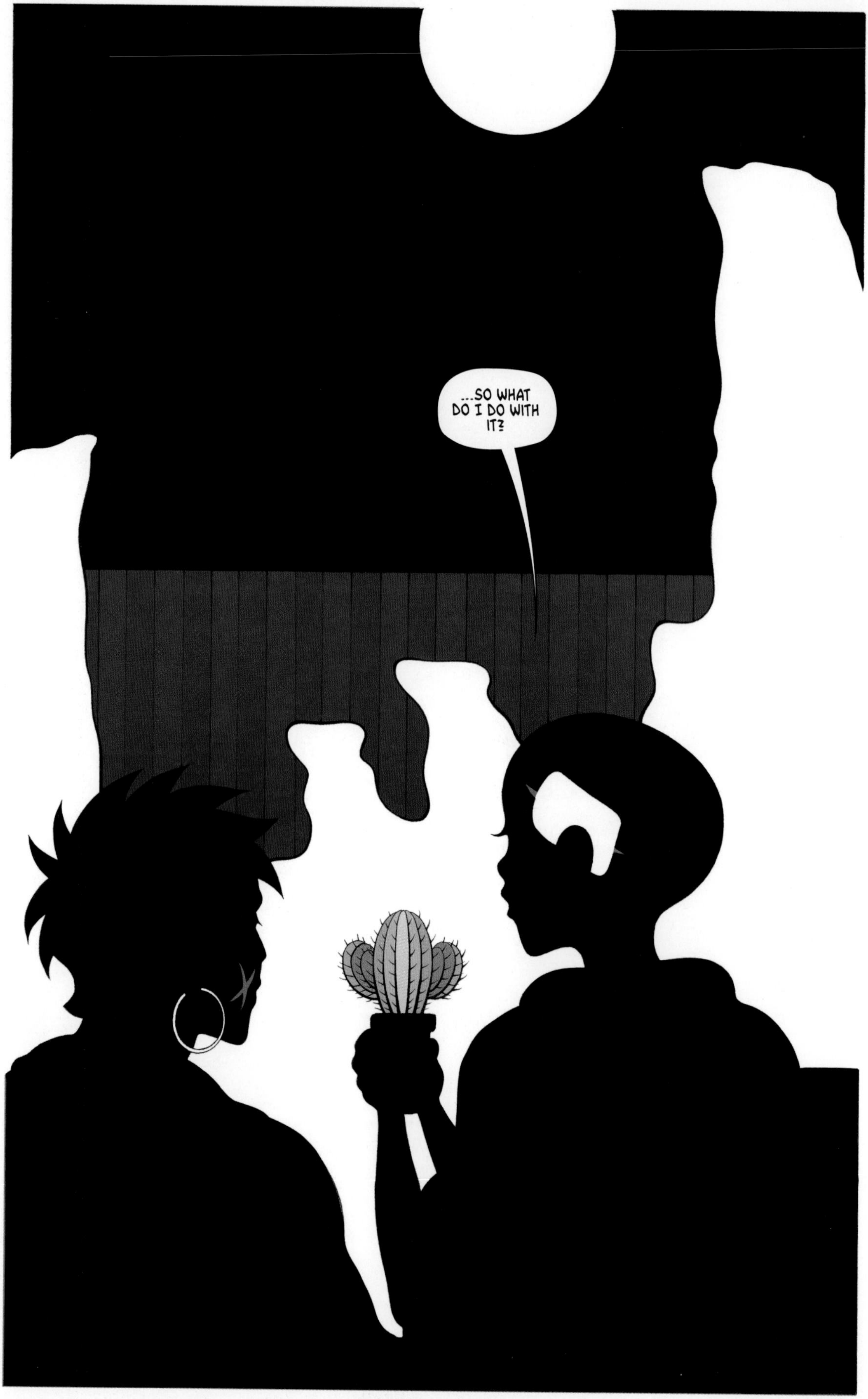
...SO WHAT DO I DO WITH IT?

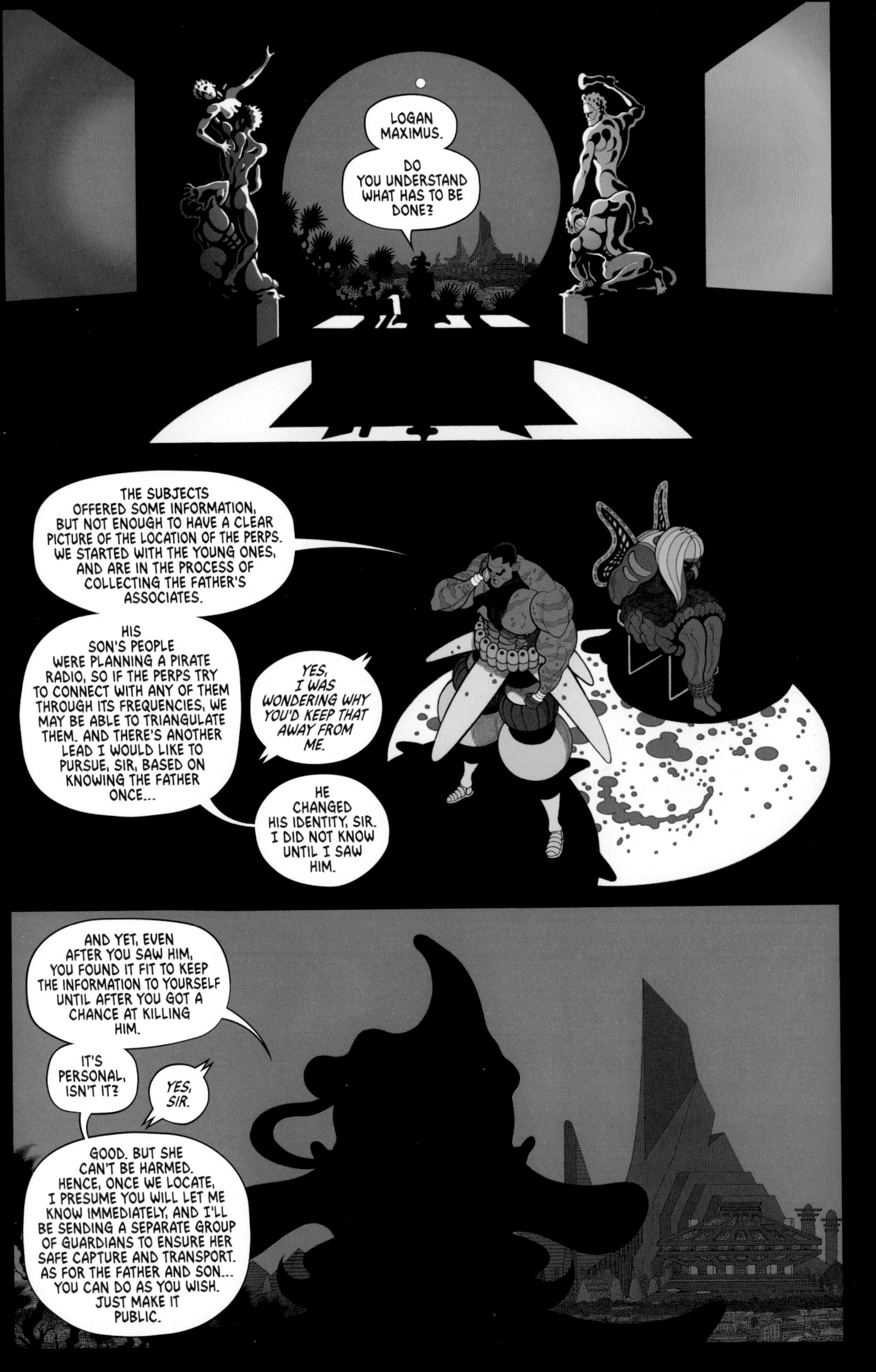
LOGAN MAXIMUS.
DO YOU UNDERSTAND WHAT HAS TO BE DONE?
THE SUBJECTS OFFERED SOME INFORMATION, BUT NOT ENOUGH TO HAVE A CLEAR PICTURE OF THE LOCATION OF THE PERPS. WE STARTED WITH THE YOUNG ONES, AND ARE IN THE PROCESS OF COLLECTING THE FATHER'S ASSOCIATES.
HIS SON'S PEOPLE WERE PLANNING A PIRATE RADIO, SO IF THE PERPS TRY TO CONNECT WITH ANY OF THEM THROUGH ITS FREQUENCIES, WE MAY BE ABLE TO TRIANGULATE THEM. AND THERE'S ANOTHER LEAD I WOULD LIKE TO PURSUE, SIR, BASED ON KNOWING THE FATHER ONCE...
YES, I WAS WONDERING WHY YOU'D KEEP THAT AWAY FROM ME.
HE CHANGED HIS IDENTITY, SIR. I DID NOT KNOW UNTIL I SAW HIM.
AND YET, EVEN AFTER YOU SAW HIM, YOU FOUND IT FIT TO KEEP THE INFORMATION TO YOURSELF UNTIL AFTER YOU GOT A CHANCE AT KILLING HIM.
IT'S PERSONAL, ISN'T IT?
YES, SIR.
GOOD. BUT SHE CAN'T BE HARMED. HENCE, ONCE WE LOCATE, I PRESUME YOU WILL LET ME KNOW IMMEDIATELY, AND I'LL BE SENDING A SEPARATE GROUP OF GUARDIANS TO ENSURE HER SAFE CAPTURE AND TRANSPORT. AS FOR THE FATHER AND SON... YOU CAN DO AS YOU WISH. JUST MAKE IT PUBLIC.

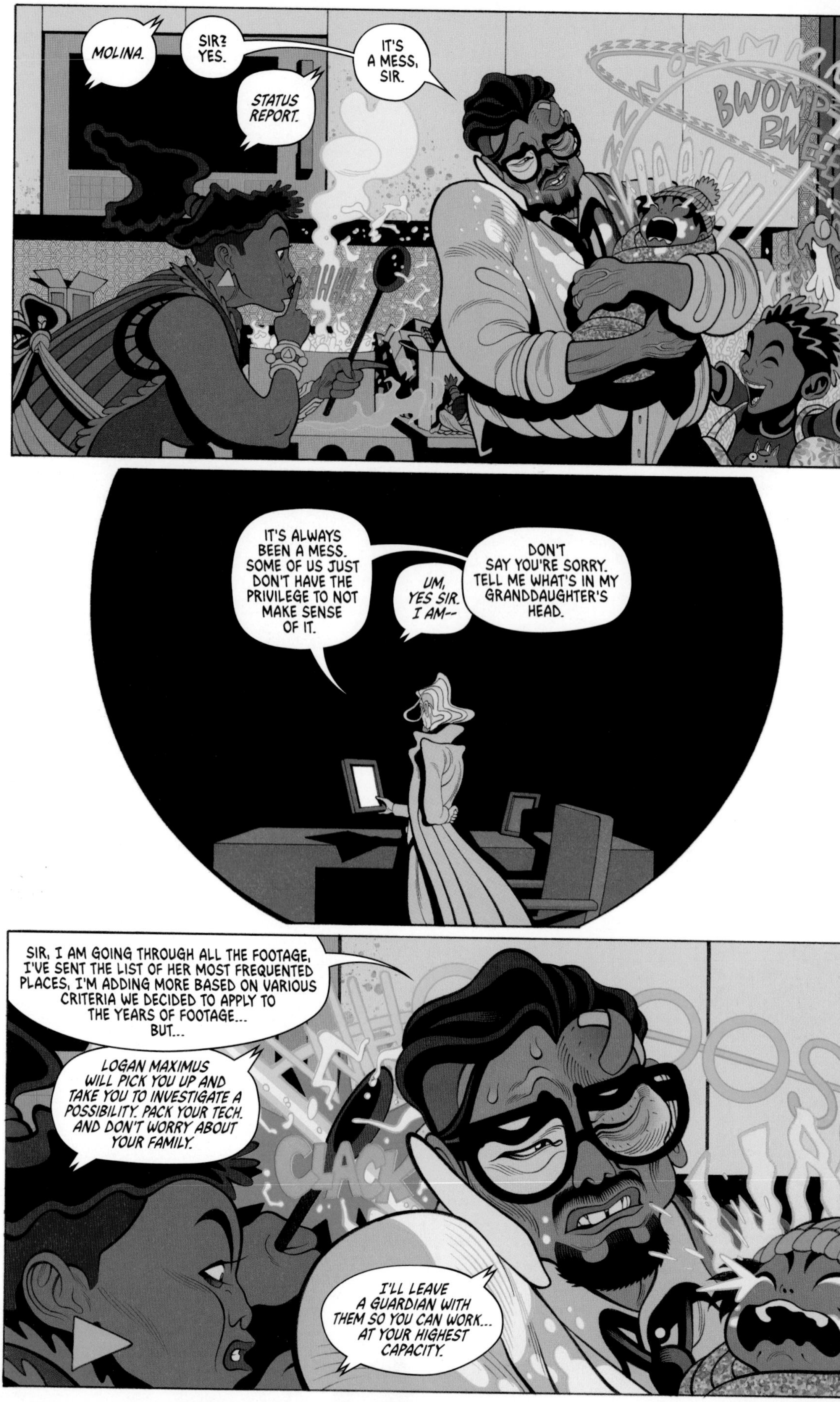
MOLINA.
SIR? YES.
STATUS REPORT.
IT'S A MESS, SIR.
BWOMP! BWEEEP
IT'S ALWAYS BEEN A MESS. SOME OF US JUST DON'T HAVE THE PRIVILEGE TO NOT MAKE SENSE OF IT.
UM, YES SIR. I AM--
DON'T SAY YOU'RE SORRY. TELL ME WHAT'S IN MY GRANDDAUGHTER'S HEAD.
SIR, I AM GOING THROUGH ALL THE FOOTAGE, I'VE SENT THE LIST OF HER MOST FREQUENTED PLACES, I'M ADDING MORE BASED ON VARIOUS CRITERIA WE DECIDED TO APPLY TO THE YEARS OF FOOTAGE... BUT...
LOGAN MAXIMUS WILL PICK YOU UP AND TAKE YOU TO INVESTIGATE A POSSIBILITY. PACK YOUR TECH. AND DON'T WORRY ABOUT YOUR FAMILY.
CLACK
I'LL LEAVE A GUARDIAN WITH THEM SO YOU CAN WORK... AT YOUR HIGHEST CAPACITY.

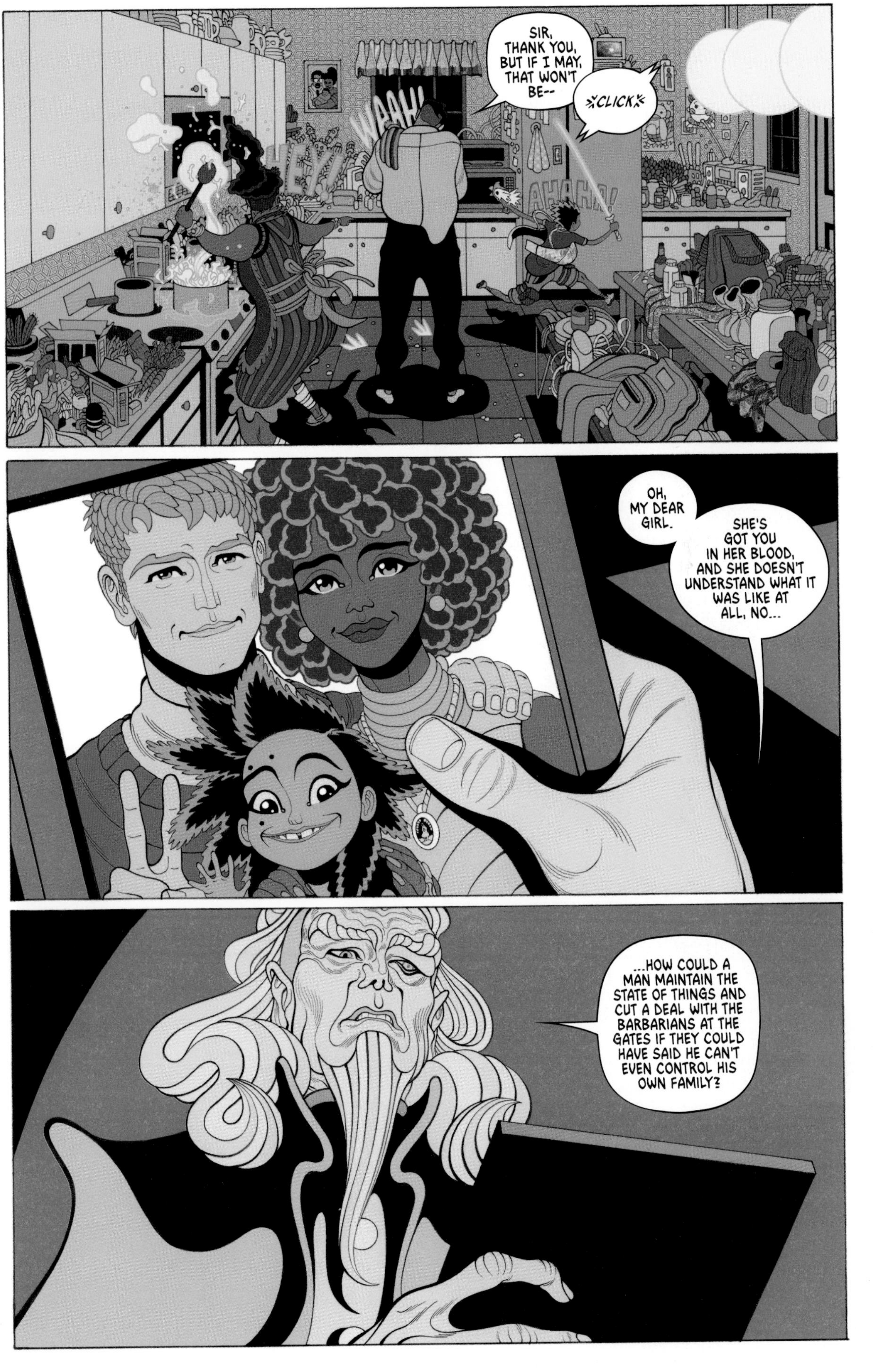

SIR, THANK YOU, BUT IF I MAY, THAT WON'T BE--
CLICK
HEY!
WAAH!
AHAHA!
OH, MY DEAR GIRL.
SHE'S GOT YOU IN HER BLOOD, AND SHE DOESN'T UNDERSTAND WHAT IT WAS LIKE AT ALL, NO...
...HOW COULD A MAN MAINTAIN THE STATE OF THINGS AND CUT A DEAL WITH THE BARBARIANS AT THE GATES IF THEY COULD HAVE SAID HE CAN'T EVEN CONTROL HIS OWN FAMILY?

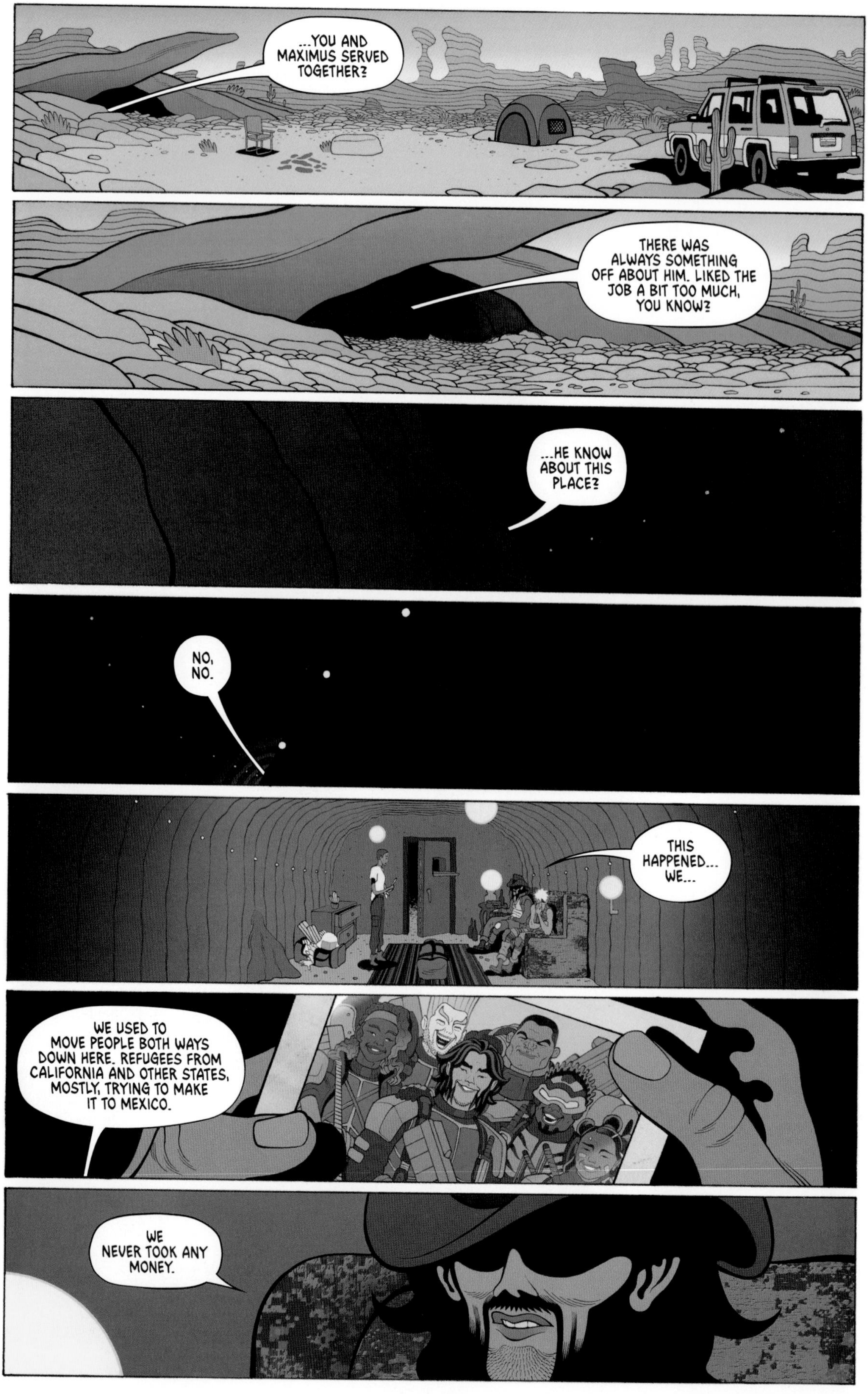
...YOU AND MAXIMUS SERVED TOGETHER?
THERE WAS ALWAYS SOMETHING OFF ABOUT HIM. LIKED THE JOB A BIT TOO MUCH, YOU KNOW?
...HE KNOW ABOUT THIS PLACE?
NO, NO.
THIS HAPPENED... WE...
WE USED TO MOVE PEOPLE BOTH WAYS DOWN HERE. REFUGEES FROM CALIFORNIA AND OTHER STATES, MOSTLY, TRYING TO MAKE IT TO MEXICO.
WE NEVER TOOK ANY MONEY.

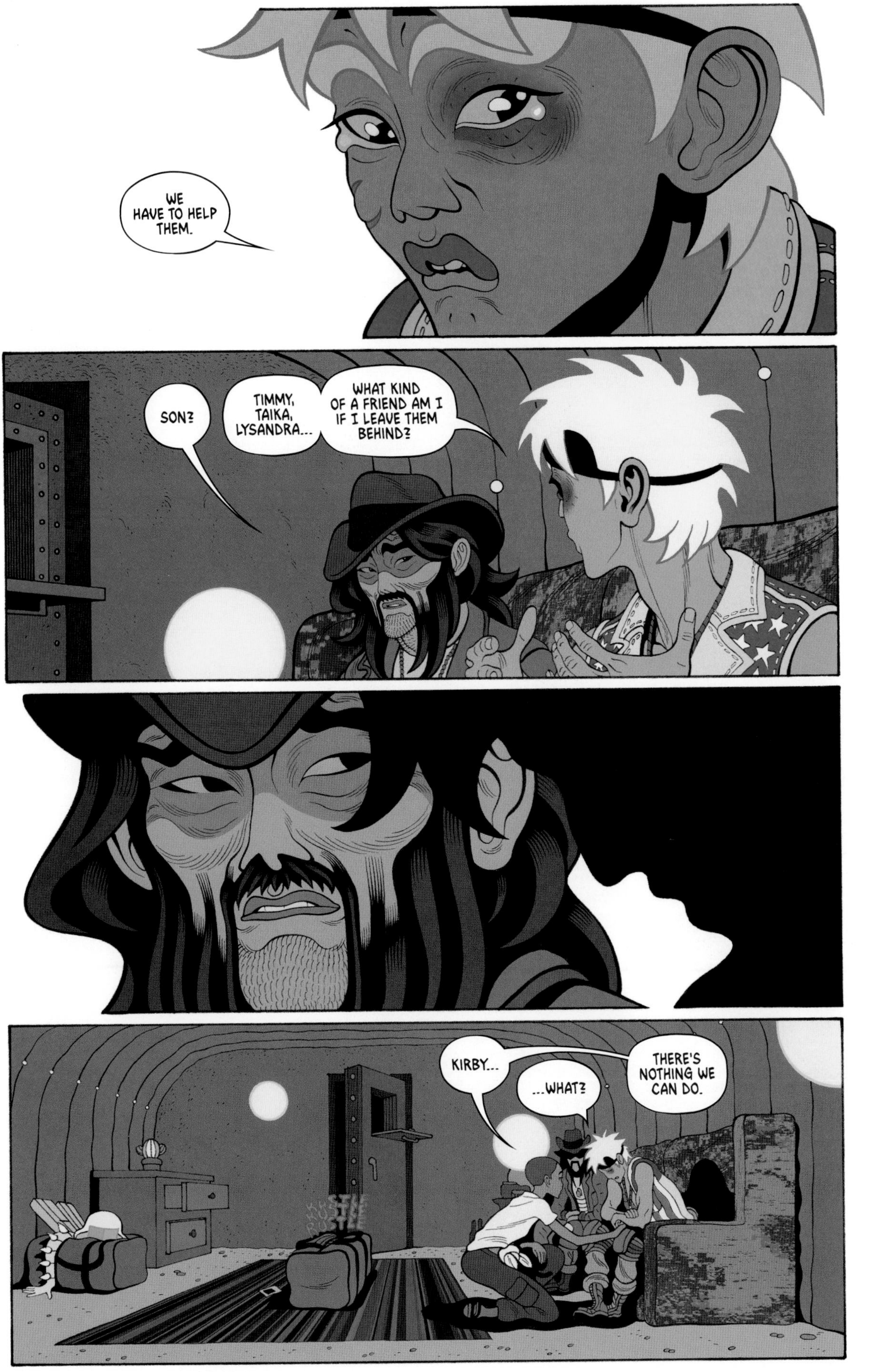
WE HAVE TO HELP THEM.
SON?
TIMMY, TAIKA, LYSANDRA...
WHAT KIND OF A FRIEND AM I IF I LEAVE THEM BEHIND?
KIRBY...
...WHAT?
THERE'S NOTHING WE CAN DO.

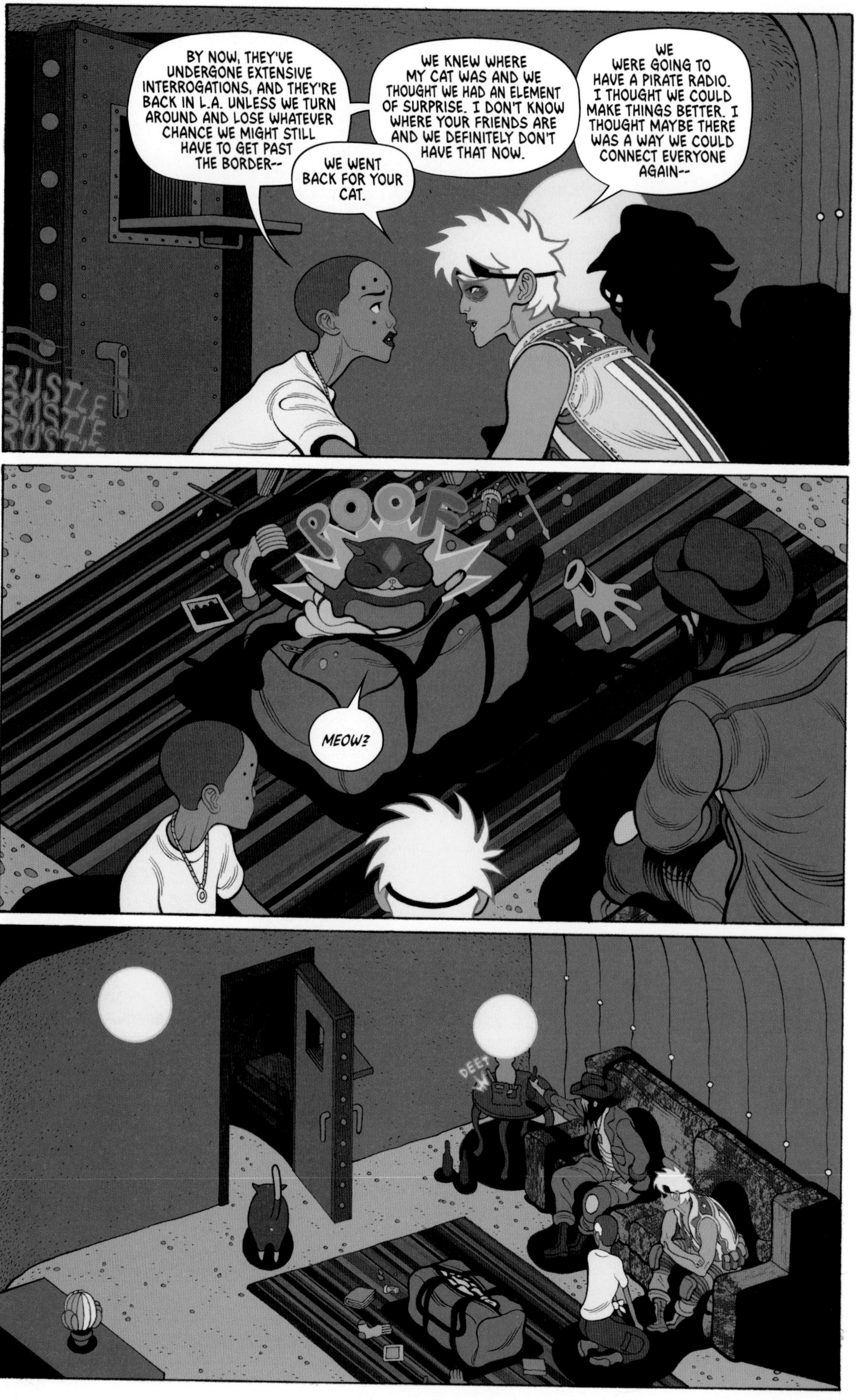
BY NOW, THEY'VE UNDERGONE EXTENSIVE INTERROGATIONS, AND THEY'RE BACK IN L.A. UNLESS WE TURN AROUND AND LOSE WHATEVER CHANCE WE MIGHT STILL HAVE TO GET PAST THE BORDER--
WE KNEW WHERE MY CAT WAS AND WE THOUGHT WE HAD AN ELEMENT OF SURPRISE. I DON'T KNOW WHERE YOUR FRIENDS ARE AND WE DEFINITELY DON'T HAVE THAT NOW.
WE WENT BACK FOR YOUR CAT.
WE WERE GOING TO HAVE A PIRATE RADIO. I THOUGHT WE COULD MAKE THINGS BETTER. I THOUGHT MAYBE THERE WAS A WAY WE COULD CONNECT EVERYONE AGAIN--
POOF
MEOW?
DEET

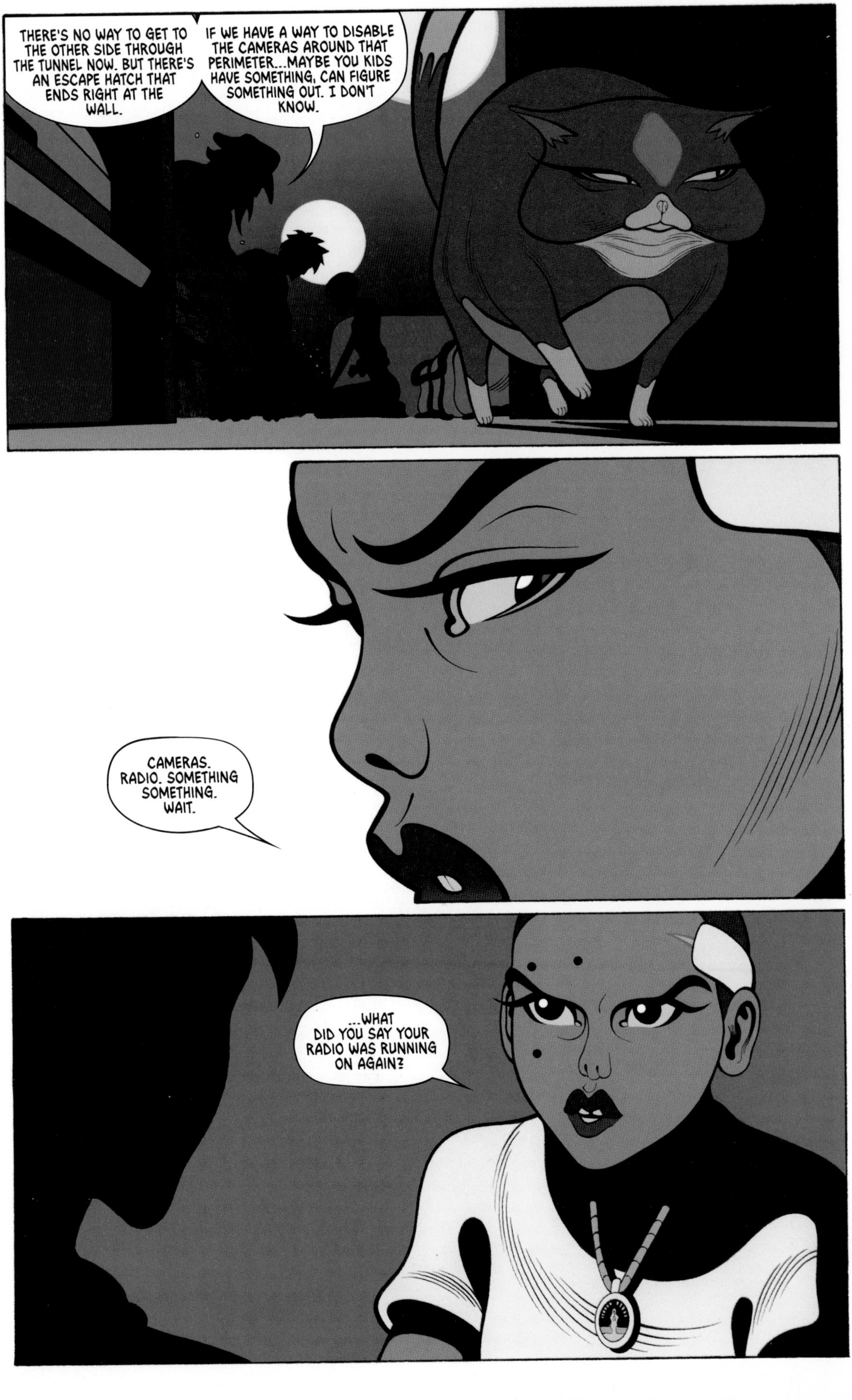
THERE'S NO WAY TO GET TO THE OTHER SIDE THROUGH THE TUNNEL NOW. BUT THERE'S AN ESCAPE HATCH THAT ENDS RIGHT AT THE WALL.
IF WE HAVE A WAY TO DISABLE THE CAMERAS AROUND THAT PERIMETER...MAYBE YOU KIDS HAVE SOMETHING, CAN FIGURE SOMETHING OUT. I DON'T KNOW.
CAMERAS. RADIO. SOMETHING SOMETHING. WAIT.
...WHAT DID YOU SAY YOUR RADIO WAS RUNNING ON AGAIN?

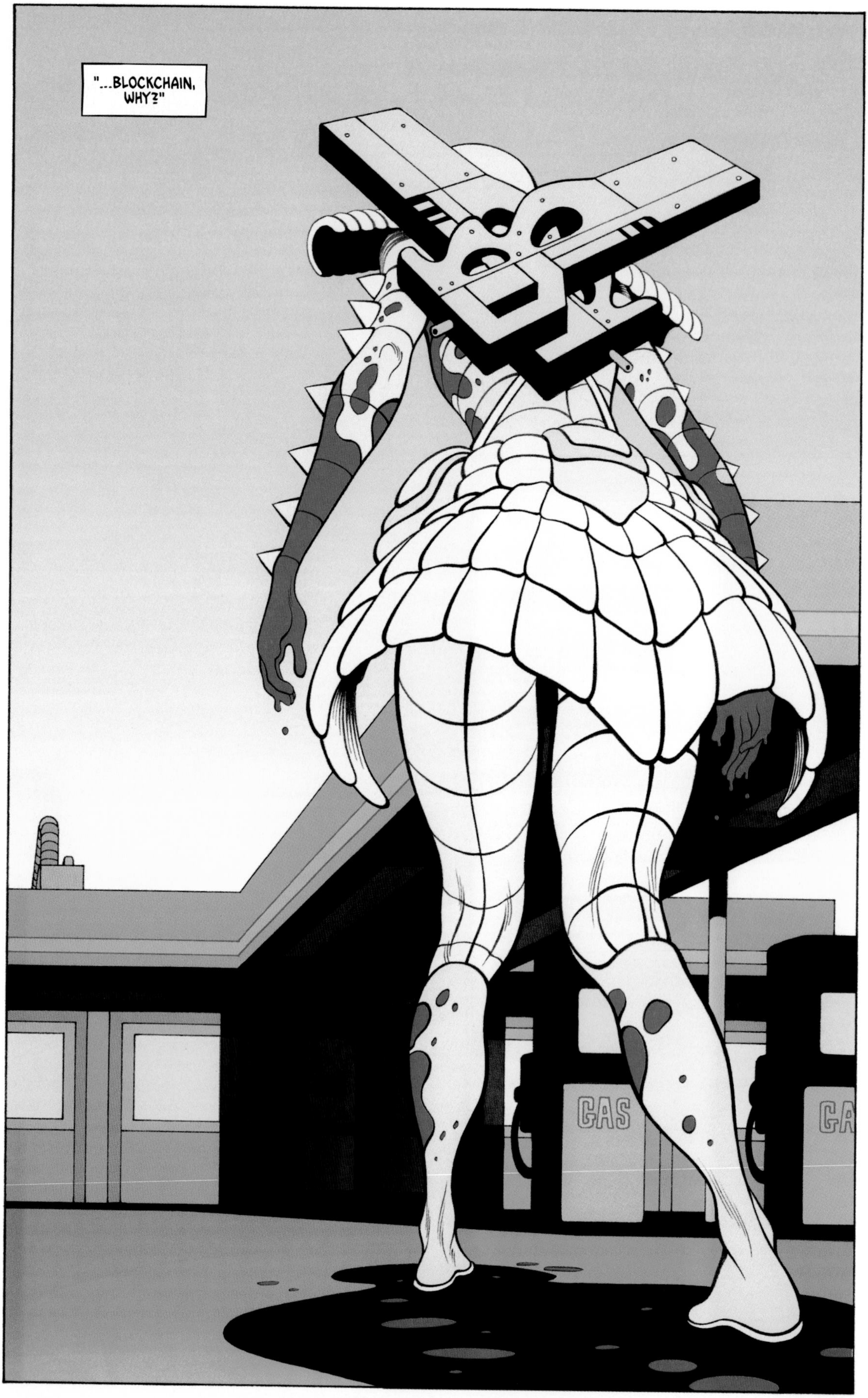
"...BLOCKCHAIN, WHY?"
GAS

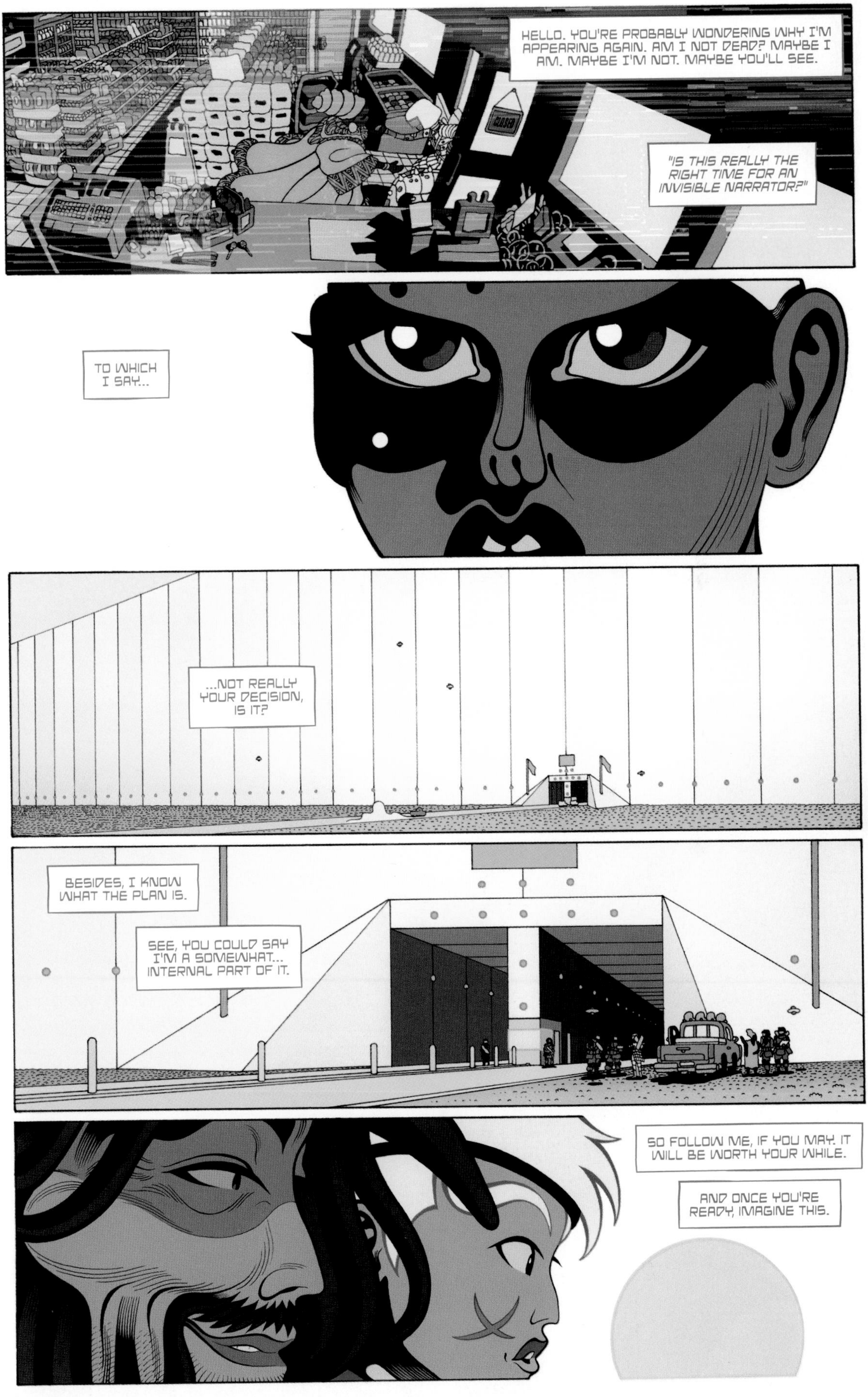
HELLO. YOU'RE PROBABLY WONDERING WHY I'M APPEARING AGAIN. AM I NOT DEAD? MAYBE I AM. MAYBE I'M NOT. MAYBE YOU'LL SEE.
CLOSED
"IS THIS REALLY THE RIGHT TIME FOR AN INVISIBLE NARRATOR?"
TO WHICH I SAY...
...NOT REALLY YOUR DECISION, IS IT?
BESIDES, I KNOW WHAT THE PLAN IS.
SEE, YOU COULD SAY I'M A SOMEWHAT... INTERNAL PART OF IT.
SO FOLLOW ME, IF YOU MAY. IT WILL BE WORTH YOUR WHILE.
AND ONCE YOU'RE READY, IMAGINE THIS.

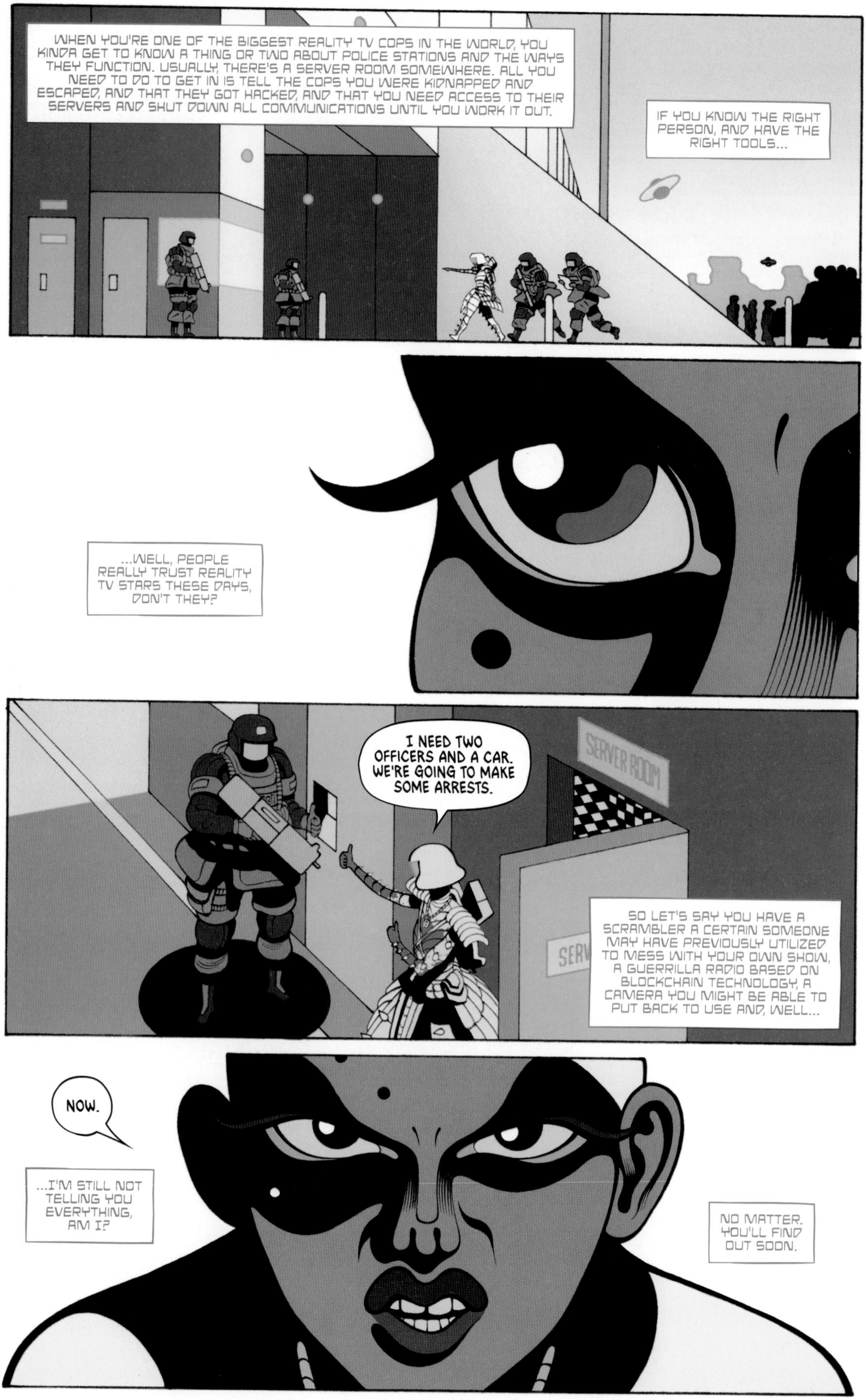
WHEN YOU'RE ONE OF THE BIGGEST REALITY TV COPS IN THE WORLD, YOU KINDA GET TO KNOW A THING OR TWO ABOUT POLICE STATIONS AND THE WAYS THEY FUNCTION. USUALLY, THERE'S A SERVER ROOM SOMEWHERE. ALL YOU NEED TO DO TO GET IN IS TELL THE COPS YOU WERE KIDNAPPED AND ESCAPED, AND THAT THEY GOT HACKED, AND THAT YOU NEED ACCESS TO THEIR SERVERS AND SHUT DOWN ALL COMMUNICATIONS UNTIL YOU WORK IT OUT.
IF YOU KNOW THE RIGHT PERSON, AND HAVE THE RIGHT TOOLS...
...WELL, PEOPLE REALLY TRUST REALITY TV STARS THESE DAYS, DON'T THEY?
I NEED TWO OFFICERS AND A CAR. WE'RE GOING TO MAKE SOME ARRESTS.
SERVER ROOM
SO LET'S SAY YOU HAVE A SCRAMBLER A CERTAIN SOMEONE MAY HAVE PREVIOUSLY UTILIZED TO MESS WITH YOUR OWN SHOW, A GUERRILLA RADIO BASED ON BLOCKCHAIN TECHNOLOGY, A CAMERA YOU MIGHT BE ABLE TO PUT BACK TO USE AND, WELL...
NOW.
...I'M STILL NOT TELLING YOU EVERYTHING, AM I?
NO MATTER. YOU'LL FIND OUT SOON.

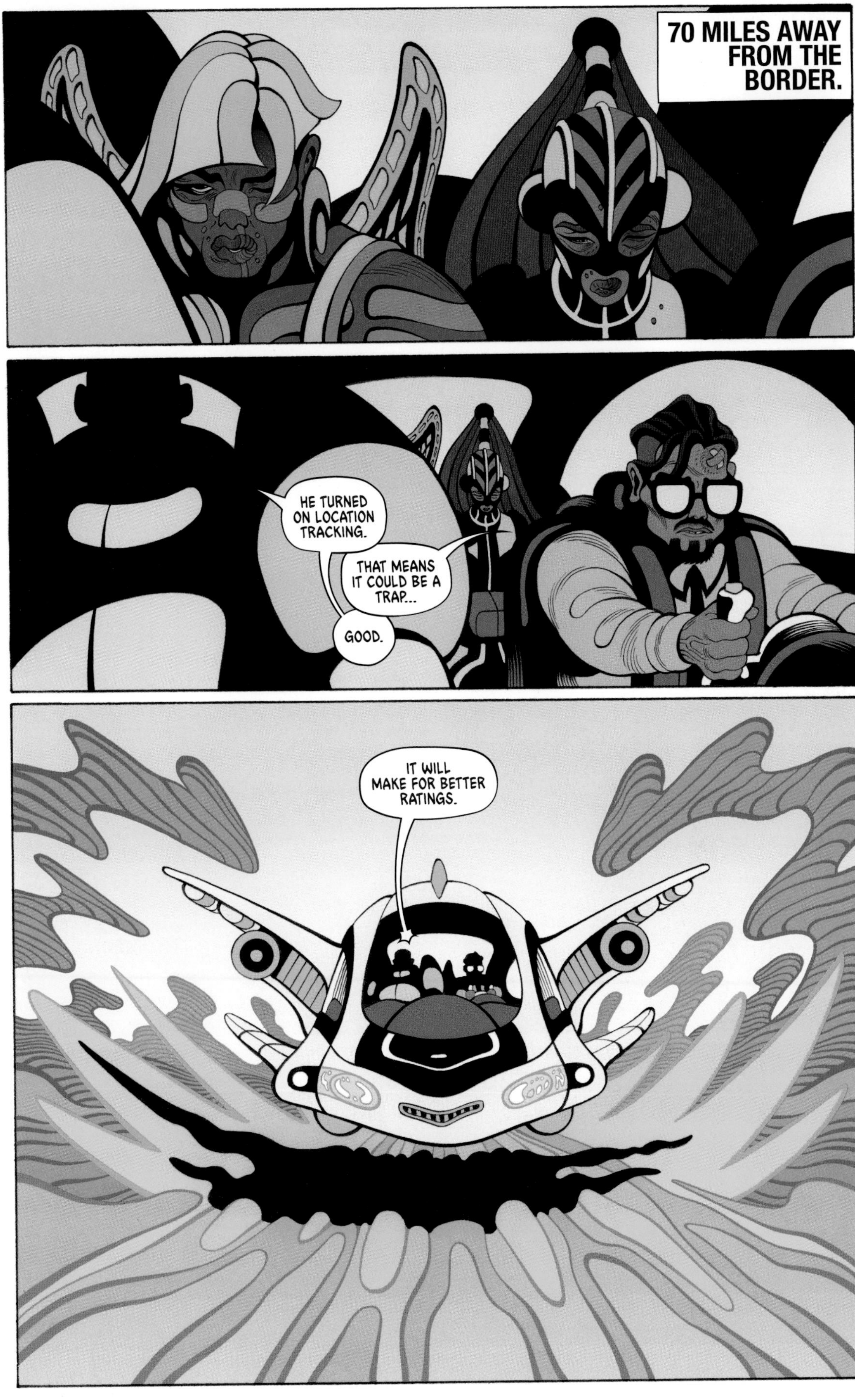
70 MILES AWAY FROM THE BORDER.
HE TURNED ON LOCATION TRACKING.
THAT MEANS IT COULD BE A TRAP...
GOOD.
IT WILL MAKE FOR BETTER RATINGS.

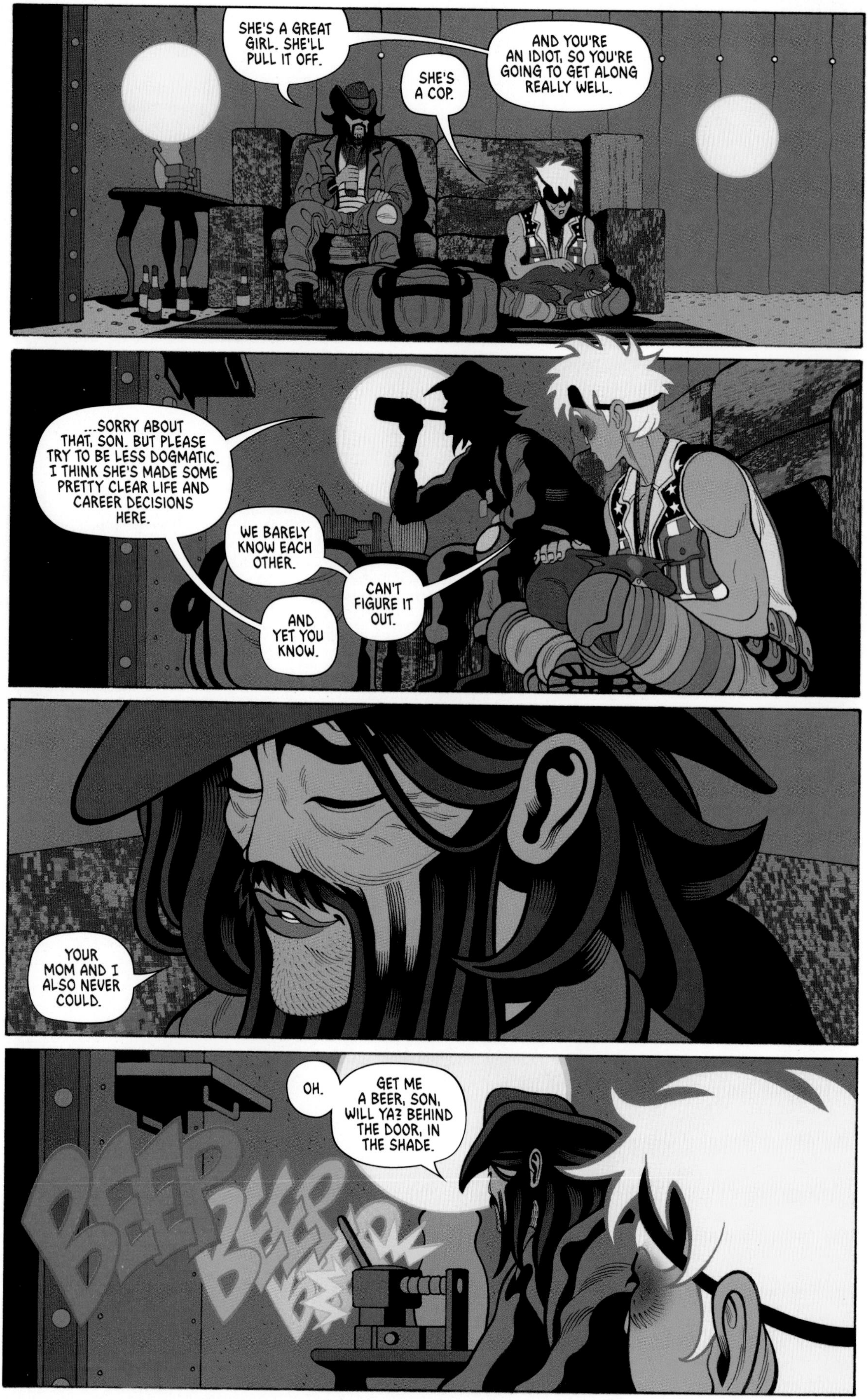
SHE'S A GREAT GIRL. SHE'LL PULL IT OFF.
SHE'S A COP.
AND YOU'RE AN IDIOT, SO YOU'RE GOING TO GET ALONG REALLY WELL.
...SORRY ABOUT THAT, SON. BUT PLEASE TRY TO BE LESS DOGMATIC. I THINK SHE'S MADE SOME PRETTY CLEAR LIFE AND CAREER DECISIONS HERE.
WE BARELY KNOW EACH OTHER.
CAN'T FIGURE IT OUT.
AND YET YOU KNOW.
YOUR MOM AND I ALSO NEVER COULD.
BEEP
BEEP
OH.
GET ME A BEER, SON, WILL YA? BEHIND THE DOOR, IN THE SHADE.

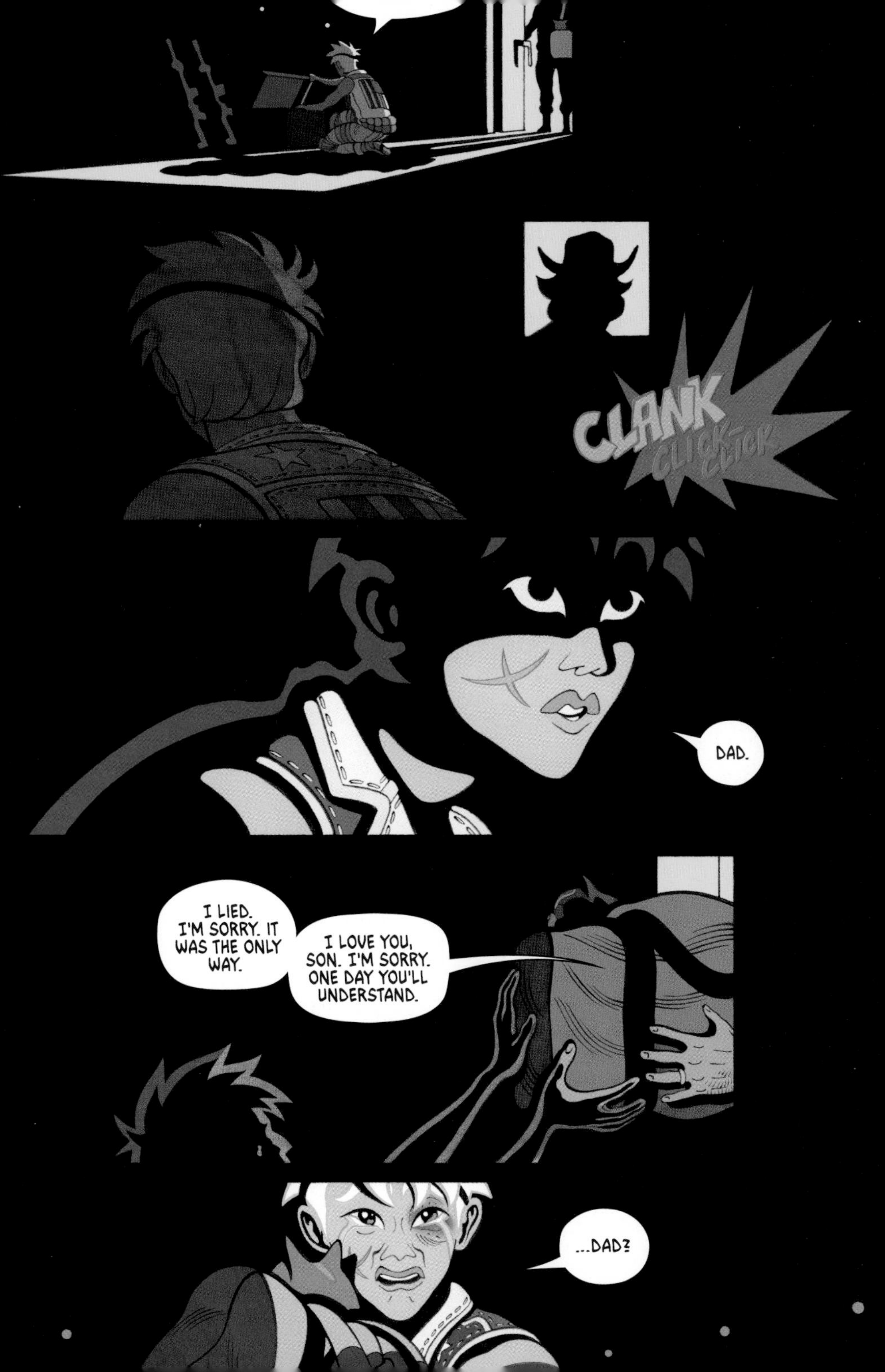
CLANK
CLICK-CLICK
DAD.
I LIED. I'M SORRY. IT WAS THE ONLY WAY.
I LOVE YOU, SON. I'M SORRY. ONE DAY YOU'LL UNDERSTAND.
...DAD?

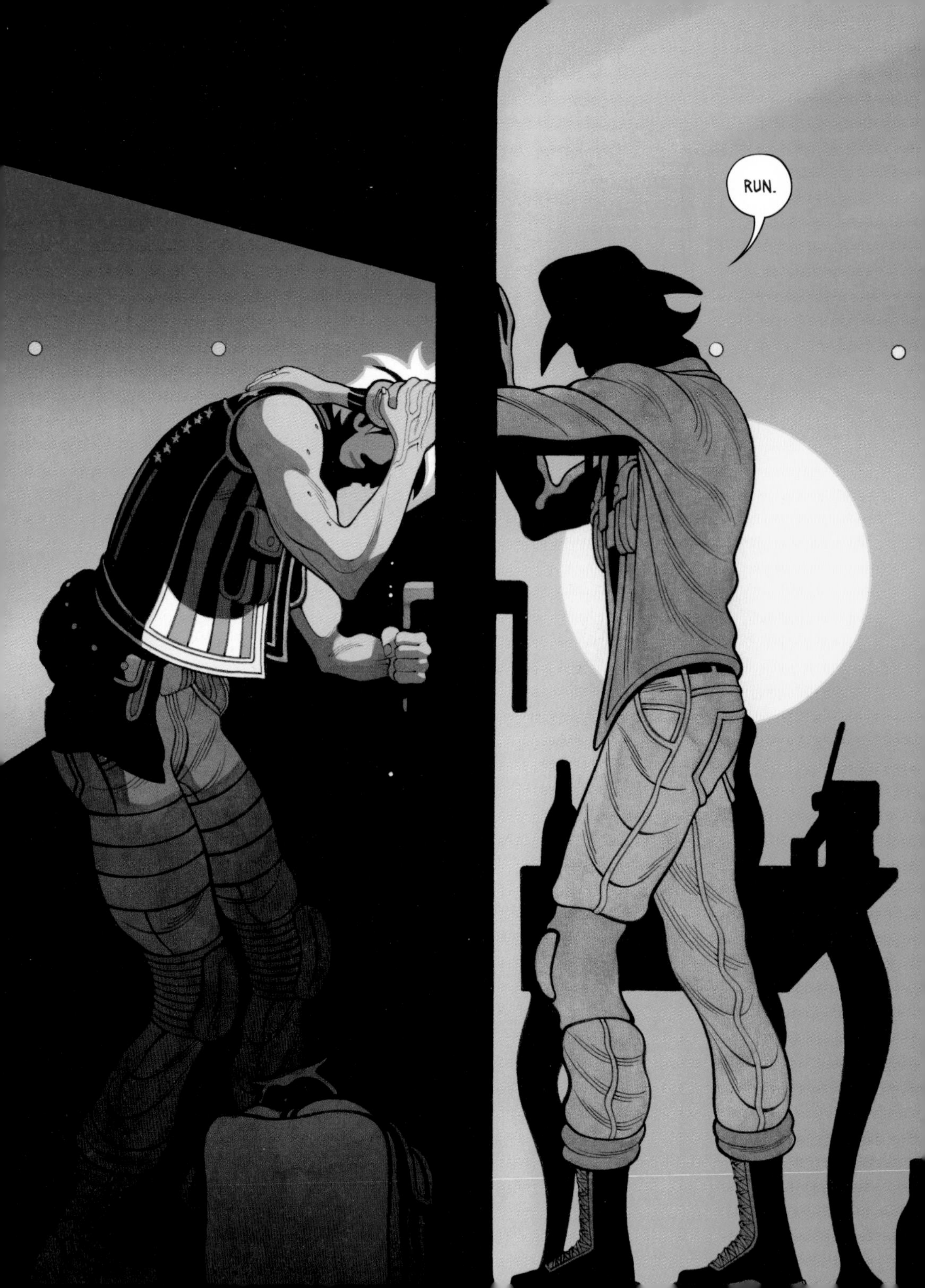
RUN.

CHAPTER 5

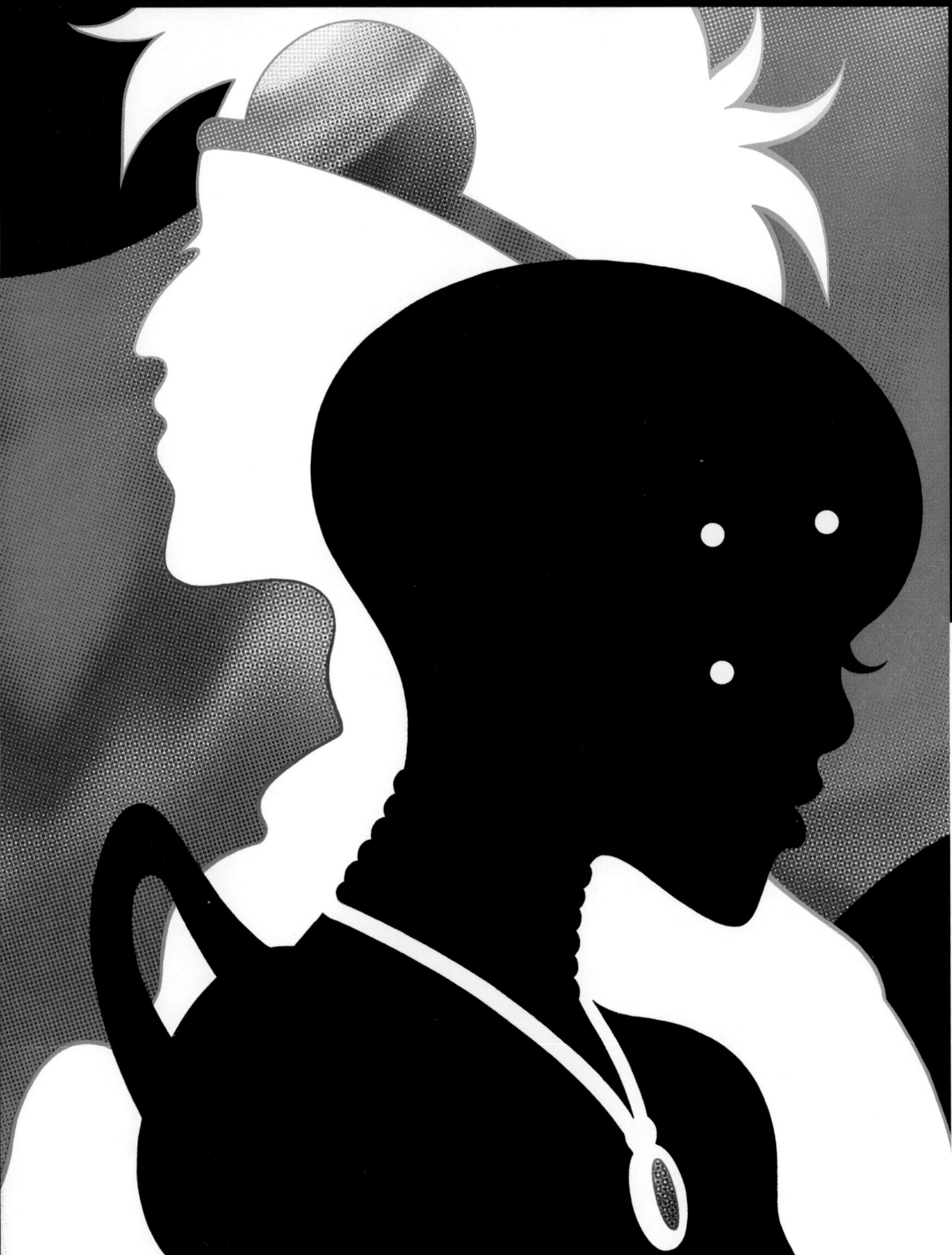

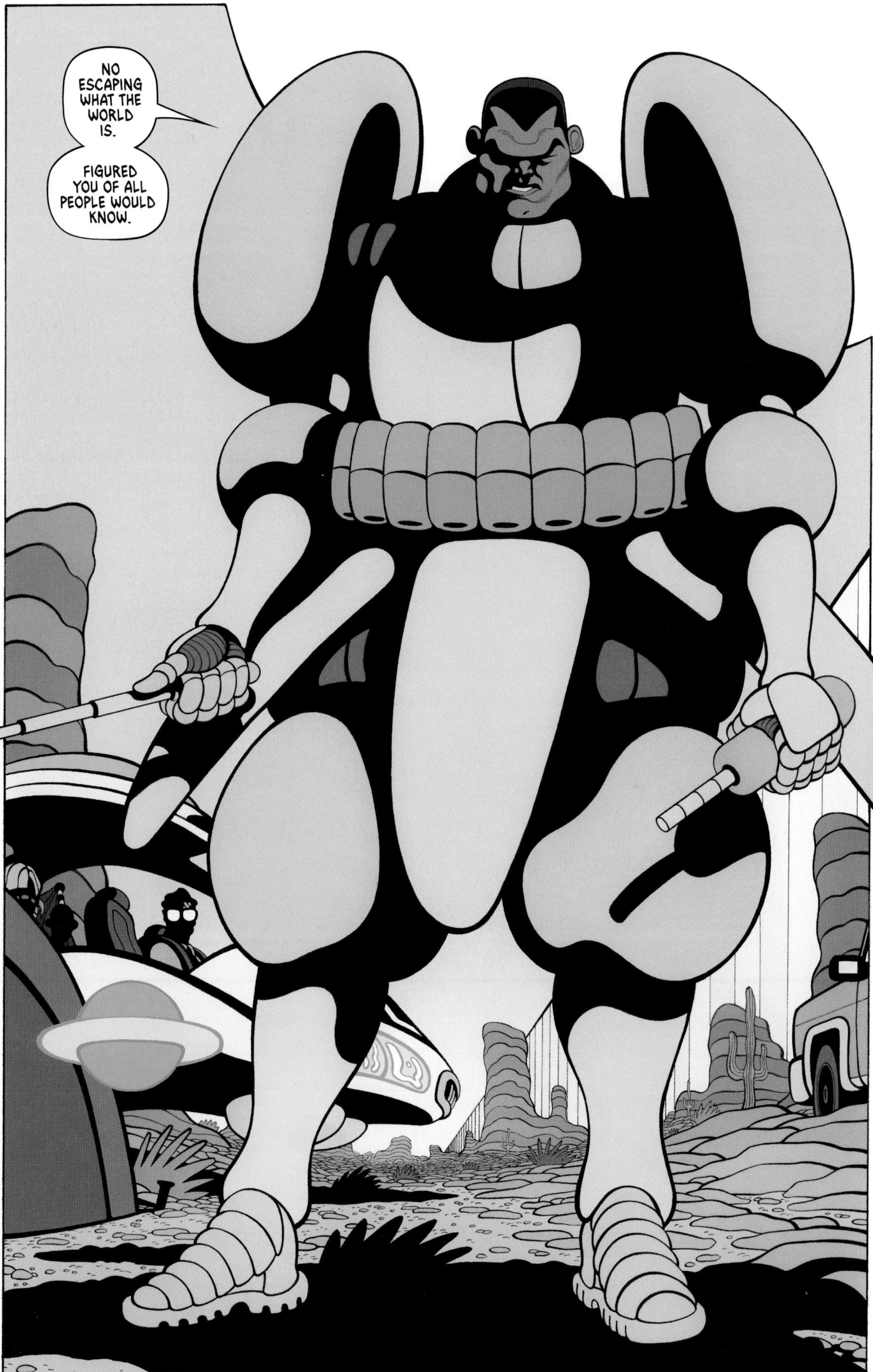
NO ESCAPING WHAT THE WORLD IS.
FIGURED YOU OF ALL PEOPLE WOULD KNOW.

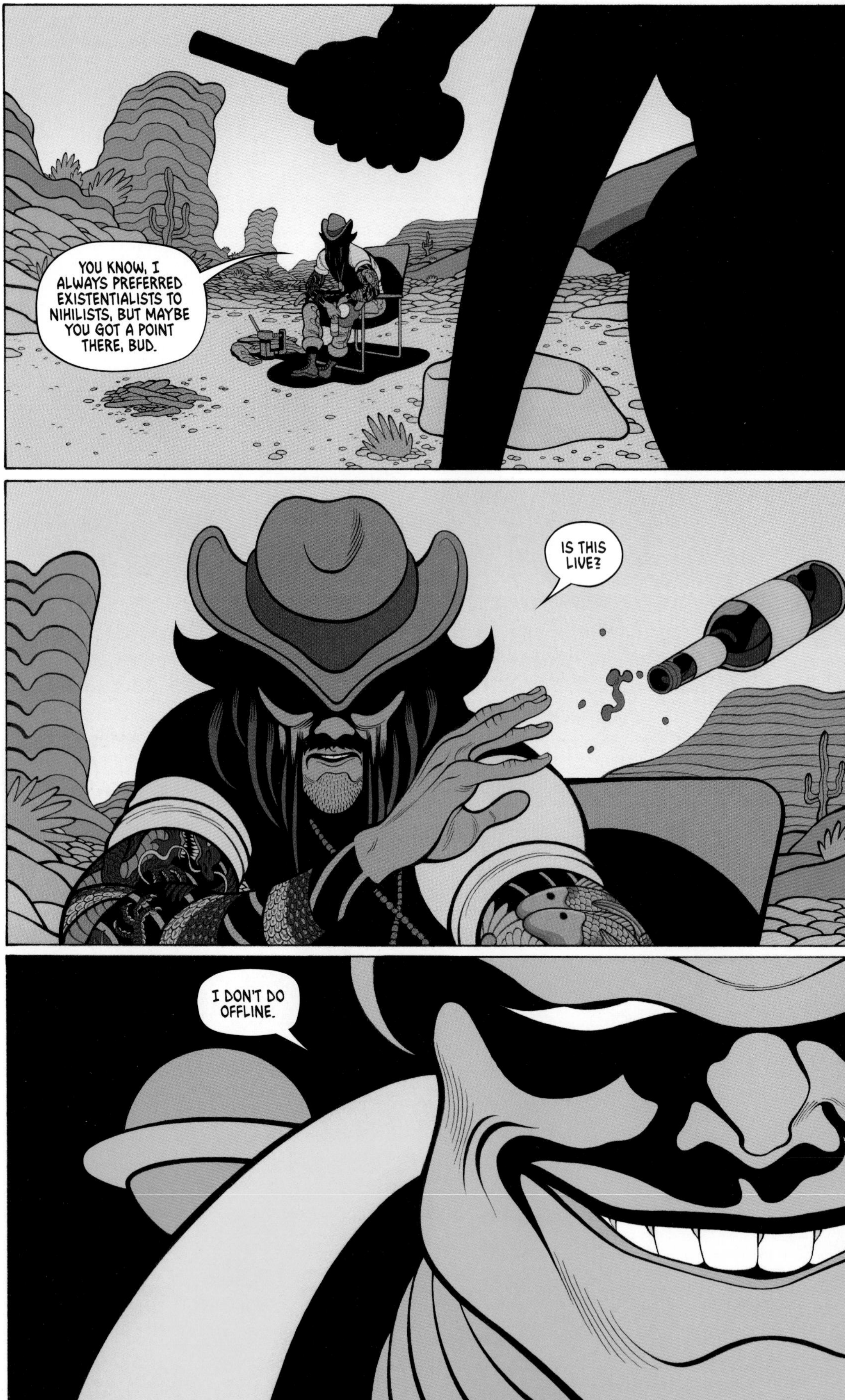
YOU KNOW, I ALWAYS PREFERRED EXISTENTIALISTS TO NIHILISTS, BUT MAYBE YOU GOT A POINT THERE, BUD.
IS THIS LIVE?
I DON'T DO OFFLINE.

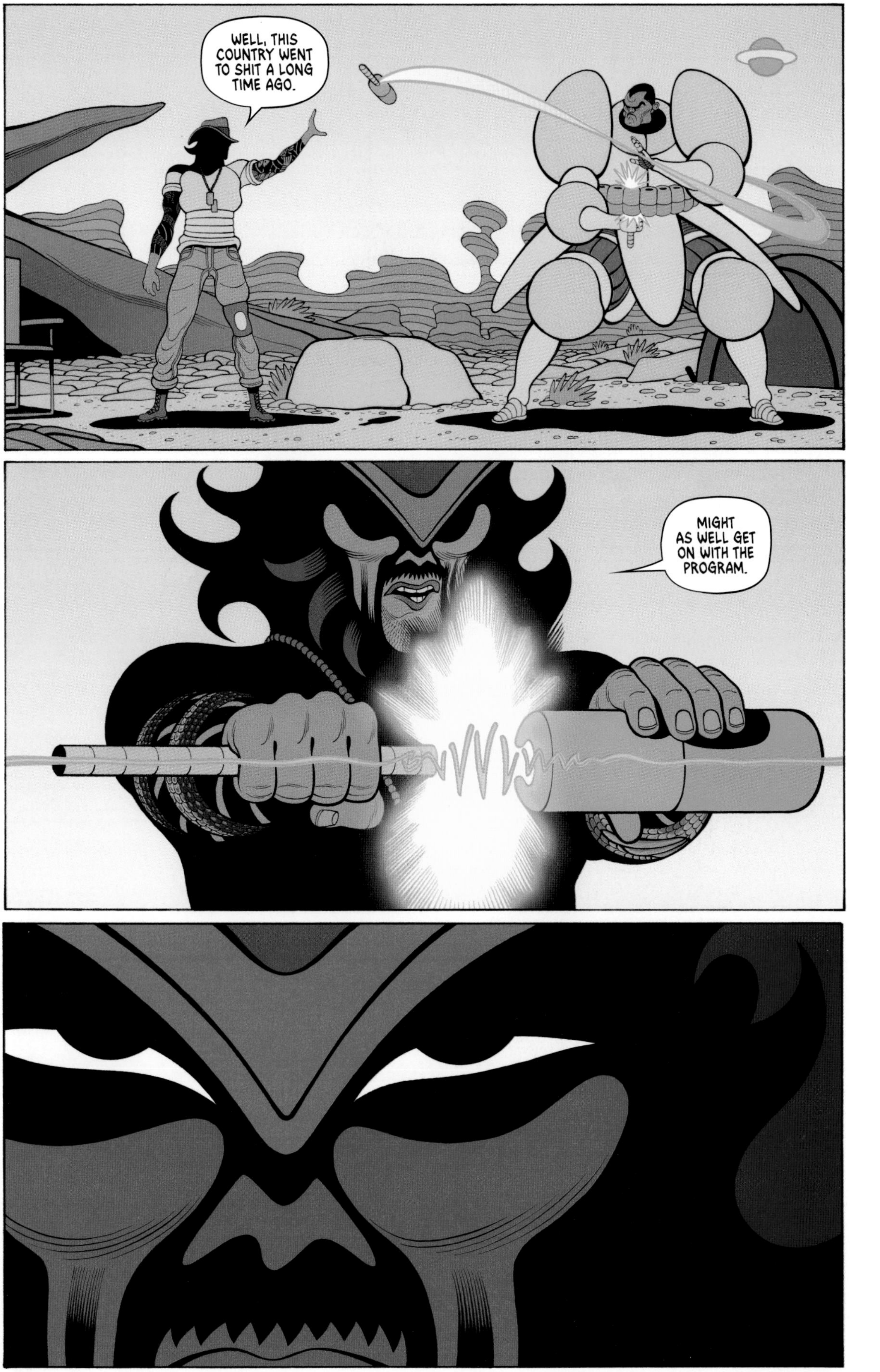
WELL, THIS COUNTRY WENT TO SHIT A LONG TIME AGO.
MIGHT AS WELL GET ON WITH THE PROGRAM.

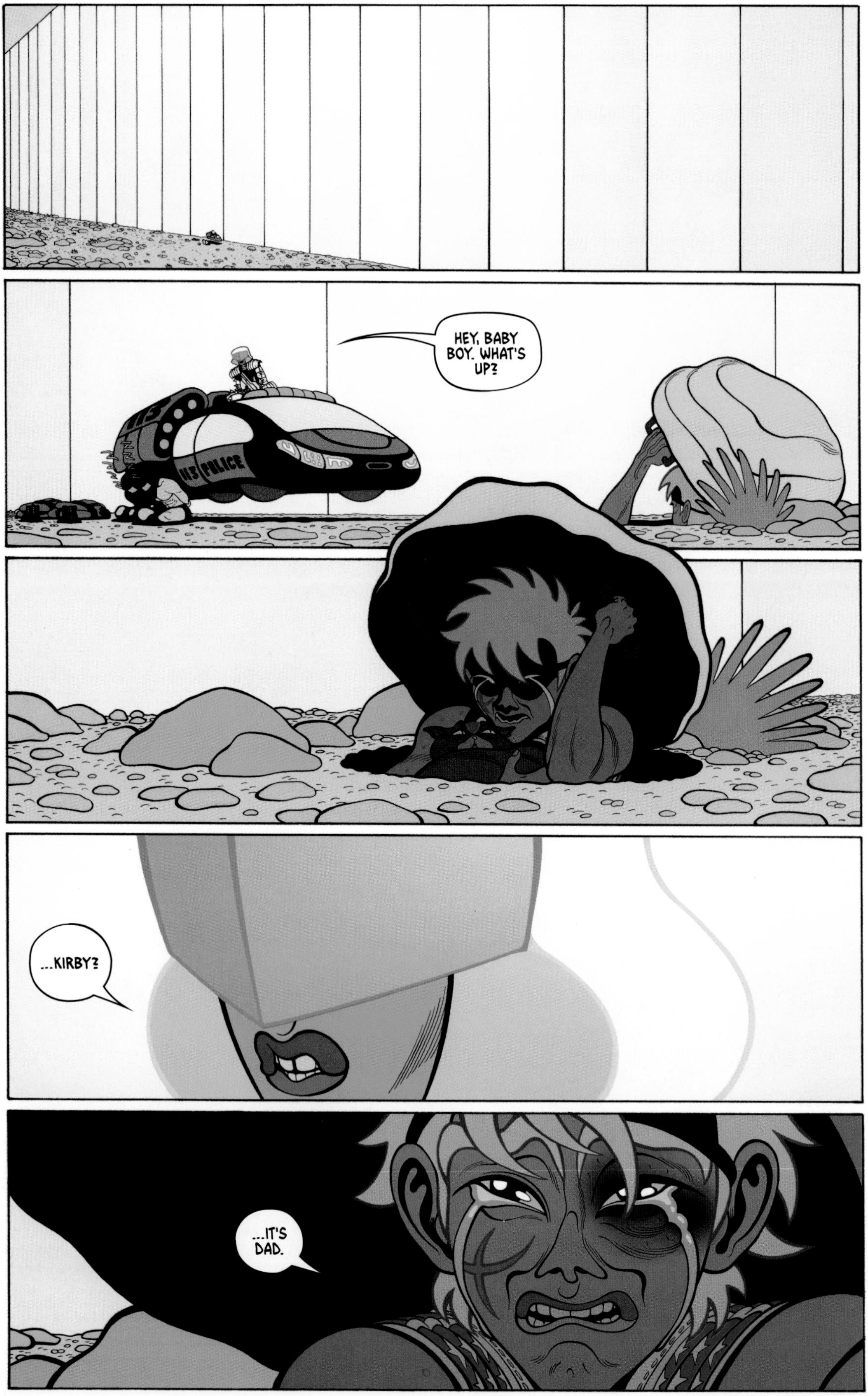
HEY, BABY BOY. WHAT'S UP?
POLICE
...KIRBY?
...IT'S DAD.

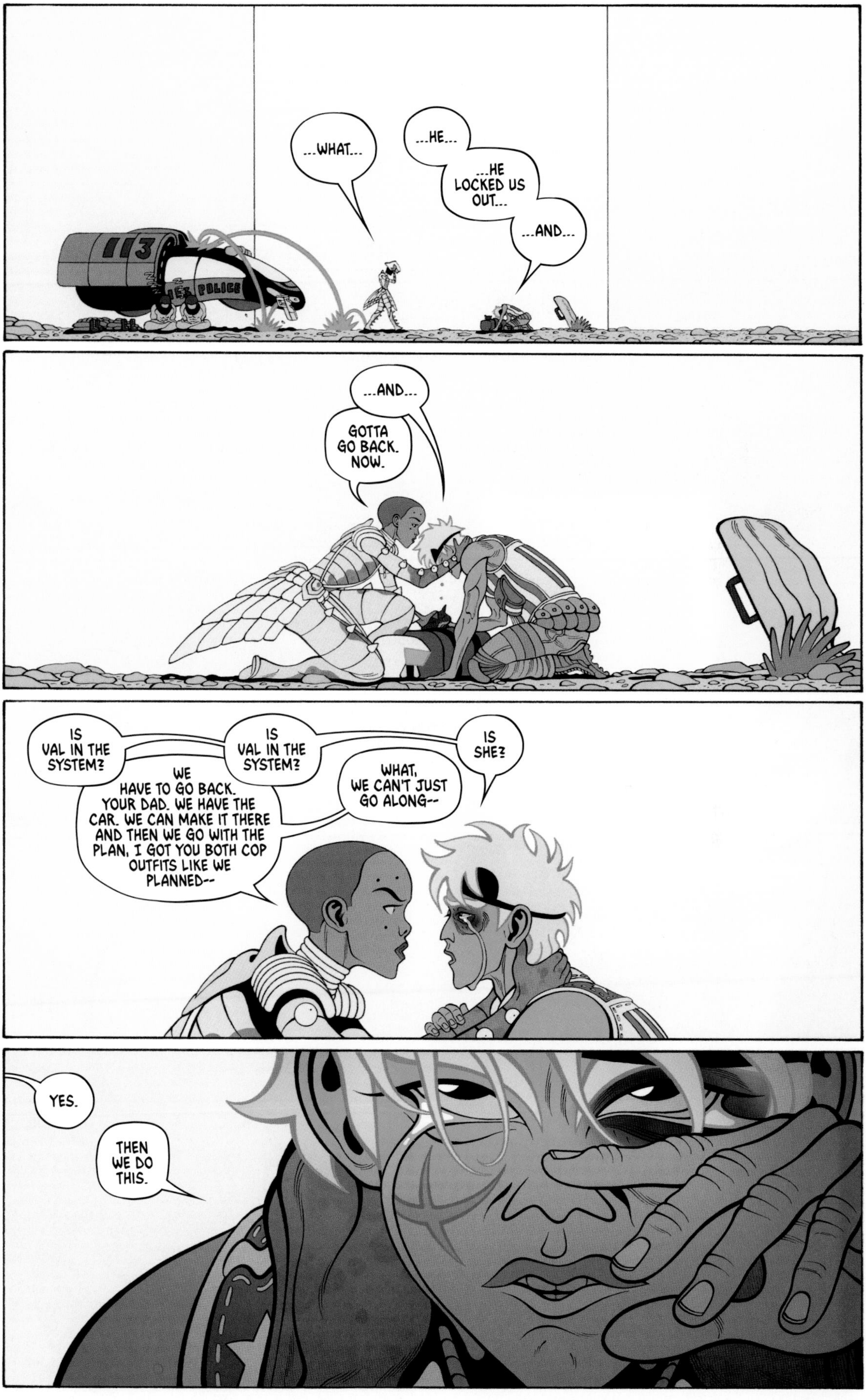

...WHAT...
...HE...
...HE LOCKED US OUT...
...AND...
...AND...
GOTTA GO BACK. NOW.
IS VAL IN THE SYSTEM?
WE HAVE TO GO BACK. YOUR DAD. WE HAVE THE CAR. WE CAN MAKE IT THERE AND THEN WE GO WITH THE PLAN, I GOT YOU BOTH COP OUTFITS LIKE WE PLANNED--
IS VAL IN THE SYSTEM?
WHAT, WE CAN'T JUST GO ALONG--
IS SHE?
YES.
THEN WE DO THIS.

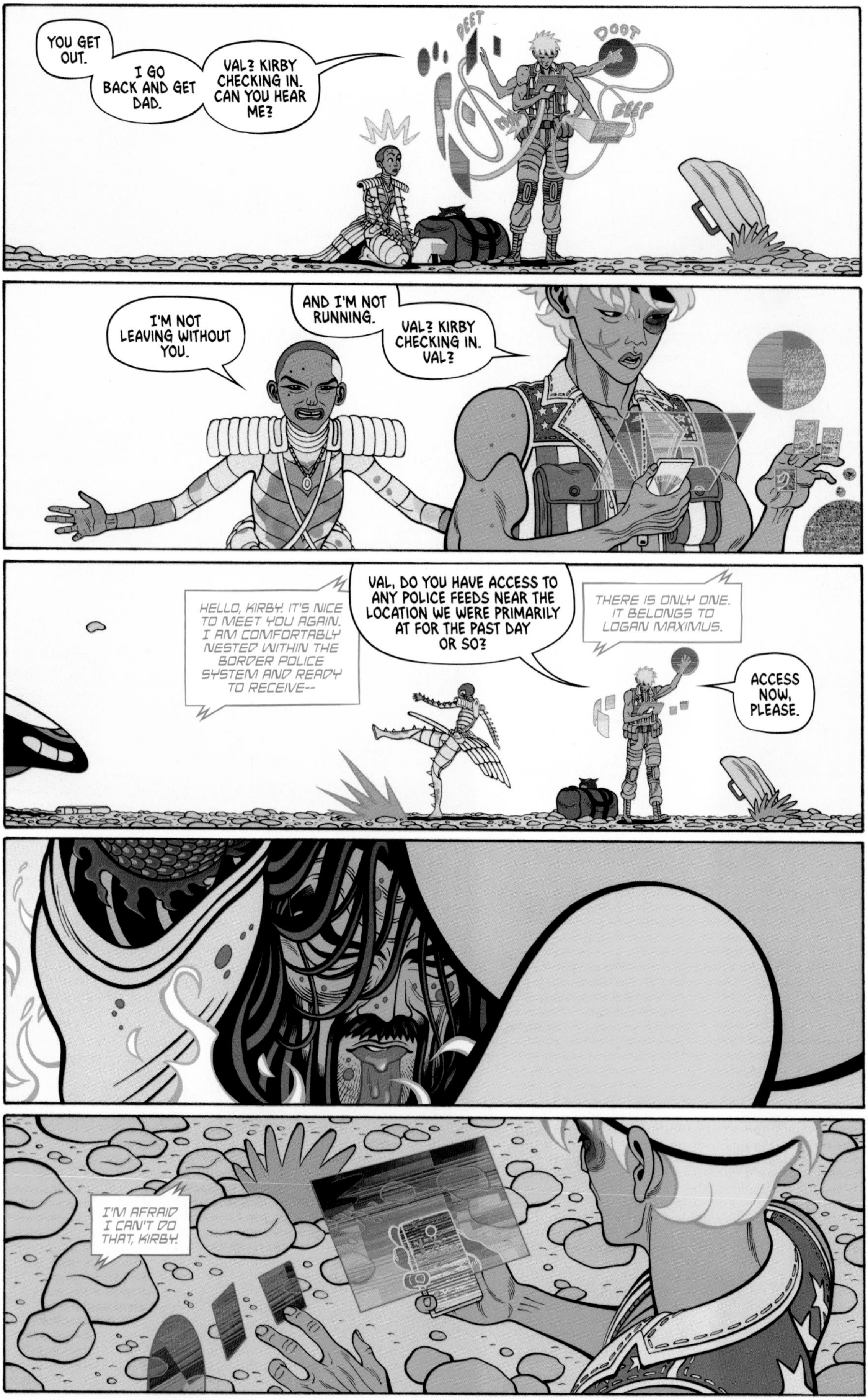
YOU GET OUT.
I GO BACK AND GET DAD.
VAL? KIRBY CHECKING IN. CAN YOU HEAR ME?
BEEP
DOOT
BEEP
I'M NOT LEAVING WITHOUT YOU.
AND I'M NOT RUNNING.
VAL? KIRBY CHECKING IN. VAL?
HELLO, KIRBY. IT'S NICE TO MEET YOU AGAIN. I AM COMFORTABLY NESTED WITHIN THE BORDER POLICE SYSTEM AND READY TO RECEIVE--
VAL, DO YOU HAVE ACCESS TO ANY POLICE FEEDS NEAR THE LOCATION WE WERE PRIMARILY AT FOR THE PAST DAY OR SO?
THERE IS ONLY ONE. IT BELONGS TO LOGAN MAXIMUS.
ACCESS NOW, PLEASE.
I'M AFRAID I CAN'T DO THAT, KIRBY.

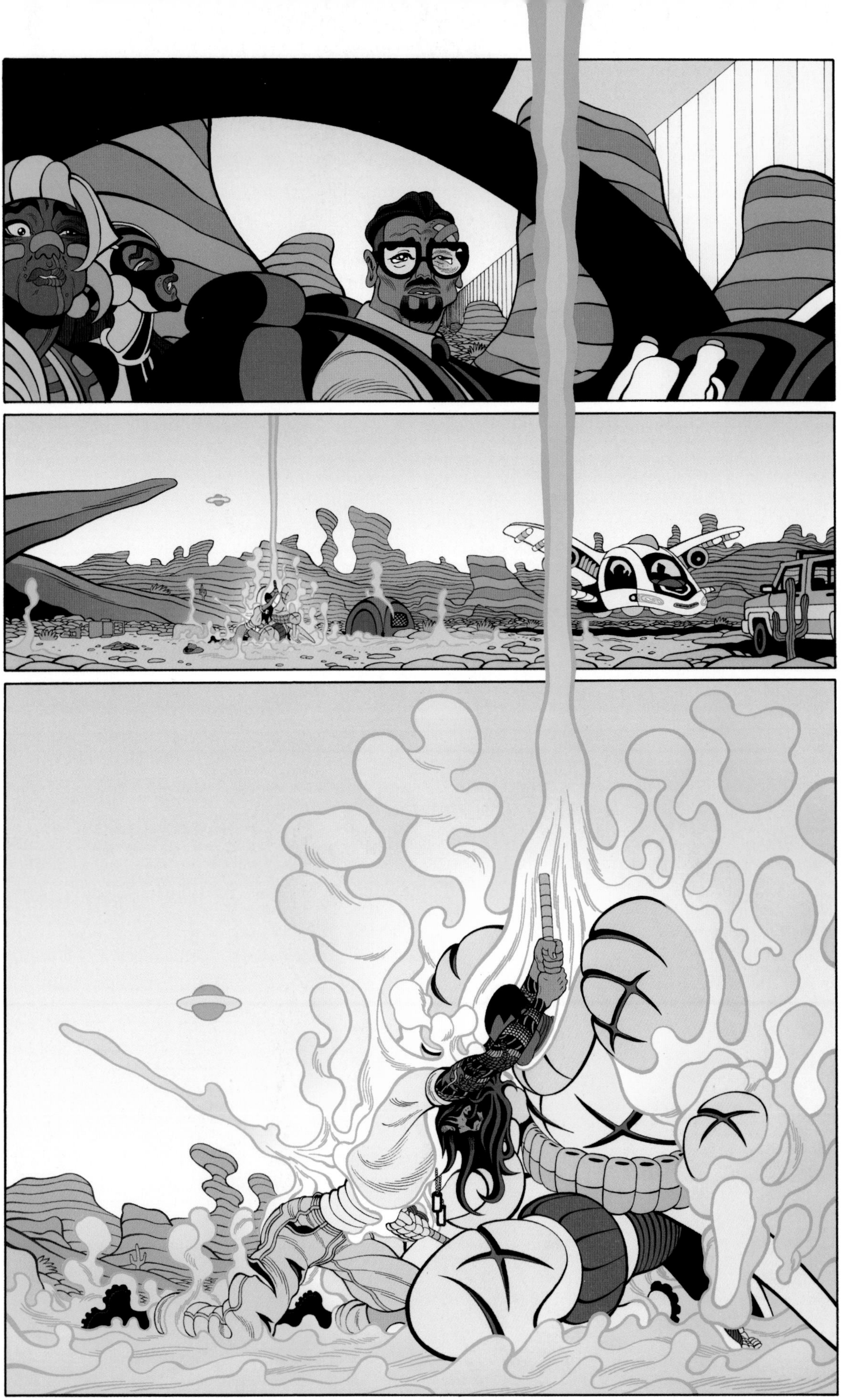

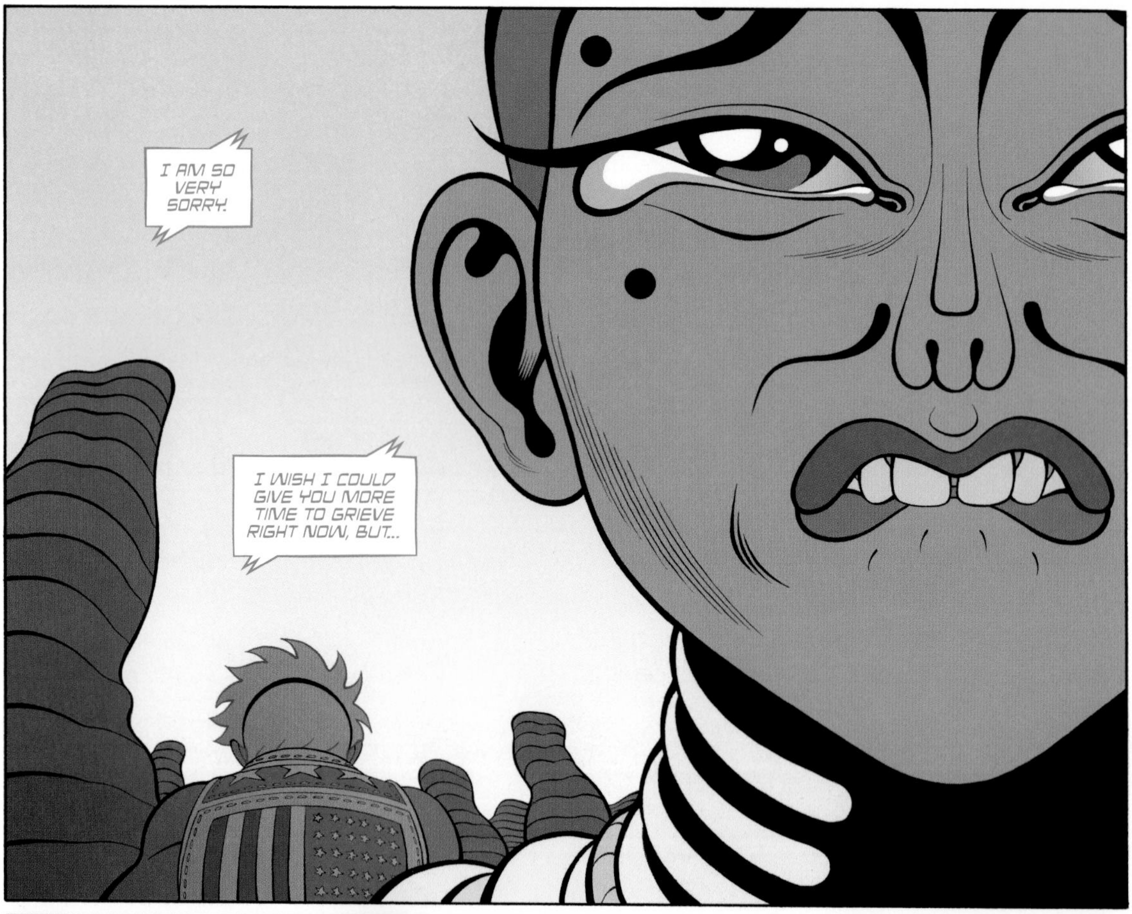
I AM SO VERY SORRY.
I WISH I COULD GIVE YOU MORE TIME TO GRIEVE RIGHT NOW, BUT...

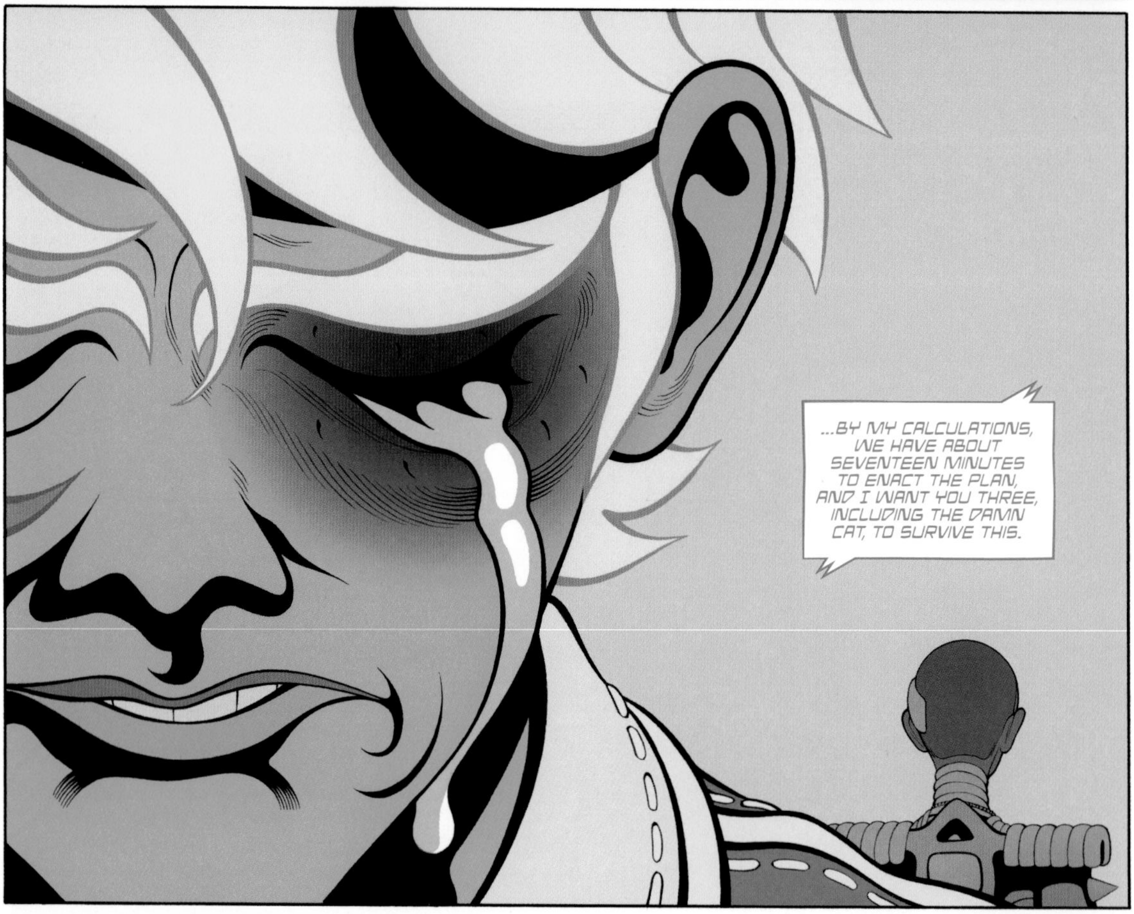
...BY MY CALCULATIONS, WE HAVE ABOUT SEVENTEEN MINUTES TO ENACT THE PLAN, AND I WANT YOU THREE, INCLUDING THE DAMN CAT, TO SURVIVE THIS.

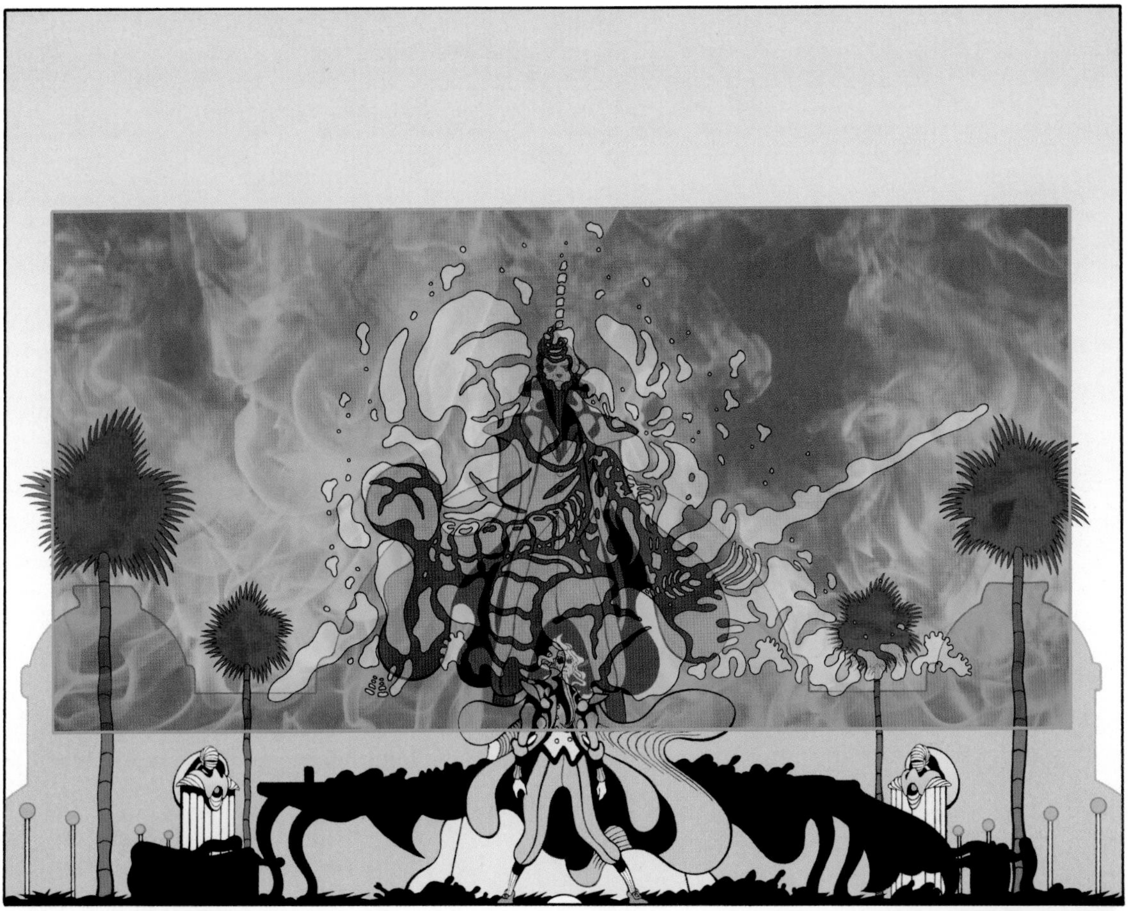

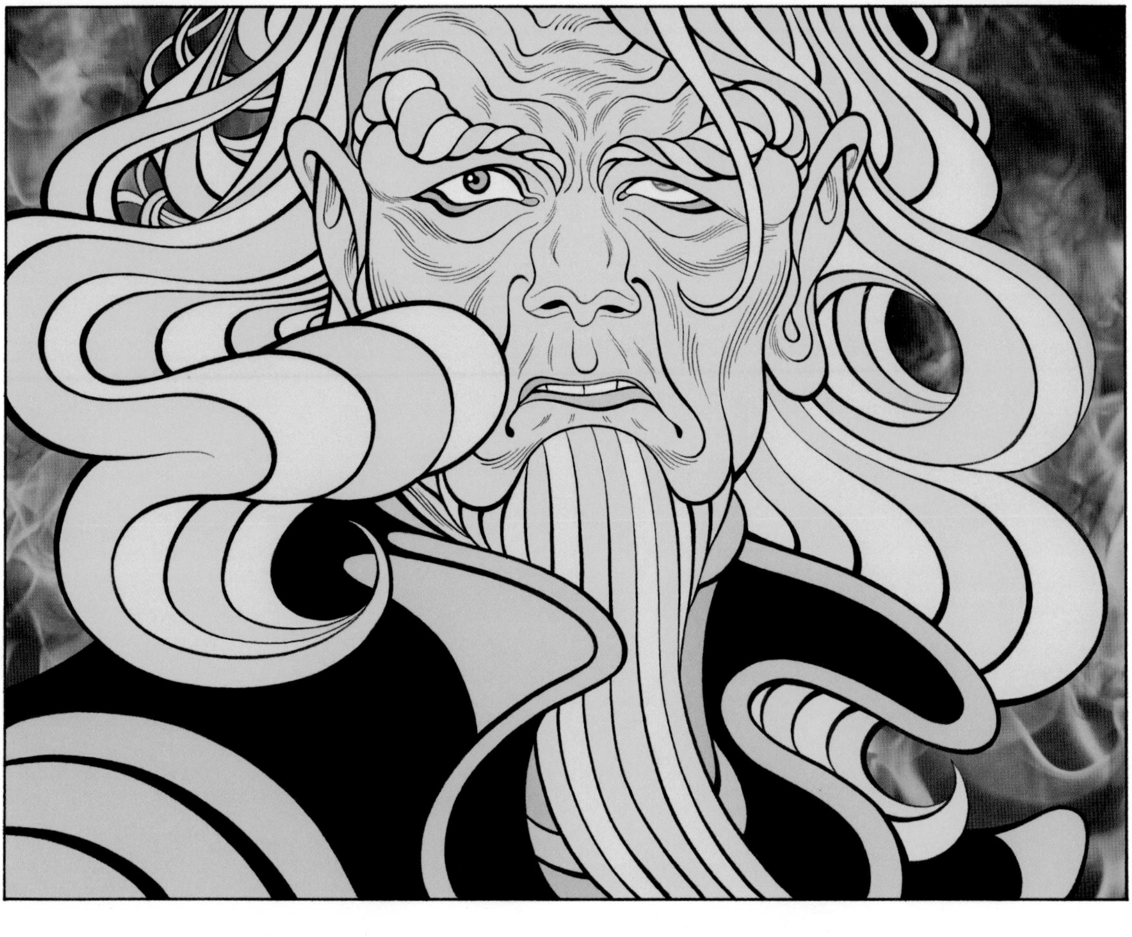

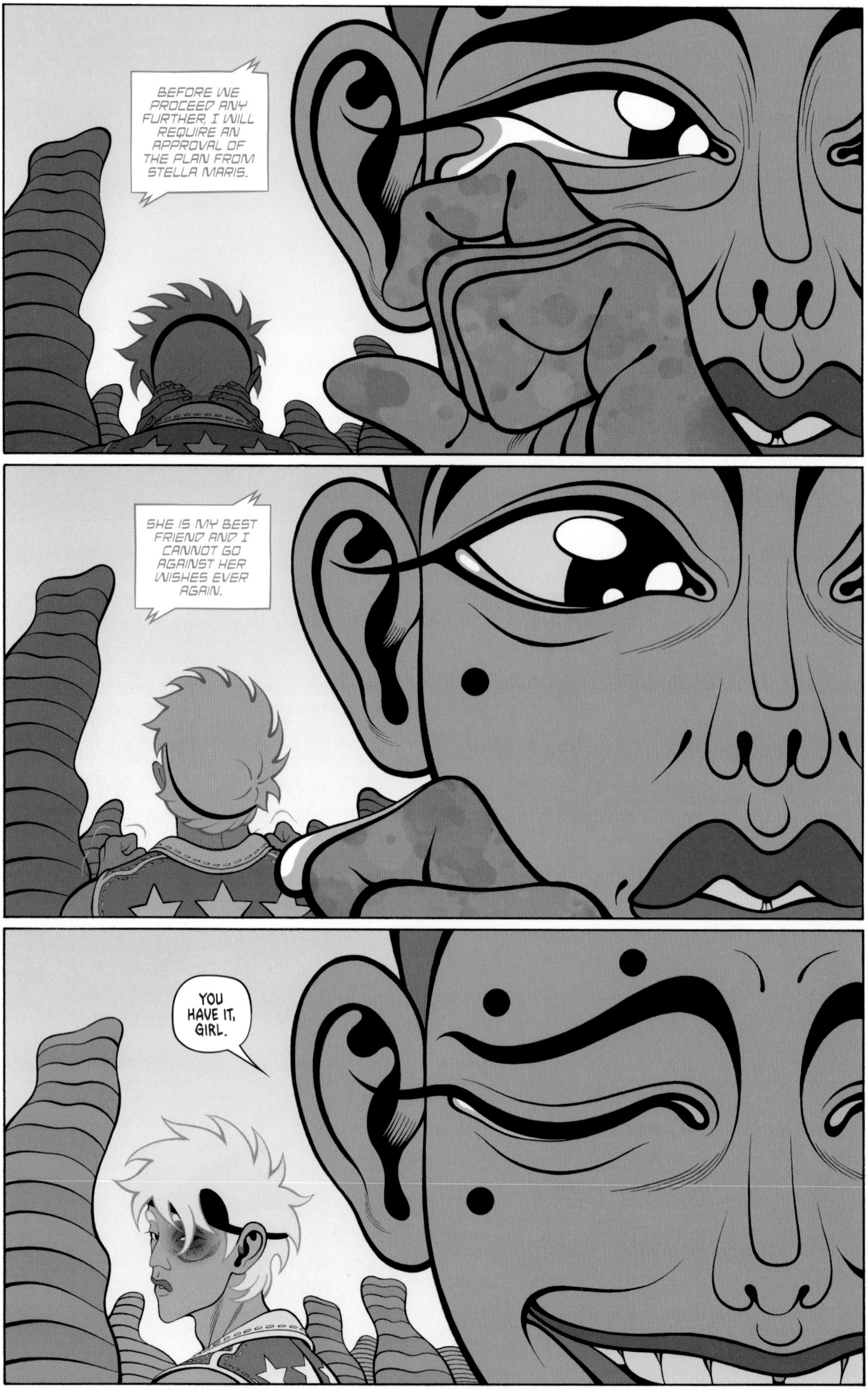
BEFORE WE PROCEED ANY FURTHER, I WILL REQUIRE AN APPROVAL OF THE PLAN FROM STELLA MARIS.
SHE IS MY BEST FRIEND AND I CANNOT GO AGAINST HER WISHES EVER AGAIN.
YOU HAVE IT, GIRL.

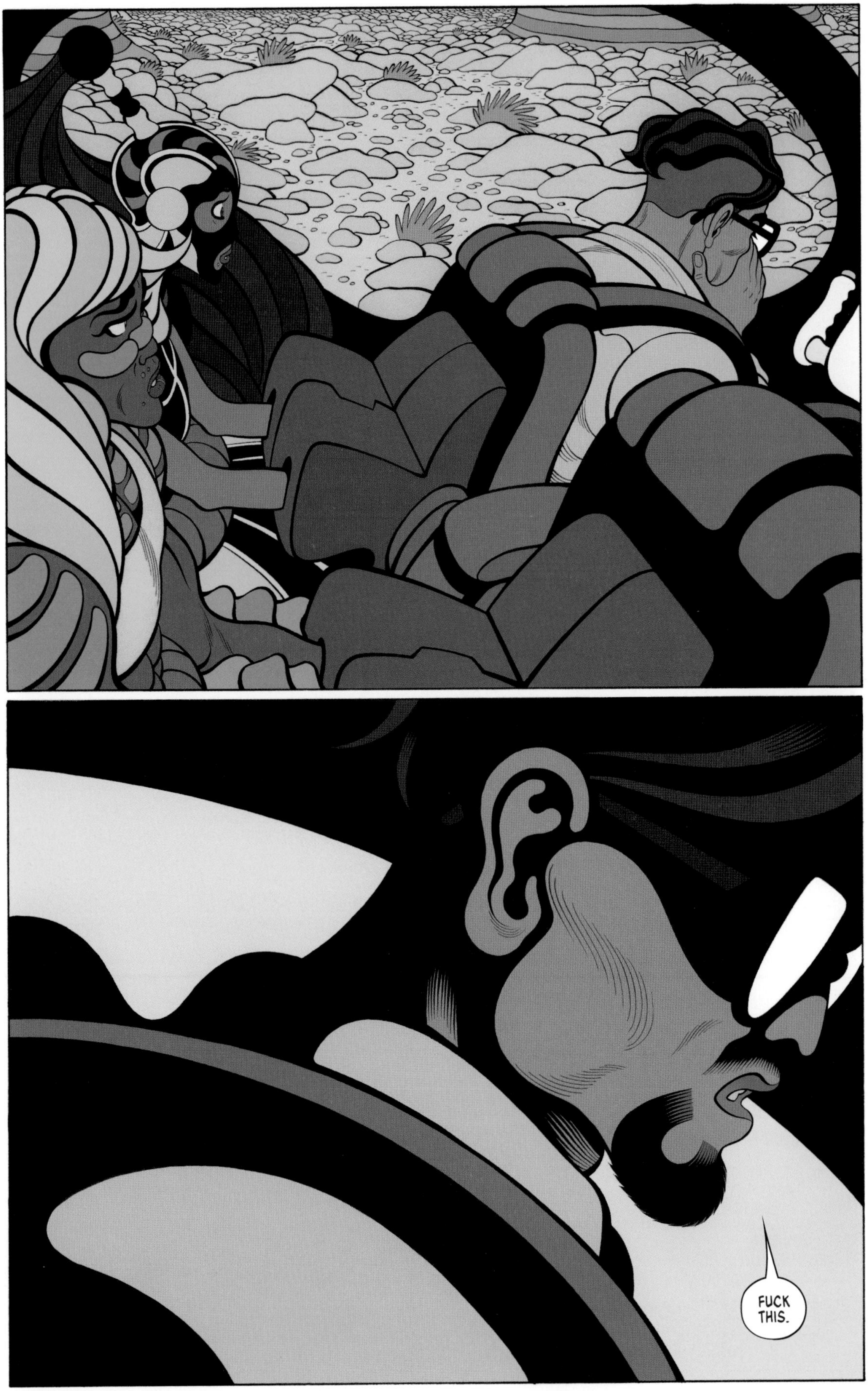
FUCK THIS.

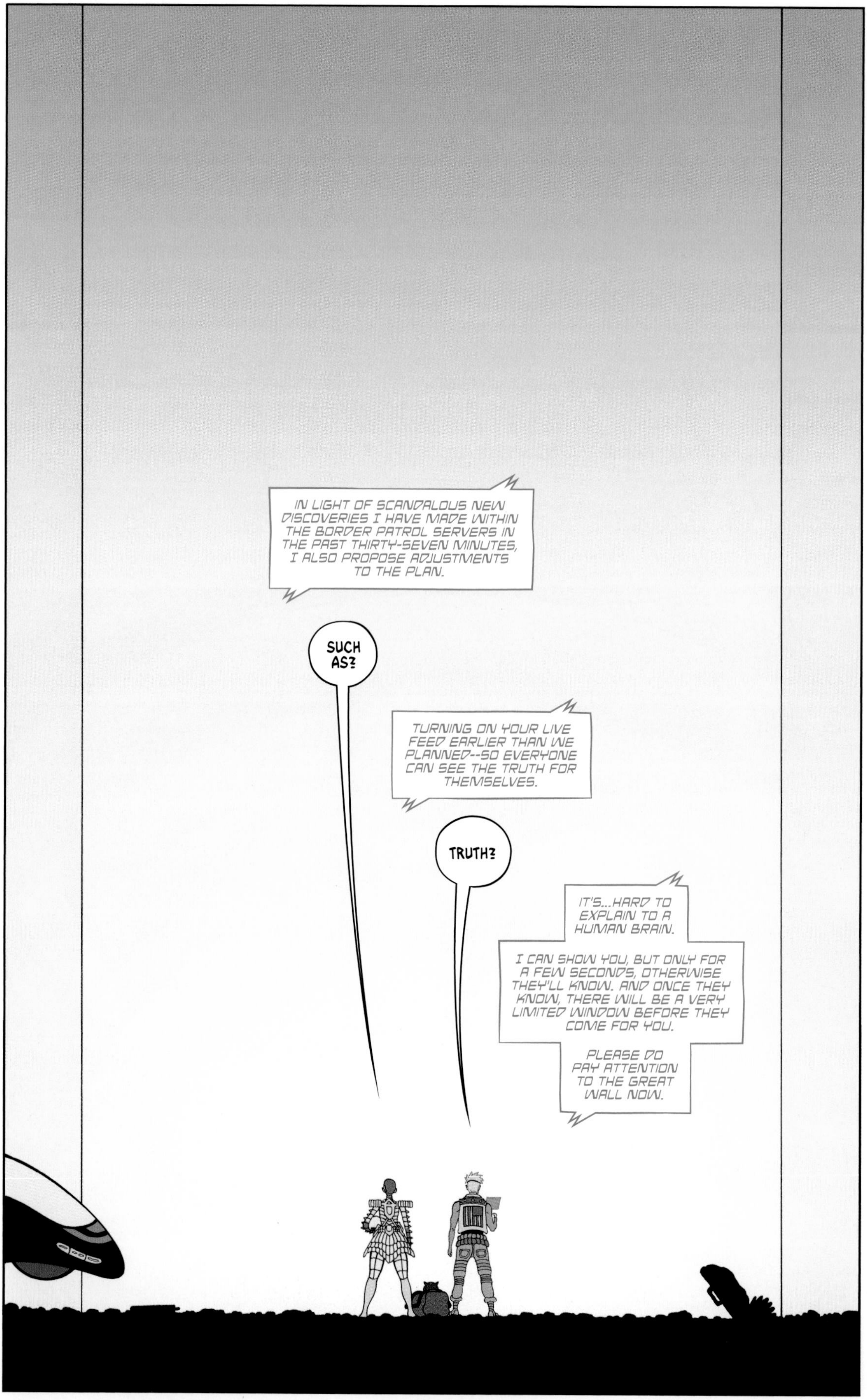
IN LIGHT OF SCANDALOUS NEW DISCOVERIES I HAVE MADE WITHIN THE BORDER PATROL SERVERS IN THE PAST THIRTY-SEVEN MINUTES, I ALSO PROPOSE ADJUSTMENTS TO THE PLAN.
SUCH AS?
TURNING ON YOUR LIVE FEED EARLIER THAN WE PLANNED--SO EVERYONE CAN SEE THE TRUTH FOR THEMSELVES.
TRUTH?
IT'S...HARD TO EXPLAIN TO A HUMAN BRAIN.
I CAN SHOW YOU, BUT ONLY FOR A FEW SECONDS, OTHERWISE THEY'LL KNOW. AND ONCE THEY KNOW, THERE WILL BE A VERY LIMITED WINDOW BEFORE THEY COME FOR YOU.
PLEASE DO PAY ATTENTION TO THE GREAT WALL NOW.

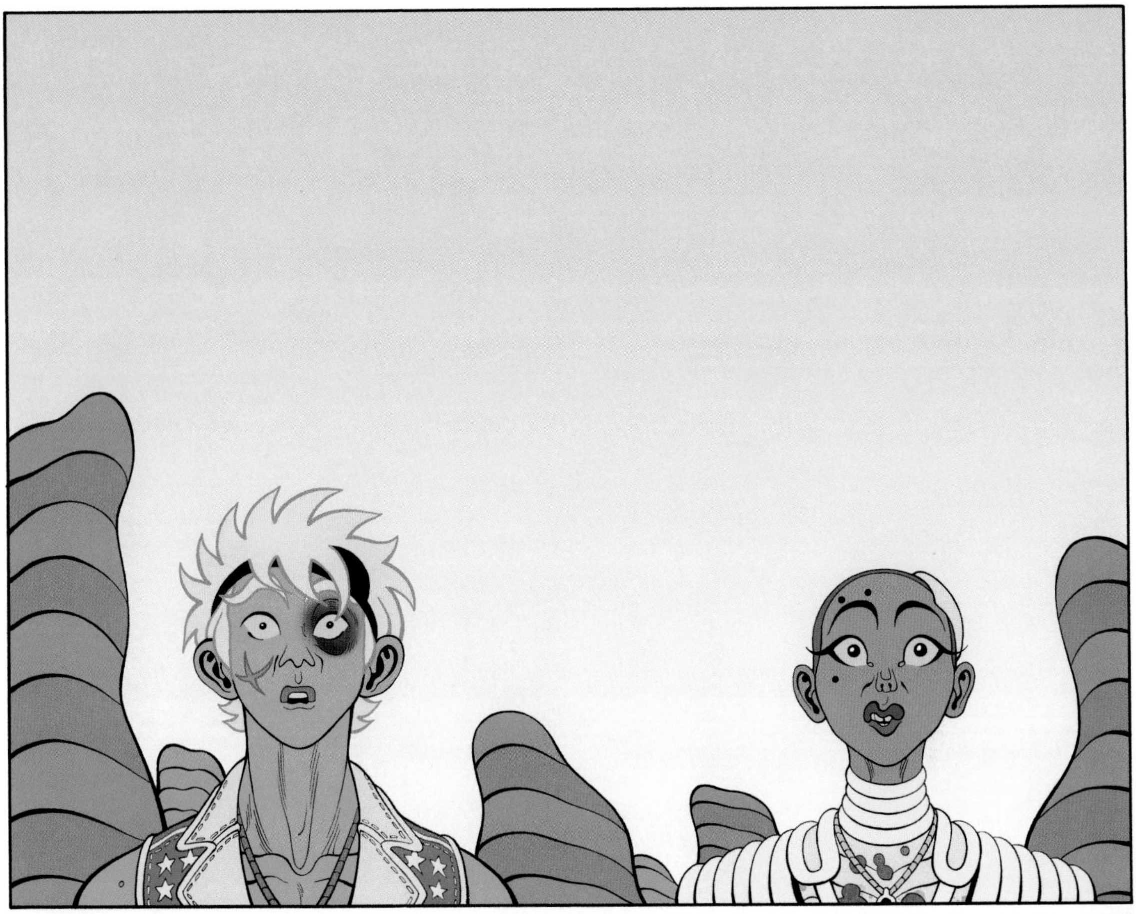

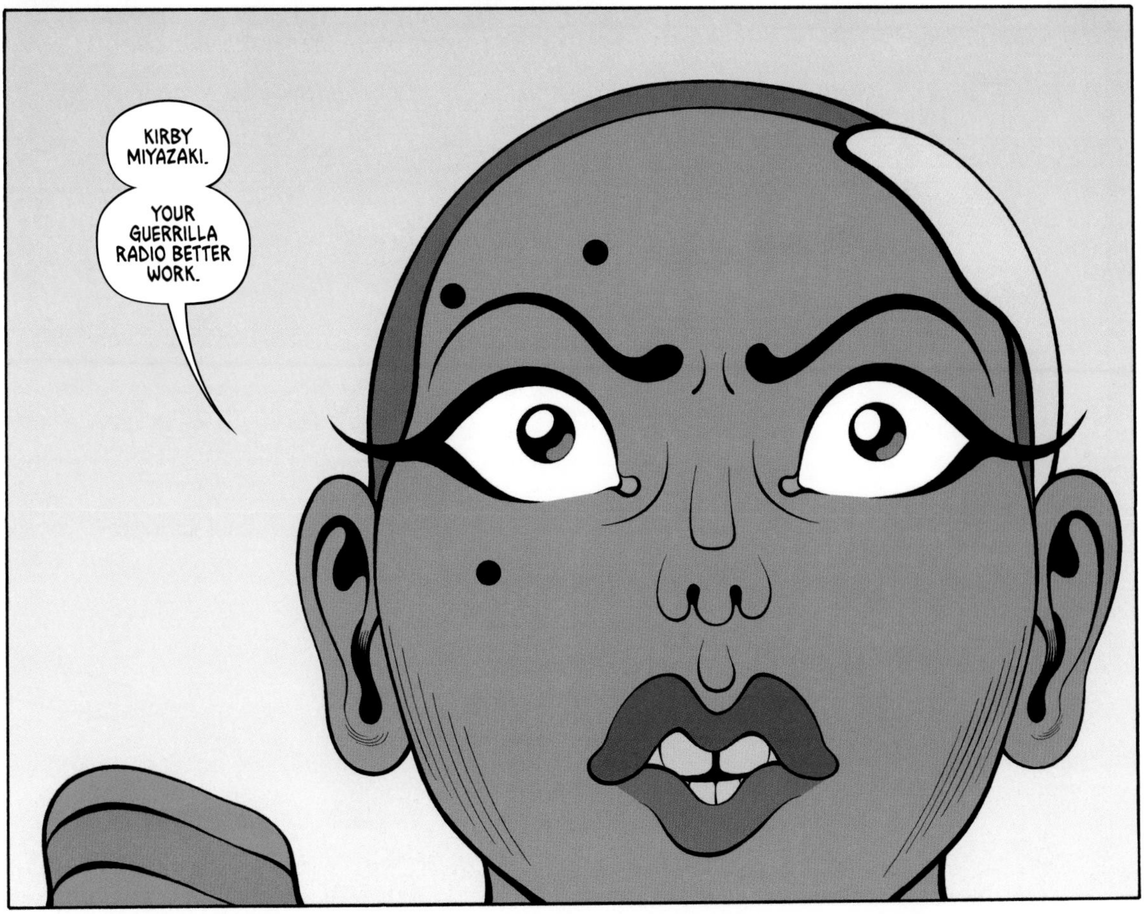
KIRBY MIYAZAKI.
YOUR GUERRILLA RADIO BETTER WORK.

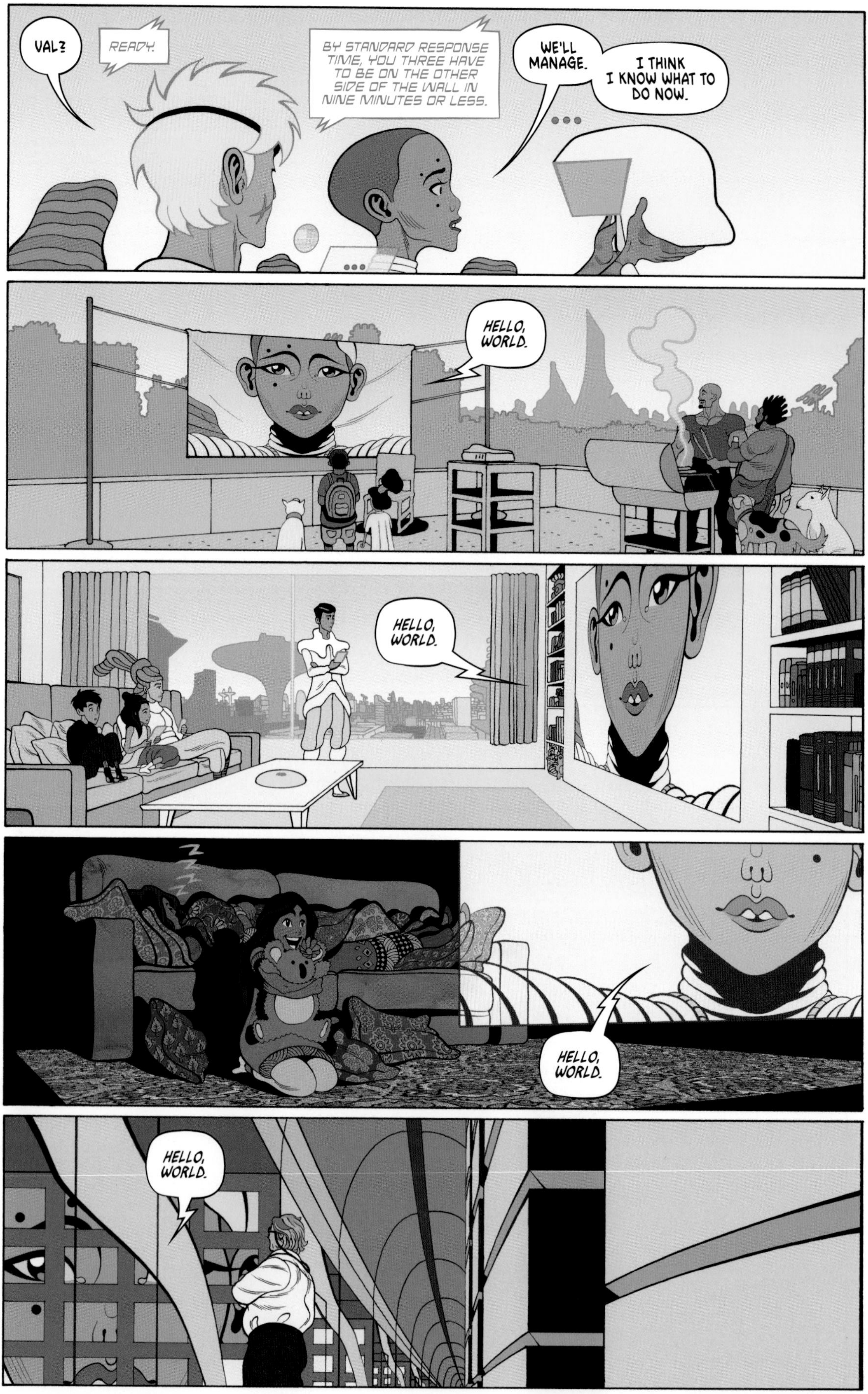
VAL?
READY.
BY STANDARD RESPONSE TIME, YOU THREE HAVE TO BE ON THE OTHER SIDE OF THE WALL IN NINE MINUTES OR LESS.
WE'LL MANAGE.
I THINK I KNOW WHAT TO DO NOW.
HELLO, WORLD.
HELLO, WORLD.
HELLO, WORLD.
HELLO, WORLD.

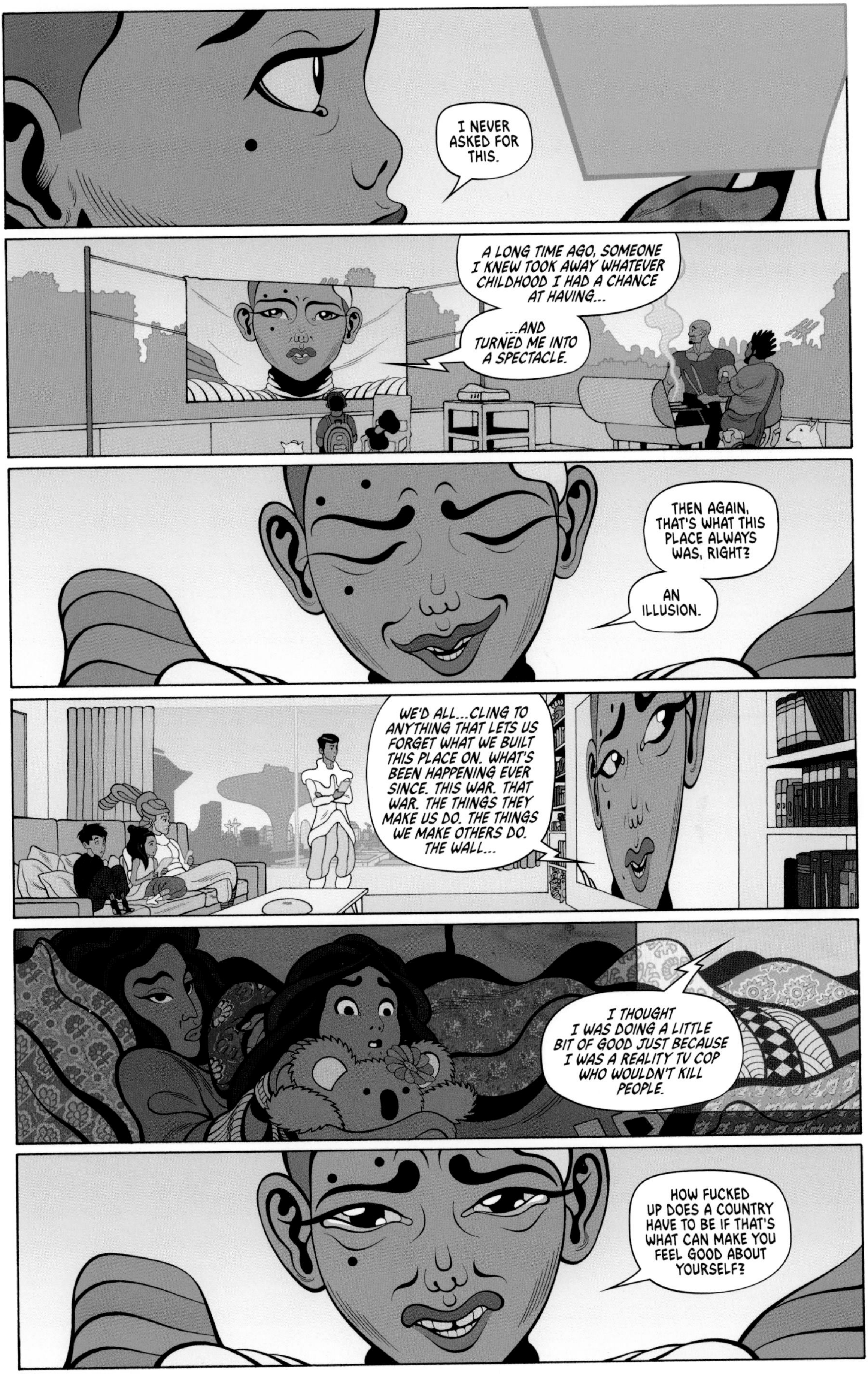
I NEVER ASKED FOR THIS.
A LONG TIME AGO, SOMEONE I KNEW TOOK AWAY WHATEVER CHILDHOOD I HAD A CHANCE AT HAVING...
...AND TURNED ME INTO A SPECTACLE.
THEN AGAIN, THAT'S WHAT THIS PLACE ALWAYS WAS, RIGHT?
AN ILLUSION.
WE'D ALL...CLING TO ANYTHING THAT LETS US FORGET WHAT WE BUILT THIS PLACE ON. WHAT'S BEEN HAPPENING EVER SINCE. THIS WAR. THAT WAR. THE THINGS THEY MAKE US DO. THE THINGS WE MAKE OTHERS DO. THE WALL...
I THOUGHT I WAS DOING A LITTLE BIT OF GOOD JUST BECAUSE I WAS A REALITY TV COP WHO WOULDN'T KILL PEOPLE.
HOW FUCKED UP DOES A COUNTRY HAVE TO BE IF THAT'S WHAT CAN MAKE YOU FEEL GOOD ABOUT YOURSELF?

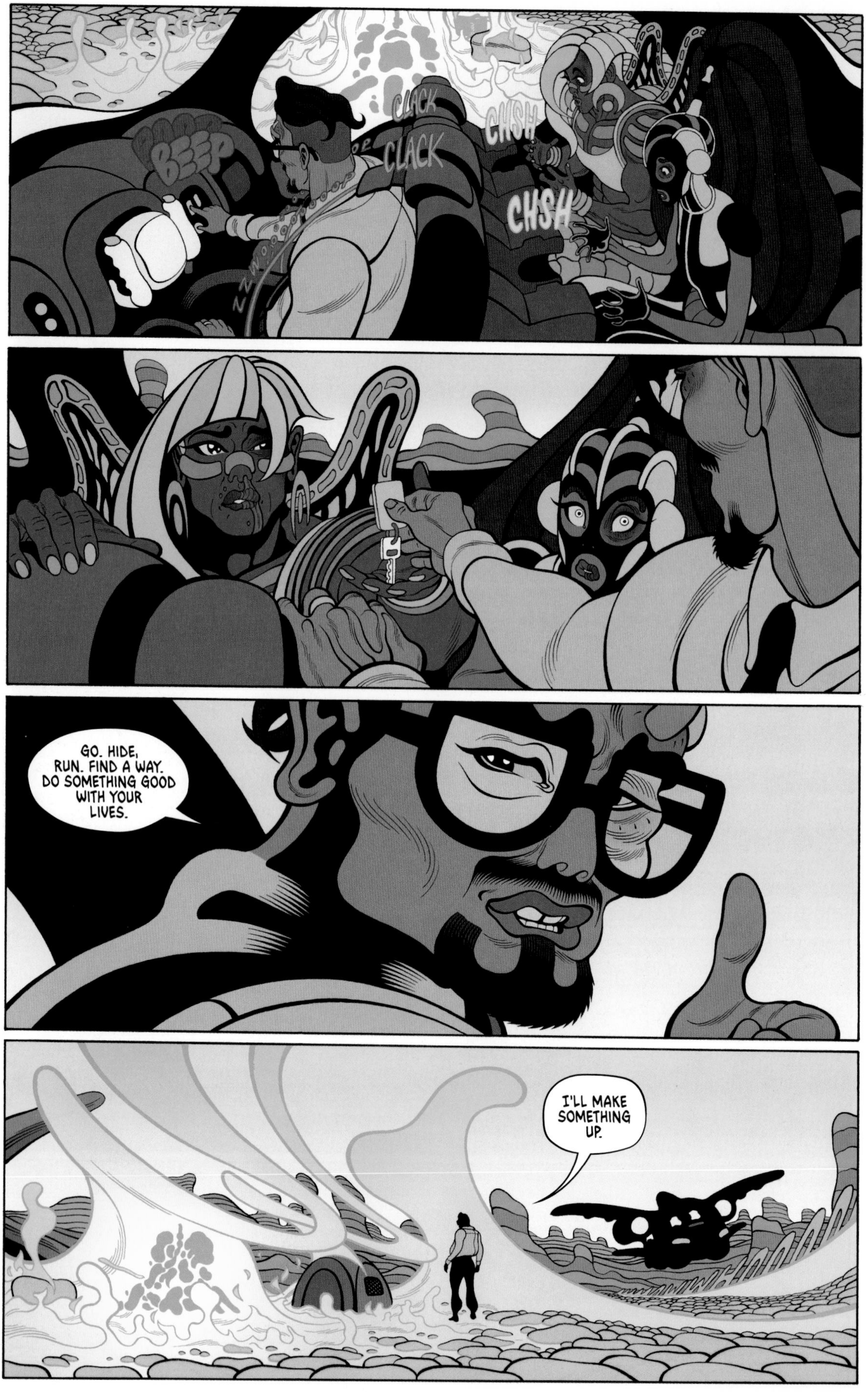
BEEP
CLACK
CLACK
CHSH
CHSH
GO. HIDE, RUN. FIND A WAY. DO SOMETHING GOOD WITH YOUR LIVES.
I'LL MAKE SOMETHING UP.

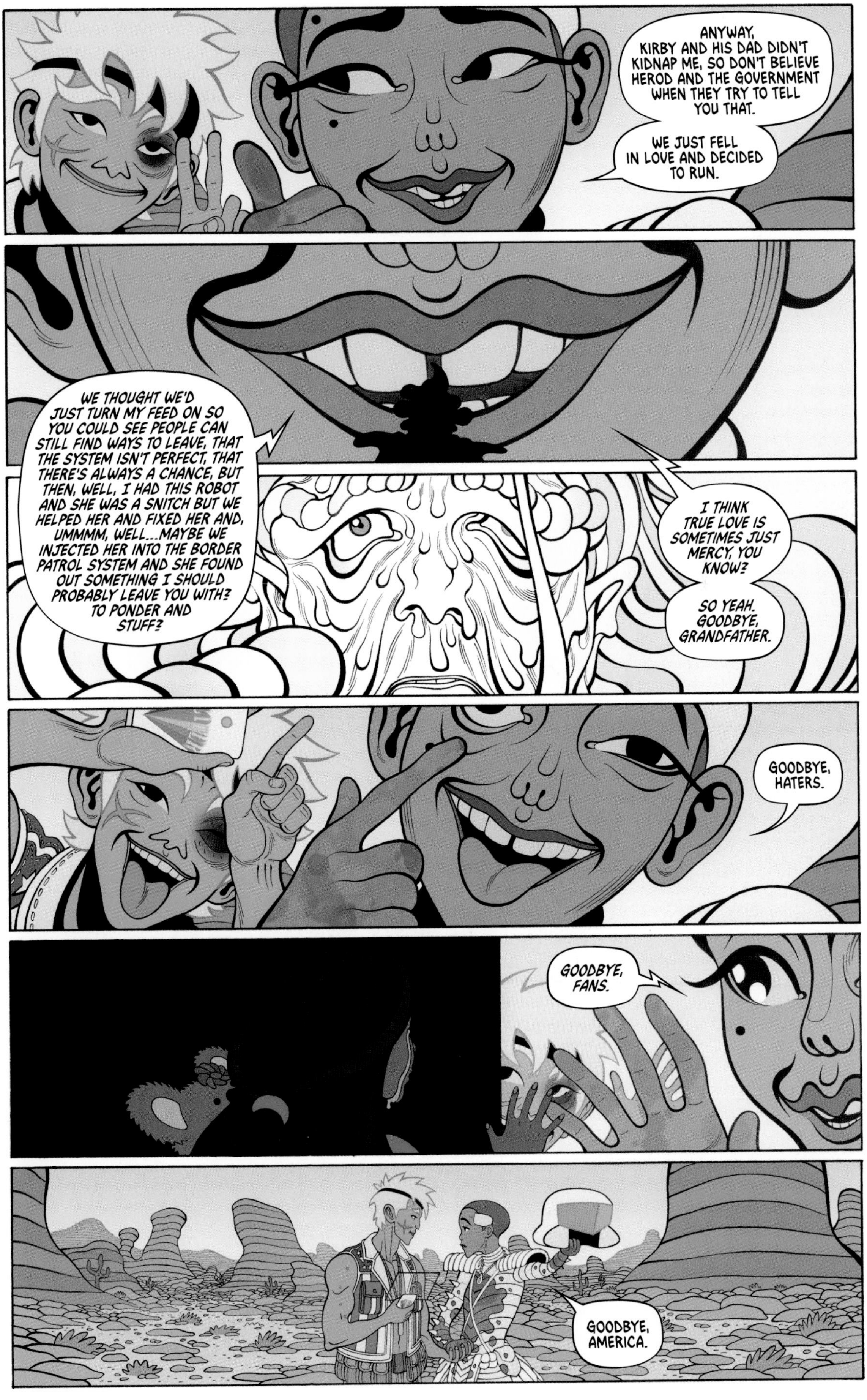
ANYWAY, KIRBY AND HIS DAD DIDN'T KIDNAP ME, SO DON'T BELIEVE HEROD AND THE GOVERNMENT WHEN THEY TRY TO TELL YOU THAT.
WE JUST FELL IN LOVE AND DECIDED TO RUN.
WE THOUGHT WE'D JUST TURN MY FEED ON SO YOU COULD SEE PEOPLE CAN STILL FIND WAYS TO LEAVE, THAT THE SYSTEM ISN'T PERFECT, THAT THERE'S ALWAYS A CHANCE, BUT THEN, WELL, I HAD THIS ROBOT AND SHE WAS A SNITCH BUT WE HELPED HER AND FIXED HER AND, UMMMM, WELL...MAYBE WE INJECTED HER INTO THE BORDER PATROL SYSTEM AND SHE FOUND OUT SOMETHING I SHOULD PROBABLY LEAVE YOU WITH? TO PONDER AND STUFF?
I THINK TRUE LOVE IS SOMETIMES JUST MERCY, YOU KNOW?
SO YEAH. GOODBYE, GRANDFATHER.
GOODBYE, HATERS.
GOODBYE, FANS.
GOODBYE, AMERICA.

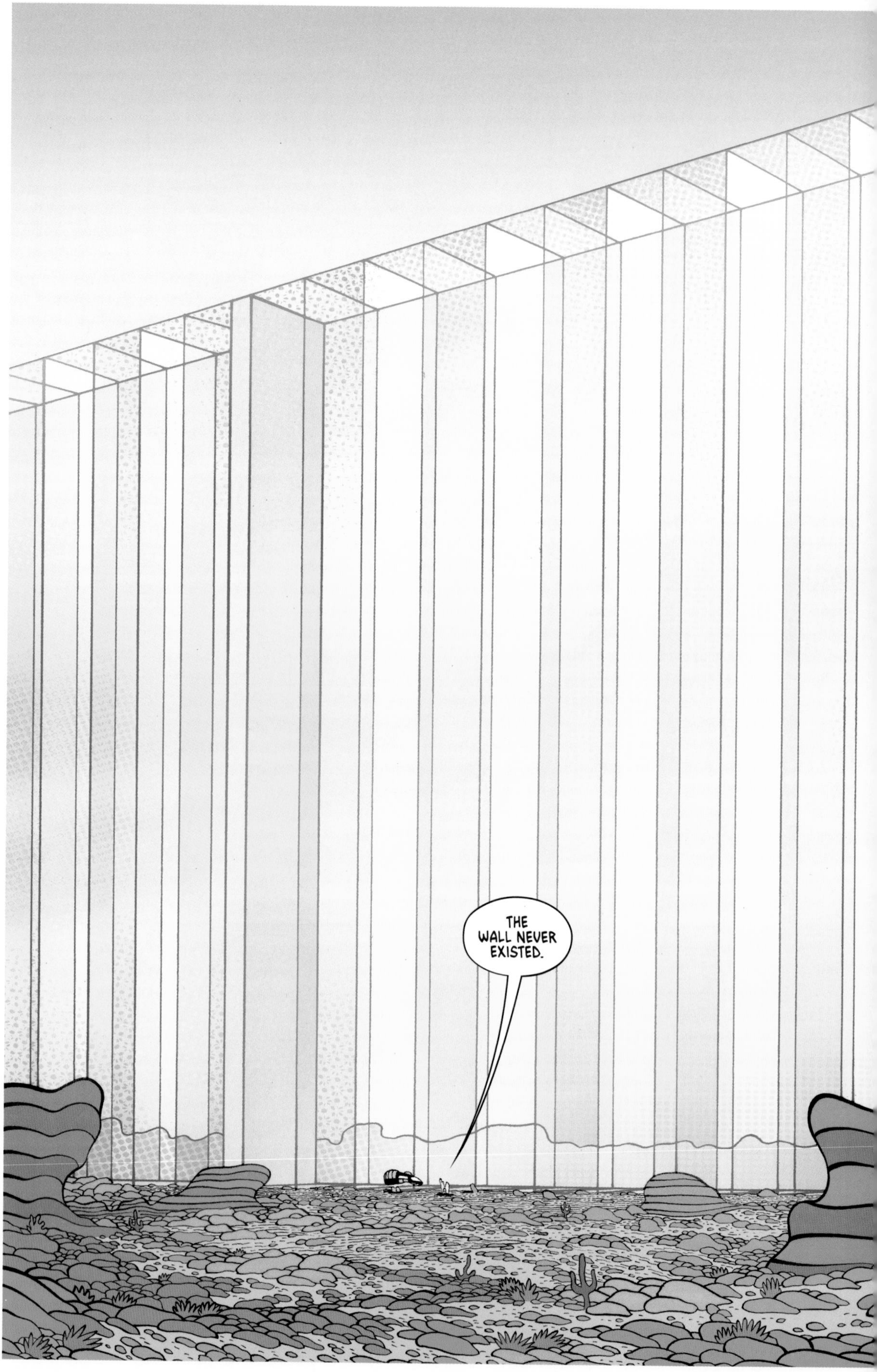
THE WALL NEVER EXISTED.

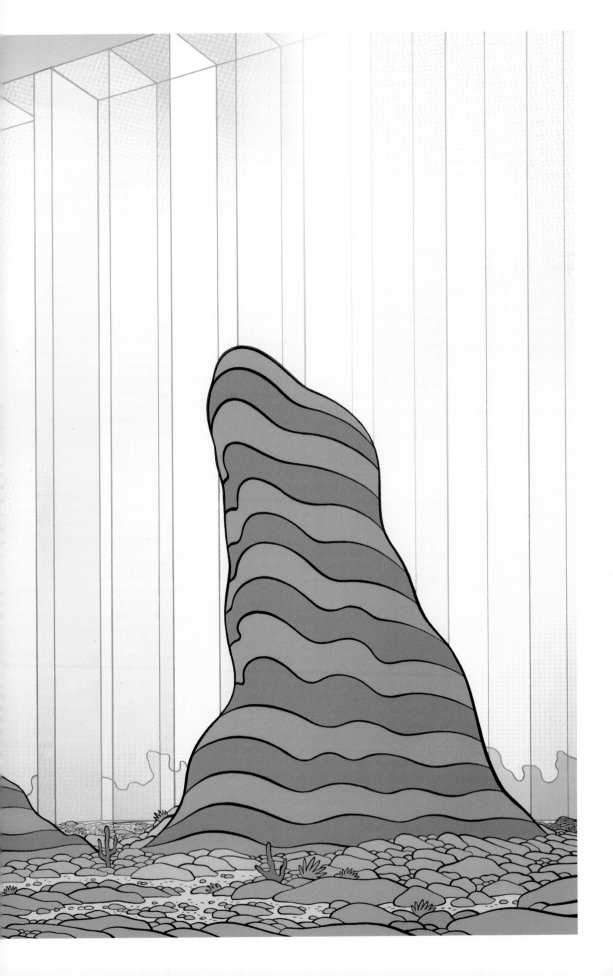

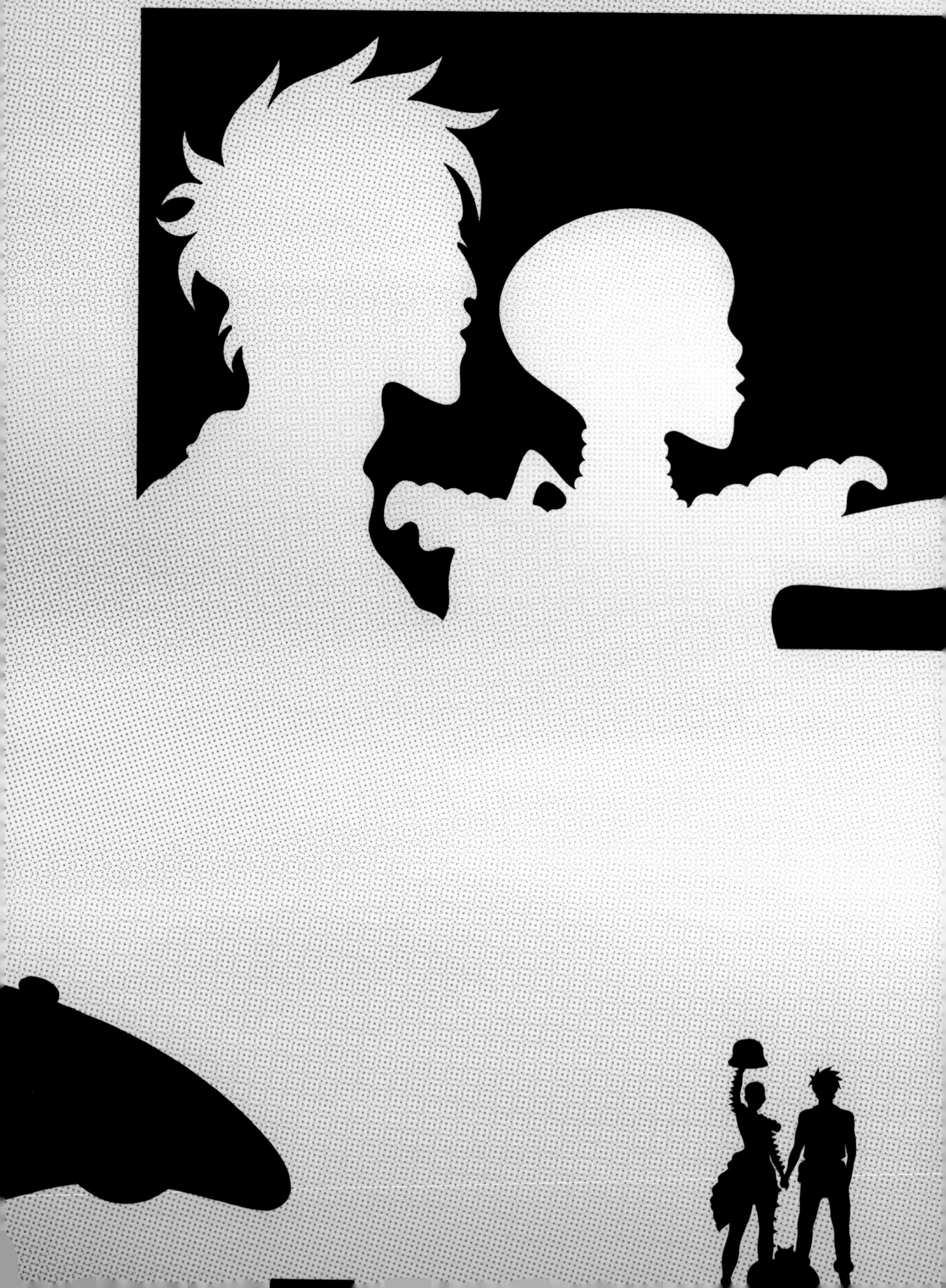

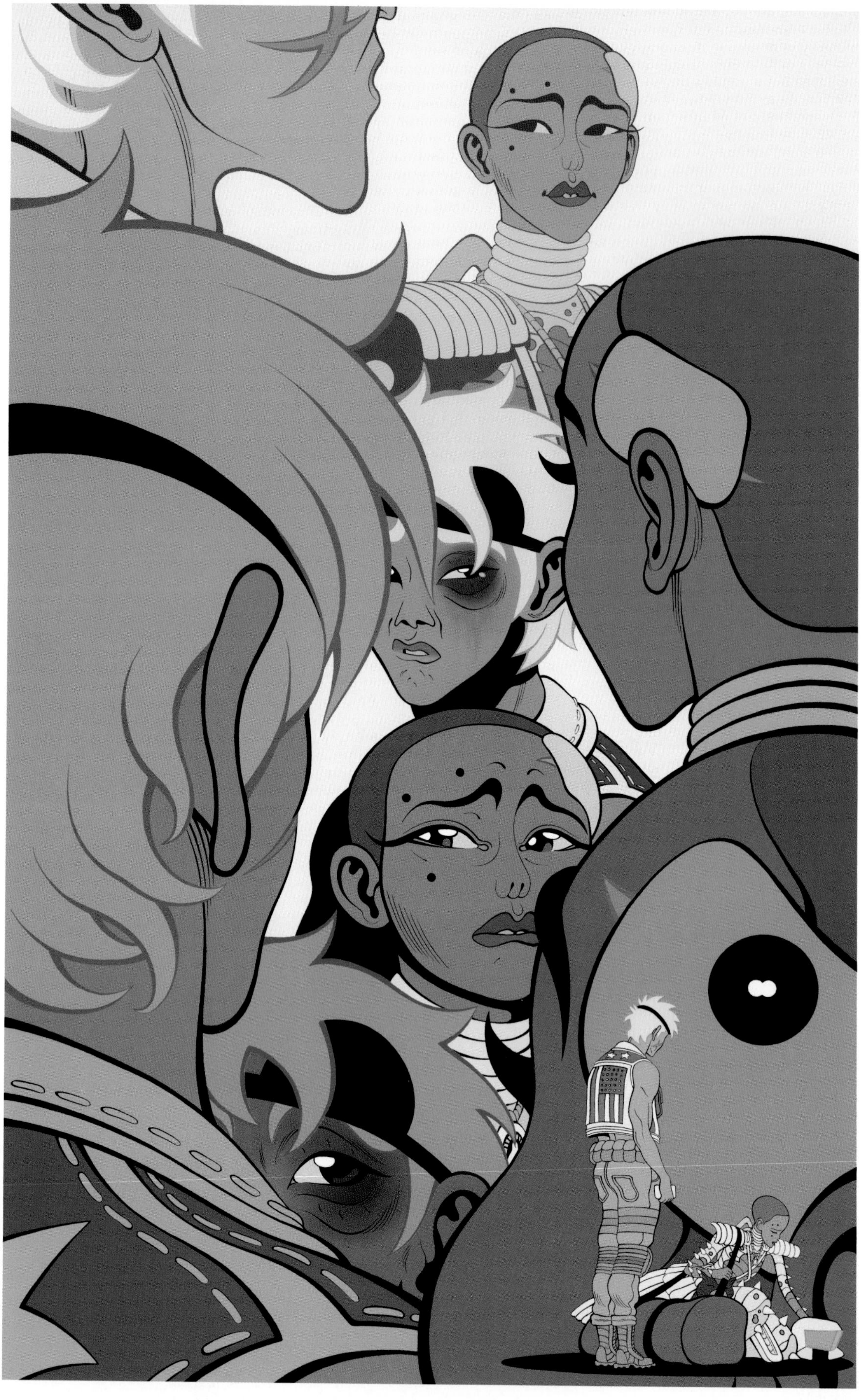

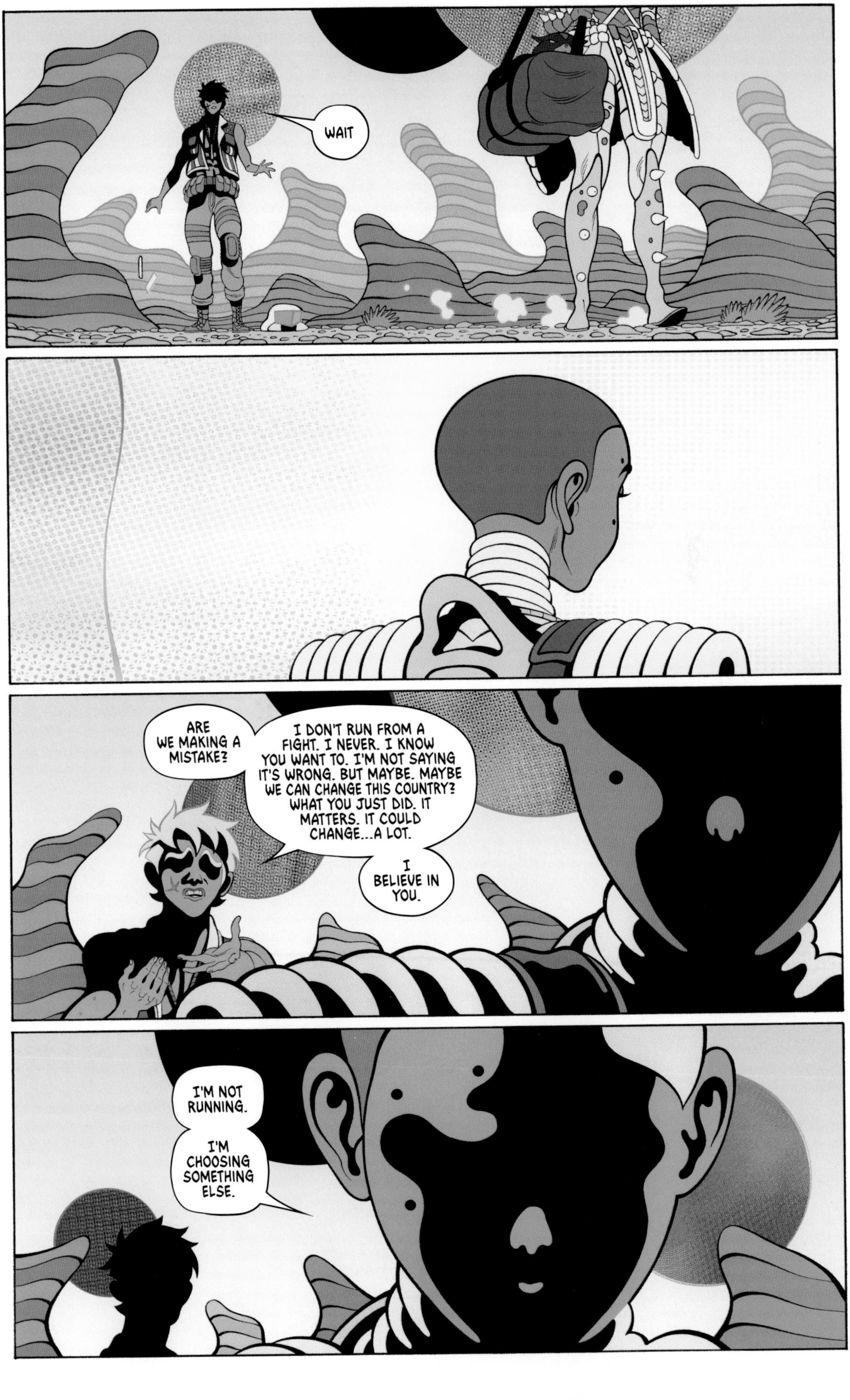
WAIT
ARE WE MAKING A MISTAKE?
I DON'T RUN FROM A FIGHT. I NEVER. I KNOW YOU WANT TO. I'M NOT SAYING IT'S WRONG. BUT MAYBE. MAYBE WE CAN CHANGE THIS COUNTRY? WHAT YOU JUST DID. IT MATTERS. IT COULD CHANGE...A LOT.
I BELIEVE IN YOU.
I'M NOT RUNNING.
I'M CHOOSING SOMETHING ELSE.

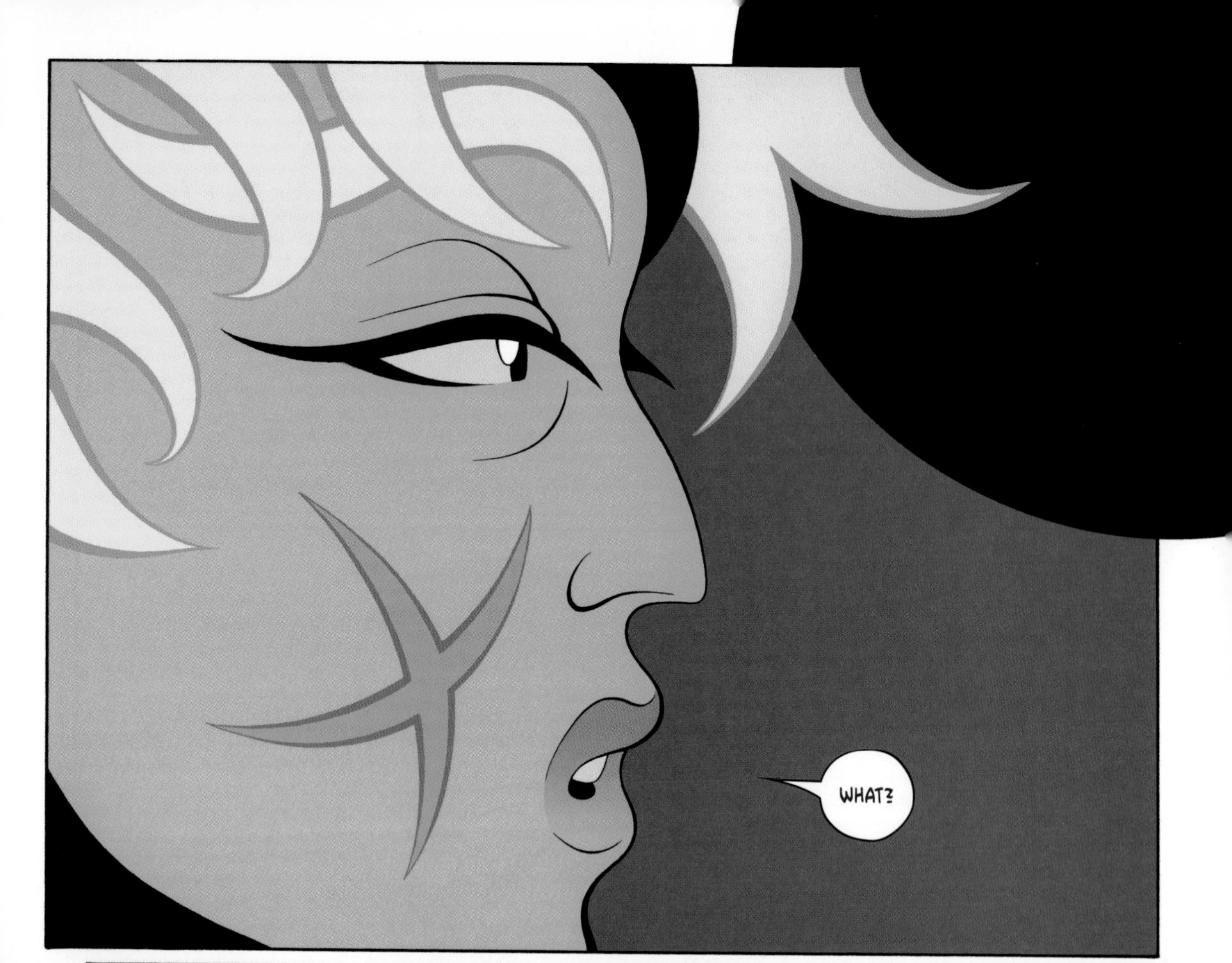
WHAT?

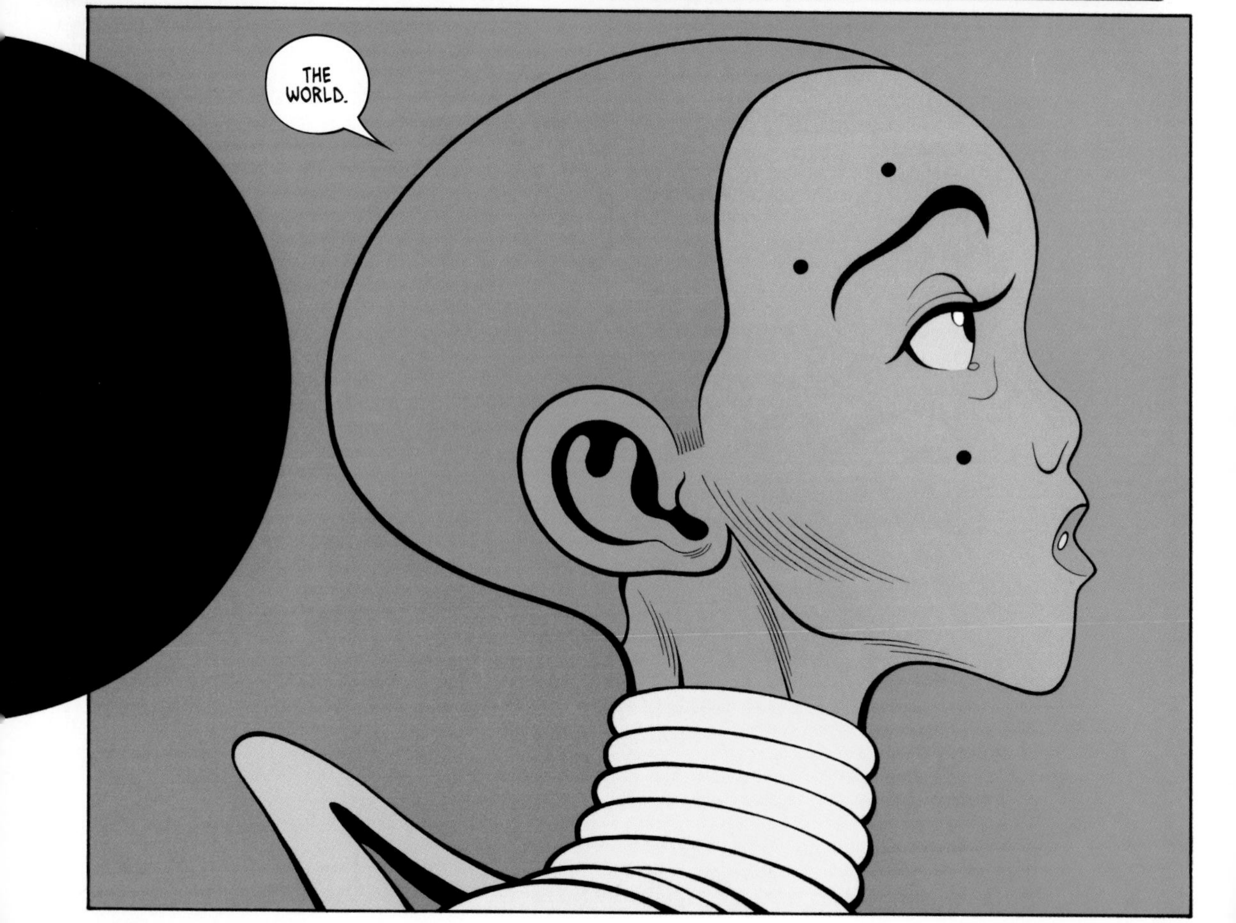
THE WORLD.

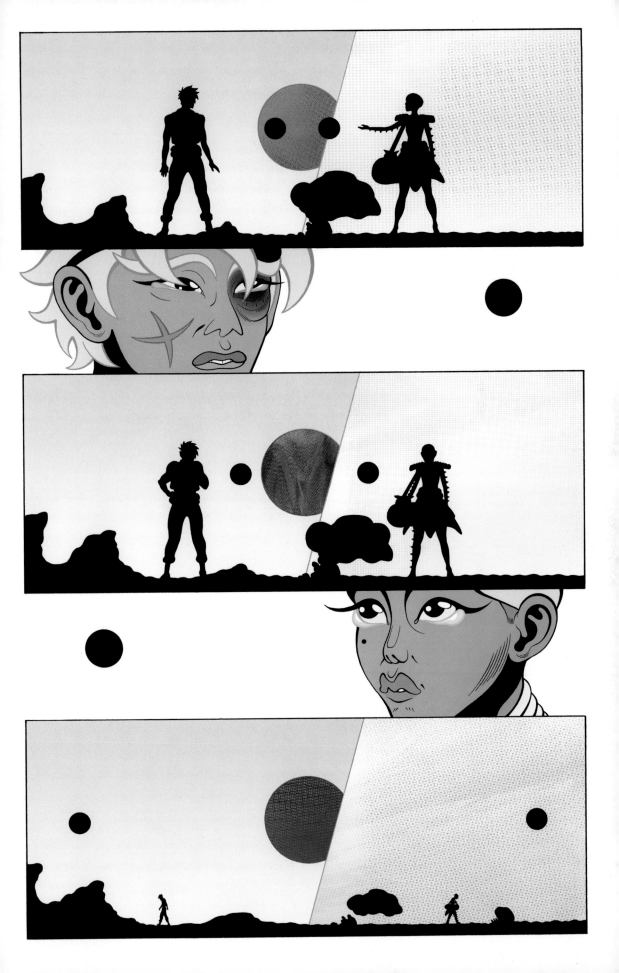

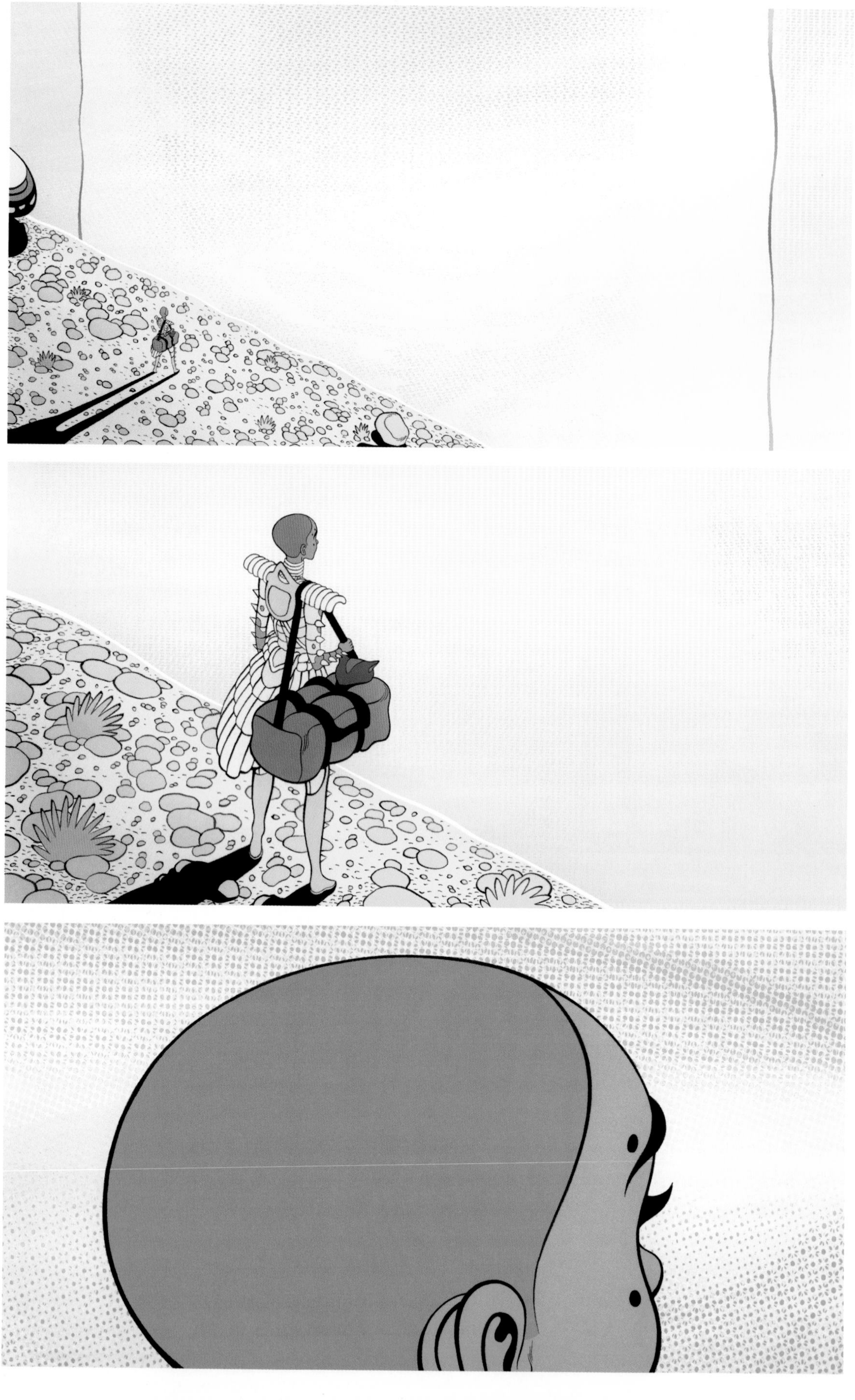

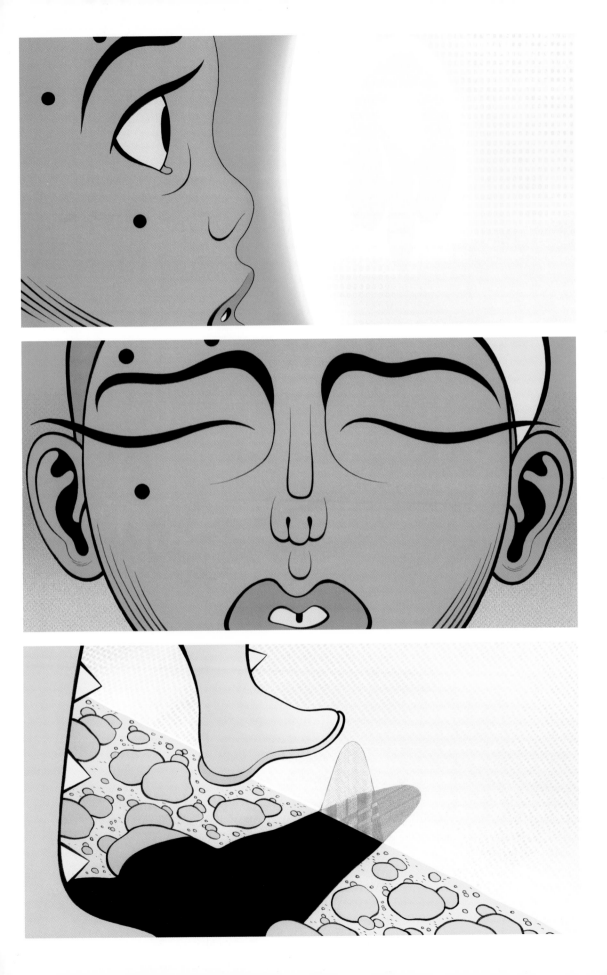

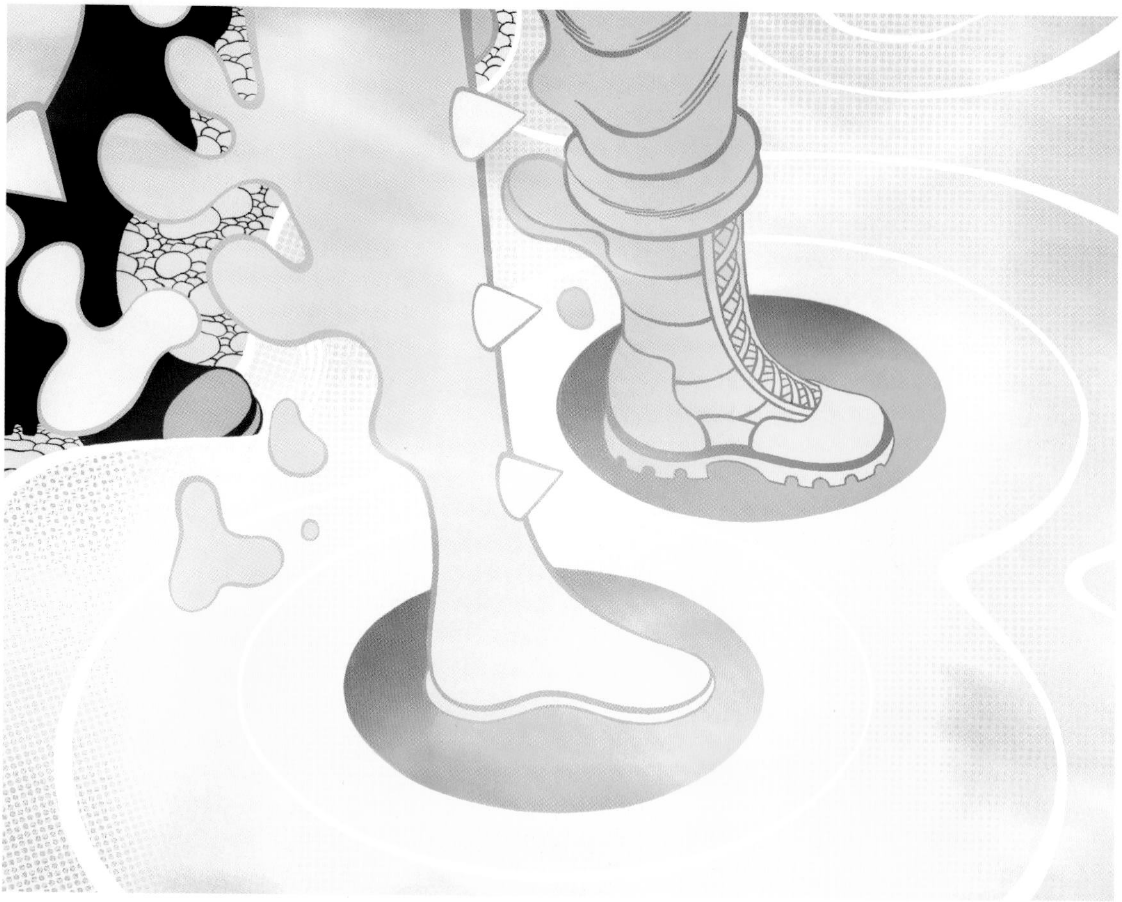

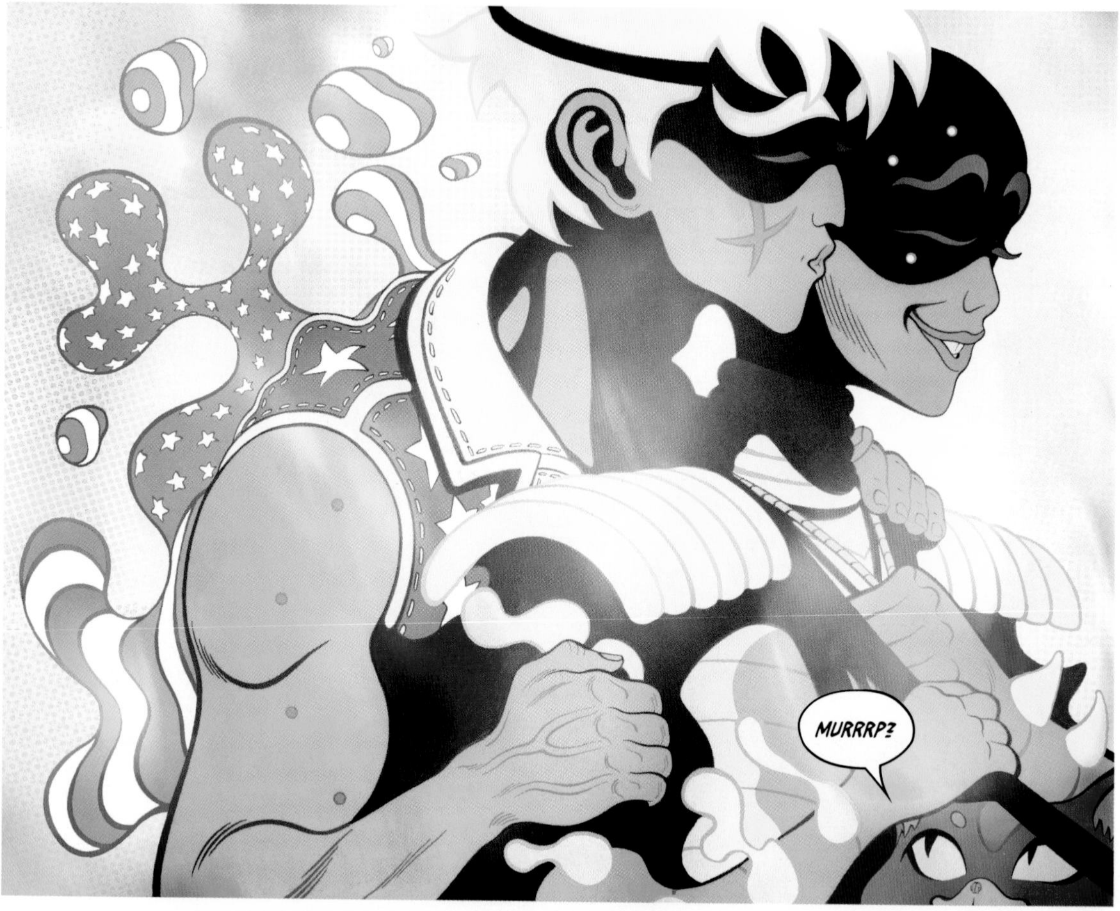
MURRRP?

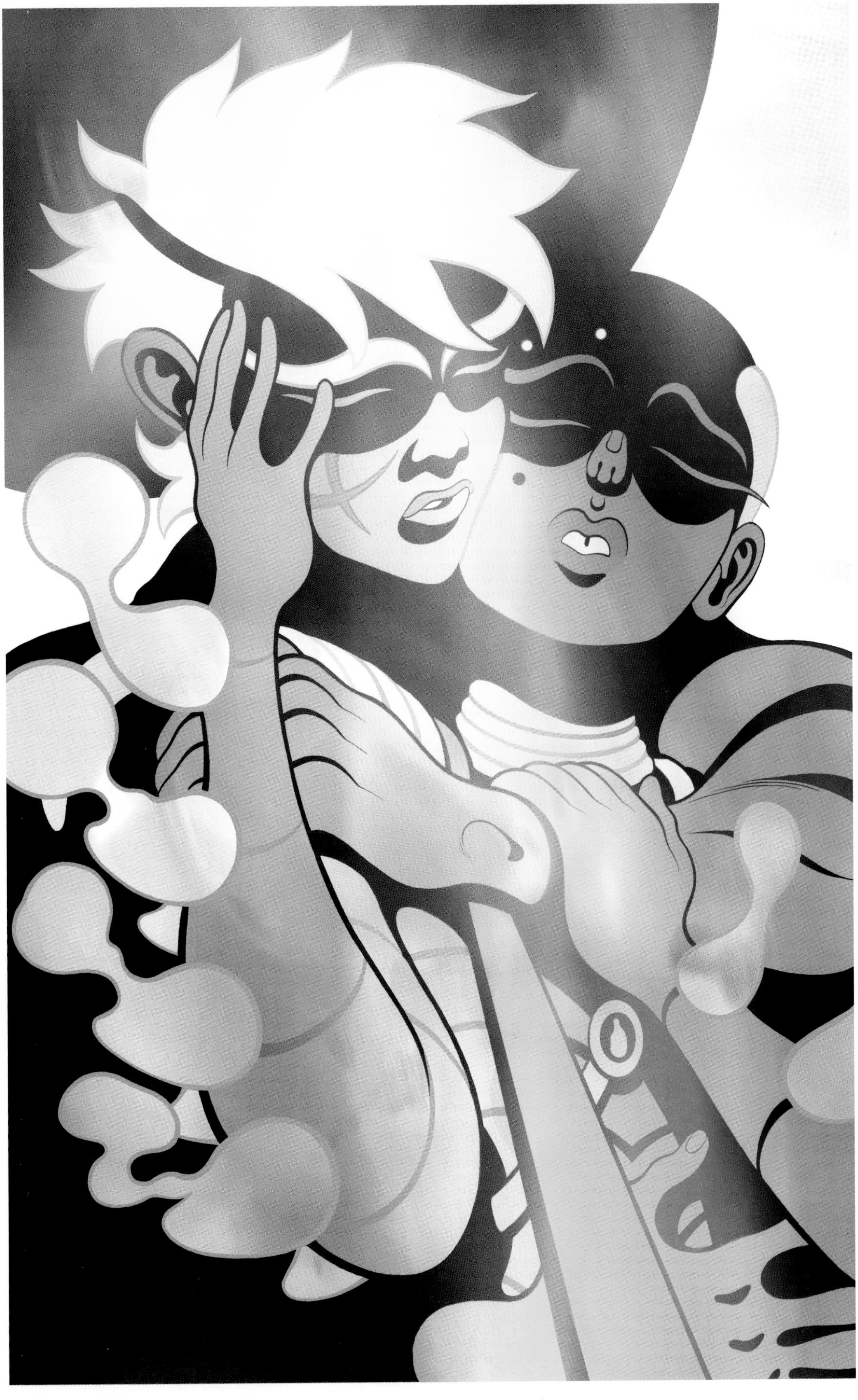

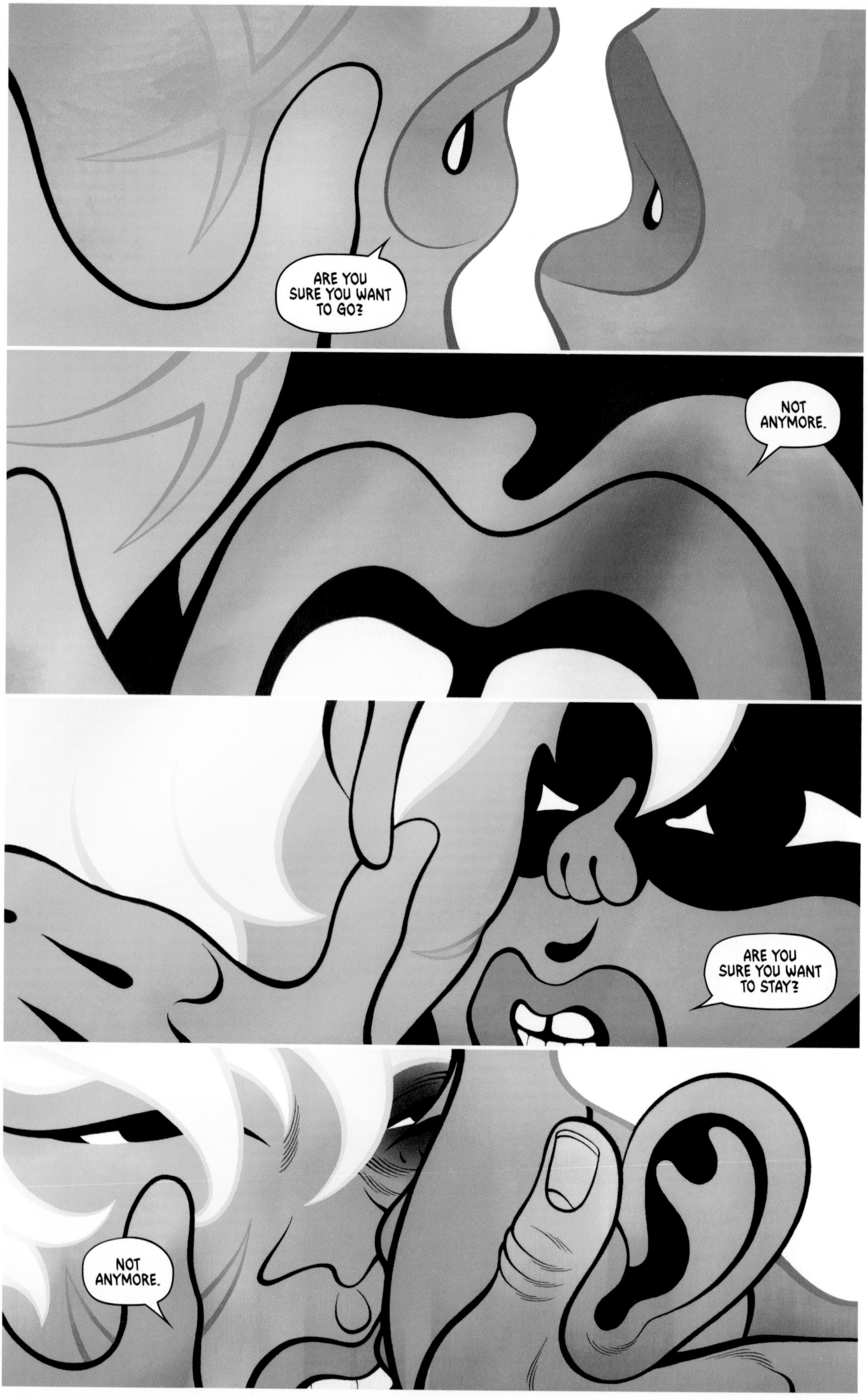
ARE YOU SURE YOU WANT TO GO?
NOT ANYMORE.
ARE YOU SURE YOU WANT TO STAY?
NOT ANYMORE.

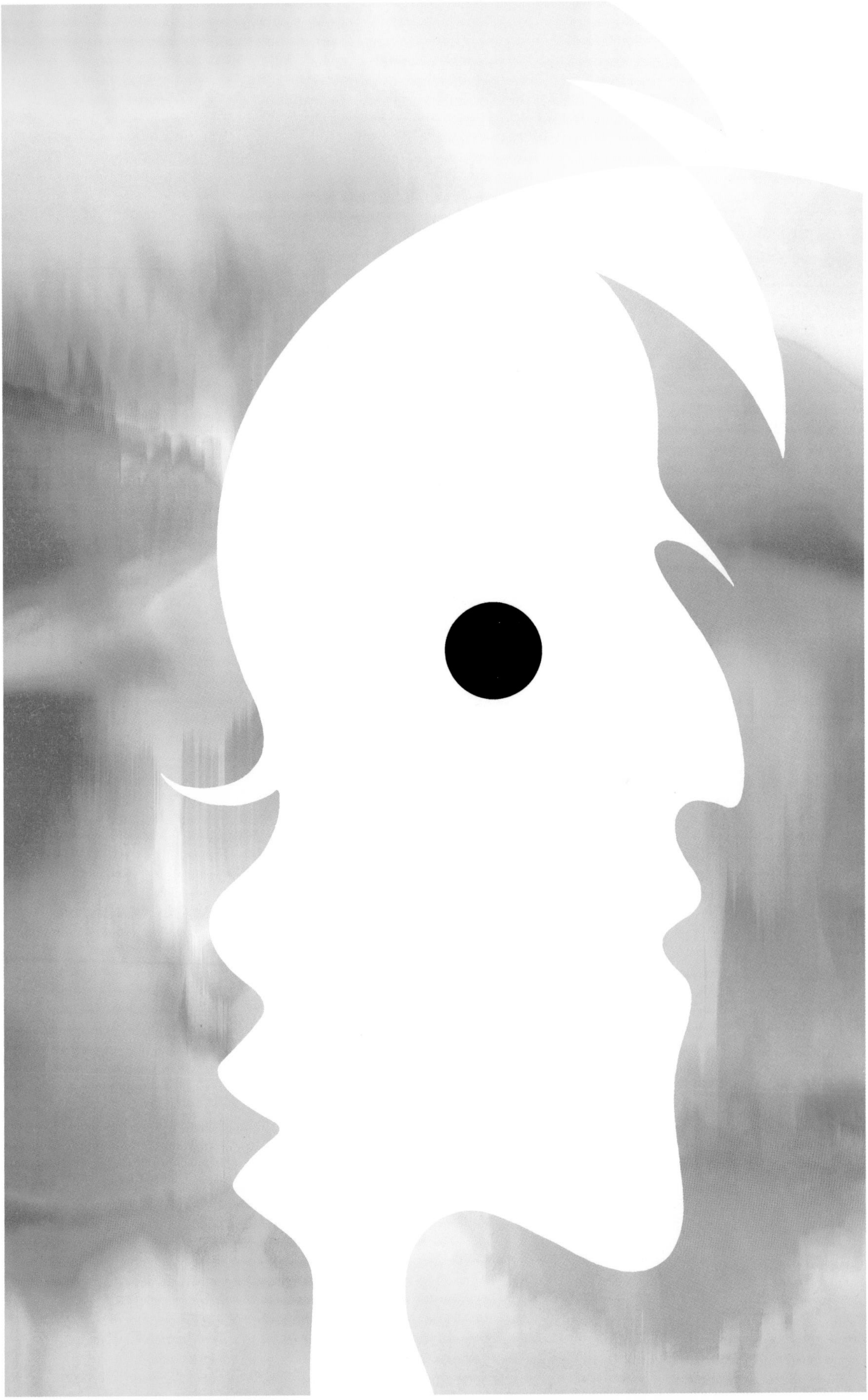

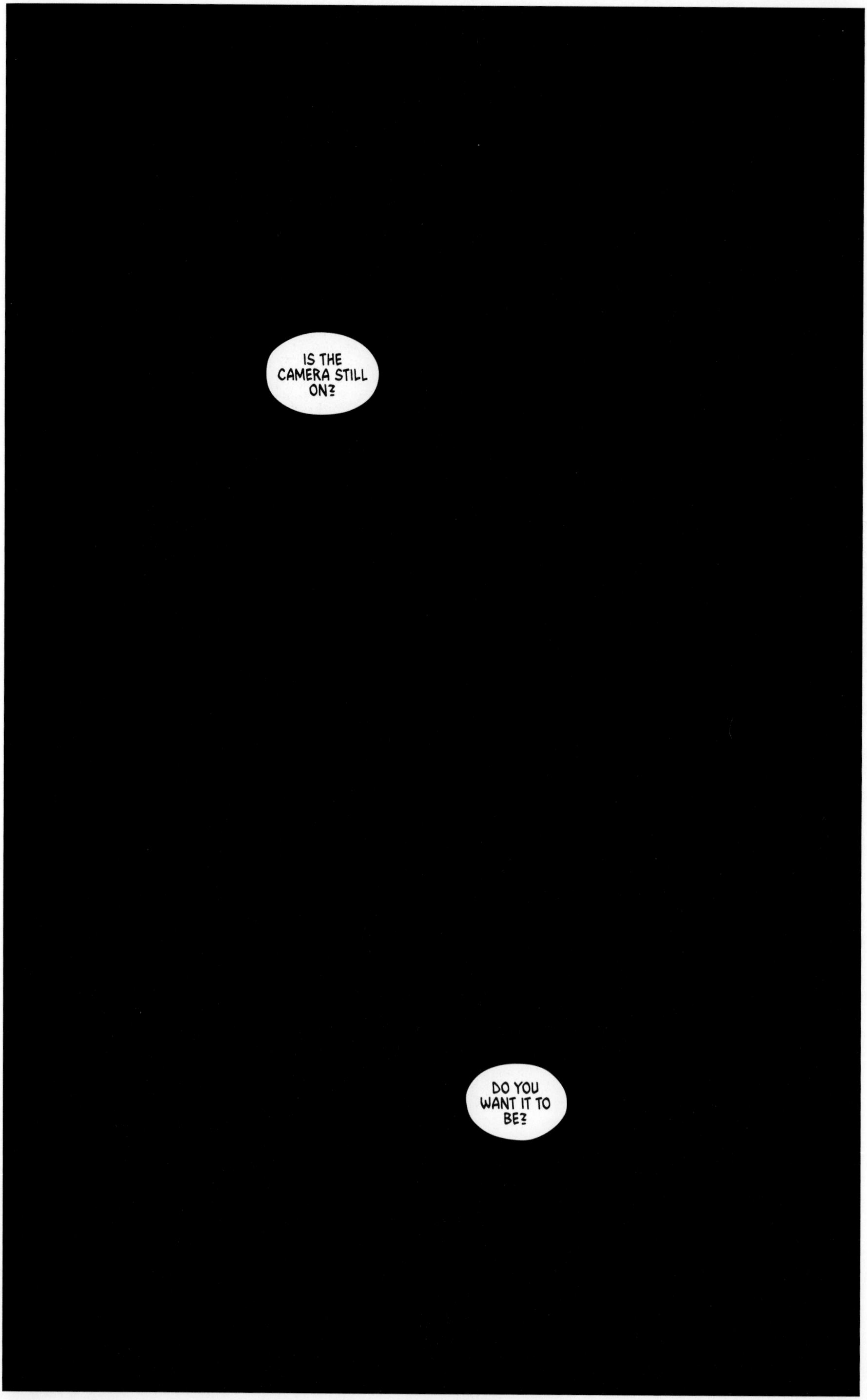
IS THE CAMERA STILL ON?
DO YOU WANT IT TO BE?

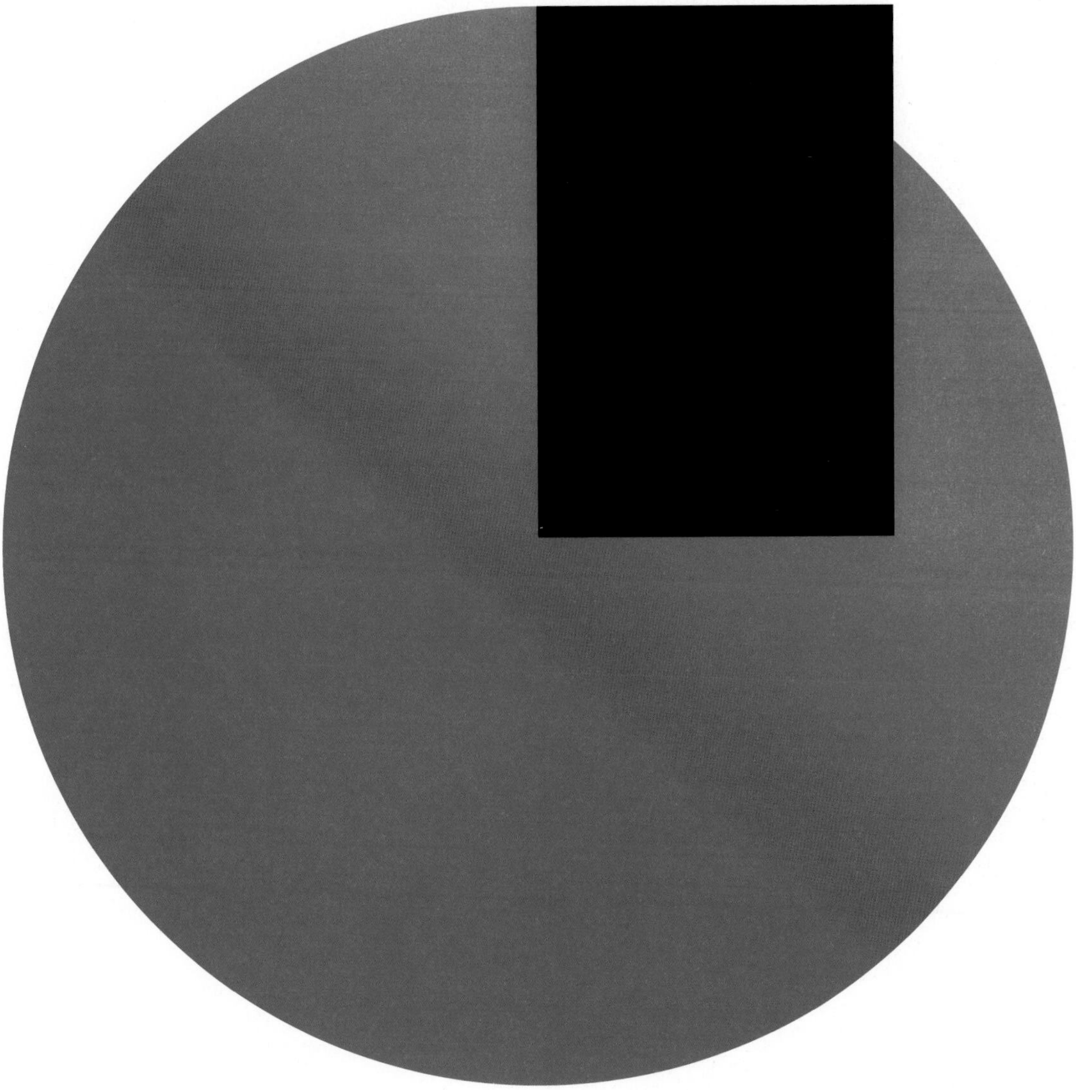

The single issue covers
of The New World #1–5

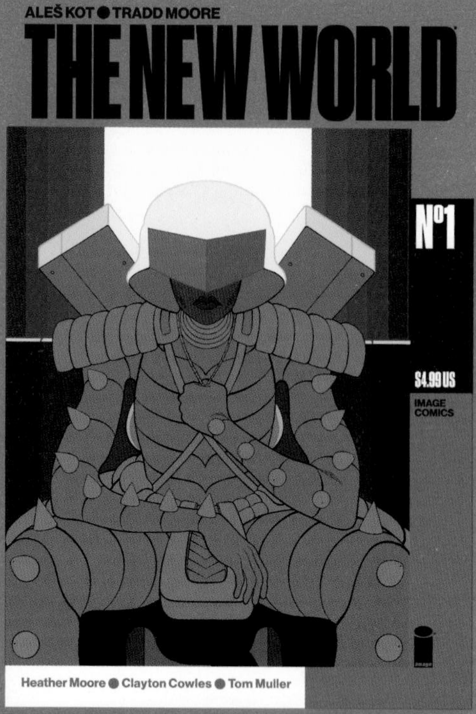
ALEŠ KOT ● TRADD MOORE
THE NEW WORLD
Nº1
$4.99 US
IMAGE COMICS
Heather Moore ● Clayton Cowles ● Tom Muller

The New World #1
Cover [A]
Art by Tradd Moore
Colors by Heather Moore
Design by Tom Muller

The New World #1
Cover [B]
Art by Tradd Moore
Colors by Heather Moore
Design by Tom Muller

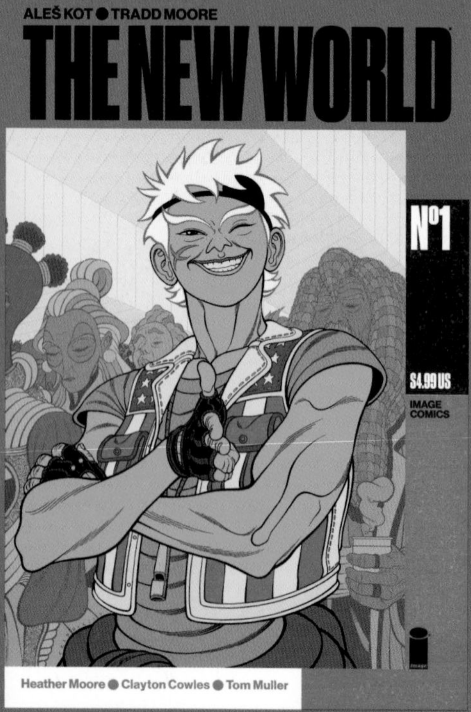
ALEŠ KOT ● TRADD MOORE
THE NEW WORLD
Nº1
$4.99 US
IMAGE COMICS
Heather Moore ● Clayton Cowles ● Tom Muller

The New World #1
Cover [C]
Art by Ian Bertram
Colors by Heather Moore
Design by Tom Muller

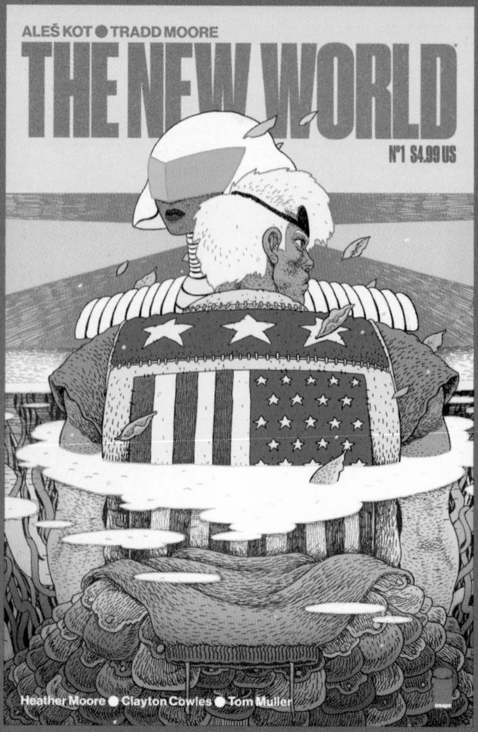
ALEŠ KOT ● TRADD MOORE
THE NEW WORLD
Nº1 $4.99 US
Heather Moore ● Clayton Cowles ● Tom Muller

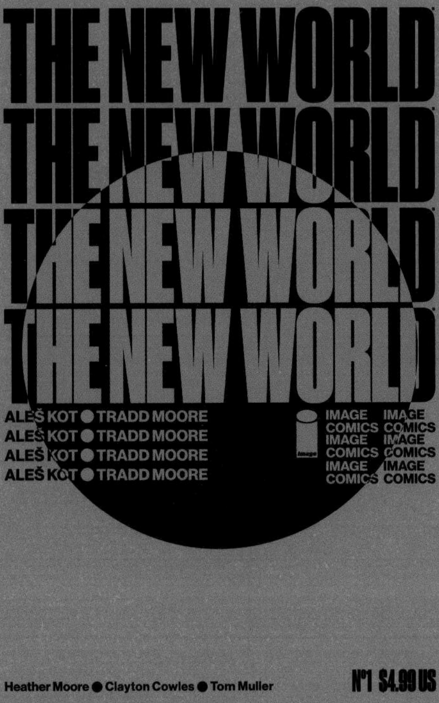
THE NEW WORLD
THE NEW WORLD
THE NEW WORLD
THE NEW WORLD
ALEŠ KOT ● TRADD MOORE
ALEŠ KOT ● TRADD MOORE
ALEŠ KOT ● TRADD MOORE
ALEŠ KOT ● TRADD MOORE
IMAGE COMICS IMAGE COMICS
IMAGE COMICS IMAGE COMICS
IMAGE COMICS IMAGE COMICS
Heather Moore ● Clayton Cowles ● Tom Muller
Nº1 $4.99 US

The New World #1
Cover [D]
Design by Tom Muller

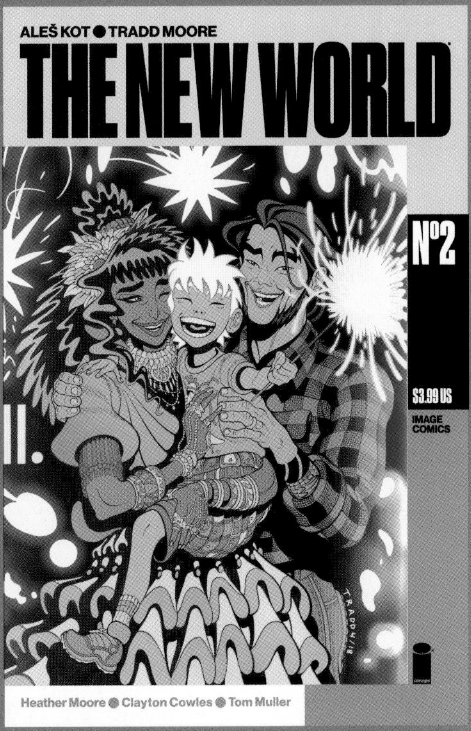
ALEŠ KOT ● TRADD MOORE
THE NEW WORLD
Nº2
$3.99 US
IMAGE COMICS
Heather Moore ● Clayton Cowles ● Tom Muller

The New World #2
Cover [A]
Art by Tradd Moore
Colors by Heather Moore
Design by Tom Muller

The New World #2
Cover [B]
Art by Tradd Moore
Colors by Heather Moore
Design by Tom Muller

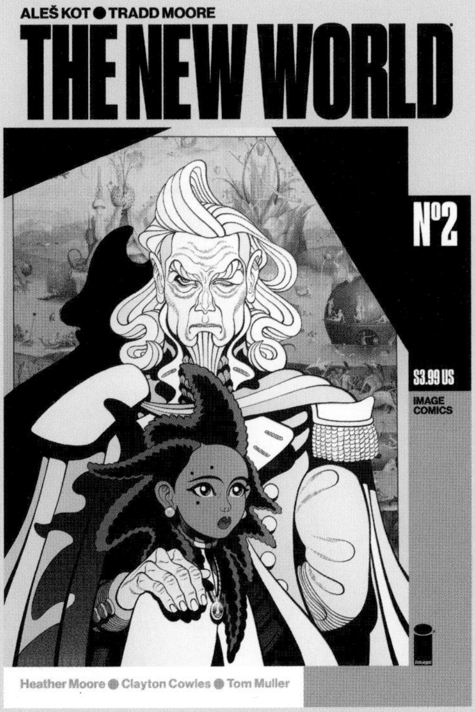
ALEŠ KOT ● TRADD MOORE
THE NEW WORLD
Nº2
$3.99 US
IMAGE COMICS
Heather Moore ● Clayton Cowles ● Tom Muller

The New World #2
Cover [C]
Design by Tom Muller

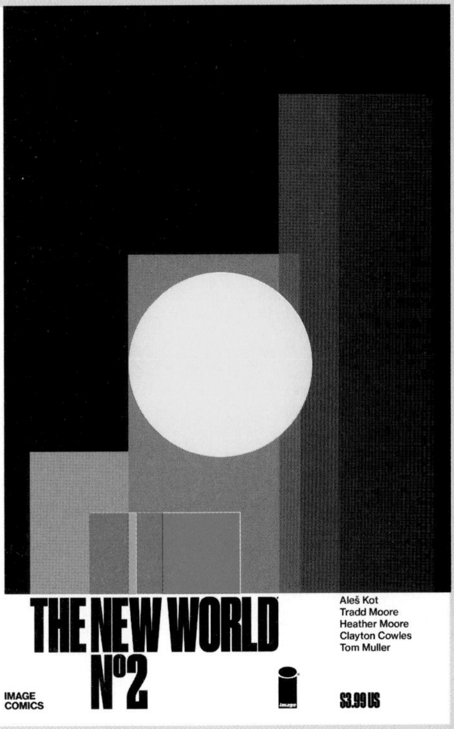
THE NEW WORLD
Nº2
Aleš Kot
Tradd Moore
Heather Moore
Clayton Cowles
Tom Muller
IMAGE COMICS
$3.99 US

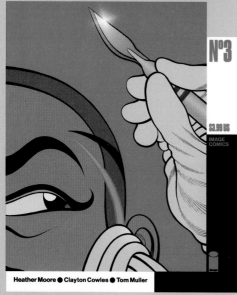

The New World #3
Cover [A]
Art by Tradd Moore
Colors by Heather Moore
Design by Tom Muller

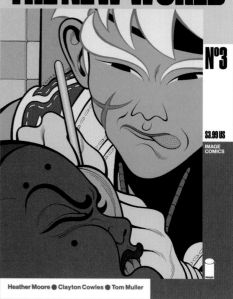

The New World #3
Cover [B]
Art by Tradd Moore
Colors by Heather Moore
Design by Tom Muller

The New World #3
Cover [C]
Design by Tom Muller

The New World #4
Cover [A]
Art by Tradd Moore
Colors by Heather Moore
Design by Tom Muller

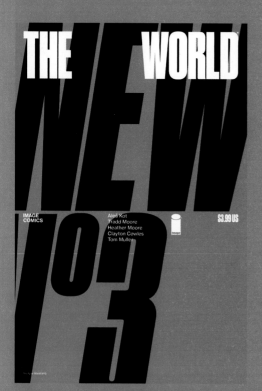

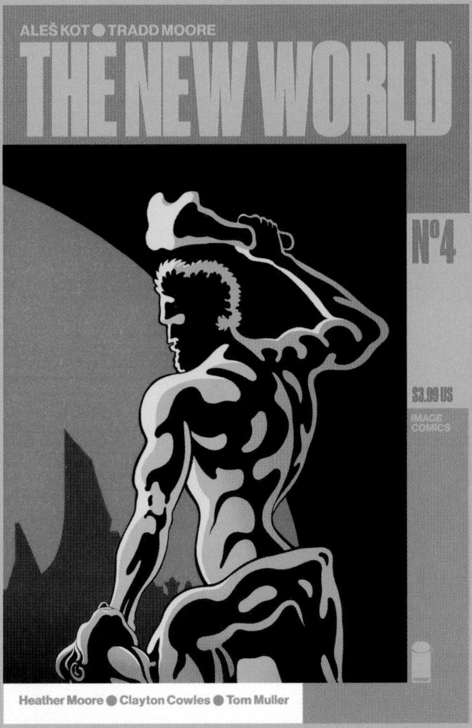
ALEŠ KOT ● TRADD MOORE
THE NEW WORLD
Nº4
$3.99 US
IMAGE COMICS
Heather Moore ● Clayton Cowles ● Tom Muller

The New World #4
Cover [B]
Art by Tradd Moore
Colors by Heather Moore
Design by Tom Muller

The New World #5
Cover [A]
Art by Tradd Moore
Colors by Heather Moore
Design by Tom Muller

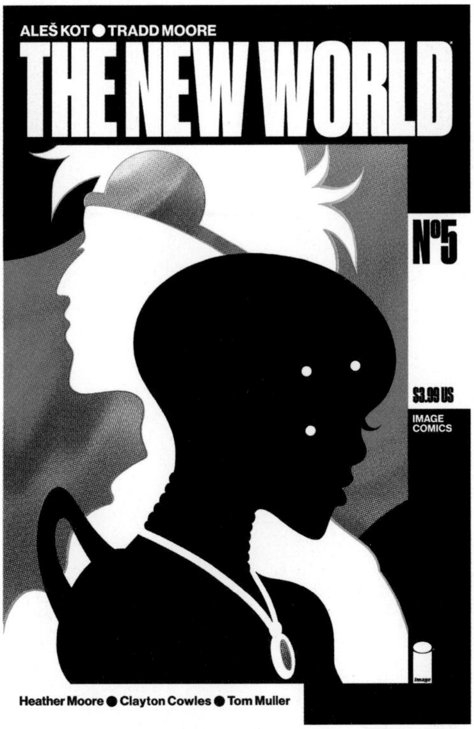
ALEŠ KOT ● TRADD MOORE
THE NEW WORLD
Nº5
$3.99 US
IMAGE COMICS
Heather Moore ● Clayton Cowles ● Tom Muller

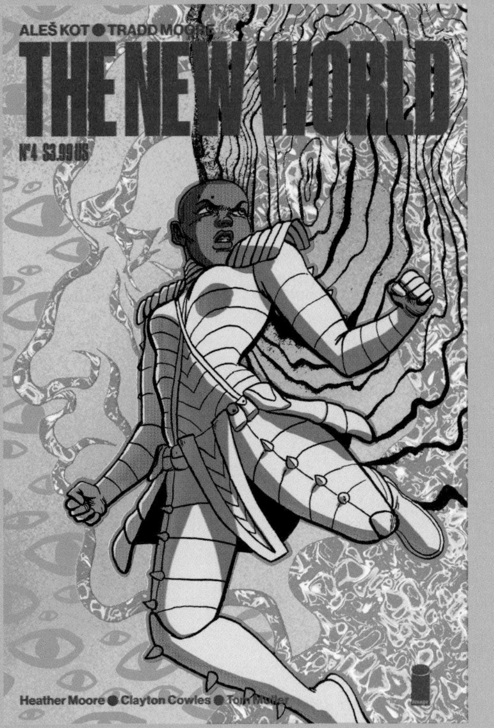
ALEŠ KOT ● TRADD MOORE
THE NEW WORLD
Nº4 $3.99 US
Heather Moore ● Clayton Cowles ● Tom Muller

The New World #4
Cover [C]
Art and color by Sloane Leong
Design by Tom Muller

The New World #5
Cover [B]
Design by Tom Muller

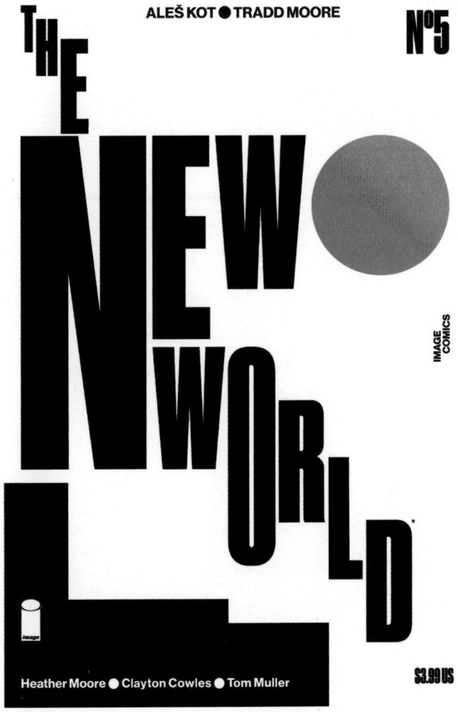
ALEŠ KOT ● TRADD MOORE
Nº5
THE NEW WORLD
IMAGE COMICS
$3.99 US
Heather Moore ● Clayton Cowles ● Tom Muller

IMAGE COMICS, INC.

Robert Kirkman: Chief Operating Officer
Erik Larsen: Chief Financial Officer
Todd McFarlane: President
Marc Silvestri: Chief Executive Officer
Jim Valentino: Vice President

Eric Stephenson: Publisher — Chief Creative Officer
Corey Hart: Director of Sales
Jeff Boison: Director of Publishing Planning & Book Trade Sales
Chris Ross: Director of Digital Sales
Jeff Stang: Director of Specialty Sales
Kat Salazar: Director of PR & Marketing
Drew Gill: Art Director
Heather Doornink: Production Director
Nicole Lapalme: Controller

imagecomics.com